After the Flying Saucers Came

AFTER THE FLYING SAUCERS CAME

A Global History of the UFO Phenomenon

Greg Eghigian

OXFORD
UNIVERSITY PRESS

OXFORD
UNIVERSITY PRESS

Oxford University Press is a department of the University of Oxford. It furthers
the University's objective of excellence in research, scholarship, and education
by publishing worldwide. Oxford is a registered trade mark of Oxford University
Press in the UK and certain other countries.

Published in the United States of America by Oxford University Press
198 Madison Avenue, New York, NY 10016, United States of America.

Some of the ideas and sources previously appeared in "Making UFOs Make Sense:
Ufology, Science, and the History of Their Mutual Misunderstanding," *Public
Understanding of Science* 26 (2017): 612–626 and "'A Transatlantic Buzz': Flying
Saucers, Extraterrestrials, and America in Postwar Germany," *Journal of
Transatlantic Studies* 12 (2014): 282–303.

CIP data is on file at the Library of Congress
ISBN 978–0–19–086987–8

DOI: 10.1093/oso/9780190869878.001.0001

Printed by Sheridan Books, Inc., United States of America

For those donating their time and energy to preserving the records of the flying-saucer era

CONTENTS

ACKNOWLEDGMENTS

I think I first began looking seriously into the history of UFOs and alien contact in 2013, but it was hardly my first encounter with the subject. Growing up, I was fascinated with the topic. I spent a good deal of my childhood sickly—diagnosed with juvenile rheumatoid arthritis—and as a result of having to stay home a lot, I became an avid reader. Reports of flying saucer sightings and alien encounters were a regular part of my reading diet, and I devoured works by John Fuller, Allen Hynek, Charles Berlitz, Erich von Däniken, and Carl Sagan. By the time I entered high school and then college, my health had improved, and new interests led me in new directions. I eventually pursued a career as a historian, with a special interest in the history of medicine and psychology. Unidentified flying objects took a back seat to other matters.

One day at a conference, a colleague of mine was talking about a book she was editing on the history of the occult in twentieth-century Germany. I asked her whether she had come across any stories about Germans after the war spotting flying saucers, as had been the case in the United States. She didn't know but urged me to look into it. I balked. I was too busy, I said. But when I fell ill the following summer and couldn't travel to archives and libraries as I normally did at that time of year, I began scouring on-line databases of German newspapers from the late 1940s and 1950s for reports of flying saucers. Sure enough, there they were. I decided to write an article about them.

I had forgotten that people across the globe had reported witnessing UFOs. I wondered how many of my fellow professors of history had written books on the subject. I was dismayed to find out only one had: Temple University historian David Jacobs published his dissertation in 1975 (only to become part of the story himself, as I discuss in Chapter 8). The oversight was glaring. Although I thought I had moved on from the topic of UFOs, it seemed time for another visit.

Researching the history of UFOs and alien contact has been gratifying and fascinating. On the one hand, it's been a homecoming of sorts, as I have been reintroduced to people and events that are like childhood friends. On the other hand, I now see them with much older eyes and through the lens of a historian. When I undertook the project, I knew it would be involved, but I soon realized these were very deep waters. Without a doubt, working with the historical records about UFOs has been more challenging for me than any other archive I have encountered, pervaded as it is with secrecy, hype, distrust, rumor, innuendo, and acrimony.

I have tried to do justice to all these aspects and to all those who contributed to making the UFO phenomenon a part of world history. A book can only do so much, however. I know I have left out individuals, groups, locales, and events that others consider pivotal. I will leave it to them and future historians to bring their stories to a wider audience. This is not intended to be the final history of the UFO phenomenon but hopefully the beginning of a new phase in writing its tale.

I have so many people and institutions to thank for their assistance along the way. First, I need to thank those organizations that helped fund research for this project: the American Historical Association, the American Philosophical Society, NASA, Penn State University, and the Smithsonian National Air & Space Museum.

I could not have navigated the complex world of ufology without the invaluable help of prominent and talented UFO researchers and archivists who all welcomed me with open arms and gave me fabulous advice. Håkan Blomqvist, Anders Liljegren, and Clas Svahn at the Archives for the Unexplained in Sweden gave me full access to their holdings as well as to their insights. I am so very indebted to them. Isaac Koi has been an invaluable resource, and his efforts preserving UFO ephemera warrant special recognition. Will Bueche bent over backward in supporting my curiosity about the work of John Mack, while Karin Austin at the John E. Mack Institute has been remarkably generous in sharing her knowledge with me. Michael Swords has been all too kind in indulging my questions and including me in conversations with veteran researchers. Jan Aldrich, Eddie Bullard, Jerome Clark, Tom Deuley, Barry Greenwood, Bill Murphy, Dave Marler, Mark O'Connell, Mark Rodeghier, and Tom Tulien in particular have been a great help to me in my work. Just as generous have been a host of other remarkable UFO investigators and students of the field: Philippe Ailleris, Alejandro Agostinelli, Ignacio Cabria, Curt Collins, Tom Deuley, Pierre Charles Dubreuil, Luis R. González, Milton Hourcade, David Jacobs, Jeff Knox, Stephen Miles Lewis, Vicente-Juan Ballester Olmos, Edoardo Russo, Gene Steinberg, Paolo Toselli, and Diego Zúñiga. I cannot thank you enough.

A host of academic colleagues, journalists, writers, and librarians have also provided me with invaluable assistance. I need to single out David Clarke for being a most steady and even-handed guide. At the National Air & Space Museum, special thanks go out to Paul Ceruzzi, David DeVorkin, Roger Launius, Cathleen Lewis, Teasel Muir-Harmony, Allan Needell, Michael Neufeld, Matthew Shindell, Alex Spencer, Bob van der Linden, and Margaret Weitekamp. Thanks as well to Christopher Bader, Matthew Bowman, Jonathan Berman, Linda Billings, Simon Bronner, Lila Brooks, Mike Cifone, the Consortium for the History of Science, Technology, and Medicine, Steven Dick, Kate Dorsch, Alexander Geppert, Alexey Golubev, David Halperin, George Hansen, Matthew Hayes, Marcia Holmes, Keith Kloor, Ravi Kumar Kopparapu, Sarah Marks, Matt McAllister, Michele Mekel, Richard McNally, Jacob Haqq Misra, Richard Noll, Eric Novotny, Christian Peters, Mark Pilkington, Sarah Scoles, Sonu Shamdasani, Shyam Sundar, and Jason Wright.

I owe a special debt of gratitude to my editor at Oxford University Press, Susan Ferber. Her initial encouragement helped me face down what seemed at times to be a hopelessly daunting task. At the same time, her insights and suggestions have helped bring greater clarity and vividness to my oftentimes awkward prose.

Finally, thanks to Natascha and the rest of my family and friends for having the patience to listen to my animated stories about UFOs and aliens over the past decade.

Introduction

Lyndia Morel got off work late that night.[1] For some time, she had worked as a masseuse at the Swedish Sauna in Manchester, New Hampshire, and on November 2, 1973, she left work at around 2:45 a.m. After getting in her 1964 Chevy Corvair, she stopped at Ben Roy's Restaurant, where she had some coffee and chatted with a co-worker for forty-five minutes. After they parted, Lyndia took the opportunity to get some gas from the station across the road.

She then headed off to her home in Goffstown, about twenty minutes away. As she went through Pinardville, traveling northwest on Mast Road (Route 114a), she noticed a large, bright yellow light that flashed red, green, and blue in the sky off to her left. She continued driving, and after about a mile, she looked again and saw that it seemed to be in the same position but appeared brighter. Upon reaching the intersection of Routes 114 and 114a, Lyndia lit a cigarette and noted that the light she had been watching had gone out. That seemed odd for a planet, she thought. For the first time she began considering the possibility that she was seeing one of those "unidentified flying objects" or UFOs people talk about. Soon after, the light appeared again.

As Lyndia drove on, she noticed the light continued its pattern of alternately going out and coming back on, all the while staying in the same position in the sky. And then suddenly, after crossing the intersection of Routes 114 and 13, there was the light, this time straight ahead down North Mast Road. Now it was larger, closer, and lower than it had been before, maybe 1,600 feet away from her car.

At this point, she could make out the contours of an odd-looking object: an orange and gold honeycombed globe, covered in hexagonal panels, with the exception of one oval window. She could see that the flashing, colored lights were actually beams coming from the center of the sphere. All the while, the object emitted a high-pitched whining noise, a sound that produced a tingling sensation throughout her body.

Until this moment, Lyndia mostly had been awestruck by what she saw. But then, events took a different turn. Without warning, she felt unable to remove her hands from the steering wheel, and her eyes seemed to be eerily and inexorably drawn to the UFO. Somehow, the sphere was taking control of her body. As far as she knew, Lyndia later recalled, she kept driving. But for around a half a mile, she experienced what she described as a "loss of memory," after which she realized she no longer had full control of the car as it sped down the road ever closer to the object.

When she came within about five hundred feet of the UFO, she could see that it was about the size of a three-story building. And then, something else caught her eye. In the window was a humanoid figure, standing behind what was perhaps a control board. Its round head was grayish, lacking a nose and ears, the face wrinkled like an elephant's hide with a slit for a mouth, completed by two large "egg-shaped" eyes dotted with dark pupils. As she stared at the creature, she had the distinct impression that it was telling her, "Don't be afraid."

If the being meant to put her at ease, it had the opposite effect. Lyndia became terrified, convinced she was about to be abducted. As she passed by the local cemetery, she noticed a house on the left-hand side of the road. Shielding her eyes from the bright lights of the sphere with one arm, she used her other hand to veer the car onto the lawn of the home of a couple by the name of Beaudoin. With her car engine running and headlights still on, Lyndia ran up to the house and pounded on the kitchen door, shouting, "Help me! Help me! Help me!"

Roused from their sleep, the couple stumbled downstairs. When Mr. Beaudoin opened the door, Lyndia fell into his arms, crying, "Help me! I'm not drunk! I'm not on drugs! A UFO just tried to pick me up!" The couple brought her into the house and phoned the police. It was 4:30 a.m. Goffstown patrolman Daniel Jubinville arrived ten minutes later and interviewed the agitated household. In his report, Jubinville noted that "the subject was quite shaken up, and this writer did not note any evidence of alcohol or drug influence."

Despite its astonishing nature, this account of an eerie encounter was not altogether out of the ordinary by the last third of the twentieth century. Elements of the story seemed to have been taken from a science fiction movie: spacemen with superpowers traveling in an unusual craft chasing down a terrified woman for some unknown purpose. Disturbingly enough, the details were not penned by a Hollywood screenwriter but rather came from a hard-working New Hampshire resident whose daily life was suddenly interrupted by an extraordinary event.

Lyndia Morel was neither the first nor the last to report seeing an unidentified flying object and its strange occupants. Soon after the end of the Second World War, people all over the world began catching glimpses of unfamiliar things sometimes zipping across and sometimes hovering in the sky. As news spread about this odd phenomenon, it left witnesses, government officials, journalists, and the general public bewildered. Were these objects real? If so, what were they? Where were they from? Who invented them and why? Speculation soon turned to beings from another world, aliens. This marked the beginning of a new worldwide preoccupation. It was the dawn of the flying saucer era.

UFOs inspired both conjecture and controversy, and they continue to do so.[2] In December 2017, the *New York Times*, the *Washington Post*, and *Politico* all featured articles on the existence of a secret US government program investigating unidentified flying objects during the years 2007–2012. The Advanced Aerospace Threat Identification Program—AATIP, as it was called—appeared to have been charged with investigating sightings mostly by US military personnel and determining whether any of the reported objects posed a threat to national security. All told, as the early reporting had it, AATIP received around $22 million in funding over the life of the program.

Part of what made the AATIP news stories in 2017 and 2018 so compelling is that they were accompanied by two videos released to the media, with a third following months later. The footage purported to show US Navy jet encounters with unusually shaped, fast-moving aircraft. In addition, a charismatic career military intelligence officer named Luis Elizondo came forward to say he had run the program and believed the military was far too dismissive in its handling of these sightings by personnel of the armed forces. He soon became the heroic face of a movement demanding government disclosure about what had been and was still going on.

Skeptics raised questions about the video footage and witness reports, and subsequent reporting suggests that AATIP existed largely in name only and that the federal funds were almost exclusively used to explore various paranormal phenomena of interest to defense contractor Robert

Bigelow. Nevertheless, when several influential American politicians took up the cause and Harvard astronomer Avi Loeb raised the possibility that the first interstellar object ever seen to enter our solar system might be an alien spacecraft, talk of UFOs and alien visitors entered the mainstream. Government officials sought to distance themselves from the association of unidentified flying objects with aliens by adopting a new terminology: "unidentified aerial phenomena" (UAP). After the Office of the Director of National Intelligence released an intelligence assessment in June 2021 in which it stated that most of the objects reported were real and unexplained, however, the tone of public discussion changed. UFOs and those who had spent years insisting on their existence appeared to finally gain the official recognition many had sought. In the summer of 2022, the US government established an office dedicated to collecting and analyzing information about sightings—the All-Domain Anomaly Resolution Office (AARO)—and relabeled UAP "unidentified anomalous phenomena." UFOs were back.

In fact, they had really never gone away. Even if most media outlets hadn't been paying attention for quite some time, there were still individuals catching sight of inexplicable things in the sky. Few had encounters as disquieting as Lyndia Morel's. More common was the experience of a man in Sheffield, England, who described seeing some sort of triangle-shaped object overhead one day. He couldn't be sure when this happened—sometime in the 1990s—and it was all over so fast, but it left him wondering over the years. When he happened upon a picture of a similar thing someone else had seen, he began thinking maybe he hadn't imagined it after all. "I've got to say, I'm not obsessed by this. But I find it very, very interesting. I'm curious to try and think, try and work out what could this have been," he later recalled. "I still to this day think, could I have made a mistake? But having seen the second picture, I think not. If I did see this, it raises all sorts of questions, you know."[3]

What has consistently drawn people to unidentified flying objects is not so much UFOs themselves as the mystery behind them. Often opaque, unanticipated, fleeting, blurry, and weird, their qualities have roused generations to study them, look for them, read about them, talk about them, write about them, and speculate about them. Whatever they are, if these things have been trying to make a secret of themselves, they have been only partly successful.

Our responses to the UFO phenomenon are an integral part of that phenomenon. Take Lyndia Morel's encounter in 1973. She had a curious experience. But her experience only became widely known through the story publicizing it, one that has its own history. Lyndia's account was pieced

SOURCES: Presents data from NUFORC; Military OneSource, "Military Installations," webpage, undated; FAA, "Special Use Airspace," dataset, updated April 20, 2023d.

NOTE: IGRA weather stations and civilian airports are included in the analyses but not shown on the map because the number of points reduces map legibility. See Figure A.2 in the appendix for these locations.

Fig. I.1 Locations of Unidentified Anomalous Phenomena (UAP) Sighting Clusters, Military Installations, and Military Operations Areas (MOA), 1998–2022. Researchers found that reported sightings during this time tended to cluster within 30 km of airspace where the military engaged in activities like combat maneuvers, air intercepts, and low-altitude tactics. Marek N. Posard, Ashley Gromis, and Mary Lee, *Not the X-Files: Mapping Public Reports of Unidentified Aerial Phenomena Across America* (Santa Monica, CA: RAND Corporation, 2023). https://www.rand.org/pubs/research_reports/RRA2475-1.html.

Fig. I.2 Sketches of UFOs made by witnesses in the Soviet Union, 1989. AFU.

together by Walter Webb, a man at the time dedicated to investigating UFO sightings. He collaborated with a good friend of Lyndia's, Betty Hill, who was already well known at that time for being one of the first women to claim to have been abducted by aliens in 1961. Webb in turn published his account in a UFO newsletter, and that newsletter was the product of an organization devoted to studying UFOs. So, behind the case of Lyndia Morel stood a lot of people and a lot of hard work that more often than not go unacknowledged.

UFOs don't make history; people make UFOs make history. This book chronicles that history. It aims to tell the story behind the story of unidentified flying objects and alien contact. And that tale at times proves just as strange, puzzling, and unsettling as UFOs themselves.

The aim of this book is not to prove that unidentified flying objects are from outer space and that aliens have been visiting us here on earth. At the same time, it does not set out to debunk UFOs and reports of alien encounters. Instead, it takes historical actors and what they say about their experiences seriously, but it does not always accept their description of things as offering a complete picture of events. This refusal to "pick a side" will no doubt frustrate some readers. However, examining the history of a topic that has inspired passionate, even nasty, debate in this way reveals a new and at times unexpected perspective on this baffling phenomenon.

UFOs and the way in which human beings have responded to them are part of human history. Whether they are the products of alien beings, secret military technology, natural phenomena, or optical illusions, and whether those claiming to have met extraterrestrials were lying, deluded, or describing a reality, it doesn't change the fact that human experiences, reactions, and speculations have been shaped invariably by the times and places in which these took place. Thus, this book tries to recover those backgrounds in order to get a better view of how they mutually shaped one another.

At an early stage in the history of sightings, it was evident that unidentified flying objects did not respect national boundaries. It was and still is a global phenomenon. For this reason, the geographical scope here extends to much of the world. That said, the reporting and study of UFOs have had hubs that have played a decisive role in the spread of international interest. At the heart of it all has been the United States. It was there that the first sighting and talk of "flying saucers" took off, and American reports, reporting, and investigations have disproportionately triggered and steered responses throughout the rest of the world. However, western Europe, South America, and Australia and New Zealand have also directed traffic in the international exchange of information about UFOs.

This book features a changing cast of characters and groups. No one person was ever in control of the direction that interest in UFOs—let alone the UFOs themselves—took. To be sure, many wanted to control the narrative and lead the movement in gaining acceptance of the phenomenon, but their hopes were always dashed. Yet while the UFO scene appears to have had a life of its own, certain pivotal figures and organizations consistently emerged to help stabilize and shift it in important ways. Some were dogged investigators, others were confused witnesses, still others were working journalists, aloof intelligence officials, dedicated scientists, engrossed engineers, and dubious academics.

Sociologist Arnaud Esquerre has astutely observed that what has made UFOs so mysterious has not been their appearance but rather their *dis*appearance.[4] Their fugitive nature has left uncertainty in their wake. The ambiguity surrounding sightings has repeatedly set in motion a cycle of bewilderment and speculation. While some have greeted reports of flying saucers and alien visitors with excitement and others with alarm, for most observers over the decades UFOs have left them in a state of suspense. What are they? Are they real? What will they do next? Should I believe the witnesses? What does the government know? Will the answers ever be revealed?

The suspenseful character of the UFO mystery is no accident. It is the result of the way in which the story of UFOs has unfolded. Much like true-crime podcasts, the UFO mystery has played out as a serial drama, with new cases popping up, new details about old cases gradually revealed, and those following every new development invited to contribute their own theories and even help in the investigation. Anyone can become part of history by helping to solve the ongoing riddle of unidentified flying objects.

Like other serialized dramas, the story of UFOs and alien encounters is often cast as a saga—a lengthy tale, marked by a successive series of startling events, replete with heroic crusaders and diabolical villains. For the very start, there has been a melodramatic quality to much of the lore surrounding UFOs. To be sure, many enthusiasts have been interested solely in the nuts-and-bolts of the objects or in collating data points. But both UFO researchers and the mass media have repeatedly presented sightings, encounters, and investigations in the form of human-interest stories, piquing our curiosity, eliciting our sympathy, and triggering our sense of outrage.

This book chronicles the rise and spread of the world's preoccupation with UFOs. It begins with a series of unsettling reports of unusual flying objects spotted soon after World War II that first sparked global interest in the prospect that extraterrestrials might be surveilling earth. Some had already entertained this possibility decades and even centuries before, but outside of the world of science fiction, their musings never had the kind of impact that the postwar sightings did. It was only the flying saucers of the 1940s and 1950s that moved military and intelligence officials to collect and analyze data about them, that inspired the creation of local, national, and international organizations dedicated to their study, and that fueled widespread suspicions that governments knew more about these events than they were letting on.

This history traces the major players and developments in the UFO phenomenon from its beginnings in the late-1940s through the first decades of the twenty-first century. It follows the oftentimes surprising twists and turns in the fascination people had with the subject, as newspaper and magazine reports gave rise first to military investigations and civilian sleuths, followed by flying saucer study groups, bestselling books, crusading whistleblowers, and blockbuster films.

Reports of sightings often came in bursts. Concentrated over a small area for a limited period, these were dubbed "flaps," while a surge of sightings made over a lengthier period of time (usually months) across one or more countries became referred to as a "wave."[5] Not surprisingly, public attention toward UFOs also has tended to come in fits and starts. There have been times—like today, the mid-sixties, and the early fifties—when enthusiasts, news outlets, and politicians have eagerly followed events. And there have been other moments—like the early 2010s and early seventies—when veteran investigators and observers openly wondered whether the UFO craze had lost all its momentum and finally reached its end.

It is not only the attention paid to UFOs that has varied. The descriptions of the encounters people had with UFOs changed considerably over time and across regions of the world. For example, the first widely publicized cases of individuals claiming to have had contact with extraterrestrials popped up in the United States in the early 1950s, in the form of stories of attractive, benevolent visitors offering spiritual messages of hope. These reports, however, often diverged from those emerging out of South America and Europe during the fifties and sixties involving meetings with speechless and mischievous tiny men. By the 1980s and 1990s, both sets of narratives had been largely eclipsed by terrifying accounts of kidnappings at the hands of unfeeling intruders from outer space.

After the Flying Saucers Came details the evolution of these and other UFO accounts and sets them against the backdrop of ongoing political, social, technological, and cultural developments. Throughout, it remains anchored in the words and memories of those who were directly involved. Newspapers and magazines, government reports, and radio and television recordings provide one set of important historical sources. Even more revealing, however, are the vast number of sources left behind by UFO researchers, debunkers, and organizations: personal papers, newsletters, periodicals, case reports, minutes of meetings, even tape-recorded phone calls. These have been supplemented with my own informal conversations, interviews, and correspondence with well over one hundred witnesses, contactees, and researchers.

It is said that we see things not as they are but as we are. Because the true nature of unidentified flying objects—in fact, even their very existence—remained an open question, UFOs functioned as a blank canvas onto which observers projected their decidedly earthbound desires and hopes as well as their anxieties and resentments. UFOs did not invite just any random set of aspirations and fears, however. Because conjecture centered on the anticipation that advanced extraterrestrial civilizations were piloting these objects, a primary focus of discussion was the scientific and technological capabilities of their inventors. As a result, the UFO presented a way for people to weigh and forecast the promise and pitfalls of modern technoscience, to see in alien achievements versions of our own potential futures.

The history of this speculation also assumes a prominent role in this book. Unidentified flying objects have raised questions about the trust being placed in some of society's most influential institutions. Science, engineering, medicine, organized religion, professional expertise, universities, government, mass media: UFO devotees have never tired of disputing the authority and integrity of each. If mystery stamped the UFO phenomenon from the very start, suspicion followed close on its heels. Present-day conspiracy theorists and science doubters have inherited a good deal of their rhetoric from this past. The fascination with UFOs did not create the "post-truth" world of today, but it has contributed to its making, and it has thrived in its online arenas.

The targets of distrust were hardly arbitrary. They, like UFOs, were part of the cultural landscape shaped by a looming presence of the second half of the twentieth century: the Cold War. For most of its history, the geopolitical conflict and arms race between the United States and the USSR relentlessly haunted the UFO phenomenon. The trappings of the Cold War turned up time and again in sightings, reports, investigations, and assessments: atomic bombs, nuclear energy, military secrets, espionage, counterespionage, the communications revolution, computing, missiles and rockets, experimental aircraft, satellite surveillance, space exploration, the threat of global annihilation. They fueled interest, shaped perceptions, fed fears, and informed theories. The unidentified flying object as we know it is unimaginable without the specter and legacy of the Cold War.

UFOs are not just seen. They have made people wonder, fret, question, probe, and argue. In that regard, they have revealed more about human beings than about alien worlds. And that is a story worth investigating.

1
Arrival

It all began, so the story goes, on June 24, 1947. That was when Kenneth Arnold, a private pilot working in Chehalis, Washington, decided to take his airplane on a trip toward Yakima in the hope of spotting a downed transport plane and collecting a $5,000 reward. Taking off around 2 o'clock that afternoon, Arnold flew toward the high plateau of Mount Rainier, reaching an altitude of a little over 9,000 feet.

In the process of making a 180-degree turn, he was suddenly startled by a bright flash of light. Fearing he might be close to colliding with another aircraft, Arnold began scouring the sky for other planes. Another flash. Then he noticed what appeared to be nine bright objects flying in close formation at what he estimated to be around 1,200 miles an hour. As he explained later,

> What startled me most at this point was the fact that I could not find any tails on them. I felt sure that, being jets, they had tails, but figured they must be camouflaged in some way so that my eyesight could not perceive them. I knew the Air Force was very artful in the knowledge and use of camouflage. I observed the objects' outlines plainly as they flipped and flashed along against the snow and also against the sky. . . . They didn't fly like any aircraft I had ever seen before. In the first place, their echelon formation was backward from that practiced by our Air Force. The elevation of the first craft was greater than that of the last. They flew in definite formation, but erratically. As I described them at the time, their flight was like speed boats on rough water or similar to the tail of a Chinese kite that I once saw blowing in the wind. Or maybe it would be best to describe their flight characteristics as very similar to a formation of geese, in a rather diagonal chain-like line, as if they were linked together.[1]

Upon landing in Yakima, Arnold apparently told others what he had seen and later reported the incident to the Air Force. He then headed off to Pendleton, Oregon, on a business trip. There he visited the offices of the *East Oregonian* newspaper to described what he had witnessed. The way in which Arnold eventually came to describe the objects he observed quickly became as important as the experience he had in the skies over Washington state. The aircraft were, he said, "flat like a pie pan and somewhat bat-shaped."

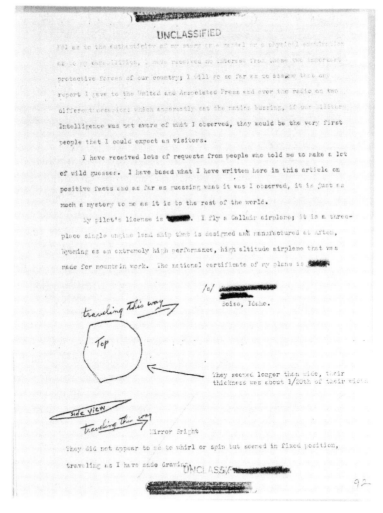

Fig. 1.1 Kenneth Arnold submitted a report to the US Army Counter Intelligence Corps in July 1947. The officer who interviewed him described Arnold as "very outspoken and somewhat bitter" toward the Army and FBI "for not having made an investigation of this matter sooner." National Archives (HMS/MLR-A1-294E, NAID 28929152).

Pressed about how they moved, he noted that the objects "flew like a saucer would if you skipped it across water."

What Arnold did not do at the time was utter the phrase "flying saucer."[2] This term, it appears, was first used in an article sent out by the Associated Press wire service on June 25. Was the choice of wording a happy accident, or simply a logical shorthand? Cognitive psychologist and writer Gilles Fernandez has pointed out the term "flying saucer" had already been around for over a half century, used to refer to the clay pigeons used in skeet shooting.[3]

In any event, newspapers throughout the world rapidly adopted the expression. Just weeks after Arnold's sighting, a Gallup poll revealed that nine out of ten Americans were already familiar with the moniker. Within months, the phrases "flying saucer" and "flying disk" had become not only ubiquitous but virtually synonymous with sightings of unusual aircraft. To witness an unknown flying object in the sky meant seeing a flying saucer.

In the days following Arnold's announcement, the American press picked up the story and began reporting on more sightings along similar lines. "Don't sell those strange flying objects reported whizzing around Western Washington short," an Associated Press story on June 26 insisted, "until the reports are all in—a flyer claimed today he saw one flash over Oklahoma City."[4] A study of 140 newspapers in ninety cities done by UFO researcher Ted Bloecher in the 1960s found that there were seventy-nine UFO-related news pieces in twenty-five states over the six days following Arnold's sighting. The pace picked up considerably after July 3. The Fourth of July that year fell on a Friday, and Bloecher found that from Friday through Monday there were at least 481 reports of unidentified flying objects.[5] The flying saucer era had begun.

And yet often neglected by the attention paid to Kenneth Arnold's strange encounter that June is that it was not, in fact, the start of the postwar world's obsession with unidentifiable flying objects. That began about a year earlier and several thousand miles away, across the Atlantic Ocean in Scandinavia.

GHOST ROCKETS

On May 21, 1946, as they would later recount to police, two separate motorists witnessed a long rocket- or zeppelin-like object in the skies over Stora Mellösa in southern Sweden. While one of the witnesses claimed to have seen two wings on the aircraft, the other did not, but was able to track it with his family for some five minutes. Meteor sightings a few days later then sparked the interest of local journalists, who reported that some witnesses said the shooting stars were reminiscent of the kinds of "flying bombs" they had seen during World War II. At first, the newspaper *Aftonbladet* referred to the objects as "rocket bombs," but then on May 28 it ran a story about the sighting of a silent and wingless projectile under the headline "Ghost Rocket Chased by Car Through Roslagen." Like American reporters would succeed in doing the following year, their counterparts in Sweden turned an experience—seeing something odd moving in the sky— into an object with a name. Over the next six months, reports of "ghost rockets" inundated Sweden. By summer's end, Swedish Defense Staff had registered almost a thousand sightings, with thousands more likely never even reaching its desk.[6]

It is not surprising that bright, moving objects in the sky might conjure up images of rockets for Swedes at the time. From the mid-1930s to the end of the Second World War, scientists and engineers in Nazi Germany successfully developed armed missiles—referred to as "*V-Waffen*" or "*Vergeltungswaffen*" (Vengeance Weapons)—that were intended to be released against enemy civilian populations. Conducting their work at a secret military base in Peenemünde on the northern coast of Germany, developers relied on the assistance of tens of thousands of slave laborers to create two lethal weapons. The V-1, an operational cruise missile dubbed the "buzz bomb" for the loud noise it made during flight, carried a one-ton, high-explosive warhead. It was followed by the V-2, the world's first long-range ballistic missile, with a maximum range of two hundred miles. First deployed against enemy targets in June 1944, more than twenty thousand V-rockets were eventually launched by the Third Reich before the end of the war.[7]

Though Britain remained the principal target for German rockets during the war, a number of V-1 rockets crashed in Sweden in 1943 and 1944. On the afternoon on June 14, 1944, a V-2 rocket inadvertently exploded over Bäckebo in the southern part of the country, scattering thousands of gleaming pieces of wreckage and creating a huge boom that blew out windows and felled trees. Local residents at first were both baffled and frightened. Many wondered if a plane had crashed. Some suspected it was the beginning of a German invasion, while others heard that the Soviets had bombed a nearby town.

Even decades later, the jarring nature of the event fueled wild speculation among the town's inhabitants. One theory held that the crash had been the result of a deliberate attempt by the Germans to test the rocket's capabilities. Speaking with archaeologists around 2004, some Bäckebo residents told of a mysterious hearse bearing a white coffin being spotted directly after the crash—a sign, they said, that German agents were there on the scene to collect the wreckage for study.[8]

In any event, the Swedish Home Guard was quickly onsite to seal off the area near the rocket's impact crater and to organize the gathering of intact parts. The largest piece proved to be the combustion chamber of the projectile's motor, around five and a half feet in length. Curious residents, aware that their town had been visited by a marvel of modern technology, grabbed any available fragments they could as souvenirs. Calls by the police for people to place seized parts on their front steps for collection by authorities were only partly heeded. The remains gathered were eventually sent to Stockholm and then to London for the Allies to analyze.

When Swedes in 1946 reported seeing odd flying objects, the notion that they were witnessing rockets seemed well within the range of possibility. Throughout the summer, ghost rocket reports grew in number and detail. In August, for instance, a Swedish Air Force pilot, Gunnar Irholm, and his signaler encountered an unidentifiable aircraft during a training exercise. As Irholm described it decades later in an interview, "Just over the horizon I could see an elongated object without the typical features of an aircraft. It had no tail fin, for example. What we saw was the picture of a cigar, a torpedo." In the official report he filed that day, Irholm claimed that he attempted to follow the object, "but I soon realized that we were not able to catch up with the craft, whose speed I estimate to be between 370 and 430 miles per hour."

One of the most spectacular sightings occurred around Lake Kölmjärv, in the north. In an interview with journalist Clas Svahn in 1984, farmer Knut Lindbäck recounted being at work around noon on July 14, 1946, when he and others heard a humming sound above. "Since I thought it was an aircraft, I looked up. But instead, I saw a rocket-like object crash right into the lake," followed by what seemed to be an explosion. Frideborg Tagebo, at the time a fourteen-year-old girl cleaning at home with her mother, told Svahn a similar story. "Suddenly we heard a roaring thunder as from an engine. My mother yelled to me to close the windows. She thought it was a heavy storm coming. Then there was a loud bang as coming from an explosion, and I saw a huge splash of water out in the lake. . . . Afterwards there was a total silence, and we could see a lot of debris floating on the surface of the lake." Military and defense engineers were dispatched to the location to test for signs of metal or radioactive material, but none were found.[9]

Until early July, reports of ghost rockets garnered relatively little attention from the Swedish press and government. This changed following a flurry of sightings on July 9 and 10 and the appearance of an article the following day in the *Aftonbladet* claiming that the Russians were responsible for conducting aviation experiments over Sweden. In response, the Swedish military issued a call to the general public to report any unusual aerial observations and to send any debris found to authorities for expert analysis. More than 250 reports came in and had the effect, as the British embassy in Stockholm put it at the time, "of opening the floodgates of publicity and given (sic) rise to speculation of a somewhat 'silly season' variety."[10]

July proved to be the busiest month yet for sightings. Reports of ghost rockets came in from Denmark, Finland, and Norway. Witnesses told of seeing "vividly shining balls of fire with tails," blue-white or blue-green in color, along with the more familiar "silver sparkling oblong items shaped like torpedoes."[11] Observations made in Finland indicated that the projectiles were flying dangerously close to Helsinki.

Reports, however, were not altogether consistent. Some claimed to see a wingless missile, others a ball, still others a cigar-shaped aircraft. Some witnesses described the machines as making a whistling sound, while others heard nothing. Observers in some locations reported the objects moving along a low, flat trajectory, yet other reports indicated the objects to be flying as high as thirty-two thousand feet.[12]

Among the Scandinavian public, the overwhelming consensus was that the rockets must be Soviet in origin. British and American observers at the time noted that residents in the region were awash in wild speculation about the Russians' intentions. Were these military experiments being carried out over neighboring countries for technical reasons? Were they a response to recent American nuclear tests in the Bikini Atoll? Or were they meant to send an intimidating message to the Scandinavians not to get too cozy with the Western allies?[13] Fearing that unbridled conjecture might provoke a massive war scare and upset relations with the USSR, Finland had already imposed a news blackout on all ghost rocket reports on June 10. Sweden and Norway followed suit just over a month later.

The government news bans reflected the extent to which European nations still remained on a war footing even a year after the end of the Second World War. The early reaction of Scandinavian authorities to ghost rocket reports was to downplay them before the public. Even privately, Swedish officials appeared to be surprisingly disinterested in the sightings through June. The rash of reports on July 9 and 10, however, led the Swedish government to commission investigations, request dedicated funding, and call on its citizens to aid in reporting incidents.[14]

Likewise, the British and American intelligence communities became especially concerned about the reports beginning in July. Sources at first appeared to confirm what public opinion was suspecting: the Soviets were testing captured V-1 rockets. Launch sites in Estonia, Germany, and off the coast of Sweden were all considered possible points of origin.

By August, however, doubts were being voiced. The Intelligence Division of the US Naval Attaché in Stockholm wondered aloud whether the Swedes themselves actually might be behind the reports. It seemed odd that no military personnel had yet "seen any fragments, photographs, radar tracks, points of impact, or other evidence of any kind to prove that guided missiles have actually been seen over Swedish territory." American officials were getting the distinct impression that Swedish military and defense officers were being evasive when questioned. "Their contradictory and confusing communiqués," staff noted, "are not typical of those which an alarmed and alert military would issue in the event of an enemy threat." The report concluded that, while it remained likely that the objects were either hysterical responses to natural phenomena and conventional aircraft or of Russian origin, one option was that the Swedes themselves were experimenting with V-rockets or deliberately trying to encourage anti-Soviet sentiments.[15]

But a week later, the US Joint Chiefs of Staff advised President Harry Truman that the consensus of the intelligence community was that the rockets were in fact real and being launched by the Soviets from Peenemünde for the purpose of testing guided missiles.[16] For their part, British officials continued to be dubious. Staff surrounding Prime Minister Clement Attlee stated boldly that they found it impossible to believe that all sightings were of genuine missiles, since not a single one had ever crashed on land.

> We are not convinced that there have been any missiles over Scandinavian territory (or over Greece, France, etc) at all. A very high proportion of all observations are accounted for by just two meteors visible, one by day and one at sunset, in Sweden on 9 July and 11 August respectively. . . . The residue of observations are random in time, place, and country and cannot unreasonably be attributed to fireworks, swans, aircraft, lightning, etc., and imagination. Such mass delusions are in our experience not unusual in time of public excitement.[17]

From the fall of 1946 through the spring of 1947, there was a marked decline in ghost rocket sightings throughout Scandinavia. Every now and again, the press would report on some strange incident, like the case of an amateur astronomer in Helsinki in January 1947 who tracked a yellow- and red-lit object in the night sky that seemed to release something like a parachute just before it disappeared from sight.[18] By April, however, US intelligence officials in Sweden issued a final report on the subject, concluding "that the widespread press reports last summer were not based on available factual evidence, that it is very doubtful if any of the reported missiles landed in Sweden." The matter, it was explained, "has in the past few months been allowed to die a quiet death, and Swedish officials prefer to dismiss it as an unexplained press sensation."[19] Attention shifted to gathering intelligence about Soviet efforts at developing guided missiles.[20]

In fact, there were more sightings over Scandinavia and the United States during the second half of 1947 and the summer and fall of 1948. Investigators from the US Air Force informed the Chief of Staff in October 1948 that in addition to cigar-shaped rockets and missiles and flat, saucer-like disks, witnesses were reporting seeing a "large, round ball-shaped object that could stop, hover, and go off at terrific speed."[21] The general view of American military and intelligence officials was that the objects were either Soviet guided missiles most likely for reconnaissance purposes or the figments of over-excited imaginations fueled by Cold War hysteria.[22] To this day, it remains a mystery who or what—if anyone or anything—was behind the ghost rocket scare of 1946.

SUMMER 1947

Back in the United States, in the immediate aftermath of Kenneth Arnold's "flying saucer" sighting at the end of June 1947, things played out much like they had in Sweden the previous year. Another July, another flurry of odd sightings, more intense media coverage, more head-scratching. So common was talk of flying saucers that newspaper cartoonists were already widely using their images to reflect on everything from the Cold War to higher taxes.[23]

By the end of the first week of July, almost every US state had at least one report of a flying saucer sighting. Witnesses described seeing flying disks that weaved and wobbled in erratic ways—some that even glowed— and that darted out of sight in a flash. Then came reports of some of the objects actually being recovered, the most famous coming out of Roswell, New Mexico, where supposedly a crashed flying saucer had been retrieved by the 509th Bombardment Group at the airfield there.[24]

Newspaper reports at that time turned to the same set of words to describe the objects: they were "eerie," "strange," "almost unbelievable." Very quickly talk turned to needing to find out what was behind "the mystery of the flying saucers."[25] The head of the Veterans of Foreign Wars Louis E. Starr spoke for many when he told an assembly soon after the Fourth of July, "Too little is being told to the people of this country."[26]

Fig. 1.2 Within weeks of Kenneth Arnold's sighting, the American press had widely adopted the term "flying saucers." And just as quickly, as one newspaper pointed out in late July, cartoonists across the country found the image a useful metaphor for taking on all sorts of political issues. *The Wilmington Morning Star* (Wilmington, NC), 19 (20 July 1947): 7. *Chronicling America: Historic American Newspapers*, Library of Congress, https://chronicling america.loc.gov/lccn/sn78002169/1947-07-20/ed-1/seq-7/.

Reports and speculations about the disks spread so swiftly in large part due to the extensive reach of newswire agencies like the Associated Press and the United Press. With a national and international presence, both had been operating as news wholesalers for decades, feeding stories to local newspapers across the United States.[27] Scattered reports of flying saucer sightings were ideal for just this kind of coverage. Throughout 1947, American newspapers from coast to coast printed the same stories—often verbatim—time and again.[28] Readers in California, Idaho, and Texas therefore could share a common collection of descriptions, stories, and conjectures with readers in Connecticut, Illinois, and Massachusetts.

So what theories were being bandied about at the time? What did people think was going on? While the possibility that aliens from another planet were visiting us was raised, it was done very rarely and treated often as ridiculous.[29] One columnist wrote a spoof in which extraterrestrials carried him off into their flying saucer, mistaking him for Orson Welles.[30] Kenneth Arnold himself was said to have encountered a woman in an Oregon café, who, after spotting him, ran out shrieking, "There's the man who saw the men from Mars" and "sobbing that she would have to do something for the children."[31]

If it wasn't aliens, then who were considered to be the likely suspects? Kenneth Arnold, for one, was convinced the US Air Force was responsible, telling the commanding officer at Wright Field in Ohio, "It is with considerable disappointment you cannot give the explanation of these aircraft, as I felt certain they belonged to the government. They have apparently meant no harm but used as an instrument of destruction in combination with our atomic bomb, the effects could destroy life on our planet."[32] Others shared the view that the disks were somehow linked to experiments with atomic energy.[33]

A number of war veterans guessed the saucers were actually radio-controlled "crystal balls" or "foo fighters," the same experimental weapons presumably used by the Germans during World War II to deter British and American bombers.[34] The United Press and most other observers, however, thought it likeliest that the Soviet Union somehow had a direct hand in the matter.[35]

To cloudy the picture still further, a new group of individuals appeared on the scene, ones who would come to play a prominent role throughout the history of UFOs—hoaxers. In these early days of the flying saucer era, hoaxers were looking to do little more than cause a mild scare or get a good laugh.[36] Four teenage boys in Idaho got more than they bargained for, however, after they planted a home-made disk—"replete with a plexiglass dome, radio tubes, burned wires, and glistening sides of silver and gold"—on a neighbor's lawn one night.[37] Police, army intelligence, and the FBI were all called in the next day to investigate, eventually solving the mystery after one of the boys admitted it had all been part of a prank.

And then, just as quickly as it had gained momentum, the news coverage fizzled out. By the end of August, the media had begun to move on to other topics. To be sure, throughout the remainder of 1947, a steady trickle of flying saucer stories appeared in American newspapers. But by the end of the year, more often than not, they were no longer being featured on the front page, and the content was often retrospective in nature, reflecting on the events of the previous summer.

———

UFO enthusiasts have long pointed to the similarities in the reports coming out of Scandinavia and the United States to bolster their contention that weird, rocket- or disk-like objects were in fact flying overhead at high speeds and in unusual patterns at the time. But bearing in mind what we now know—namely, that this was only the beginning of the world's preoccupation with unidentified flying objects—it is equally striking how many elements present in 1946 and 1947 would later become a staple in reports about UFO sightings. Warm, summer days, a time when people tended to be outside. Seemingly credible witnesses. Flying objects shrouded in mystery. A widespread belief that they were high-tech, piloted vehicles. An eager press, on the lookout for captivating stories during slow news cycles.

Suspicions of a military involvement. Skeptical responses on the part of governments and intelligence agencies. Hoaxes. In a way that no one could have known at the time, the ghost rocket and flying disk episodes provided the building blocks for countless other reports that would soon follow in their wake.

The two events also reveal something else worth noting: flying saucers were born under the cloud of world war. Regardless of whether Scandinavian or American witnesses at the time saw something real or not, their experiences were instantly and repeatedly filtered through the lenses of World War II and the Cold War by those who reported and passed on their stories. When the first wave of reports of unidentified flying objects over northern Europe began circulating in May and June of 1946, observers turned to the recent past to cast the things as rockets akin to those encountered during the last stages of World War II. The popular consensus was therefore that the UFOs must be military in origin, the only question being to which military they belonged. An answer was readily at hand. Since the Soviets had captured Peenemünde, the launch site for V-rockets during the war, they had to be the source. Whether the objects represented a show of strength or an attempt at experimentation, the ghost rockets (many believed) were being used as chess pieces in the wider game of geopolitical dominance.

A year later, the same kind of guesswork was at play. Could the flying saucers be experimental weapons of the US Air Force, maybe atomic in nature? Or perhaps they were based on German technologies from the war? There must be a Soviet connection, still others reckoned.

One war had ended, and another—a cold one—was just beginning. Both gave reason for many to consider the existence of unidentified flying objects not only real but also potentially dangerous. The number and fleeting nature of sightings, combined with the lack of any concrete evidence of actual projectiles, lent an aura of mystery and eeriness to the reports of ghost rockets and flying disks. For now, few considered anyone other than earthly superpowers, mischievous kids, or overwrought hysterics responsible for their appearance. That would soon change.

2

Apparitions, Airships, and Aliens

Weird lights and curious objects in the sky. Reports of extraordinary, seemingly impossible flying machines. Speculation about their inventors and pilots. Suggestions of secret military projects. Even talk of visitors from outer space. A media frenzy, and a public both mesmerized and more than a little fearful. This was the scene in the United States and parts of Europe by the fall of 1947.

It all happened so quickly. The characters and events may seem to have come straight out of a Hollywood production meeting, but no one person or group directed the action. While newspapers certainly helped stoke the fire, they too were scrambling to catch up with the wave of reports coming from the general public. As Kenneth Arnold himself noted at the time, no individual had the ability to take control of the story. It seemed to have a life of its own.

The response to the reports of ghost rockets and flying saucers is as much a riddle as the unidentified flying objects themselves. Were there, in fact, odd new objects in the skies during the second half of the 1940s? Why did suspicion immediately fall on the militaries of the United States and the Soviet Union? Why did some draw the conclusion that aliens from another world were involved? What was it about these reports that so captivated the public and news media?

To find answers requires considering just how unusual all this was—not just the sightings themselves, but also how people reacted to the news and what were considered plausible explanations at the time. This means looking back, back before there were "ghost rockets" and "flying saucers," to earlier accounts of mystifying and fleeting objects.

History is, in fact, replete with chronicles of awe-inspiring and sometimes downright alarming visions of what are commonly referred to as "celestial wonders." Longtime UFO researcher Jacques Vallee and his collaborator Chris Aubeck have compiled a sampling of around five hundred accounts of these apparent "wonders in the sky."[1] Ancient Roman and Chinese texts speak of contemporaries seeing fireballs, spears, soldiers, ships, and chariots floating above them.[2] Medieval and early modern sources from Europe, Asia, and the Near East depicted and wrote about apparitions of flying dragons and serpents, multiple moons and luminous globes, fiery crosses and soaring lanterns, battling armies, and gliding warriors. While some witnesses supposedly cowered in fear, others reported being amazed, like the Italian artist Benvenuto Cellini (1500–1571), who recalled that, once, "(o)n horseback, we were coming back from Rome. Suddenly, people cried, 'Oh God, what is that great thing we see over Florence.' It was a great object of fire, twinkling and emitting enormous splendor."[3]

For their part, Vallee and Aubeck dwell on the similarities between these descriptions and the flying saucer sightings and alien contact reports of the twentieth century. To be sure, combing over these descriptions one after the other, it's easy to wonder what this all adds up to. But that has as much to do with how Vallee and Aubeck present these tales as it does with the tales themselves. Their book offers these vignettes with little or no context surrounding them. Instead, they are set up alongside one another, leaving one to read them all the same way, each treated as a sort of journalistic account in its own right.

If a historical account of an event appears bizarre to us, however, this likely has something to do with the fact that the writer or artist was operating with a different frame of mind from ours. These figures lived in worlds with social relations, values, and expectations largely unfamiliar to us today. The whole point of their anecdotes often was not to dispassionately relate a series of events, but rather to attest to some timeless truth or to teach a lesson.

Histories of celestial wonders, unlike the work of Vallee and Aubeck, set depictions within their peculiar time and place, unpacking the purpose of their authors and the ways in which the stories circulated. What they reveal is as fascinating as the sightings themselves.

At least as far back as the ancient Babylonians (roughly 1500–1250 BCE), observers attempted to make out and recreate patterns in the movements of things in the heavens. But one of the things that distinguishes modern-day astronomy from its earlier predecessors was the latter's assumption that those objects had a direct impact on events here on earth, indeed on the very health of individuals and the fate of communities. This was because it was believed that the gods or the one God used cosmic events to express themselves and intervene in human affairs. What we now refer to as astrology was for centuries inseparable from star- and planet-gazing.[4] In such a universe, celestial objects had not only movements but also meanings, and these meanings had to be deciphered. Ancient, medieval, and early modern observers, then, did more than track the skies; they read the skies.

When it came to aerial anomalies, arguably nothing drew more commentary than comets and meteors. While a firm distinction between the two would have to wait until the end of the 1600s, both learned elites and commoners since ancient times agreed they were portents of looming calamity. The Romans considered them monsters and harbingers of earthquakes, tidal waves, and bad harvests. Medieval chroniclers believed they could herald the death of kings and warn of imminent war. Theologians such as Thomas Aquinas and Martin Luther expected them in advance of the Day of Judgment.[5]

During the sixteenth and seventeenth centuries, pamphlets, chronicles, treatises, and broadsides in Europe regularly recorded sightings of mysterious celestial apparitions.[6] In a period beset by religious enmity, plague, and war, the visions were especially unsettling. While some observers believed the manifestations to be the work of Satan or warnings from God, many contemporaries thought it more likely they were optical illusions, symptoms of mental disorder, or simply natural phenomena misunderstood by the misinformed.

Amazing sightings have come in other forms besides airborne spectacles. Medieval and Renaissance mapmakers frequently drew all sorts of sea monsters on their maps, based less on actual encounters than on legend.[7] European travelers in the Middle Ages reported coming across marvelous creatures, such as giant snakes, sea serpents, and dog-headed humans. While it was believed that these remarkable species testified to some basic moral truth about God's order, the existence of monstrous prodigies was something else entirely. More often than not, Europeans considered the birth of a "monster"—a term often applied to an individual with a pronounced congenital deformity—to be a sign from God, who was communicating displeasure with some particular action or circumstance.[8]

Still another variation on the theme of strange observations comes from mariners, who have long shared stories of eerie, sometimes horrifying, experiences while at sea. Legends of phantom ships and of sailors being lured to their doom by strange underwater voices date back to ancient times and are common among seafaring communities.[9] A Japanese author by the name of Hokusai (1760–1849), for example, recounted the unsettling tale of fishermen from Cape Kamagasaki near Osaka. Around the beginning of November, he recounted,

> the fishermen don't believe in throwing out any nets at all. If they do, as they pull their nets in, their boat is surrounded secretly underwater by naked men with ladles in their hands who circle the boat. They sing sad and reproachful songs, and with these ladles they fill the boat so quickly with water that it goes down. Then the strange men cry, "Come along with us! Come along with us!" and vanish in the sea. This is supposed to mean that those who have drowned in the sea near this spot are calling for more comrades. So they say.[10]

Folklorists point out that tales like these were meant to do more than strike fear in listeners. As stories that were shared over generations, they served as cautionary lessons, reminding seafarers to keep in mind their survival depended not simply on their own skills but on their fellow sailors and villagers as well.

Seamen weren't alone in reporting encounters with the spirits of the dead. Ghost stories appear to be universal, occupying a place in every society's lore. That said, haunting specters have been described in a variety of ways. Seventeenth- and eighteenth-century Europeans, for instance, referred to them interchangeably as "ghosts," "demons," "the returned dead," "apparitions," "phantoms," and "shades."[11] Some spirits are said to be fully formed, walking-and-talking entities, while others manifest themselves solely as a sound, a light, a movement, or a change in room temperature. Still, since ancient times, most accounts have accepted that these presences all bear a message for the living—typically a warning or an avenging truth.[12]

It is difficult, if not impossible, to tease out the religious aspects from the other elements in all these remarkable sightings and stories. By their very nature, wonders were divine, even if they were deeply troubling at times. Although less beholden to religious institutions and authorities, the modern world has also managed to find a place for holy apparitions.

Take for instance the so-called Marian cult. The phenomenon has been a form of reverence expressed toward the Virgin Mary, in which followers claim to have visions of the Holy Mother. According to one estimate, since the fourth century there have been around twenty-one thousand apparition experiences, with more than two hundred taking place between 1928 and 1975. Witnesses have described their encounters as "heavenly," "unearthly," "radiant." The encounter itself, however, typically has involved more than just a sighting of Mary. She is said to have conversations with observers, in which she predicts future events, condemns popular vices, heals and comforts the sick, shows witnesses heaven or hell, issues calls for peace, and imparts secret knowledge.[13]

Celestial wonders, phantom ships, ghosts, marvelous animals, and saintly visions had much in common with the first flying saucer sightings. All were spectacles, arresting observations of amazing things. They weren't just extraordinary; they were rare and, in most cases, fleeting. Who knew when such a vision would appear and to whom? As a result, they inspired attempts to somehow capture them figuratively, in paintings, illustrations, engravings, photographs, and, most especially, words.[14] Wonders sparked stories, which were then passed on to others, who in turn would pass them on to still others. It wasn't necessary to see a marvel to know what one looked like.

On the other hand, in the ghost rocket and flying saucer reports following World War II, there seems to have been no religious or sacred element in the responses to the very first wave of UFO sightings. Like the missiles and disks themselves, the supernatural, too, left little, if any, trace. For that very first group of witnesses and trackers of the UFOs, it didn't occur to them that the flying objects were anything other than solid, manmade artifacts.

This would not remain the case. Within a few years of Arnold's sighting, flying saucers started provoking a very different reaction among some observers. But at the start of the flying saucer era at least, the speculation was decidedly earthbound. Why did people respond in the way they did? Or put another way, why didn't they respond like their ancestors had?

MODERN WONDERS

The status of the kinds of wonders that had captivated ancient and medieval observers began to change alongside the sciences of the seventeenth and eighteenth centuries. The so-called mechanical philosophy—one that treated the natural world as a machine whose parts could be broken down and measured in terms of size, shape, and motions—won over researchers and academic institutions and led natural scientists to increasingly turn their backs on religious, supernatural explanations of things like celestial marvels. Eighteenth-century philosopher David Hume, for example, spoke for many when he adamantly spurned belief in wonders as lazy and vulgar, a superstitious vice of the lower classes.[15] Before the French Revolution of 1789, even clergymen in an overwhelmingly Catholic country like France were voicing their skepticism about claims of things like miracle healings: growing worries about fanatical witnesses, enthusiastic crowds, and new, popular religious cults helped lend credence to the view that miraculous experiences were best left matters of private faith.[16] By the beginning of the nineteenth century, the field of meteorology in Britain no longer saw the sky as a canvas for divine signs, but rather as a scientific object for chemical and statistical analysis.[17]

This process of secularization did not so much destroy interest and belief in grand marvels as it channeled them in new directions. And in the 1800s, industrial capitalism gave rise to one of these new outlets: technology. Industrialization relied on manufacturers using powerful, new machines to take on tasks in the factory. Industrialists didn't just make use of machines, however. They also made contraptions and innovations that accelerated life itself. Some, like the cotton gin, sped up production. Others, like the telegraph, sped up communications. But novelties such as the steamboat, the steam-powered locomotive, the propeller, the internal combustion engine, and the diesel engine made it possible to accelerate travel like never before.

Not everyone greeted these inventions with enthusiasm. The new railway journey, for instance, left some passengers bored with the experience of travel, finding it difficult to focus on the landscape as carefully as they had earlier by horse-drawn carriage. Others found the speed and size of locomotives terrifying. Highly publicized train crashes reinforced their fears, with some travelers complaining of suffering from nervous pains, paralyses, and fatigue due to the strain put on them during the trip.[18]

By the turn of the century, much of the talk about new technologies dubbed them "modern wonders," attributing to them almost supernatural properties. What had once been a regard reserved for God's creations was applied to things like ocean liners and motion pictures. News outlets and advertisers celebrated them as the culmination of technical innovation, confirming the public perception that one was living in a time of unprecedented progress.[19]

Nothing seemed to justify this excitement more than the attempts and ultimate success at mastering human flight. While the first untethered and manned hot air balloon took off in 1783, it was not until the 1880s that a successfully navigated flight was possible. Enthusiasts would have to wait until the first decade of the twentieth century for Ferdinand Graf von Zeppelin to successfully fly a long rigid-hulled dirigible and the Wright brothers to achieve the first powered flight of an airplane.

Yet even before these turn-of-the-century achievements, aviation captured the imagination of ambitious inventors and a curious public, especially in the United States. It started in 1822 with Philadelphian James

Bennett, a mathematician claiming to have invented a machine with which one can fly "through the earth's air, can soar to any height, steer in any direction, start from any place and alight without risk or injury." A host of entrepreneurs soon came forward with flying machine projects of their own. The press proved only too happy to indulge these ventures, as the *Liberty Hall and Cincinnati Gazette* did toward the end of June 1834. It reported to its readers that "one of our ingenious local citizens has invented, and has now in preparation, the model of an *aerial steamboat*, in which he proposes to ascend on the fourth of July."[20]

Nothing ever came of that effort in the end, but enthusiasts were not deterred. Fame and fortune seemed to await any future designer of a navigable airship, and encouragement came not only from the public. The prestigious *Scientific American* during the years 1845–1865 published fifty-seven articles alone on aerial navigation as well as an offer of a $1,000 prize in 1860 for anyone creating a worthy airship by September 1861. The American Civil War brought even more urgency to the idea of manned flight, inspiring inventors to consider the military applications of an aerial contraption. One, New Jersey resident Solomon Andrews, offered his services directly to President Abraham Lincoln, promising to build an airship capable of sailing five to ten miles for reconnaissance missions. Andrews eventually succeeded in designing a craft he dubbed the *Aereon*, made of three cigar-shaped cylinders inflated with hydrogen and held together by a frame and netting. While the *Aereon* proved itself capable of flight, it was hardly reliable, and the War Department eventually decided not to fund its further development.[21]

By the century's end, attitudes about the potential for airships ran the gamut from eagerness to dread. Some imagined a bold, new world opening up. In January 1895, the *Scandia Journal* of Kansas imagined that in "a few years" a refined woman could instruct her servant, "Tell my daughter that she must not forget that dinner will be an hour early to-day. She is in Egypt." The servant then telephones a "pyramid station," after which the lady of the house remarks, "I see the airship from Market Street, Japan nearing the window. . . . Here comes my daughter on her bi-wind flyer just in time for dinner."[22]

At the same time, there were stories of eccentric figures reported to be at work making their own flying machines, but whose sanity seemed in question. An elderly Kentuckian named Judge Fenley apparently was spending lengthy periods of time in trees to prepare for what he planned to be a trip to the moon. Pinning his hopes on an airship powered by boilers and a series of cannons, he proclaimed, "I can reach the moon in 10 or 12 days, traveling at the rate of 10,000 miles an hour and allowing for a variation of the course," reassuring those concerned, "I have become accustomed to being in high places, and I can now stand on any limb that will bear my weight and look down without the least feeling of fear or dizziness."[23]

The potential of a piloted airship could also be cause for worry. When one American "aeronaut" announced his plans to make a steel airship capable of flying ten miles up in the air and doubling as a boat, one newspaper wondered aloud, "will the dynamite and the destructive chemical bearing airship ever be a reality of the war of the future?"[24]

The attention heaped on aviation schemes, in turn, sparked something else as well—reports of airship sightings. One of the earliest sightings recorded supposedly took place in Ohio in 1838, reported some years after the event by a devout Mormon, John Pulsipher:

> Signs and wonders were seen and heard which caused the Saints to rejoice. One pleasant day in March, while I was at work in the woods, about one mile from the Temple, with father, Elias Pulsipher and Jesse Baker, there was a steamboat past over Kirtland in the air! It was a clear, sunshine day. When we first heard the distant noise, we all stopped work. We listened and wondered what it could be. As it drew nearer, we heard the puffing of a steamboat, intermingled with the sound of many wagons rattling over a rough stony road. We all listened with wonder but could not see what it was. It seemed to pass right over our heads; we all heard the sound of a steamboat as plain as we ever did in our lives. It passed right along and soon went out of our hearing.[25]

Here again was a familiar tale of sacred wonders and awesome miracles, of signs of God's grace. And yet the aircraft passing by was in the shape of a steamboat, a commercial success of the industrial age. Pulsipher's account manages to mix elements of the old with elements of the decidedly modern.

Later reports of sightings, however, largely did away with any reference to divine signs and God's handiwork. There were wonders to be seen in the sky, there waiting to be read. Their messages, however, were far more mundane, and they came in the form of advertisements.

In England, the first advertising in the air came from a theater company, which fixed a balloon carrying its name on to the roof of the theater. Balloon advertising spread quickly, with others using electricity to light their balloons so they could be seen at night. Balloons were just the beginning. There were lit "sky signs," large wooden or metal letters fixed on iron frames and set onto roofs of businesses. Airships had company logos painted on their sides. By the early 1920s, airplanes were commissioned for "sky writing," with planes flying over large gatherings of people and spelling out a message or company name with a smoke trail. This was followed by the use of searchlight projectors in the 1930s to achieve a similar effect at night.[26]

THE MYSTERIOUS AIRSHIP CRAZE OF 1896–1897

The end of the nineteenth century not only ushered in a period of innovation in aviation but also launched the first wave of odd airship sightings throughout the world. The American press in particular expressed fevered interest in the subject.[27]

The Sacramento Evening Bee reported on November 17, 1896, that an enterprising New Yorker planned on flying an airship, decked with a device to project light, westward to California and arriving within a couple of days. According to the paper, that evening between 6 and 7 p.m., hundreds of Sacramento residents "saw coming through the sky, over the housetops, what appeared to them to be merely an electric lamp propelled by some mysterious force." The device rose and descended, worrying witnesses that it might well crash, but instead it sailed along above the streets. Even more curiously, observers said they heard voices coming from the object. "Lift her up, quick!" one of them said to another. "You are making directly for that steeple!" As the paper explained, the voices were "not the whisperings of angels, not the sepulchral mutterings of evil spirits, but the intelligible words and the merry laughter of humans."[28]

Newspapers in San Francisco, Oakland, and San Jose quickly picked up the story. Opinion was divided on what exactly it all added up to. Some believed the witnesses, noting as one article did, that "all the stories coincide." Surely this had to be one of those newfangled airships. Others thought it more a case of mistaken identity, pinning blame on the brightness of Mars or Venus. Still others, however, considered the whole thing a hoax, most likely perpetrated by local newspapers themselves. This was the view of The Sunday Oregonian, which accused San Francisco journalists of printing "little else" but fake news. The uncivilized savagery of California bred a "fake spirit" there, the Oregonian explained, producing "a peculiar mental receptivity of marvelous, horrible and obscene fiction, by uniting in the typical Californian of today the credulity of the barbarian with the depraved taste of mature civilization. He will believe any lie, but he likes best lies well spiced with horror and indecency."

Genuine or not, the Sacramento story proved to be only the beginning. Over the following three weeks, dozens of newspapers across California, from Chico to Riverside, reported local sightings. It didn't take long for

Fig. 2.1 Reports of mysterious airships made front-page news across the United States in 1896 and 1897. Stories like this one portrayed the crafts as ingenuous modern marvels. Note that the artist's drawing was based on second-hand information. *The San Francisco Call*, 80 (23 November 1896), *Chronicling America: Historic American Newspapers*, Library of Congress, https://chroniclingamerica.loc.gov/lccn/sn85066387/1896-11-23/ed-1/seq-1/.

word of sightings to emerge in Oregon, Washington, Nevada, and Arizona. Publication of artist sketches based on witness descriptions graphically confirmed the sense that there must be something to these reports.

By mid-December, press interest had begun to wane, but picked up again in the middle of January 1897. A flurry of reports appeared in the press again in April, before petering out for good in May. These sightings were not confined to the West Coast. Papers in Oklahoma, Missouri, Minnesota, Wisconsin, Michigan, Indiana, Kentucky, and Pennsylvania all reported local witnesses seeing some kind of weird flying object. In most cases, the accounts offered little by way of description. When they did, the object was often described as cigar-shaped, sailing like a balloon. On other occasions, it was supposedly oblong and winged. Many of the vessels were said to be equipped with propellers, but the most prominent feature reported was a searchlight that scoured the night sky.

For those putting stock in the sightings, the big mystery of course was identifying the mastermind behind the airships. Rumors of wealthy entrepreneurs with a knack for invention fueled wild speculation. In other cases, lawyers came forward claiming to represent a client who was responsible for the device.

The most common view was that the airship was the creation of an "ingenious mechanic," a talented—if not quirky—tinkerer. Stories from witnesses who alleged they actually met the crew or inventor helped encourage this impression. There was a San Jose electrician who told reporters that the inventor took him to a secluded spot where he helped install the ship's motor, after which he was given a ride to Hawaii and back. And a sailor said that a pilot gave him a ride north of Los Angeles and was accompanied by a woman who spoke Spanish.

There were scattered reports of witnesses whose encounters were of an extraterrestrial variety—encounters with men from Mars. Few in number and mostly concentrated during the wave in April and May, these sensational stories are unusual in the amount of detail that alleged witnesses provided. One of the earliest of these was related by Colonel H. G. Shaw of Stockton, California, at the end of November 1896.[29]

As Shaw told it, he and a companion by the name of Spooner were riding in a carriage on their way back from Lodi at around 6 p.m., when the horse suddenly stopped at the sight of "three strange beings." Around seven feet tall and slender, they had fingers without nails, no facial hair, large eyes, mouths without teeth and were naked, yet covered in some kind of natural growth that made their skin as soft as velvet. Odder still were their feet, twice the size of most men's, and "they were able to use their feet and toes much the same as a monkey." Yet, Shaw found them to be possessed "of a strange and indescribable beauty. . . . They were graceful to a degree and more divinely beautiful than anything I have ever beheld."

The colonel asked them where they were from, but the response was an unintelligible guttural warble. The beings showed just us much interest in the two men and their horse and carriage and inspected them with small flashing lights they carried. At one point, the entities even tried to lift Shaw up to carry him away, but their muscles were too weak for them to move him.

Months later, similarly bizarre accounts popped up. On April 19, 1897, the *Dallas Morning News* reported that an airship had crashed into a windmill in the town of Aurora, leaving in the wreckage the dead and mangled body of its pilot, who was said to be "not an inhabitant of this world." Around this same time, a farmer in Kansas was roused by a three-hundred-foot-long airship hovering over his cows that scanned them with a searchlight. He tried his best to stop the ship's curious inhabitants from absconding with one of the heifers, but to no avail.[30]

Stories like these were fanciful rarities at the time. By far, the over-whelming majority of reports about the mysterious airships of 1896–1897 were of two kinds. They either provided few, if any, details at all about the object sighted, or they described a contraption that can best be termed a composite of nineteenth-century innovations and aerial won-ders. Entrepreneurial inventors, balloons, dirigibles, experimental winged crafts, steam engines, motors, screw propellers, electricity, lights in the sky: newspaper accounts of the airships were filled with the century's most famous devices and characters.

The press, of course, played a pivotal role in the whole affair. The ex-travagance of some accounts raises a question: did the newspapers just make up the whole thing? Some fellow editors and publishers, including mogul William Randolph Hearst, certainly thought so. Articles about the occult and strange things at the frontier of the known world were a popular genre in papers at the time.[31] However, it wasn't altogether necessary for the industry to perpetually concoct new tall tales to keep the airship wave afloat. The very nature of journalism at the time operated in a way that encouraged the kinds of stories associated with the airship craze.

By the 1890s, a news story could spread quickly and easily. The Associated Press enjoyed unique access to Western Union's national net-work of telegraph lines. It allowed the AP to sell identical news items to multiple local newspapers. At the same time, a new trend had emerged in journalism: illustrated news. Using multiple sources to reconstruct scenes like natural disasters and coronations, sketch artists and journalists came up with graphic renditions of events based on the information of witnesses.

A master illustrator would then often take that and translate into a more compelling vision. The final product was thus something far removed from those directly connected to the event. Since most papers looked to highlight human-interest stories to bolster their sales, it's no surprise that reports and images of encounters with a mysterious airship could flourish at the end of the century.[32]

The great airship wave of 1896–1897 appears to have been the first of its kind. It demonstrated how the promise of modern technology, the allure of human flight, and the power of the press could converge to create a mass social phenomenon. What's most striking is the way it inspired amazement and wonder. The tales of baffling lights, extraordinary airships, and oddball inventors did more than report them, they celebrated them.

THE AIRSHIP SCARES OF THE EARLY TWENTIETH CENTURY

In the spring of 1909, another spate of airship sightings surfaced, but this time events played out differently. The reason has a lot to do with where and when the sightings took place.

The setting was England, at a time when residents feared that their island nation might soon find itself under attack. Their worries centered chiefly on one European power: Germany. One measure of this can be found in literature. Between 1871 and the start of World War I in August 1914, English writers imagined invasions of the British homeland in over sixty different works of fiction, forty-one of which involved the Germans.[33]

There was good reason for Britons to feel unsettled by Germany, which over the last quarter of the nineteenth century transformed itself into an industrialized and thriving nation with colonial ambitions. Starting in 1898, under its bombastic emperor Wilhelm II, the country embarked on massive build-up of its naval fleet in a bid to upend Britain's historical dominance of the seas. Between 1905 and 1908, the United Kingdom and Germany openly engaged in a naval arms race that led observers to openly wonder if war between the two was imminent.

Adding to the anxieties was word of spectacular successes in aviation. Chief among these was the rigid dirigible developed in Germany, which carried its developer's name—the zeppelin. For much of his career, Count Ferdinand von Zeppelin had been one of hundreds of inventors trying to develop a practical airship, when he first attempted (unsuccessfully) to get state funding in 1894. Originally intended for military reconnaissance, Zeppelin went ahead without government assistance to work on a design using aluminum, eventually flying the building-sized machine in July 1900.

By the beginning of July 1908, he had demonstrated that his dirigible was capable of flights of twelve hours in length.

The German media hailed the count as a hero and the zeppelin as a shining symbol of national achievement. Opinion was decidedly different outside Germany, where the dirigible's potential military application was cause for unease. In July 1908, German nationalist and imperialist writer Rudolf Martin told the British newspaper the *Daily Mail* that he could imagine an invasion plan in which 3,500 aerial machines could land 350,000 German soldiers in the United Kingdom within thirty minutes. Statements like these threw many British residents in a panic.

The German zeppelin threat fired the imagination of writers and artists in 1908. In France, writer Pierre Giffard and illustrator Albert Robida published *The Infernal War* in weekly installments, an illustrated children's adventure story that envisioned a monumental German attack on London using airships. That same year, English novelist H. G. Wells serialized his illustrated book *The War in the Air*, a story in which an invading German air fleet bomb and destroy American dreadnoughts as well as the city of New York. When asked about the inspiration for his portrayal of heartless Germans in the novel, Wells pointed to Rudolf Martin.[34]

It was in early May 1909 that the first sightings began. A trigger may have been the comments of British War Secretary Richard Haldane. In an interview, he was quoted as saying, "Our insularity vanished with the nineteenth century. . . . A hostile airship, hovering over London, would be unassailable, and could inflict enormous damage."[35] Soon the *Evening News* and the *Daily Express* began reporting on witnesses claiming to have seen a cigar-shaped dirigible at least 100 feet long flying overhead. A couple from Clacton-on-Sea alleged to have found a steel bar presumably dropped by an airship, with the words "Müller Fabrik Bremen" printed on it. More ominously, stories were circulating that foreigners "speaking with a guttural accent" were wandering around and asking questions of witnesses. Almost two weeks after the supposed discovery in Clacton, the husband in question told the *East Anglian Daily Times* that two male foreigners appeared at the back of his house, "where the stables are situated, and where for some time I kept the article. The men hovered about my house persistently for five hours—until 7 o'clock in the evening."[36] Others, too, claimed to have had exchanges with the crew of the airship and testified that they looked German in appearance.

The British government dismissed any talk of actual German airships over England. The necessary technology, officials insisted, was still beyond the capabilities of zeppelin makers. By the end of May, the wave of sightings was over. Nevertheless, a similar scare took place in New Zealand during the summer of 1909. There, too, suspicion lighted on German aviators.[37]

With war looming on the horizon, another wave of reported sightings took place across Europe and Russia from the fall of 1912 to the spring of 1913.[38] In Great Britain, there were descriptions of lights in the sky, long cigar-shaped aircraft, sounds of an engine or propeller, suspicions of German reconnaissance. The editors of the London Daily Mirror dismissed the sightings as a form of mass hallucination. A case of "airshipitis," they called it. This didn't stop Parliament from passing a bill granting officers the right to fire at any mysterious airship spotted.[39]

The outbreak of the First World War in August 1914 sparked a new, more intense wave. Reports this time came from Australia, Canada, South Africa, and the United States.[40] But once again, Great Britain proved itself a hub for sightings.

During the summer and fall of 1914, rumors swirled that the Germans not only had set up an extensive spy and sabotage network within the United Kingdom but had also installed gun platforms and zeppelin bases on British soil. Along with reports of strange lights, mysterious airplanes, and dirigibles in the skies, local police and vigilantes across the British Isles conducted searches for evidence of possible storage facilities for the aircraft. In some cases, they found what they considered to be "very clear evidence" of their existence.[41]

Germany eventually would use zeppelins to attack British military and civilian targets, starting in January 1915. Over the course of the war, there were seventy-five zeppelin raids on England, causing around 2,000 casualties.[42] German aerodromes in the English countryside were not real, but the fear about them was. The airship scares of the First World War highlight a new sense of vulnerability the general public felt at the time. Theirs was the first generation for whom death at the hands of piloted aircraft passed from the world of imagination and fiction to the world of military strategic planning and civil defense. This was a world where rumor and xenophobia crashed head on into actual mechanized warfare and indiscriminate carnage.

OTHER WORLDS, OTHER BEINGS

In August 1909, during the airship scare in New Zealand, a man on the North Island was said to have seen an airship drop a package. Upon opening it, he found a note inside. "A Message from Mars. We are delighted with

Gilmour Thomson's Scotch whisky. Send 10,000 cases by first airship." At the very least, the story was an artful advertising stunt.

Another resident at the time entertained the possibility rather more seriously. When it came to the recent spate of airship sightings, the individual told a local paper, it is "more likely to be the beginning of an invasion from Mars. Water being scarce on that planet, the Martians are . . . looking out for a new world to inhabit; and New Zealand being a conspicuous object on our globe, they will probably attack us first."[43]

These anecdotes—one involving a prank, the other a lot of speculation—could be dismissed as minor footnotes in the history of airship sightings. After all, the overwhelming attitude at the time was either that the whole thing was the work of Germans or that it amounted to little more than a case of mass hysteria. However, Martians also had cropped up in the stories surrounding the sightings in the United States in 1896–1897. Why would Martians come up in the first place? Why would it occur to someone to propose this possibility, even as a joke?

Far from being an outlandish opinion, educated observers since ancient Greece entertained the notion that the universe was likely filled with other worlds and civilizations like our own. The philosopher Epicurus, believing the cosmos to be composed of moving, colliding, and sticking atoms, thought it undeniable that "there are infinite worlds both like and unlike this world of ours. For the atoms being infinite in number, as already proved, are borne on far out into space."[44] Others, like Aristotle, disagreed, insisting instead on the uniqueness of our heaven and earth. While the subject garnered some debate over the ensuing centuries, prominent astronomers in the eighteenth century re-energized the discussion. Based on telescopic observations of planets as well as on theological assumptions about God's unlimited powers of creation, it seemed undeniable, as philosopher Immanuel Kant put it in 1781, "that, at least, some one of the planets, which we see, is inhabited." Around this same time, English astronomer William Herschel, believed he had found evidence from his lunar observations of there being forests, roads, canals, and even pyramids on the surface of the moon.[45]

Throughout the nineteenth century, the possibility of intelligent extraterrestrial life continued to attract the attention of thinkers of various stripes. Religious figures were especially taken with the subject. In 1832, the founder of Mormonism, Joseph Smith, began developing the idea of there being three heavens organized in a hierarchy through which all spirits might pass and whose pinnacle was the "celestial kingdom."[46] For his part, Rev. Thomas Dick of Scotland believed the question of alien life warranted a more quantified analysis. In 1837, he calculated the number of residents of known planets and moons in the solar system based on his own estimates of the population density of England at the time. Venus, he announced, likely had around 53.5 billion inhabitants, but Jupiter might well boast almost 7 trillion dwellers. Others, however, such as Ellen G. White, one of the founders of the Seventh-Day Adventist Church in the United States, had no need for computations like Dick's. In the 1840s, she claimed that the Lord had given her "a view of other worlds," visions that included meeting the "noble, majestic, and lovely" inhabitants of other planets.[47]

The last third of the century brought a renewed liveliness to discussions over the possibility of extraterrestrial life. Prolific English astronomer Richard Proctor became a leading spokesman for the view that planets, suns, and moons evolved from a "sunlike state" to what was eventually "planetary decrepitude." This meant, he contended, that every orb in space invariably enjoys periods when it sustains living creatures. Meanwhile astronomer Camille Flammarion was influencing a generation of French readers through his popular books—including some of the earliest examples of science fiction—in which he did more than insist on the existence of life on the sun, the moon, and Mars. He declared that humanity was a "citizen of the sky," that "the earths which hover in space have been considered by us . . . as the future regions of our immortality. There is a celestial home of many dwellings, and there . . . we recognize those places which we will one day inhabit."[48]

Scientific and theological speculations about the existence of alien life intersected with budding occult religions to spark interest in a new venture: the prospect of actually communicating with extraterrestrials. Already in the eighteenth century, Baron Emanuel Swedenborg had claimed to have the ability to speak with inhabitants of "other earths," including residents of the moon and Mercury. Two new movements repurposed this line of thinking. Spiritualism, emerging in the mid-nineteenth century, offered the promise of receiving and transmitting messages from and to the spirits of the dead through so-called mediums, who did so telepathically and through "automatic writing" while often in a dream-like trance. A few decades later, the movement of theosophy proposed a new mystical worldview that wedded the latest trends in astronomy and geology with the occult tradition's emphasis on discovering the secret keys to sacred wisdom. Theosophy's leading figures, Madame Helena Blavatsky chief among them, combined Buddhist and Hindu practices and lore, belief in the interconnected "astral" properties of all natural things, and a faith in the power of magic to encourage the converted to embark on a journey of ever greater spiritual enlightenment.[49]

These ideas would later have a direct impact on the UFO phenomenon by providing the building blocks for the New Age religious movements following the Second World War. Back in the late nineteenth century, however, spiritualism and theosophy inspired some "gifted" individuals to claim they had special powers allowing them to leave their bodies and visit with extraterrestrials. One of the more remarkable examples was the amateur Swiss medium "Hélène Smith," born Élise-Catherine Müller. Smith was working as a salesperson in a silk shop in Geneva when she was discovered by psychologist Théodore Flournoy, who had been keen on finding a spiritualist medium to study. For five years, Flournoy observed and interviewed the woman, eventually publishing a book about her in 1899.[50]

Starting in November 1894, Smith claimed to have begun having visions of Mars. After an interruption of some fifteen months, the visions returned in February 1896 and lasted until at least 1899. During seances, Smith would provide witnesses with elaborate descriptions of the Martian landscape, including its hills, fauna, and flora. Later, in a waking state, she went on to draw a number of portraits of what she was witnessing.

Mars was teeming with life, she said, and this included alien beings not unlike us. Flournoy recalled one of her first descriptions of them:

> Carriages without horses or wheels, emitting sparks as they glided by; houses with fountains on the roof; a cradle having for curtains an angel made of iron with outstretched wings, etc. What seemed less strange, were people exactly like the inhabitants of our earth, save that both sexes wore the same costume, formed of trousers very ample, and a long blouse, drawn tight about the waist and decorated with various designs.[51]

Smith quickly got to know the Martians and their folkways, guided particularly by one named Astané. In order to communicate with the red planet's inhabitants, Hélène Smith learned to speak, read, and write what she claimed to be the Martian language. She eventually transcribed the Martian script for Flournoy, who turned to his linguist friend Ferdinand de Saussure for his assessment. Two years later, French philologist Victor Henry analyzed it in his book *Le Langage Martien* (The Martian Language), arguing that what Smith had concocted offered unique insights into how languages arose.[52] Ultimately, Flournoy disappointed Smith and members of the spiritualist community when he concluded that she was nothing but a victim of "mental dissociation" and multiple personality.

Yet the idea of contact with extraterrestrials was far from exclusive to mediums, mystics, and "madmen." Most scientists and intellectuals at the time also considered it likely that the moon, Mars, and Venus were

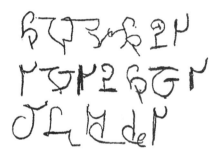

Fig. 2.2 The medium Hélène Smith claimed she was able to visit Mars by entering a trance state. In August 1897, she provided the first of several examples of Martian script that were transmitted to her through visual hallucination. Th. Flournoy, *From India to Planet Mars* (New York: Harper & Brothers, 1900).

populated by civilizations and that communicating with the beings there might be a viable option. And from the late-1860s through the 1920s, a number of prominent figures offered their proposals for doing so.

Eugenics founder Francis Galton and Russian rocket innovator Konstantin Tsiolkovskii, for instance, both suggested using giant mirrors to reflect sunlight toward inhabited planets to make contact. In 1901, inventor Nikola Tesla announced that he had encountered odd electrical disturbances in his lab, "with such a clear suggestion of number and order" that he believed they could only be considered signals from Mars. "The feeling is constantly growing on me," he explained, "that I had been the first to hear the greeting of one planet to another. A purpose was behind these electrical signals." News that in 1909 Mars once again would be in opposition and thus would be especially close to the earth sparked even more fevered discussions, including a proposal for funding a $10 million cluster of mirrors in the desert of the American southwest. Another inventive plan called for using battery-powered searchlights to send out Morse code signals to the Red Planet.[53]

While Mars had always seemed to be a likely candidate for intelligent life, interest in the prospect peaked from the late nineteenth through the early twentieth centuries. Italian astronomer Giovanni Schiaparelli sparked this new wave of speculation after he announced that he had observed markings on the surface of Mars, which he dubbed "*canali*" in 1877. In Italian, the term could mean "channels" or "canals." Either way, to many the wording seemed to imply the presence of water and a measure of engineering (perhaps no coincidence given the recent completion of the Suez Canal).

Media interest in the "Martian canals" was booming in the 1890s, when American businessman and astronomy enthusiast Percival Lowell took it upon himself to make his own observations of the canals and announce his remarkable findings in a series of works published between 1894 and 1908. The canals were artificial, he concluded, designed as a system of irrigation by a desperate civilization attempting to get water from the polar ice cap to the rest of the surface.

A talented speaker and writer, Lowell spread his ideas with infectious enthusiasm. Newspapers reveled in the "mystery of the canals," and they portrayed Lowell and his fellow astronomers as modern-day explorers of unknown lands. The talk helped inspire works of science fiction, such as *War of the Worlds* by H. G. Wells and Edgar Rice Burroughs's *A Princess of Mars*. By 1930, however, astronomers working with large telescopes solved the riddle of the canals for good. The "*canali*" were not fine lines on the surface of Mars, but rather dark patches that smaller instruments were unable to properly detect—an optical illusion mistakenly assumed to be ducts. Over the next two decades, some scientists held out hope for there being vegetation on the planet but saw little cause to believe Mars was inhabited by intelligent beings.[54]

This fact hardly deterred fiction writers with an interest in alien encounters. In novels and in pulp magazines like *Wonder Stories* and *Astounding Science Fiction*, they offered up a parade of extraterrestrial oddities over the course of the 1920s and 1930s. David Lindsay introduced the residents of Tormance, whose multi-colored skin changed hue with their every thought and emotion and who communicated telepathically. Stanley G. Weinbaum's story "A Martian Odyssey" (1934) invented a world inhabited by birdlike beings, silicon creatures, and a tentacled "dream beast" that could project illusions in the minds of others. In 1938, John W. Campbell Jr. presented a nightmare scenario in which researchers in the Antarctic inadvertently reanimate a frozen alien pilot capable of killing any living thing and assuming its body and identity.

At the same time, serials featured the exploits of outer space heroes like John Carter and Flash Gordon fighting and making friends with a host of exotic outer space civilizations. A mere decade before the first reports of flying saucers, the global reach of these serialized adventures was striking. Already by the late thirties, the *Flash Gordon* comic strip, one of its creators claimed, had been translated into eight foreign languages, was published in at least 130 newspapers, and was being read by around fifty million people.[55]

One man, however, believed encounters with aliens were more likely here on earth. A former newspaper man, New Yorker Charles Fort received an inheritance around the end of World War I that allowed him to pursuit his life-long passion of research into paranormal events in the modern world. In a series of books he published between 1919 and 1932, Fort detailed a dizzying number of reported cases of bizarre, seemingly unexplainable phenomena—"damned" facts and knowledge, as he put it—that science simply dismissed or ignored. There were ghost sightings, weird footmarks found in snow, and examples of teleportation, levitation, and spontaneous human combustion, among other things. So original was his approach to the synchronicities of such oddities that weird and anomalous phenomena eventually became known simply as "Forteana."

In his first book, entitled *The Book of the Damned*, Fort laid out a litany of out-of-place things seen falling from the sky, including black rain, frogs, fish, stones, showers of blood, even flesh. He noted the number of sightings as well of eerie manifestations spotted in the sky, like mysterious lights, dirigibles, odd clouds, shadows, and triangles. There must be, he surmised, an alien presence positioned outside earth's atmosphere. But if so, why weren't they communicating with us directly? Perhaps we simply weren't worth the effort. "I think we're property. I should say we belong to something," he ominously mused. "That once upon a time, this earth was No-man's Land, that other worlds explored and colonized here, and fought among themselves for possession, but that now it's owned by something. That something owns this earth—all others warned off."[56]

ATTACKS FROM THE AIR, ATTACKS FROM THE AIRWAVES

By the mid-1930s, the world once again seemed to be on the brink of total war. Civil war gripped China and then Spain, an increasingly aggressive Japan invaded Manchuria, Italy attacked Abyssinia, and bellicose fascist and communist movements extolled the virtues of combat.

Already in the early twenties, Italian military theorist Giulio Douhet had predicted that strategic bombing by independent air forces would prove decisive in the next war. A decade later, his vision of a coming war in which bombers deliberately targeted major cities in order to undermine civilian morale drew the attention of numerous European observers. The picture he painted was grim:

> Within a few minutes, some 20 tons of high-explosive, incendiary, and gas bombs would rain down. First would come explosions, then fires, then deadly gases floating on the surface and preventing any approach to the stricken area. As the hours passed and night advanced, the fires would spread while the poison gas paralyzed all life. By the following day the life of the city would be suspended.[57]

The British again proved especially jittery. The experience of zeppelin raids and Imperial Germany's willingness to use poison gas during the Great War led military writers and politicians in the early 1930s to insist that the residents of the United Kingdom needed to steel themselves for the inevitable assault from the air. Science fiction writer H. G. Wells once again added fuel to the fire when he published *The Shape of Things to Come* (1933), a futuristic novel that conjured up a world in which cities were devastated by heavy bombing from the air. By the spring of 1935, word that Nazi Germany enjoyed air parity with Britain helped spark a panic in the press, with newspapers painting scenarios in which tens of thousands of urban dwellers were likely to lose their lives and limbs due to German air raids.[58]

In April 1937, gruesome reality imposed itself on nightmarish fantasy. With Spain in the throes of civil war, forces loyal to the nationalist government of General Franco carried out an aerial bombing raid against Basque loyalists in the town of Guernica. Seventy percent of the city's center was destroyed, and hundreds of civilians were killed, including women and children. The results, which drew international media coverage, shocked many in Europe and elsewhere.[59]

But it was in the United States in 1938 that the specter of unbridled carnage from the skies converged with speculation about life on other planets in a most unexpected way. On October 30, twenty-three-year-old director and actor Orson Welles and his company, The Mercury Theatre on the Air, broadcast live on CBS radio an hour-long adaptation of H. G. Wells's *The War of the Worlds*. What made the broadcast so distinctive was the manner in which the players told the story. Throughout most of the show, Welles and his fellow actors simulated a normal broadcast of live music, periodically interrupted by news bulletins announcing a developing story about strange objects landing in and around the New York metropolitan area. Very quickly, reporters "on the scene" revealed that the objects were piloted spaceships from Mars, equipped with deadly heat rays and poison gas. Martians, it would seem, had begun all-out attack on planet earth—starting with Grovers Mill, New Jersey.

In the days immediately afterward, newspapers along the East Coast offered up accounts of the alarm the show had inspired that night. The *New York Times* told of frenzied phone calls to local police stations by people claiming to have seen smoke "from the bombs" and described a group of families in Newark rushing "out of their houses with wet handkerchiefs and towels over their faces to flee from what they believed was to be a gas raid." Newark's *Star-Eagle* claimed that police there had seen panicked residents rushing down streets. The *Philadelphia Inquirer* reported that "thousands of Philadelphians were terrorized," and the *Washington Post* could only acknowledge that "[f]or an hour, hysterical pandemonium gripped the Nation's Capital and the Nation itself."

Two years later, Princeton University social psychologist Hadley Cantril and his team of researchers published the results of a series of surveys and interviews with residents in the area about their experiences that night. At first glance, *The Invasion from Mars: A Study in the Psychology of Panic* appeared to confirm early media reports. Cantril estimated that at least 1.2 million listeners had been "frightened," "disturbed," or "excited" by the broadcast. Given that perhaps over six million listeners had tuned in, it was clear that actually most had remained unruffled. Cantril concluded that individual responses to the broadcast depended on one's "standards of judgment," on a person's relative degree of suggestibility under given circumstances.[60]

More recent studies of Cantril's team of investigators and how they worked together reveal that their book—like news outlets in the days after the broadcast—greatly exaggerated the extent of the panic. Eager to secure funding for the project from the Rockefeller Foundation, Cantril and his collaborator Paul Lazarsfeld hyped their results, while also downplaying the most obvious and mundane findings—that most listeners were not at all upset and that those who were agitated often simply contacted friends, family, or authorities to see what was going on. Far from triggering mass hysteria among a gullible public, the 1938 *War of the Worlds* broadcast demonstrated that the power of mass media had clear limits and that listeners still placed their trust in their immediate circle of personal relations.[61]

That said, the world quickly learned that earthly powers by themselves were more than capable of wreaking unprecedented havoc and devastation from the skies. The Second World War saw combatants on both sides of the conflict turn to massive strategic bombing campaigns, unapologetically aimed at densely populated urban centers and intent on destroying enemy infrastructure and eroding morale. Berlin, Dresden, Hamburg, Kobe, London, Milan, Rotterdam, Tokyo, Turin, Warsaw, and scores of other cities were targeted. Millions were killed, injured, or left homeless by the attacks. The bloodletting of conventional bombing only foreshadowed what was to come in 1945.[62] On August 6 and August 9, the United States dropped two atomic bombs on the Japanese cities of Hiroshima and Nagasaki. By December of that year, an estimated 150,000 to 200,000 residents there had died.[63]

The massive destruction and loss of life associated with the bombing campaigns of World War II would have a profound impact on the postwar flying saucer phenomenon. The war also contributed another legacy to the flying saucer era. Beginning in October 1944, Allied pilots flying over Western Europe began reporting seeing "balls of light" chasing their aircraft—most often at night—at remarkably fast speeds and maneuvering in a deliberate fashion. Early speculation was that the lights were, in the words of an Associated Press report, German "jet and rocket propelled planes and various other 'newfangled' gadgets against Allied night fighters."

As more pilots across Europe claimed to have encountered the suspicious objects from November 1944 through February 1945, American news outlets reported that the fiery balls had been given a nickname: foo fighters. The origin of the term remains in doubt. Some believe "foo" to have been a corruption of the French term for "fire" (*feu*). Others trace it to the popular comic strip *Smokey Stover*, whose goofy main character was a firefighter, but referred to himself as a "foo fighter." Either way, the moniker stuck. "A foo fighter picked me up at 700 feet and chased me 20 miles down the Rhine Valley," Lt. Donald J. Meiers of the 415th Night Fighter Squadron related to journalists in January 1945. "I turned to starboard, and two balls of fire turned with me. We were going 260 miles an hour and the balls were keeping right up with us."[64]

Reporting on the sightings that same month, *Time* magazine said that explanations of the phenomenon among pilots, radar technicians, and scientists ran the gamut—from innovative remote-controlled devices intended to confuse pilots, interfere with radar, or perhaps even cut a plane's ignition, to simple instances of St. Elmo's Fire.[65] When the CIA formed a scientific advisory panel in 1953 to evaluate reports of unidentified flying objects, the group considered the foo fighters of World War II as well. In the end, the panel seemed to side with the skeptics. Foo fighters were apparently "electrostatic (similar to St. Elmo's fire) or electromagnetic phenomena or possibly light reflections from ice crystals in the air, but," they added, "their exact cause or nature was never defined."[66]

———

Well into the eighteenth century, astonishing things—both glorious and ominous—could appear in the sky. And why not? After all, the sky included the heavenly realm of deities and sacred beings. Observers greeted these sightings alternately with amazement, awe, dread, and, at times, alarm. Dating back to medieval travel narratives, the eyewitness experience was considered critical, for credibility could be bestowed only on those who had directly observed these wonders.[67]

Even after modern elites and the mass public began seeing the world around them in more tangible, less spiritual terms, the skies continued to be populated by wondrous things. In the nineteenth and early twentieth centuries, products of human invention became the objects of marvel and speculation. The creation of piloted balloons in the late eighteenth century helped kindle visions of powered airships made by ingenious entrepreneurs. Soon enough, the skies began to fill with billboards, lit signs, dirigibles, and, finally, airplanes themselves. To many, this only confirmed they were living in an age of unbridled progress. Fueled by a combination of nationalism, marketing, the thrill of adventure, and a fascination with technology, aviation was able to recover much of the former enthusiasm and wonder the skies had traditionally inspired.

Never very far off the horizon lay a dark side. Early science fiction writers captured the nagging apprehension that, in the mastery of flight, some would invariably see a military advantage to be had. The airship scares of the turn of the century revealed that the public felt a palpable sense of vulnerability about modern states harnessing aircraft to realize their dreams of national glory. The two world wars affirmed their fears.

Science fiction and pulp magazines were also responsible for adding another element to the mix of enthusiasm and anxiety about air travel: extraterrestrials. The belief that alien civilizations existed dated back to the ancient world, and while it remained a subject of sometimes animated debate, astronomers and theologians by the eighteenth century largely agreed that the prospect seemed likely. Between 1877 and the start of the First World War I, observations of the moon and Mars led some to argue that there was proof of intelligent life there. That said, it was rarely argued that these beings had yet visited earth (Charles Fort being the chief lovely Earth maidens. What they intended to do with them was never made clear.[13]

Here were all the ingredients of the old westerns transplanted to outer space, a style some critics by the early 1940s referred to as "space opera."

In early 1948, Palmer also began overseeing publication of a new magazine called *Fate*. With it, he and his associate Curtis Fuller—editor of *Flying* magazine—looked to capitalize on the budding interest in flying saucers by publishing a pulp magazine that focused on the unidentified flying objects as well as a catalog of paranormal and occult phenomena. Ghosts, psychedelic drugs, Yeti, religious cults, black magic, X-ray vision: all found a home in *Fate*. Like its predecessors, the magazine developed its own style, replete with pulp covers, fantastic claims, doubts about conventional thinking and authorities, and an invitation to readers to send in their own stories of paranormal encounters.

Fate's debut issue promised to uncover "the truth about flying saucers" and featured Kenneth Arnold's account of his encounter with the odd disks. Arnold's story was accompanied by a commissioned piece from aeronautic expert John C. Ross, who noted similarities between what Arnold claimed to have seen and some new aircraft in development. But if Arnold's description of what he saw was correct, Ross admitted, "I do not believe they were manufactured in the United States or in the Soviet Union or even on the Planet Earth itself."[14]

Through *Fate*, the flying saucer sighting met the world of science fiction fantasy. Even before this, there had been a meeting of minds between Ray Palmer and Kenneth Arnold. In fact, the two struck up a partnership and friendship soon after the pilot's famous sighting and eventually published a book together, *The Coming of the Saucers* (1952).

As they later recounted, Arnold's brush with flying saucers had not ended in June of 1947. A few weeks later in July, Palmer had asked Arnold to go to Tacoma, Washington, to check out the story of two harbor patrolmen— Harold Dahl and Fred Crisman—who had sent Palmer a package containing what they claimed were fragments of a flying saucer. Arnold reluctantly agreed.

After Arnold checked in to his hotel, Dahl paid him a visit and told him that in June he and a crew had had their own sighting of "six very large doughnut-shaped craft" with portholes while boating off Maury Island. One of the craft appeared to be having mechanical trouble, he said, and debris from the vessel fell to earth, some of which he and his crew picked up. The next day, a stranger in a dark suit came to Dahl's home and invited him to breakfast. Dahl obliged. Once at the diner, the mysterious figure exception). Instead, public intellectuals put forward plans to try to send signals to our extraterrestrial neighbors, while mediums attempted to contact them telepathically.

It was science fiction writers who brought the aliens to earth. In both the novel and the radio broadcast of *The War of the Worlds*, the visions historically associated with aviation converged with longstanding discussions about extraterrestrial civilizations. Wells and Welles provided an arresting set of images, sounds, and emotions to at least imagine what a global encounter with aliens might look like. World War II did nothing to discourage the belief that one day space travel too would likely be exploited for the purpose of conquest.

Looking back from the present day, it seems at first so self-evident that all the elements in the flying saucer phenomenon were there decades earlier than Kenneth Arnold's flight around Mt. Rainier. Mysterious flying machines. Alien worlds. Extraterrestrial communications. Remarkable achievements in aviation, science, and engineering. Global warfare and public anxiety.

And yet, as haunting as cases of telepathic contact with extraterrestrials, the airship scares, *The War of the Worlds* broadcast, and foo fighters were, they were fleeting episodes in history. They failed to inspire sustained media interest, to launch a mass movement, or to shape an international pastime. It would take flying saucers to do this.

And that presents a new riddle. Why did flying saucer sightings become such a pervasive and persistent obsession, when earlier versions of the phenomenon did not?

3

Spaceships, Conspiracies, and the Birth of the UFO Detective, 1948–1953

By the end of 1947, a skeptic about flying saucers might well have concluded that reports of sightings were fast becoming a thing of the past. In the United States at least, media interest was fading. Flying saucers appeared ready to go the way of airships, wartime foo fighters, and postwar ghost rockets: here today, gone tomorrow.

But on January 8 and 9 in 1948, newspapers across the country announced that flying saucers may have claimed their first casualty. A twenty-five-year-old Kentucky Air National Guard pilot, Thomas Mantell, died while pursuing an unidentified flying object. Mantell and two other pilots in the vicinity had spotted the object and attempted to track it down. The others eventually gave up the chase. Mantell did not. A witness reported, "The plane circled three times, like the pilot didn't know where he was going, and then started into a dive from about 20,000 feet. About halfway down there was a terrific explosion."[1] The official explanation was that Mantell mistook the planet Venus for an aircraft, flew too high, and eventually lost consciousness and control of his plane. Over the years, UFO enthusiasts have cast doubts on this explanation, noting Mantell's considerable flight experience.

Then, in the early hours of July 24, two Eastern Airlines pilots, Clarence Chiles and John Whitted, were flying their DC-3 around five thousand feet over Alabama, when they spotted what appeared to be a wingless, cigar-shaped object traveling rapidly within five hundred feet of their plane. The men described the fuselage as having two rows of windows, about one hundred feet in length, and moving at an estimated seven hundred mph. It looked like "one of those fantastic Flash Gordon rocket ships in the funny papers," Whitted later explained. After passing the DC-3, the object quickly darted out of sight.

Upon landing in Atlanta, Chiles and Whitted found that news of the sighting was already public knowledge, and the two were subsequently interviewed on the radio and by newspapers. The Pentagon's initial public response was to say that the object spotted was a weather balloon, but it soon backed away from that explanation.[2] Internally, officials in the US Air Force responsible for tracking unidentified flying objects were rattled. As Edward Ruppelt, director of the operation from 1951 to 1953, later put it, "According to the old timers at ATIC [Air Technical Intelligence Center], this report shook them worse than the Mantell Incident. This was the first time two reliable sources had been really close enough to anything resembling a UFO to get a good look and live to tell about it."[3] At this point some officials apparently went on record to declare to their superiors it was now their assessment that flying saucers were interplanetary vessels.

Public opinion would come to change too. When George Gallup in August 1947 published the results of a survey he conducted just weeks after Kenneth Arnold's sighting, he revealed that 9 out of 10 Americans had heard of flying saucers (compared to only about half who had heard of the Marshall Plan). As to what the objects might be, 33 percent at the time didn't have an answer, 29 percent thought witnesses were mistaken, and 15 percent thought they were secret American weapons. If anyone thought they were spaceships, their answer was buried within the 9 percent under "other."[4]

Ten years later in August 1957, Trendex conducted another survey of the American public, asking "From what you have heard or read, do you believe that there is some possibility that they [flying saucers] may be objects from outer space?" Most (52.9 percent) rejected the possibility outright or didn't know (21.8 percent). But a little over 25 percent said yes.[5]

Within a decade, speculation that flying saucers were visitors from another planet went from being an opinion associated with "crackpots" to a seemingly legitimate explanation alongside others. Even if most Americans remained dubious, by the mid-1950s the proposition that flying saucers were extraterrestrial in origin had earned its place in public debate. How did this happen? Did the general public arrive at this themselves? Or were they inspired by others?

SATURATED SKIES

People were, in fact, seeing new things in the sky. Never before had there been so much traffic overhead. Military and civilian air travel had arrived.

Civil aviation in the United States was first regulated beginning in 1926 with the Air Commerce Act of 1926. Over the next six years, air traffic over the country grew, though technical hurdles limited this growth. During the late twenties and thirties, the impact of regulation was especially felt in air safety, where the passenger fatality rate was cut in half in just two years. The establishment of beacons, course lights, and two-way radio communication between air and ground made it possible for increasing miles of airspace to be navigable at night and in bad weather. This benefited both airmail and passenger traffic. During the years 1929–1932, the number of airline passengers carried domestically rose from 160,000 to 474,000 and some 127 million passenger-miles were flown. The introduction of the DC-3—larger, faster, and with a greater range than previous planes— into regular passenger service in 1936 made it possible, for the first time, for passenger traffic to produce more revenue for airlines than their mail services.[6]

World War II helped make airplanes more ubiquitous in more places than ever. Building some 330,000 aircraft during the war, military aircraft were flying constantly. And since the US government needed bases for all these planes, aircraft could be seen all over the country, particularly in the Southwest where the weather was especially favorable. The first overseas flights by a US airline on a regular basis were those by Northeast Airlines, beginning in the North Atlantic in February 1942. Northwest, TWA, and Eastern Air Lines followed suit that same year with flights to and from Brazil, the Caribbean, the Middle East, Siberia, and the South Atlantic. Between 1943 and 1947, the number of passengers carried by domestic airlines quadrupled.[7]

In the aftermath of the war, both domestic and international air travel experienced a stunning boom. By the end of 1949, lower coach class fares were widely available, with a coast-to-coast flight on TWA available at $110. The entire country was soon being serviced by a network of national, so-called trunk, airlines, while secondary carriers served less populated areas. In 1945, the total passenger miles flown on domestic and American flag carriers was over 3.5 billion; within one year, the figure had risen to 6 billion, increasing to over 8 billion in 1950 and 14.7 billion in 1953. Meanwhile, Pan Am, Braniff, and United established scheduled routes connecting the United States with Asia, Europe, Mexico, and South America. By the early fifties, planes had effectively displaced ships as the chief form of travel for international passengers.[8]

During those first seven or eight postwar years, the selling off of military aircraft like the DC-3 and the airlines' introduction of newly designed airplanes had a pronounced impact on the aerial landscape. Not only were more planes in the air, but they were also flying at higher altitudes and faster speeds than had previously been the case. In 1947, the average speed of a domestic aircraft was just over 168 mph, but by 1953 it had reached almost 200 mph. The result, as aviation historian R. E. G. Davies has observed, was "increased congestion at airports" and "the saturation of air space." Already during the war, airports and landing fields sprouted up to accommodate the growing traffic, and the trend only continued in the postwar period; the number of airports and airstrips rose from 2,331 in 1940 to 4,026 in 1945 and 6,760 in 1953. But without adequate controls and coordination between authorities, the situation was precarious. This was made grimly evident at Newark Airport in 1952, when three crashes and more than one hundred deaths forced the New York Port Authority to close it down on February 11.[9]

The existence of so many flying objects undoubtedly contributed to the rise of UFO sightings. A lot was going on above Americans' heads. But this hardly explains why people came to believe that something otherworldly was also making its presence known.

THE MAN WHO INVENTED FLYING SAUCERS?

Pulp fiction editor and Milwaukee native Ray Palmer cut a striking figure. The blonde-haired and blue-eyed Palmer stood at four feet, eight inches tall and was hunchbacked, the result of a botched surgery following a car accident in childhood. What he might have lacked in stature he more than made up for in enthusiasm and drive.

From his youth, Palmer had been an avid reader of early science fiction, particularly the magazine *Amazing Stories*. By 1938, he had gone from being an adoring fan to editor of the periodical. He relished his chance to mesmerize readers with tales of the bizarre. Among his most successful launches were a series of what were billed as "true stories" by Richard Shaver, beginning in 1945. In them, the author told of there being a monstrous subterranean race of beings who kidnapped surface-dwellers, abused scantily clad women, and used powerful rays to make humans do their bidding. Promoted by Palmer as "The Shaver Mystery," the yarns helped *Amazing Stories* sell hundreds of thousands of issues.[10]

Shaver's fantastic accounts, though inventive, were not a new thing. Decades earlier, a whole new genre of literature had emerged to serve a growing niche market: pulp fiction. Developed at the end of the nineteenth century, the pulps were magazines printed on cheap paper and often in a large format, with eye-catching colored images on their covers. During the twenties and thirties, the magazines offered millions of readers a steady stream of serialized adventures involving star-crossed lovers, daring flying aces, hard-boiled detectives, gun fighters of the Old West, macabre horror stories, and, of course, breath-taking tales of science fiction. When it launched in 1926, *Amazing Stories* was the first all sci-fi magazine in the United States. By the start of World War II, it had been joined by an array of others, all with titles promising mind-boggling thrills, including *Science Wonder Stories*, *Astounding Stories of Super-Science*, *Startling Stories*, and *Planet Stories*.

Popular especially among working-class and younger readers, the magazines inspired an enthusiastic fan base. Seeing an opportunity to promote sales, *Amazing Stories* editor Hugo Gernsback began publishing fans' letters along with their home addresses so that they could get in touch with one another and form their own readers' clubs. "The point we wish to make," Gernsback told readers in 1929, "is that our correspondents themselves must organize the clubs, recognizing that we are interested in it, and will be, in the future when it takes shape, delighted to give its progress space in our columns."[11] The ploy worked. By the end of the year, a number of "science correspondence clubs" had sprouted up throughout the country, many of whose members included sci-fi authors themselves.

Ray Palmer and fellow enthusiast Walter Dennis were among those who founded their own club. In 1930, they took the fan experience a step further, starting one of the first ever fanzines, a ten-page mimeographed newsletter called *The Comet*.[12] Others followed, with names like *The Planet*, *Science Fiction Digest*, *The Fantasy Fan*, *Alchemist*, and *Spaceways*. The newsletters gave sci-fi followers a chance to read fan book reviews, keep up on club outings and get-togethers, and generally share common interests. After the war, fan clubs and fanzines like these came to serve as a model for the flying saucer clubs and newsletters of the 1950s.

By 1938, publisher Bernard George Davis handed over *Amazing Stories* to the exuberant Palmer. Davis, however, made it clear he expected stories and human interest to be center stage, not science. Palmer obliged and added another element common among some of the other pulps of the time: risqué covers, with images of scantily clothed damsels in distress. Under his watch, *Amazing Stories* adopted a tried-and-true formula for its tales: they were fast-moving, melodramatic, suspenseful, with a tinge of sex. As one staff writer described a typical Palmer story,

> A raygun was a raygun, a space warp a space warp, and no scientific details need apply. Alien invaders from west of Sirius were beaten back by armadas of Earth's spaceships commanded by steel-thewed heroes; bug-eyed monsters pursued

described the entire episode Dahl had experienced the previous day and left him with a warning that "if he loved his family and didn't want anything to happen to his general welfare, he would not discuss his experience with anyone."[15]

Arnold went on to speak with Dahl's associate Fred Crisman, who confirmed the story. Afterward, the men showed Arnold some of the supposed debris, which to him looked like lava stone. Unconvinced by the men's claims, Arnold invited two acquaintances working in army intelligence— Capt. Davidson and Lt. Brown—to come to Tacoma to look into the matter themselves. After interviewing Crisman and examining the debris, they dismissed the whole thing as nothing more than an elaborate hoax. Davidson and Brown flew back to their base that night.

The next morning, Arnold was given the news that the B-25 bomber Davidson and Brown were flying had exploded twenty minutes after takeoff, killing them both. The *Tacoma Times* newspaper ran the banner headline, "SABOTAGE HINTED IN CRASH OF ARMY BOMBER AT KELSO: Plane May Hold Flying Disc Secret." As Arnold later recalled, "Suddenly I didn't want to play investigator any longer." He decided to call Palmer in Chicago "and get out of this mess." Adding to his dread, a United Press newswire reporter in Tacoma whom Arnold knew told him that informants were saying the plane had carried some specially guarded cargo and that it may well have been shot out of the sky deliberately. "I'm just giving you sound advice," the reporter told Arnold. "Get out of this town until whatever it is blows over. . . . I'm concerned with your welfare."[16]

Before leaving town, Arnold tried to track down Dahl and Crisman. They were nowhere to be found. When Arnold went by Dahl's home, he found the entire house emptied of all its furniture. A few days later, Crisman and Dahl were questioned by the FBI in Tacoma, where they told investigators a different story: they had made the whole thing up. Neither worked for the harbor patrol, and the fragments were never from a flying saucer. They insisted Ray Palmer had pressured them so much they simply gave in and said what they thought he wanted to hear. In the end, the report of flying saucers over Maury Island was officially dismissed as a hoax. But Palmer never tired of suggesting that a conspiracy lay behind the affair and that at its center was the shady figure of Fred Crisman.

The Maury Island episode would become the stuff of flying saucer lore. Over the decades, most UFO researchers accepted that Dahl and Crisman had perpetrated a fraud. Others insisted that the incident proved that insidious figures loomed over the flying saucer phenomenon, prepared to stop at nothing to silence any talk of extraterrestrial visitors.[17]

The events surrounding the Maury Island incident established a precedent. The case set in motion the way in which countless other flying saucer reports would be investigated, analyzed, and written about. By enlisting the aid of Kenneth Arnold—a businessman and sometime aviator who had witnessed unidentifiable flying objects—to play private investigator to the bizarre claims of two strangers who proved to be hoaxers, Ray Palmer helped orchestrate a marriage of fact and fiction that extended beyond the written page and spilled over into real life. Reports of a bizarre sighting, questionable physical evidence, amateur sleuths, nefarious and mysterious characters, suspicious disappearances, federal agents, accusations of a hoax, and fears about a conspiracy. Palmer, Arnold, Dahl, and Crisman unwittingly provided the blueprint for and themselves became characters in what would become the recurring melodrama of ufology.

Decades later, John Keel, a writer about the paranormal, would credit Ray Palmer with being "the man who invented flying saucers." Palmer, he said, "assigned artists [for *Amazing Stories*] to make sketches of objects described by readers, and disc-shaped flying machines appeared on the covers of his magazine long before June 1947."[18] Religious studies scholar David Halperin has since questioned Keel's assessment. The images of flying saucers that illustrated issues of *Amazing Stories* in the late-forties and early-fifties, he notes, came after the first sightings. "It was the UFO phenomenon that impacted science-fiction, not the other way around."[19]

In the end, Ray Palmer did not invent flying saucers, but did introduce them to the world of pulp science fiction. Talk about unidentified flying objects would never be the same.

THINGS GET REAL

In 1949, most observers considered flying saucer sightings to be genuinely puzzling. Yet despite the musings of science fiction buffs, there is little evidence to indicate that most Americans at the time took seriously the idea that extraterrestrials were behind the flying disks. Most instead were drawn to more earthly explanations.

In April and May of 1949, freelance writer Sidney Shalett published a lengthy piece in the *Saturday Evening Post* in which he laid out the most plausible of these explanations.[20] Shalett researched the article for two months, interviewing witnesses, scientific experts, and officials in the Air Force. And he reexamined some of the prominent sightings, including the cases of Kenneth Arnold, Thomas Mantell, Chiles and Whitted, and Maury Island.

Shalett acknowledged that the spate of flying saucer reports over the previous two years could not be dismissed as hoaxes or the ramblings of disturbed minds. The roll of witnesses, he thought, included too many reputable professionals like police officers, airline pilots, businessmen, and astronomers. His sources told him there were a number of things that could account for the growing number of reports.

Among those Shalett cited was Ohio State University astronomer J. Allen Hynek, who was serving as a consultant to the Air Force in its study of flying saucers. Hynek estimated that around 25 percent of sightings could be pinned on planets, shooting stars, and other natural objects in space. But there were other suspects as well. Military and weather balloons—especially gyrating radar-wind target balloons that operated between forty thousand and sixty thousand feet and Navy skyhook balloons designed to detect nuclear bomb tests and able to reach one hundred thousand feet in the air—were commonly mistaken for flying saucers. Air beacons and searchlights also fell into the category. And, Shalett noted, both the US Air Force and Navy were known to be experimenting with new types of supersonic planes and missiles. The skies were teeming with curious but manmade objects.

Shalett's article was a textbook example of another kind of intervention in the conversation about flying saucers, one that would repeatedly turn up over the coming decades: the skeptic attempting to explain away sightings. Like others that followed, the piece also came with a moral lesson. "The Great Flying Saucer Scare," Shalett emphasized, "showed us to be, when frightened, as credulous as anyone else." The brouhaha over unidentified flying objects, it seemed, offered a cautionary tale about how easily fear and gullibility could overthrow our sense of rationality.

Yet Shalett himself showed at least one major organization was taking flying saucers seriously. Since July 1947, the US Air Force Office of Intelligence had been looking into the most credible reports and concluded that unidentified aerial objects with unusual features were indeed being spotted. Aeronautic analysts at the Technical Intelligence Division at Air Materiel Command Headquarters at Wright-Patterson Air Force Base in Dayton, Ohio were given the task of assessing the situation more fully. In December, they decided there was enough evidence to warrant the creation of a classified task force to look into reports in a more systematic fashion. In public, journalists like Shalett referred to the Air Force's UFO program as "Project Saucer." Within a few years, however, the official names were made public: Project SIGN and Project GRUDGE.

SIGN began operations in January 1948. The division at Wright-Patterson Air Force Base responsible for the project was an intelligence unit tasked with assessing potential aerial threats to national security. The memory of prominent experimental weapons programs during the Second World War—like Nazi Germany's V-rocket program and America's Manhattan Project—along with growing fears about the Soviet Union and its military capabilities, framed the project's task.[21] Its goal was to determine whether flying saucers were in fact aircraft, and if so, whether they were the work of a foreign power, some other US agency, or something else entirely.

Staff at Wright-Patterson Air Force Base served as the project's analysts, under the direction of Capt. Robert Sneider. Consultants called upon to help included astronomer J. Allen Hynek, experts at Project RAND, and members of the Scientific Advisory Board to the Air Force Chief of Staff.

All in all, Project SIGN combed through more than 250 reported saucer sightings. Its primary focus was on the objects being observed and their movements. In general, observers reported seeing one of four kinds of shapes: flying disks, torpedo-shaped objects, spherical objects, and balls of light. Report details were then matched with information about the location of guided missiles, research facilities, airfields, radio beacons, radar stations, and meteorological stations, as well as the presence of known celestial phenomena and the flight paths of migrating birds. Consideration was also given to such psychological effects as vertigo and optical illusions.

During the first half of 1948, team members appear to have been drawn two explanations: Soviet technology or human error. Then during the last week of July news of the Chiles-Whitted Eastern Airlines sighting reached the group. Investigators were sent to interview the two commercial pilots, and the team found their claims compelling.

Based on the Chiles-Whitted case and several other seemingly credible sightings, a number of Project SIGN analysts were said to have become convinced that none of the conventional explanations sufficed. They decided to write an "Estimate of the Situation" report to their superiors.[22] Flying saucers, it declared, "were interplanetary."[23]

Or so it is said. The report itself may have been sent off in late September 1948, but the chief source vouching for its existence was Edward Ruppelt, former head of the Air Force's UFO task force Project Blue Book. UFO historian Michael Swords points out that two other officials went on record saying they too read it. Historian Kate Dorsch has been more dubious and points out, "No other corroborating evidence suggesting even the existence of this document—let alone its contents—has ever been uncovered. No drafts, no mentions either before or immediately after from either military personnel or consulting scientists, not a single surviving copy (even though Ruppelt claims a few were saved 'as mementos of the golden days') of the many that were allegedly distributed."[24]

If claims of the situation report's existence are accurate, however, it made its way up the chain of command, with officials taking different sides. As Michael Swords has put it, debate largely pitted can-do pilots, engineers, and technicians—professionals prone to thinking "that one could build things that worked, that advances were possible, but that certain things were not yet available"—against dubious scientists inclined to dismiss the extraordinary as impossible or absurd.[25] One of these scientists was the Air Force consultant and Nobel Prize–winning chemist Irving Langmuir. Asked to examine thirty to forty of the best cases as a consultant, Langmuir concluded that photographic evidence and witness statements were murky and inconsistent and that most sightings were likely of Venus.[26] Some Air Intelligence analysts agreed, believing it much more likely that the USSR was flying experimental aircraft over the United States in order to frighten Americans and Europeans into recognizing Soviet military superiority. As the story goes, the "Estimate" finally reached Gen. Hoyt Vandenberg, the Air Force Chief of Staff; he made it clear he wanted to hear nothing of aliens from another planet. The report was rejected and sent back for revision.

Whatever the truth may be about the "Estimate of the Situation" memo, in its final report released internally in February 1949, Project SIGN declared it could find "no definite and conclusive evidence" to prove or disprove the existence of actual unidentified aircraft.[27] "It is unlikely," the report concluded, "that positive proof of their existence will be obtained without examination of the remains of crashed objects." Still, SIGN recommended that further investigations be carried out, but once a "sufficient number of incidents are solved to indicate that these sightings do not represent a special threat to the security of the nation," the project should be terminated.

The report did acknowledge that analysts had considered the possibility of extraterrestrial visitation, but it conceded "the actions attributed to 'flying objects' reported during 1947 and 1948 seem inconsistent with the requirements for space travel." According to the assessments of two consultants—a missile specialist and a nuclear physicist—this left nowhere to turn but to "the efforts of all the science-fiction writers" and "conjure up a large number of hypothetical methods of transportation like gravity shields, space overdrives, teleports, simulators, energy beams and so on." In the end, "all information so far presented on the possible existence of space ships from another planet or of aircraft propelled by an advanced type of atomic power plant have been largely conjecture."

In February 1949, Project SIGN was renamed Project GRUDGE. Running until March 1952, it has been widely seen as little more than an effort aimed at debunking reports of unidentified flying objects. GRUDGE consulted with Swedish Defense Staff about their experience with "ghost rockets," astronomer J. Allen Hynek, the Air Weather Service, MIT physicist George E. Valley, psychologist P. M. Fitts, and the RAND Corporation, examining some 375 incidents.

As a report written in August 1949 shows, just six months into its work, staff had concluded that UFOs did not pose a threat to national security. Unidentified flying objects, the report stated, were the result of the following:

a. Misinterpretation of various conventional objects.
b. A mild form of mass hysteria or "war nerves."
c. Individuals who fabricate such reports to perpetrate a hoax or to seek publicity.
d. Psychopathological persons.[28]

GRUDGE recommended that the investigation of flying saucers "be reduced in scope" and the conclusions shared with the public. For the most part, the only benefit the nation could derive from UFOs would be as a propaganda tool for inciting mass hysteria in enemy populations.

Still, the assessment of Project SIGN and the dismissive conclusions of Project GRUDGE are revealing. Already in the late 1940s some technology experts appeared willing to entertain the possibility that unidentified flying objects were from outer space. At the same time, the association of flying saucers with pulp literature and comics led many—especially scientists and top military officials—to view them as belonging more properly to the world of science fantasy than to the world of science fact. Events in 1950 served only to further widen the gulf separating believers and unbelievers.

THE ALIENS FIND THEIR ADVOCATES

1950 proved to be a pivotal year in shaping the course of UFO history. For the first time, a series of publications pieced together the scattered sightings and fragmented news reports into a compelling, cohesive storyline. The case for visitors from outer space found its first crusaders—and its first plots.

In 1949, the pulp men's magazine *True* asked one of its writers, Donald Keyhoe, to take a look at the flying saucer phenomenon. Keyhoe, who had previously written articles on aviation for the monthly periodical, was a natural choice. A graduate of the US Naval Academy, he became a lieutenant in the Marines and eventually injured himself in a plane crash in 1922. The injury led to his retirement, which gave him a chance to pursue an interest in writing. His stories—with titles like "The Master of Doom" and "The Mystery of the Singing Mummies"—began to appear in the pulp adventure and science fiction magazines *Weird Tales* and *Dr. Yen Sin*.[29]

After becoming an aide to the renowned transatlantic pilot Charles A. Lindbergh in 1927, Keyhoe published his first book entitled *Flying with Lindbergh*. Soon, Keyhoe was writing for mainstream outlets, including the *Saturday Evening Post* and *Reader's Digest*, and eventually published his second book, *M-Day: If War Comes, What Your Government Plans for You* in 1940. When war did come in 1941, he went back to active duty, serving in the Naval Aviation Training Division. After leaving the service, he retired at the rank of major.[30]

By the time Donald Keyhoe began writing about flying saucers for *True* magazine, he had over two decades of publishing experience, firsthand knowledge of aviation, and contacts in the military. These backchannels enabled Keyhoe to gain access to government information about unidentified flying objects. As the chief of the press section at Wright-Patterson Air Force Base (home to Projects SIGN and GRUDGE), Albert Chop, later recalled in an interview, "While the rest of the press, maybe once in six months they say something about UFOs. But Don Keyhoe was at my desk three times a week . . . And he used to bug the hell out of me! I'd come to work and he'd be in my chair! Waiting for me!"[31]

Keyhoe further augmented his knowledge by subscribing to a news clipping service, which provided a steady supply of newspaper articles about flying saucer sightings from across the country. This allowed him to keep tabs on reports that the Air Force and national news outlets often missed or ignored.[32]

On December 26, 1949, the January 1950 edition of *True* magazine hit the shelves, featuring Keyhoe's article "The Flying Saucers Are Real." He would expand the piece into a book by the same title a few months later.[33] It became the first UFO bestseller, selling around five hundred thousand copies.

Keyhoe regaled his readers with the story of Thomas Mantell's crash, the Chiles and Whitted Eastern Airlines encounter, as well as the case of Lt. George Gorman, a National Guard pilot, who claimed to have gotten into a dogfight with a fast-moving light over Fargo airport in October 1948. He pointed out that odd disks and rocket-shaped craft had been reported across the globe, from Sweden to New Guinea, from the Philippines to Paraguay. He consulted with aeronautic engineers on the feasibility of disk-shaped flying machines. And he revealed that a segment of the US intelligence community believed that flying saucers were being controlled by "an interplanetary craft hovering at high altitude." Flying saucers were not only real, they were from outer space.

Much of Keyhoe's book was dedicated to speculating about just what the interplanetary visitors might be up to. Exploration? Research? Reconnaissance? For the time being at least, the saucers seemed content to hover, to merely observe. What their end game was remained a mystery. But investigators believed it most likely that their recent interest in earth had been sparked by spotting the explosion of atomic bombs beginning in 1945.

It was not the only mystery, in Keyhoe's estimation. His contacts in the military had given him access to information about the investigations that had been conducted by the Air Force, what he called Project "Saucer." Yet, despite evidence from reliable witnesses, officials seemed intent on brushing off any suggestion of aliens. Keyhoe described himself as "certain that Project 'Saucer' was trying hard to explain away the sightings and hide the real answer."[34] But why? With Orson Welles's 1938 *War of the Worlds* broadcast still fresh in their minds, authorities seemed to fear touching off a mass panic. The government would need to be pressured to unveil its secrets to the public.

In all this, Keyhoe was breaking new ground. Bringing his skills as a writer and journalist to bear, he fashioned himself as an intrepid investigative reporter trying to get to the bottom of the flying saucer phenomenon. Where were the disks from? What were their intentions? How were they being powered? Why were they here? Keyhoe's own speculations took their cues from those of military officials, classified reports, and aeronautic specialists. Kenneth Arnold may have been the first to play amateur UFO sleuth. But it was Donald Keyhoe who fashioned himself into the first professional ufologist.

Beyond this, he provided the basic building blocks for generations of theorists about unidentified flying objects. Collect reports of curious sightings. Weigh the credibility of witnesses. Assess the technologies being used. Speculate on visitors from other worlds and their puzzling motivations. To these he added one more important element: confronting a government conspiracy of silence. Ufologists from this point on had two goals. They would have to solve the riddle of the flying saucers, and they needed to force the-powers-that-be to disclose the information they were guarding.

Several months after the publication of Keyhoe's book, in the fall of 1950, Frank Scully delivered the next UFO bestseller entitled *Behind the Flying Saucers*.[35] A columnist for the entertainment industry magazine *Variety*, Scully already had used his column in the fall of 1949 to recount an

Fig. 3.1 Donald Keyhoe (left) with his longtime associate at the National Investigations Committee on Aerial Phenomena, Richard Hall, in November 1966. Photo by Duane Howell/ The Denver Post via Getty Images.

extraordinary tale. A group of scientists revealed to him they had just had the opportunity to inspect the remains of a flying saucer that had crashed in the Mojave Desert. The disk was around one hundred feet across and contained elaborate controls, food capsules, technologies of unknown composition, and heavy water "like the water found in Norway, which the Nazis figured would help them to be the first to make an atomic bomb." Even more astonishingly, the scientists said they had seen the dead bodies of sixteen alien crew members, each the size of "Singer midgets" and charred black by the crash. Those investigating believed the creatures had come from Venus and that the saucer likely operated on magnetic power.[36]

Like Keyhoe, Scully developed his story into a book, setting it against the backdrop of the Cold War and the government's preoccupation with secrecy. "Between the people and government today lies a double standard of morality," he insisted.

Anything remotely scientific has become by government definition a matter of military security first; hence of secrecy, something which does not breed security but fear. If we see anything unusual, even in the skies, we the people must either freeze our lips, like a Russian peasant at the sight of a commissar, or give our names, addresses, business connections, and testimony to be screened and filtered by anonymous intelligence officers.

Also like Keyhoe, Scully cast himself as a champion of full disclosure. "There is only one thing to do under such a setup. Expose their tactics," he demanded. "Show that more offenses are committed under the word 'defense' than this world dreams of. Insist that what we say is the whole truth, and what they say is not the whole truth."[37]

"The truth" that Scully went on to chronicle involved two men: a geophysicist in the oil industry named Silas Newton and a magnetics engineer and defense contractor who went by the pseudonym Dr. Gee. Newton had introduced Scully to Dr. Gee. Gee went on to recount how he and Air Force investigators had examined three crashed flying saucers and the corpses of their occupants. He described the uniformed spacemen as being thirty-six to forty inches in height, estimated to be about thirty-five to forty years of age, and "perfectly normal in their development." As an engineer, it was the ship that drew Gee's attention—disk-shaped, with an aluminum-colored shell, all its dimensions oddly divisible by nine. And he had kept an unknown metal artifact from the saucer for testing purposes.

Dr. Gee's claims seemed to confirm Keyhoe's main points. Not only were flying saucers from outer space real, the government knew they were real, but was hiding that fact.

Two years later, an enterprising writer, J. P. Cahn, decided to check out Scully's account. He interviewed Scully and Newton and tracked down Dr. Gee, eventually publishing his findings in *True* magazine.[38] Dr. Gee was in fact Leo GeBauer, a lab technician, and both he and Silas Newton were not accomplished researchers, but rather con men. The two had come up with the idea of developing a "doodlebugger," supposedly an oil-locating device that would invariably make any of its owners a fortune. Newton served as the front man, setting himself up as the president of Newton Oil Company, while GeBauer played the accomplished engineer. But how could they account for this miraculous machine? Captured Venusian technology offered an imaginative, albeit elaborate, explanation. At least one investor was taken in for more than $230,000.

The two men were eventually arrested, tried, and convicted for running a confidence game. They were given probation and ordered to pay restitution. Frank Scully appears to have been just another of their victims. But he never wavered in his view that the original account he gave was true.

In time, Scully receded into the background. Fans of the 1990s television series *The X-Files* have conjectured that the reporter's last name was the inspiration for that of actor Gillian Anderson's character. The show's creator Chris Carter has put that rumor to rest, however, revealing that Dana Scully was named after baseball announcer Vin Scully. Still, Frank Scully's tale of crashed saucers, dead aliens, and government intrigue left its mark. It confirmed the suspicions of some that those in power were not leveling with the general public. And it opened up the prospect of finally setting eyes on the inscrutable occupants of the flying saucers.

Keyhoe and Scully left readers with as many questions as answers. This proved to be a boon for ufology, as others were now encouraged to offer their own theories. When Gerald Heard, a prolific British author who wrote on mysteries, spirituality, and philosophy, took up the subject at the end of 1950, it was questions and not answers that drove his analysis. "The problem then arises," he wrote, "and it is an acute one, second to none in importance to all the peoples of this world: who controls these machines, who has made them, whence do they come?"[39] Based on prevailing science, the nature of the aircrafts, and how they behaved, he was led to guess that they were likely intelligent, insect-like Martians who had been observing us for some time, but were concerned that our use of atomic weapons might pose a threat to the solar system. Yet again, the specter of nuclear war haunted the visions of those trying to fathom the meaning of the flying saucers.

FLYING SAUCERS ON FILM

As the first books appeared reporting on the story of the flying saucers and venturing to unlock their secrets, fiction writers also began taking up the subject. It was in 1950 that the first novel with the term "flying saucer" in the title was published in the United States. British writer Bernard Newman, an author of espionage thrillers and travel books, penned *The Flying Saucer*, setting its plot against the backdrop of the Cold War. The story revolves around a well-intentioned hoax. A group of scientists, concerned about escalating international tensions, stage fake flying saucer crashes—replete with phony alien remains—in England, the United States, and the USSR in order to get the superpowers and their allies to put aside their differences to fight their common extraterrestrial foe. The scheme eventually succeeds, and the world's most pressing problems are resolved.[40]

The Flying Saucer was also the name of the first feature-length movie on the topic, released the same year. Though not an adaptation of the novel by the same name, the film is also more obsessed with Cold War scheming than with alien visitors. Upon hearing that Soviet spies are in Alaska to ferret out the truth about flying saucer sightings there, American intelligence officers recruit a man and a woman to work undercover and find out what the Soviets know. It turns out that there is a flying disk, but it's the invention of a scientist, whose assistant is trying to sell the device to the Russians. Eventually, the assistant takes flight in the saucer, only to have the spaceship explode in midair.

The Flying Saucer was a low-budget affair. Not surprisingly, it did poorly at the box office, and critics were left cold by its flimsy plot. The following year, audiences were treated to their first glimpses of visitors from another planet, when three films were released. *The Man from Planet X* and *The Thing from Another World* regaled viewers with stories of humanoid aliens bent on either enslaving or killing the earthlings they encountered. While the two adopted the adventure plots of earlier space operas, Robert Wise's *The Day the Earth Stood Still* offered a different spin. A flying saucer lands in the National Mall in Washington, DC. The disk is manned by a handsome looking extraterrestrial visitor named Klaatu and his oversized guardian robot Gort. Throughout the film, Klaatu announces he has an important message to relate to the world's leaders, but he is constantly thwarted in his effort to reach them. Eventually taking refuge in his saucer, a dying Klaatu explains to an assembly of scientists that he is part of an interplanetary group that has relinquished their sovereignty to robots like Gort in order to preserve peace. He leaves his listeners with a dire warning. "If you threaten to extend your violence, this Earth of yours will be reduced to a burnt out cinder. Your choice is simple. Join us and live in peace, or pursue your present course and face obliteration. We shall be waiting for your answer. The decision rests with you."

The Day the Earth Stood Still and *The Thing from Another World* showed Hollywood there was an appetite for flying saucers and spacemen, each grossing close to $4 million. Over the course of the 1950s, the studios released more films about (mostly evil-minded) visitors from another world: *It Came from Outer Space* (1953), *The War of the Worlds* (1953), *Killers from Space* (1954), *Earth Versus the Flying Saucers* (1956), *Invasion of the Body Snatchers* (1956), *The Blob* (1958), and *Invisible Invaders* (1959), among others. For the most part, the plots featured the same stock cast of characters found in earlier space opera fiction—a sage scientist or doctor, a heroic couple, futuristic technology, stymied military and police, and, of course, nefarious aliens.

Like pulp magazines, Hollywood helped bring adventure and drama—in short, entertainment—to flying saucers and extraterrestrials. By telling its stories pictorially, film offered audiences images of spaceships and aliens, making them more vivid than written prose ever could. Still, the movies remained relegated to the world of fantasy.

But in 1950, photography also began lending credence to the reality of flying saucers. In June, newspapers across the country and the venerable photojournalism magazine *Life* featured two photographs of a flying saucer taken by McMinnville, Oregon, farmer Paul Trent. The magazine largely left the images to speak for themselves, but the article described Trent as "an honest individual" and claimed the negatives showed "no signs of having been tampered with."

Trent's set of photographs were unlike anything that had appeared before them: clear, dramatic, with a defined view of the object. The photos were widely hailed as the first compelling pictures of a flying saucer.

To be sure, a number of grainy and blurry photos of flying saucers had been made public before this, dating back to just a few days after Kenneth Arnold's sighting. But none of these earlier pictures could surpass the definition and detail of Trent's photos. For decades to come, UFO enthusiasts,

Fig. 3.2 Paul Trent's set of photographs were first published in early June 1950 in the McMinnville *Telephone Register*. The photos were widely hailed as the first compelling pictures of a flying saucer. Loomis Dean/The LIFE Picture Collection/Shutterstock.

investigators, and skeptics alike puzzled over the snapshots, debating whether it was all a hoax or the real thing.[41] In the process, the McMinnville flying saucer became one of the most iconic images of an unidentified flying object and helped inspire generations of budding UFO photographers. If seeing was believing, the next best thing to capturing a flying saucer was to capture it on film.

LINGERING DOUBTS AND THE SUMMER OF THE SAUCERS, 1950–1952

Over the course of 1950 and 1951, local newspapers throughout the United States continued to carry stories about flying saucer sightings. A woman in California whose car was buzzed by something that "looked like two dinner plates." A private pilot flying over Illinois who saw a sixty-foot disk flying at great speed. A Michigan congressman who, along with other witnesses, saw an unidentified flying object in the middle of a summer afternoon. Two Massachusetts high school students who, while driving their car one night, encountered a flying disk giving off sparks that "went up and down about 20 feet each way, and made a weird, high-pitched, whistling noise. Then it went straight up and was gone in a second."[42]

What exactly did witnesses at the time think they were seeing? It's difficult to generalize. Reports were often brief and lacked detail and, of course, different people had different perspectives. The Michigan congressman, for one, insisted he believed the object was an American military aircraft.

An informal survey of witnesses conducted around this time seems to confirm that this was a common sentiment. In 1951, *Popular Science* asked a sample of people who reported seeing a flying saucer to choose which of four explanations they considered to be the most plausible for their experience. The results were revealing: 52 percent thought they saw "man-made aircraft," 28 percent weren't sure what they saw, 16 percent believed they saw "something commonplace," and only 4 percent felt they had witnessed a "visitor from afar."[43] For all the conjecture about buzzing spaceships and curious Martians, most of the public were still decidedly earthbound in their explanations.

This hardly deterred news media outlets. They continued to report on individual sightings, albeit in a more muted fashion. Then, in the spring and summer of 1952, the topic of flying saucers took on a new urgency, becoming front page news.

That April, *Life* once again took on flying saucers, this time in a lengthy article by H. B. Darrach Jr. and Robert E. Ginna Jr. entitled "Have We

Visitors From Space?"[44] Besides recaps of Arnold's sighting, the death of Thomas Mantell, and the Eastern Airlines incident, the article offered up a number of perplexing cases collected by the Air Force's UFO projects: hundreds of witnesses who saw numerous lights racing across the night sky over Lubbock, Texas, between August and November 1951; an astronomer in New Mexico who, along with his family, witnessed a bright object hovering in the clouds; an Air Force officer who tracked five objects on radar across a three-hundred-mile scope in less than four minutes. Citing an array of experts, the authors of the piece ruled out all the standard explanations. These were real, physical objects, not psychological phenomena, objects far beyond American and Soviet capabilities. There was only one plausible explanation left, they insisted, and quoted applied physicist Maurice Biot. "The least improbable explanation is that these things are artificial and controlled," Biot said. "My opinion for some time has been that they have an extraterrestrial origin."

The article had an immediate impact. Decades later, veteran UFO historian Jerome Clark recalled that he was first introduced to flying saucers when that issue of *Life* arrived in his home. "A few hours or days later, I told some playmates about 'flying saucers.' 'Some people think they're from outer space,' I said—something my dad must have told me, since I could not have read the piece myself." This began what Clark refers to as his "private 1950s," his abiding fascination with UFOs and "an ever deepening skepticism of received wisdom about all things."[45]

Life described the response to its article as "unprecedented." The Air Force reported a rise in reports from witnesses following the publication. The magazine itself received a stream of letters from readers, all suggesting their own theories for the phenomenon. "We should start construction of a suitable landing field for them," one reader wrote. Another said, "God is trying to tell the world something." Scientists also wrote in, arguing that it was more likely that things like lenticular clouds and reflections and refractions of light over desert terrain were being mistaken for flying objects. *Life* encouraged its readers to remain vigilant and report "the sighting of any strange aerial objects to the nearest Air Force representatives" and, if possible, to "photograph any such object you see."[46]

The summer months of 1952 brought with them a stunning turn of events. The number of reported unidentified flying objects sightings skyrocketed. Whereas Air Force Intelligence typically had received only 20–30 reports a month, it logged 149 in June, nearly 500 in July, and another 175 in August.[47]

One of the most alarming cases happened over the course of two consecutive weekends in late July around Washington, DC. Air traffic controllers at Washington National Airport detected a cluster of blips on their radarscopes not far from the US Capitol. A senior controller who observed the initial incident on the night of July 19/20 was emphatic that "they were not ordinary aircraft," since it was clear they were able to make "right angle turns and complete reversals of flight." Radar showed, he said, they were especially active in the vicinity of planes in the area. "They acted like a bunch of small kids playing. It was helter-skelter as if directed by some innate curiosity."[48]

Air traffic controllers weren't the only ones to take notice of the strange objects. Nearby Air Force base personnel, military and commercial airline pilots, and local residents were among a host of observers who reported seeing fast and erratically moving lights in the night sky. A Capital Airlines captain who tracked seven of the objects one night between DC and Martinsburg, West Virginia, recounted they traveled with "tremendous vertical speed," moving up, then suddenly down, speeding up, slowing down, and seemingly hanging motionless at will.[49] By July 28, it was reported that jet interceptor planes of the Eastern Air Defense Command were on twenty-four-hour alert to take off as soon as any new blips or lights were spotted.[50] The capital was caught up in a classic UFO flap.

Initially, government officials said they were baffled by the phenomenon, but adamantly denied they were secret American weapons. But it was clear they recognized that their claims of ignorance only reinforced the dubious views of some. "What more can we do or say to convince people that we are not trying to hide something," an exasperated Pentagon spokesman asked reporters, "that we feel there is honestly no reason to believe there is any inexplicable mystery at all about 'flying saucer' reports."[51] Eventually, Maj. Gen. John A. Samford, the Air Force's director of intelligence, announced that experts were of the opinion that temperature inversions—layers of warm air trapping cooler air below them—were likely responsible for bending radar and light waves, causing the bizarre sightings.[52]

That hardly closed the matter. Throughout the month of August, newspapers across the country detailed countless sightings of unidentified flying objects. The Washington flap, it appeared, was part of a wave. In upstate New York, hundreds observed "flotillas" of shiny objects racing above them. Saucer-shaped blobs were seen over Ada, Oklahoma. Observers spotted flare-like objects near Fort Bragg one afternoon. In fact, military bases were fairly common sites for sightings: Lake Erie Coast Guard Base near Niagara Falls, Lake Charles Air Force Station in Louisiana, Keesler Air Force Base in Mississippi, Hamilton Air Force Base and Travis Air Force Base in California, Ellington Air Force Base in Houston. And then there were international reports of sightings, from Peru, France, Germany, Italy, Israel,

Iran. Details from witnesses were often much the same: they told of seeing luminous objects or unusual lights, often moving in concert, accelerating at great speeds, capable of remarkable maneuvers (like climbing at steep angles or taking sharp turns) and then suddenly disappearing from view.[53]

What can be made of the wave of 1952, what some have called "the summer of the saucers"? Ufologists and skeptics would later offer their own divergent explanations for the rash of reported sightings. What can't escape notice is the prominent role the media played in not just covering UFO sightings, but also actively promoting them. Even if UFOs were in fact popping up with greater frequency, news outlets often exploited the situation for their own purposes.

Take an example from Indiana at the beginning of August 1952. Inspired by the wave of sightings following the reports from Washington, *The South Bend Tribune* decided to organize an event it called "Operation Flying Saucer." The paper enlisted the help of members of the civil defense Ground Observer Corps, local military radar sites and police, and an amateur astronomy club in scouring the skies for a mass watch to take place one Saturday evening, posting six mobile shortwave radio transmitters at select vantage points. Meanwhile, the *Tribune*'s radio station affiliate urged its listeners to stand watch and to call the newspaper's number and ask to speak to an Operation Flying Saucer staff member. The staff person was then to pass any credible sightings back to the radio station, which then would report it to listeners, so that others in the area could be on the lookout. As a final touch, a lone reporter was placed in an airplane and asked to cruise the area, while remaining in radio contact.

Two thousand were said to have packed Notre Dame stadium to look through telescopes set up there. All fifty-five civil defense posts were manned, and observers saw residents sitting out on rooftops and in yards. At the same time, the newsroom phone lines remained busy, logging hundreds of reports. To be sure, a share were gag calls, but most were thought to be sincere. Few—perhaps around one hundred—were deemed worthy of the Air Force's attention.[54]

THE CIA ENTERS THE PICTURE

Not everyone at the time considered flying saucer watching a frivolous pastime. Since the early days of sightings, the Central Intelligence Agency's (CIA) Office of Scientific Intelligence had been tracking developments. The wave of sightings in the summer of 1952 caught the eye of CIA officers and led its director, Gen. Walter Bedell Smith, to approve a UFO intelligence program in collaboration with the Air Force. The initiative foundered after it met resistance from the Air Force. The chiefs of most of the US intelligence agencies then instructed the CIA instead to recruit a number of leading scientists to examine the evidence and then decide whether a dedicated CIA program was actually warranted.[55]

The outcome was the creation of a panel whose job was to determine what, if any, threat "unidentified flying objects"—a term that had become commonplace in government circles since Project GRUDGE—might pose to the United States. The panel was headed by Cal Tech physicist and presidential scientific advisor H. P. Robertson. Robertson was joined by physicists Luis Alvarez, Lloyd V. Berkner, and Samuel A. Goudsmit, along with astrophysicist Thornton Page, missile specialist Frederick C. Durant III, and the ever-present astronomer and Air Force consultant J. Allen Hynek. All had considerable experience working with government agencies.

What became known as the Robertson Panel met three times in January and February of 1953. Intelligence and technical specialists gave the group briefings. In addition, members examined a sample of Air Force archival materials (documents, films, reports), though prominent ufologists have argued that the sample consisted solely of hoaxes and identified flying object cases.

The panel concluded that there was no evidence that unidentified flying objects were the products of space travelers and that they only indirectly posed a national security risk.[56] "Reasonable explanations" could be found for most sightings, the panel's report stated, though admittedly no one cause fit all cases. But even in those instances for which there was no obvious explanation, the sightings were typically too brief (generally only two to three seconds long) or witnesses too unclear in their descriptions to make investigation worthwhile. The absence of any "hardware" meant the UFOs had something of a "'will-of-the-wisp' nature" to them.

Even with the Robertson Panel deeming flying saucers unremarkable, it still remained an open question as to whether the government need concern itself with the phenomenon. Being a CIA operation, the inquiry considered not just unidentified flying objects themselves, but also any broad social consequences they might have. The Air Force investigations of sightings were forensic in nature, intended to look into individual cases and get to the bottom of them. By contrast, the scope of the CIA's interest in UFOs was necessarily wider, since the agency's job was to gather and analyze any intelligence that could possibly have national security implications.

The Cold War played a pivotal role in the Robertson Panel's thinking. An intelligence-gathering enterprise, the group was tasked with examining existing data, evaluating its reliability, and considering the ramifications any information related to unidentified flying objects might be having on the conflict between the two superpowers.[57] In short, it had to take seriously the fact that information about UFOs could serve military purposes, that it could be weaponized. After all, the Cold War was as much a war of words and worries as it was a conflict between armed forces.

The panel's interest in the gathering and spread of information about flying saucers is what led it to recognize that the very process of reporting sightings to the military was helping to fuel the UFO phenomenon. "The result today is that the Air Force has instituted a fine channel for receiving reports of nearly anything anyone sees in the sky and fails to understand," the panel concluded. "This has been particularly encouraged in popular articles on this and other subjects, such as space travel and science fiction. The result is the mass receipt of low-grade reports which tend to overload channels of communication with material quite irrelevant to hostile objects that might some day appear." The fact that a military agency was collecting reports of UFO sightings sent the message to the general public that "these objects were or might be potential direct threats to national security."

What worried Robertson and the others, then, were the psychological and interpersonal consequences of the UFO phenomenon: the possible misidentification of actual enemy objects, an overloading of emergency reporting channels with false information, the vulnerability of the general population to psychological warfare. "Accordingly," panel member Frederick Durant wrote, "the need for deemphasization made itself apparent."

To accomplish this, the panel recommended that the government embark on an "educational" campaign. This was neither surprising nor an issue unique to UFOs. From 1945 to 1960, US intelligence services came to see mass communication as a useful tool in steering public opinion as part of a psychological warfare campaign against communism. By the early fifties, the US government had already spent a billion dollars doing just that.[58]

In this case, the panel suggested focusing on two things: "training and debunking." Training meant giving military personnel and intelligence analysts the skills to recognize common illuminated objects and meteorological phenomena. Debunking was going to be more complicated, since it involved working with "mass media such as television, motion pictures, and popular articles." The key was to try to make UFOs less fascinating by exposing their "secrets" as mere mirages. The group encouraged all national security agencies to "take immediate steps to strip the Unidentified Flying Objects of the special status they have been given and the aura of mystery they have unfortunately acquired." More ominously, it suggested that budding flying saucer enthusiast groups—like Civilian Flying Saucer Investigators in Los Angeles and the Aerial Phenomena Research

Organization in Wisconsin—be monitored to see what effect their work was having on public sentiment. "The apparent irresponsibility and the possible use of such groups for subversive purposes should be kept in mind," the panel noted.

DEBUNKING FLYING SAUCERS

Ufologists have consistently pointed to the Robertson Panel report as evidence of an early government attempt to silence any talk of unidentified flying objects. Here is clear proof, so the argument goes, that officials were more interested in discrediting reports rather than in discovering what lay behind them. Decades later, the Robertson Panel continues to occupy a prominent place in UFO conspiracy theories and demands for government disclosure.

Few, if any, however, have reflected on the specific interest the panel showed in debunking the flying saucer phenomenon. As surveys at the time showed, the vast majority of the American public were dubious about reports of flying saucers and visitors from outer space. Why then did a group of scientists think debunking was necessary at all? What exactly was debunking? And why did prominent figures at the time consider it so critically important to debunk the UFO phenomenon? Once again, a closer look reveals that skepticism about flying saucers also has a history that was bound up in the Cold War.

The term "debunk," coined in 1923 by American journalist William Woodward, was originally meant to refer back to a couple of older terms, "bunk" and "bunkum," both synonyms for humbug or nonsense. To debunk something therefore meant to expose a claim, belief, or person as false or fraudulent.

The actual practice of debunking preceded the invention of the term and dates back centuries to a tradition of publicly disparaging widely held—typically, religious—beliefs considered to be spurious. Prominent intellectuals in ancient Rome, for instance, ridiculed the faith and rituals associated with certain foreign religions as examples of what they called *superstitio*. Those deemed superstitious were thought "to submit themselves to exaggerated rituals, to adhere in credulous fashion to prophecies, and to allow themselves to be abused by charlatans."[59] During the early modern European witch hunt craze, numerous skeptical theologians and scholars attacked the belief in witchcraft for being flawed and corrupt and argued that those claiming to be witches merely suffered from mental disorders.[60] And as the spiritualist movement inspired a renaissance in belief in ghosts and speaking with the dead over the late nineteenth and early twentieth centuries, magicians like Harry Houdini and ghost hunting sleuths like Harry Price took it upon themselves to reveal the confidence tricks being played on vulnerable clients.[61]

Skepticism's history testifies to the fact that its practitioners have laid claim to a very specific social role. On the one hand, skeptics generally directed their incredulity at what were essentially religious beliefs and assertions, their concern being that fraudulent convictions posed a danger to the moral fabric and well-being of society. At the same time, by dismissing certain beliefs as superstitious, skeptics attempted to draw and police the boundary separating legitimate from illegitimate claims. Skeptics therefore placed themselves in the position of not just arbiters of the truth, but protectors of the general welfare.[62] Theirs has been a decidedly educational and moralizing enterprise.

Debunking flying saucers arose alongside the first claims of sightings and shared the basic features associated with skepticism. Journalists, opinion writers, and Air Force investigators were among the first to dismiss spectacular reports of UFOs as cases of optical illusion, misidentification, hysterical fancy, or outright hoaxes. By the early-1950s, Nobel laureate in chemistry Irving Langmuir publicly dismissed ufology as an example of "pathological science," instances in which "there is no dishonesty involved but where people are tricked into false results by a lack of understanding about what human beings can do to themselves in the way of being led astray by subjective effects, wishful thinking, or threshold interactions."[63]

One of the first sustained efforts to portray the flying saucer craze as a pseudoscientific fad came from American popular science writer Martin Gardner. In 1952, Gardner published *In the Name of Science: An Entertaining Survey of the High Priests and Cultists of Science, Past and Present* (rereleased in 1957 under the title *Fads and Fallacies in the Name of Science*).[64] Billed as "a study in human gullibility," the book directed criticism at a wide range of "pseudo-scientists" and "cranks": Forteans, hollow earth proponents, Lysenkoists, believers in the lost continent of Atlantis, scientologist L. Ron Hubbard, and ESP proponents, among others. Flying saucers, too, drew Gardner's fire.

Gardner dismissed the elaborate stories and theories of writers like Donald Keyhoe, Frank Scully, and Gerald Heard as examples of fanciful "Forteanism" encouraged by unscrupulous characters like Ray Palmer. The skies, he explained, were teeming with weather balloons, guided missiles, and experimental aircraft, as well as commercial planes, birds, reflecting clouds, and vivid planets like Venus. At the same time, frauds further muddied the waters. Wasn't it most likely that Kenneth Arnold and

Thomas Mantell encountered Navy skyhook balloons? Didn't Paul Trent's photographs look a lot like a garbage can thrown into the air? In every case, a more mundane explanation than extraterrestrials was readily available.

Why was Gardner so bothered by all of this? Even if the speculation about visitors from another world was overblown, what harm was there in people enjoying some lighthearted entertainment? Gardner responded to this line of thinking by pointing to the public's alarmed response to Orson Welles's *War of the Worlds* radio broadcast. That panic, he emphasized, showed that the uneducated could be easily whipped into a frenzy by stories inspired by science fiction rather than science fact. Recent history showed where that could lead. "[T]he more the public is confused, the easier it falls prey to doctrines of pseudo-science which may at some future date receive the backing of politically powerful groups," he fretted. "If the German people had been better trained to distinguish good from bad science, would they have swallowed so easily the insane racial theories of the Nazi anthropologists?"[65]

"I AM THE MAN WHO SHOT SANTA CLAUS"

As psychologist Peter Lamont has pointed out, being skeptical is one thing, being a skeptic is another thing entirely.[66] To voluntarily assume the mantle of skeptic or debunker involves much more than simply voicing one's doubts about some accepted wisdom. The self-proclaimed debunker takes on a new career as a public figure, exposing hoaxes, picking holes in faulty beliefs, and defending the authority of experts. Which particular expertise is being defended, however, depends on the context. While early modern skeptics of witchcraft often criticized believers for embracing beliefs contrary to theological doctrine, Martin Gardner thought it was scientific expertise that was under assault from quacks and cultists.

This concern that superstitious beliefs were threatening scientific authority was considered by some to be especially worrisome in early Cold War America. Before the 1940s, scientists generally had little to no experience in public civic engagement, as most believed their work needed to be unencumbered by the gaze and opinion of laypeople. Following the Manhattan Project and the atomic bomb explosions over Japan, however, numerous atomic scientists began publicly sounding the alarm about the dangers of nuclear energy. They ultimately were met by resistance from government officials, who accused many of communist sympathies, demanded loyalty tests, and monitored their activities. At the same time, debates over whether science policies should be left solely in the hands of unaccountable scientists led prominent academics and writers to express the fear that science in the atomic age could be used as a tool of oppression.[67]

All this made scientists—particularly those working in the physical sciences—acutely sensitive to questions about their intentions, integrity, methods, and authority to speak about pressing issues of the day. Those pushing the flying saucer story seemed to be doing just that. None of the major public figures insisting that UFOs were the work of aliens had academic credentials or were trained scientists. Yet they were willing to put themselves forward as experts and claimed to have privileged knowledge that university professors found unreliable, if not outright absurd.

This was the setting for the rise of the first great UFO debunker, Donald Menzel. One of the first theoretical astrophysicists in the United States, Menzel served as the director of the Harvard College Observatory from 1952 to 1966, where he set up programs for research and teaching in radioastronomy and space astronomy and eagerly gave talks to schoolchildren, who nicknamed him "Donald Duck." During World War II, he had served in the Office of the Chief of Naval Communications, where he used his expertise to help match radio frequencies to radio communications. After the war, he continued to work with the military, among other things demonstrating how solar phenomena were relevant to forecasting conditions for radio signals.[68]

It's unclear exactly when Menzel began developing an interest in unidentified flying objects. Sometime between 1947 and 1950, Harvard Observatory director Harlow Shapley suggested to three of his colleagues that they each individually set about disproving what they considered to be one of the prominent pseudosciences of the time. Cecilia Payne-Gaposchkin took on the theories of Immanuel Velikovsky, Bart Bok astrology, and Donald Menzel flying saucers.[69] Menzel shared with his colleagues the conviction that academics had a social obligation to educate the public, especially young people, about science and to correct popular misconceptions.

Menzel's first public pronouncements about UFOs came in the summer of 1952. As he explained in an article he wrote for *Look* magazine that June, Menzel dismissed belief in flying saucers from outer space as a kind of "prehistoric" return to superstitious belief in personalized, supernatural forces. He surmised there were three reasons why, as he put it, "so many civilized people [have] chosen to adopt an uncivilized attitude toward flying saucers": mystery, fear, and entertainment.

First, flying saucers are unusual. All of us are used to regularity. We naturally attribute mystery to the unusual.

Second, we are all nervous. We live in a world that has suddenly become hostile. We have unleashed forces we cannot control; many persons fear we are heading toward a war that will end in the destruction of civilization.

Third, people enjoy being frightened a little. They go to Boris Karloff double features.[70]

Menzel's first book on UFOs, *Flying Saucers*, hit bookshelves during the first half of 1953.[71] In it, he rejected any suggestion that what people had been seeing might be aircraft from outer space or secret weapons from the USSR. Instead, he insisted, all the reported phenomena had perfectly natural explanations. Though he would become known for mocking and belittling the UFO craze, Menzel adopted a tone in the book akin to a slightly stuffy science teacher instructing his pupils—even providing readers with experiments to perform at home and a questionnaire to fill out for reporting sightings. Any ridicule was largely reserved for what he referred to as the "cultist" propagators of far-fetched theories. Menzel did not doubt that many observers had witnessed something unusual in the sky. In fact, he admitted he himself had seen things like "hazy disks" and "a cross flaming in the sky."

Flying saucers, as he put it, were as real as rainbows. Sure, there were "hoaxers and jokers." But by and large, what people reported witnessing were in fact products of the natural world. The culprit in most cases was light being reflected or refracted. Clouds, temperature inversions, water droplets, ice crystals, and dust, Menzel demonstrated, all had the ability to change and bend light in ways, creating shadows, flashes of light, mock suns, and phantom moons. Added to this were planes, weather balloons, kites, shootings stars, and planets that, to the uninformed observer, could create the impression of a strangely moving vehicle overhead.

Working with actual UFO reports to the Air Force, Menzel took on some of the most canonical cases, offering what he considered the most probable explanations. Kenneth Arnold, for instance, likely saw something that was the result of layers of haze just over the back side of a mountain range reflecting the sun like a mirror but tilted in unusual ways due to the jagged terrain. In the unfortunate case of airman Thomas Mantell, descriptions from other pilots in the area hours later made it likely he saw what's called a "mock sun" or "sun dog," an atmospheric phenomenon caused by ice crystals in cirrus clouds and creating a halo effect.

Fig. 3.3 Astronomer and flying saucer debunker Donald Menzel in 1967. Menzel often encouraged his readers to perform experiments that helped demonstrate his points. Mary Evans Picture Library.

Menzel's scoffing take on UFOs and his snub of flying saucer advocates has earned him the animosity of many ufologists. His close association with the military has fed speculation over the years that his work was sponsored by the CIA or that he was an actual operative for American intelligence.[72] While his debunking of UFOs did address the Robertson Panel's recommendation to strip flying saucers of the "aura of mystery" surrounding them, there is no credible evidence to support claims he was doing the bidding of government agencies. Menzel's motivation was to protect the public from what he deemed groundless beliefs and false prophets. He was well aware that in doing so he was putting himself in the position of the perennial killjoy. After all, he told a reporter in 1952, "I am the man who shot Santa Claus."[73]

The wave of peculiar aerial sightings across the United States in 1947 might well have been as fleeting as the great airship scare of 1896–1897. But if the flying saucer sighting was born in 1947, the flying saucer saga was minted over the ensuing six years. Over this time, unidentified flying objects went from being merely observations and things to being a stock set of images, characters, and stories. By the middle of 1953, to mention seeing something moving oddly in the sky instantly conjured up flying disks, Kenneth Arnold, Thomas Mantell, alien corpses, farmer Trent, Donald Keyhoe, the military, government cover-up, hoaxes, and ridiculing skeptics. The Air Force adopted the term UFO to try to rid the phenomenon of these associations, but to no avail. To this very day, for most people, to speak of a UFO is to raise the possibility of extraterrestrial visitors and all that goes with it.

Flying saucer sightings emerged from the ground up, from the reports of witness after witness, admittedly egged on at times by news coverage. The flying saucer saga, however, was the creation of writers and editors, with the particular stamp of pulp fiction publishers, pulp authors, pulp fandom, and pulp themes. The fact that intelligence officials were expressing interest in sightings, while also remaining secretive, fueled suspicions about conspiracies and plots.

Enter the ufologist and his nemesis, the debunker. The two Donalds—Keyhoe and Menzel—offered themselves up as self-styled detectives (Menzel even compared himself to Sherlock Holmes). They would use their knowledge, skills, and contacts to uncover the truth about flying saucers. Keyhoe played the single-minded investigative reporter, exposing covert reports and backroom meetings, Menzel the forensic scientist, reconstructing events before a group of eager students.

Each in his own way did something that proved critical to cementing a future for the flying saucer phenomenon. They created two competing, but compelling, stories about UFOs that took the array of ephemeral sightings and fragmented reports and bound them up into single, coherent narratives set against the backdrop of the Second World War and the looming Cold War.[74] Keyhoe's was a tale of an unbridled technological progress, capable of both great feats of exploration and grisly destruction but *covered up* by powerful elites. Menzel countered with an account of a mystery whose solution was readily at hand for those possessing proper expertise but that was being *covered over* by charlatans and zealots.

The lines were drawn for what would become a perpetual debate about unidentified flying objects between believers and skeptics. Beyond this, Keyhoe and Menzel showed that more was at stake in the flying saucer question than just the possibility of contact with aliens. UFOs touched off a host of political and social concerns and controversies—from citizens' rights to government information, to public trust in authorities, to the limits of science and technology.

These preoccupations seemed especially relevant to many Americans by the early 1950s, living as they did with memories of World War II and the prospect of atomic warfare. But that same cloud hovered over other parts of the world as well—even more so than the United States. If flying saucers were buzzing earth, surely other parts of the world were seeing them too. And if UFOs truly were global, then a global response was necessary.

4

From Mystery to Movement, 1947–1960

In 1948, the Chief of Staff of the United States Air Force was made aware of a number of unusual reports coming out of Turkey in early May of that year. The Istanbul newspaper *Yeni Sabah* reported at the time that witnesses from various parts of the country recently had been seeing "shining objects like meteors" overhead. Some believed them to be rockets. This was borne out by the fact that authorities acknowledged one of the objects had passed over the northwestern city of Adapazari, exploded in the air, and scattered parts in a nearby village, killing a dog. After the debris was inspected, it was confirmed to have been a rocket. But as an internal Air Force memo explained, this did not dissuade the spread of a now familiar canard. "According to rumors, it is possible that the rocket is connected with the 'flying disc' experiments being conducted by the Russians at the station on Mt. Alagoz close to the eastern frontiers." The Air Attaché in Ankara was asked to look into the possibility.[1]

This incident can be found documented in the files of the US Air Force's Project Blue Book. Established in March 1952 to replace Project GRUDGE, Project Blue Book was codename for the office in charge of investigating reports of unidentified flying objects. Headed first by Capt. Edward J. Ruppelt, Blue Book would continue its work into the 1960s. All told, the project filed over 12,600 reports, ranging from as few as 146 to as many as 1,501 incidents a year. 701 remained unidentified.[2]

The events in northern Turkey in 1948 call to mind the encounters residents of Sweden had had two years earlier. In fact, an enterprising ufologist might well try to connect the dots. Perhaps a case can be made that what happened over Adapazari holds the key to making sense of Scandinavia's "ghost rockets"?

The recording of this incident raises new questions about the UFO phenomenon in its early days. First, the episode in Turkey shows that after the wave of flying saucer sightings in the United States in 1947, other parts of the world also were reporting sightings. How widespread was this? Where and when? How were the objects described and explained in these other places? Second, the very presence of Project Blue Book files about these sightings demonstrates that the US Air Force was keeping tabs on UFO reports from other parts of the world. How did it do this and, especially given its professed skepticism, why? Third, the files reveal that the information about the sightings originally came from a Turkish newspaper. How common was it for the world's media to report about unidentified flying objects, and from where were outlets getting their information? And finally, records confirm that rumors about "flying saucers" were circulating at the time. Was this among US personnel? Turkish officials? The local population? How common was it for people across the world to know about flying saucers in 1948 or, say, ten years later in 1958?

After Kenneth Arnold's sighting, American newspapers informed readers of sightings throughout the country. And as reports came in, the US Air Force decided to keep tabs on the situation. A steady flow of scattered sightings punctuated by periodic flaps and waves kept unidentified flying objects in the news. Tracking and arguing over flying saucers from outer space seemed to many to be a quintessential pastime of postwar Americans. As a cultural craze, it's easy to imagine it suffering the same fate as other American fads like vaudeville, pole-sitting, or dance marathons—fun for a time, but with little staying power.

UFOs did not become a quaint footnote of American history. Over the course of the 1950s, flying saucers and speculation about them traveled the globe and stirred a generation of enthusiasts. Not content with standing on the sidelines, these "saucerers" (as the British dubbed them) and "soucoupistes" (as the French called them) would take it upon themselves to press the issue and to look into the flying saucer question themselves. In doing so, they transformed their shared curiosity into an organized, worldwide movement.

GETTING NEWS OF THE FLYING SAUCERS

Reports of Kenneth Arnold's glimpse of unusual aircraft near Mt. Rainier on June 24, 1947, also captured the attention of some outside the United States. French ufologist Henri Chaloupek recalled visiting his aunt in Prague, Czechoslovakia, at the end of June, when a newspaper lying around with an article about Arnold's encounter caught his eye, though he admitted what really sparked his lifelong interest was learning of pilot Thomas Mantell's death months later.[3]

Most people across the globe first began learning about the existence of flying saucers about a week or two after Arnold's sighting. From the end of June and until mid-July, newspapers covered the reports of flying saucers darting across America's air space.[4] French press coverage about "*soucoupes volantes*" began already in late June, and by the end of the first week of July, the daily *Le Monde* was tracking the progress American press agencies were making in coming up with explanations for the "saucers" and "flying crêpes" being observed.[5] In Belgium, *La Libre Belgique* reported on July 5 that "mysterious 'flying saucers'" were plaguing "the American sky."[6] In Spain, the first mention of the term "flying saucers" (*platillos volantes*) appeared in papers on July 8, with follow-up articles quoting US government officials downplaying the wave of sightings there.[7] On July 12, it was reported in Austria that a disk had actually landed in northern Hollywood.[8] At this same time on the other side of the Atlantic, dailies in Chile also began carrying stories about the American wave of sightings. None of these articles were based on original reporting but were gleaned from foreign news agencies.[9]

As news of the flying saucers spread, papers began guessing about what or who might behind the unidentified flying objects. Suspicions in those early days fell on some of the usual suspects: militaries testing new types of aircraft, atomic experiments, secret weapons of the United States or the Soviet Union. But some considered extraterrestrial spaceships a real possibility, finding inspiration in the comic books and science fiction of the era.

Not every country was caught up with following the developments in the United States at first. The press in Argentina, for instance, only became interested in the story once reports coming out of Europe, Japan, and Mexico began to turn up. By and large, newspapers reported on the same set of American sightings and stories, as they relied on large international news agencies for their foreign news.

Take Sweden, for example. Dailies there began reporting about American encounters with flying saucers during the first week of July 1947 based on the newswires of the Associated Press and Reuters. "'Flying saucers' haunt America," *Dagens Nyheters* reported on July 4. On July 7, *Stockholms-Tidningen* cited an AP report that hundreds of people had observed "flying platforms" moving at great altitudes. A few days later, the same paper relied on the AP to report on a possible flying saucer crash in Roswell, New Mexico. When, soon after this, Swedish papers began to publish articles on "flying plates" and a "rocket-like projectile" over Denmark, Norway, and

Sweden, their descriptions and terminology left little doubt that these were the same phenomena being described on the other side of the Atlantic.[10]

This pattern would play out across the world: flying saucers quickly went from being an American drama to a domestic one, as people globally started to report sightings at home. Italian historian of ufology Giuseppe Stilo has examined the dates of the first known UFO sightings in forty countries and has found that most were reported fourteen to eighteen days following the Kenneth Arnold sighting. In some cases—the Soviet Union, Vietnam, Portugal, and Romania—the first dated reports did not appear until 1948 or 1949.[11] More often than not, witnesses did not recount tracking an actual flying disk, but rather catching a fleeting glance of a "sphere," a "ball," an elongated shape, or a bright light traveling silently at a rapid rate. News outlets in these cases took it upon themselves to classify them as flying saucer sightings.

Argentina was one place where this was the case. On July 11, a newspaper in Buenos Aires reported that a flying saucer had been seen over the city of La Plata that day. Witnesses described it as "something like a star" that radiated different colors and moved up and down, eventually disappearing in the western sky. More reports soon followed, with observers telling of zig-zagging disks or large lights moving at high altitudes. In one case, a police officer and several of his men described watching fifty to sixty red, flashing disks moving at high speeds.

As writer Roberto Banchs has put it, Argentinian news stories during this time generally conveyed a sense of "expectation, restlessness, and suspense" about the sightings.[12] That said, they expressed mostly skepticism about reports. *La Hora* lamented the fact Argentina could not "escape the hysteria of the flying saucers," seeing in it nothing more than warmongering propaganda aimed at getting people worked up about imaginary invaders in order to gain their support for an American military build-up. The influential *La Nación* considered the sightings to be but another chapter—following in the path of the Trojan Horse, the V-1 and V-2 programs, and the Manhattan Project—in the history of nations cloaking their military inventions in secrecy. *Noticias Gráficas*, however, mused that reports were most likely the work of pranksters and fame seekers. Most Argentinian dailies treated the phenomenon as light entertainment. Cartoonists there referenced flying disks in conjuring up images of airborne dishes, fruits, and vegetables being thrown by the likes of irritated wives and workers.[13]

Brazil, too, got caught up in the excitement.[14] Newspaper coverage there was concentrated during the first two weeks of July. Witness descriptions of the size and shape of the objects they saw varied and were frequently vague. The press borrowed heavily from the English language terms being bandied about to refer to the phenomena. They spoke of "flying disks" (*discos voadores*), "flying saucers" (*pires voadores*), and "flying platters" (*pratos voadores*). In the end, the media settled on the term "flying disks."

In contrast to Argentina, the Brazilian press communicated a sense of astonishment and wonder about flying saucers, describing sightings with words like "sensational," "mysterious," "incredible," and "fantastic." Getting many of their stories from phone calls from witnesses, papers like *O Noite* did little fact checking. In Rio de Janeiro, where competition between morning, afternoon, and evening newspapers was intense, the flying saucer story was given considerably more space in the latter—papers that were popular mainly with workers, housewives, and young people.

Early explanations in Brazil for the sightings varied, with some taking seriously the possibility of visitors from outer space. But opinion largely broke along two lines of thinking. One camp argued that the disks were real objects, mostly likely secret weapons of the superpowers. The other— one that included most scientists who went on record—thought it likelier that the phenomenon could be chalked up to fevered imaginations and misperceptions. Advocates on both sides agreed that memories of the Second World War and the specter of the Cold War were playing a major role in the phenomenon. Columnist Guilherme de Almeidia mused in *Diário de São Paulo* that recent events showed the world was resolute in its desire to refine and test its secret weapons. And writer Austregésilo de Athayde noted that America was following the example of Sweden's panic over ghost rockets. "Hallucination, my friends, pure hallucination" was behind the whole thing, he contended. "Fear is the father of these fantastic visions."[15]

THE FLYING SAUCER'S INVENTOR REVEALED

What the German magazine *Der Spiegel* had dubbed the "transatlantic whoosh" over flying saucers died down just as quickly as it arrived.[16] By the end of that summer of 1947, the first great wave of UFO sightings was over.

That said, flying saucers did not disappear. Isolated reports cropped up, sightings continued in the United States, and there were occasional flaps, as was the case in Italy in March 1948 and July 1949.[17] And the death of pilot Thomas Mantell while chasing a UFO made international headlines.[18] Flying saucers stayed on people's minds even across the most forbidding geographical boundaries. This is clear from a case recorded in Project Blue Book files.

In December 1949, an unnamed German man was released from his internment as a Soviet prisoner of war. From August to mid-October, he had worked as a handyman in an auto repair shop in Moscow. On two occasions during his captivity, he later told American officials, he caught sight of an unusual flying disk. The center of its body was black, becoming red toward the edges and finally white at the very edge. A "flaming arch" stood atop the disk, and white hot sparks trailed behind. While he was unable to follow it for very long, he noted it was capable of hovering and then darting off at great speed. Interrogators "agreed that the man had seen something and that his statement should be taken to be reliable."[19] Not only did flying saucers travel fast and cross great distances, but the Moscow sighting also shows the news about them could pierce the boundaries of the Iron Curtain and even a prisoner of war camp.

It is one of the more striking features of the UFO phenomenon in its early years that it so swiftly entered the vocabulary and popular culture of the international community. Flying saucers spawned stock rumors and legends that moved with relative ease across the globe. As these spread, they were often tweaked, giving rise to domestic tales that borrowed elements from ones circulating abroad, but now tailored to a national audience.

One of the most prominent of these during the years 1947–1952 sounded strangely similar to stories from the nineteenth-century airship scares. These were reports about an unsung inventor of the flying saucer who had finally come forward to reveal its secrets. Both South America and Europe proved especially fertile ground for such anecdotes.

Admittedly, this particular rumor had some factual basis. Designers had begun mulling over the possibility of a flying disk-like object already by the second decade of the twentieth century. Italian architect Guido Tallei patented his model for "*dischi volanti*" in 1926.[20] In 1944, Dutch engineer and artist Alexander Weygers filed for a patent for what he dubbed a "discopter," whose rotors were enclosed within the discus body of the aircraft.[21] And during World War II, the United States and Germany both came up with their own experimental aircraft—the Vought V-173 Flying Pancake and the Horten Ho 229—that bore a striking resemblance to the flying saucer ideal.

Within weeks of Kenneth Arnold's sighting, dubious figures started coming forward to tell authorities and news outlets they had invented flying saucers years earlier. Among the first of these was W. H. Ashlin, a forty-four-year-old English engineer and former RAF pilot living in Valparaíso, Chile, who claimed to have invented a rotating flying saucer with its own special propulsion system by 1939. Ashlin claimed he had offered the technology to Great Britain to fight Nazi Germany, but officials

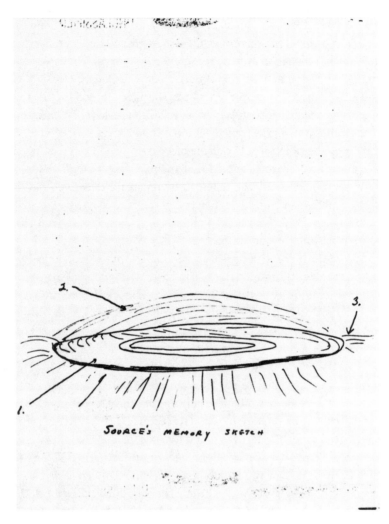

Fig. 4.1 Sketch by a former German prisoner of war of the disk he saw over Moscow in the fall of 1949. #1 was the body, #2 the arch, and #3 the trail of sparks. National Archives (341 NAID-28935719).

weren't interested, so he gave the technical details to the Chilean military in July 1947. Others soon followed suit. In Argentina, two separate men—Juan Bautista Leone and Julio Ruiz—claimed to have developed the flying saucer in the early 1940s. Like Ashlin, Ruiz maintained that he approached the Argentinian army about his "giro-plano," but without success.[22]

Brazil also had its own experience with "inventors." In August 1947, Alcides Teixeria Kopp told reporters that he was the true inventor of flying saucers and that he was guiding them using radar but was hoping the Brazilian government could provide him with resources to continue his

Fig. 4.2 During World War II, the Nazi regime earmarked 500,000 Reich Marks for the brothers Reimar and Walter Horten to develop the all-wing Horten Ho 229. When finally test-flown in 1944, however, it crashed. After the war, rumors spread that German and Italian engineers had successfully mass–produced flying saucers already in the thirties and forties, but there is no evidence to support the claims. Photo by Eric Long, Smithsonian National Air and Space Museum (NASM 2000-9339).

experiments. In 1948, a German national who was being held in a federal prison in Rio de Janeiro for espionage revealed to newspapers that he had designed radio-guided flying saucers under the Nazis for reconnaissance and anti-aircraft purposes. Jacob Johannes Starziczny (alias Niels Christian Christensen) went on to say he was ready to build one for Brazil capable of countering atomic bombs, reaching speeds of one thousand kilometers per hour, and flying without refueling for up to thirty hours. Over the next four years, Starziczny went on to revise some of his claims and made his release a condition for his aid. The Brazilian military dismissed him as a fraud.[23]

Starziczny was not the only one to claim that flying saucers were an invention of Nazi Germany. Just two weeks after Arnold's sighting, the American civilian authority in Frankfurt, Germany, received a letter from a Dr. T. Kelterborn saying that he had sketched plans for a flying saucer and had handed them over to a patent office in Berlin in 1944, though he never heard back from staff there. He therefore suspected that his work had been further developed during the war and was in the hands of the USSR, which was using it against the United States. By 1950, army intelligence officers in Germany had informed their superiors about still other claims that specialists there had developed flying disk technology during the Third Reich.[24]

The idea that flying saucers originated in Nazi Germany and its allies proved to be especially alluring to the media.[25] In March 1950, newspapers in the United States reported on a story appearing in Italian papers that a seventy-three-year-old Italian engineer named Giuseppe Belluzzo was openly saying that he had drafted plans for a flying disk thirty-two feet in diameter and equipped with explosives in 1942. Both Mussolini and Hitler, he said, were intrigued.[26] About a week later, the German magazine *Der Spiegel* quoted engineer Rudolf Schriever, who claimed he had sketched out plans for a rotating flying disk capable of moving at great speeds and hovering in place for hours. Schriever apparently had hoped to submit his drafts to Hermann Goering's office, but the Russians occupied the country before he could do so.[27]

The media coverage given over to speculation about the Nazi origins of flying saucers owed a lot to Germany's historical association with innovative science and technology as well as its wartime V-rocket program. Along with the United States and USSR, Nazi Germany seemed to be one of the few countries with the resources and determination to build such futuristic aircraft. But among a small circle of unreformed nationalists, a more sinister fantasy of Germany's connection with UFOs was being concocted: the idea that Hitler and Nazi scientists were themselves operating the flying saucers.

This elaborate neo-Nazi vision was a pastiche of various rumors, esoteric legends, and antisemitic beliefs circulating in central Europe around the Second World War. One of these—a notion that had enjoyed some cachet within the Nazi hierarchy during the Third Reich—was that it was possible for an occult elite of racially pure Aryans to establish spiritual contact with a metaphysical world center located in the Arctic and Himalayas.[28] Another contributing thread came from speculation that not just high-ranking Nazi party officials, but even Hitler himself had managed to slip away from the clutches of Allied forces. In 1947, a Hungarian national living in Argentina, Ladislao Szabó, published *Hitler esta vivo* (*Hitler Is Alive*) in which he described Hitler's supposed escape to a secret base in Antarctica. It went on to inspire a host of magazine stories into the early-1950s.

The popular fascination with German superweapons and the arrival of flying saucer sightings provided the final pieces for minting a bold, new storyline, first sketched out by Swiss engineer Erich Halik in a series of articles published between 1951 and 1955 in an esoteric Austrian magazine. According to this grand narrative, Hitler and his entourage of German scientists and technicians had managed to escape from Europe carrying their cutting-edge flying saucer technology and were now comfortably ensconced in either Antarctica or the Arctic, where they were preparing to defeat the Allied powers using their flying saucers. The result would lead to the apocalyptic revival of National Socialism. Over the course of the 1960s and 1970s, the story grew and flourished, pushed especially by neo-Nazi publishers and writers Wilhelm Landig and Ernst Zündel.[29]

THE WAVE OF 1950

As was the case in the United States, 1950 marked a watershed in the history of the UFO phenomenon throughout much of the world. In March and April, newspapers and magazines chronicled an explosion of homegrown UFO sightings. In Italy, for example, over 370 sightings were reported that year.[30] Stories of traffic jams caused by gawking crowds, reflections from experts and commentators, and ads picturing saucers and Martians helped support articles about individual sightings. A study by the Italian Center for UFO Studies in Turin of some one hundred Italian dailies found at least two thousand items involving flying saucers made it into print in 1950.[31]

Latin America also experienced a precipitous rise in reported sightings that year. Descriptions of throngs of sky-gazing onlookers blocking traffic were reported in Bolivia, Brazil, Cuba, and Uruguay.[32] In Chile, *La Nacion* reported that citizens were phoning in to recount their sightings. Based on the calls, the Santiago paper summed up, public opinion was wavering between thinking the objects were experimental weapons and suspecting they were Martian signals.[33]

Mexico got caught up in the frenzy after being largely unmoved by the flying saucer wave of 1947. The Mexican press avidly reported on sightings throughout the country in March 1950. First came a report in *Ultimas Noticias* of a group of people who witnessed a static object high in the sky near the Chihuahua Airport. This was followed by the account of two pilots claiming to have seen a flying saucer moving at high speed over Ometepec, Guerrero. Within days, thousands in Chihuahua were tracking a small bright spot in the sky for hours; two pilots spotted a red disk flying at over 250 mph; air traffic controllers, pilots, and tourists in Mexico City followed a shiny object flying in circles near the airport; and there were multiple reports of saucers crashing on Mexican soil. Meteorologists and astronomers explained that Venus, meteors, and weather balloons likely accounted for most, if not all, of the sightings.[34]

What explains this flurry of UFO sightings in March and April of 1950 across multiple countries? At the time most countries had no ufologists and no UFO investigative bodies to collect and publicize reported sightings. All the accounts in the wave of 1950 came from newspapers, magazines, and, to some extent, radio. After a period of being relatively dormant when it came to the subject, why was the international press interested in covering flying saucers?

Once again, the reason can be traced back to the United States—in particular, the publication of Donald Keyhoe's article in the January 1950 issue of *True* magazine. Take Spain, for instance. Before the article hit stands in late December 1949, speculation in Spain about the origins of flying saucers had centered on the Soviet Union. But just days after Keyhoe's piece came out, the Spanish newswire service EFE cited it in an article considering the possibility that UFOs were interplanetary vessels. CIFRA, the national branch of EFE, had a particular penchant for flying saucer stories.[35] During the first few months of 1950, newspapers continued to fuel suspicions about alien visitors, with headlines like "Flying Saucers Are Being Manned by Beings from Another Planet" and "Attack from Mars? The Mystery of Flying Saucers."[36]

Keyhoe enjoyed similar coverage throughout Latin America. After his and Frank Scully's books were published later that year, both received considerable attention in the Americas and Europe. It would be an overstatement to say that Keyhoe singlehandedly created the wave of sightings in 1950, but Keyhoe's reportage provided the impetus for influential news outlets to cover foreign and domestic sightings and explore the alien origins of flying saucers like never before.

FOLLOWING THE NEWS

After 1950, flying saucers became a mainstay of the popular press. News outlets kept tabs on developments, albeit to varying degrees. In the United States, television news organizations showed little interest in the subject until the mid-1960s, and African American newspapers carried almost no UFO stories during the first two decades of the phenomenon. Most dailies covering the story were simply content to passively report on incidents that somehow made it across their desk, playing up any human-interest and entertainment angles. Then wire services picked up a small number of these reports and circulated them nationally and internationally.[37]

While newswire agencies helped spread stories about sightings in the 1950s, a handful of larger newspapers, tabloids, and magazines actively promoted the flying saucer story. Already in 1949, the French daily *France-Soir* dedicated a periodic section in the paper to reports of mysterious lights in the skies over the United States. And in the fall of 1950, it published excerpts from Scully's *Behind the Flying Saucers*. The Brazilian illustrated weekly magazine *O Cruzeiro* featured excerpts from Keyhoe's *The Flying Saucers Are Real*, with stories about flying saucers appearing in a third of its issues in 1952.[38]

In the United Kingdom, news coverage of flying saucers picked up considerably in 1950. Between 1945 and 1949, the *Daily Mail* had printed only five stories about unidentified flying objects. But by October 1950, two competing papers had stepped up their coverage. First, the *Sunday Dispatch*—whose editor Charles Eade was good friends with Lord Mountbatten of Burma, who by then had become an avid UFO enthusiast—published a front-page story on October 1 with the headline "The Story That May Be Bigger Than Atom Bomb Wars," promising readers it would continue to follow up on developments. A week later, the *Sunday Express* serialized Gerald Heard's book *The Riddle of the Flying Saucers*. Eade and the *Sunday Dispatch* countered by publishing extracts from the books of Donald Keyhoe and Frank Scully.[39]

The increased attention to the flying disks appeared to many to lend the phenomenon a growing legitimacy, something that worried at least one prominent European scientist. In April 1951, the French monthly *Science et Vie* (Science and Life) published a piece about flying saucers in which the arguments for and against their reality were laid out, leaving it up to readers to decide what the truth was. The magazine's neutral stance on the subject outraged astrophysicist Évry Schatzman. In a series of articles, Schatzman dismissed the talk of flying saucers as "unhealthy," a "mystification" rooted in American science fiction and driven by a pervasive nervousness and anxiety running through the general public.[40] In France, as was true everywhere the flying saucers turned up, they sparked debate between two camps: the *prosoucoupistes* (pro-saucerists) and the *antisoucoupistes* (anti-saucerists).

Away from newsrooms and ivory towers, early saucerists proved to be far more dedicated and enterprising than their debunking counterparts. Many of those engrossed in the ongoing saga were not content to simply read about sightings that happened to pop up in their favorite periodical. Within months after news broke of the Arnold sighting, devotees began clipping out newspaper and magazine articles about flying saucers and keeping them in piles, files, and scrapbooks.

Some, like the famous psychologist Carl Jung, did so as adults. Many began their collections during childhood. Veteran American ufologist Barry Greenwood recalls starting when he was eleven years old, taking scissors to local newspapers in Boston during big UFO waves in the mid-1960s. He went on to expand his stockpile by swapping copies with other enthusiasts. As the number of his clippings grew over the course of the 1970s, he moved them from simple folders into loose leaf binders with sheet protectors. "At one point when I actually counted them," he recalled, "there were something like 320 large binders from letter-sized to newspaper page-sized."[41]

Once he could afford it, Greenwood—like countless others—subscribed to a press clipping service that regularly fed him articles from across the country. First emerging as a thriving business in the United States in the 1880s, press clipping bureaus offered a form of data mining to paying clients. Customers gave the service one or more search terms. Workers then scoured newspapers and magazines for articles discussing the topic, cutting them out with a blade, pasting them to a slip with a note about the publication and date, then bundled and sent them off to clients. By the first decade of the twentieth century, news clipping bureaus existed throughout Europe, Latin America, the Ottoman Empire, southern Africa, Australia, and Japan.[42]

News clipping services proved invaluable for serious UFO investigators from the early-1950s until well into the 2010s. Longtime Italian UFO researcher Edoardo Russo remembers first subscribing to Lucius (Lou) Farish's US-based UFO news clipping service in 1976 when he was still in his teens. It inspired him to cultivate and exploit similar resources in Italy. Over the next few years, Russo and a group of motivated volunteers began locating and acquiring several large personal clipping collections. By 1981, they had established their own press clipping newsletter, with a network of correspondents across Italy contributing to it throughout its quarter century of existence. Eventually in 1990, the Italian Center for UFO Studies (CISU) set up its own clipping subscription service "Eco della Stampa." By the time the service was ended in 2017, it had distributed some fifteen thousand clippings.[43]

Collecting news clippings did more than give saucer buffs a way to keep up with the latest news. In possession of their own fund of source material, it gave them a chance to intently study the phenomenon on their own. Anyone with the time and tenacity could carry out their own investigations, without relying on the likes of Keyhoe and Scully to digest the evidence for them. The first generation of ufologists was born.

THE FIRST AMERICAN SAUCER GROUPS AND NEWSLETTERS

Some buffs were clearly willing to invest a good deal of their leisure time to following developments. Many, if not most, devotees were content to indulge their interest in private, arguing about flying saucers with friends, family, and co-workers. But some followed the lead of science fiction fans in the 1930s and 1940s and decided to correspond and publicly meet with other aficionados to share their knowledge of the subject. These were the beginnings of the first flying saucer groups.

No one group started the trend. Instead, saucer clubs popped up locally across the world without any central coordination or direction. More often than not, early versions consisted of only a handful of members—sometimes as few as five or six—and functioned like a reading circle. While some met in a member's home, others convened in public halls or cafes to share UFO news and exchange views on the latest books of prominent ufologists. In short order, some clubs began hosting lecturers who spoke about the results of their own research and speculated about the flying saucer phenomenon.

From 1951 through 1954, a few groups in larger cities began staking out more ambitious agendas for themselves. Organizations like the Australian Flying Saucer Bureau in Sydney, Civilian Saucer Investigation of New Zealand in Auckland, and Civilian Saucer Intelligence in New York signaled that they were going to do what government agencies were proving too chary to do themselves: take sightings seriously, investigate cases diligently, and report findings openly.[44]

One of the earliest of these groups was the Los Angeles–based Civilian Saucer Investigation (CSI).[45] It was formed in December 1951 by a group of men who announced their interest in establishing a "coordinated civilian effort to gather the facts upon which to establish the origin, identity, and ultimate purpose of the [flying saucer] objects." CSI Los Angeles looked the part of a serious enterprise, boasting aeronautical engineers, a German rocket scientist, and author of *The Riddle of the Flying Saucers* Gerald Heard among its members.

In January 1952, Civilian Saucer Investigation acquired a post office box and invited flying saucer witnesses to write in and report their sightings. After being mentioned in articles in *True* and *Life* magazines, in newspaper pieces, and on radio and television, the group was inundated with so many first-hand reports from across the globe that it struggled to keep up. Members diligently combed through each case, logging the information, asking a panel of engineers to evaluate its details, and comparing it to similar cases. Reports considered to be "especially significant" were then copied and sent to the Air Intelligence Center at Wright-Patterson Air Force Base in Ohio.

By September 1952, Civilian Saucer Investigation had launched the inaugural issue of its newsletter. The plan was to fund the publication through member contributions and a subscription fee (50¢/copy or $2/ year). Group members wrote pieces discussing noteworthy recent UFO incidents, analyzing patterns across hundreds of sightings, and tracking developments and reports abroad. The publication and the organization proved short-lived, though: both were shut down in 1954. CSI Los Angeles explained to its followers that the revenue from subscriptions was insufficient to carry on and that the work involved "can be handled adequately only on a full-time staff basis."[46] In the decades that followed, countless UFO groups would go on to suffer the same fate, finding it impossible to sustain themselves as purely voluntary operations without a stable stream of funding.

These hurdles did not deter other Americans from trying their hand at similar ventures. Many, perhaps most, of these early "saucerists" and clubs have long since been forgotten. Some figures, however, went on to stake their own claims to fame within the UFO milieu.

One early pioneer was Leonard Stringfield, founder of Civilian Research, Interplanetary Flying Objects (CRIFO), based in Cincinnati, Ohio.[47] As a serviceman during the war, Stringfield himself had caught sight of "three unidentifiable blobs of brilliant white lights" that disrupted a flight he was on over the Pacific. Pursuing a career in advertising after the war, Stringfield thought little of the incident until he became aware of flying saucer reports in 1950. By 1952, he was convinced that UFOs were interplanetary spaceships. The sightings over Washington, DC, that summer spurred him to form his first saucer group called the Civilian Investigating Group for Aerial Phenomena. Though it never attracted any members, it did bring him some local media attention, and soon witnesses were sending him their reports of sightings.

In March 1954, Stringfield decided it was time to found his new organization, CRIFO, and to set about publishing a monthly bulletin (*Orbit*), with a first printing of two hundred copies. A few weeks later, things took a remarkable turn. On May 18, 1954, national radio broadcaster Frank Edwards—a champion of Donald Keyhoe and flying saucer speculation— encouraged his listeners to write CRIFO with their information about UFOs. Within weeks, Stringfield had achieved national fame and had to recruit his wife, two young daughters, and a family friend to help process around six thousand letters from across the world. By that fall, *Orbit* could boast of having some 2,500 subscribers.

Stringfield was so successful that in September 1955 officials with the US Air Defense Command recruited him to report up-to-the-minute sightings from the Cincinnati area through a dedicated phone line. Over the next two decades, he would continue to cooperate with government officials. And he moved on from CRIFO, becoming the chief public relations specialist for two major UFO organizations.

In contrast to Leonard Stringfield, Albert K. Bender struck a decidedly eerie note in his involvement with UFOs. An army veteran and a factory timekeeper living in Bridgeport, Connecticut, Bender founded the short-lived International Flying Saucer Bureau (IFSB) in 1952 and published its newsletter *Space Review*. Bender had a longstanding interest in science fiction and the supernatural, so it was no coincidence that the group and its bulletin resembled earlier science fiction clubs. Members came from all walks of life—a warehouse worker here, an electrician there, and the increasingly commonplace share of military veterans—and unlike CSI, women could be counted among their ranks. *Space Review* published not only sightings reported by Flying Saucer Bureau members, but also poems about flying saucers and a listing of recent science fiction books along with pulp and men's magazine articles on UFOs.

In the fall of 1953, Bender suddenly announced the closure of the Flying Saucer Bureau. In the October issue of his newsletter, Bender was cryptic with his readers:

> The mystery of the flying saucer is no longer a mystery. The source is already known, but any information about this is being withheld by orders from a higher source. We would like to print the full story in Space Review, but because of the nature of the information we are very sorry that we have been advised in the negative. We advise those engaged in saucer work to please be very cautious.[48]

Bender went on to confide to some of his colleagues at the time that he had been threatened by mysterious figures dressed in black to not reveal the truth about unidentified flying objects. Greeted with skepticism by many ufologists, Bender's fearful claims moved others to see a grand conspiracy at work behind the scenes. His close associate, the writer Gray Barker—who edited his own publication *The Saucerian* from 1953 to 1962—was probably the most famous of these. In 1956, Barker published *They Knew Too Much about Flying Saucers*, in which he detailed similar menacing encounters UFO investigators had had with ominous strangers.[49]

Eventually Bender published his own book, *Flying Saucers and the Three Men* (1962).[50] In it, he explained that the mysterious men he had encountered in 1953 had been in fact extraterrestrials, who transported him to an alien base in Antarctica where he met their leader, the Exalted One. Gray Barker and most others found Bender's new assertions hard to swallow, and over the years Bender's claims have been dismissed as either deliberate fiction or concoctions of an unwell mind. Whatever the case,

Bender and Barker together succeeded in promoting what has become a staple of UFO lore and popular culture: the existence of a mysterious group of men in black who visit and frighten those who dig too deeply into the mystery of unidentified flying objects.

If Albert Bender offered onlookers a glimpse of the freakish, New Jersey resident James (Jim) W. Moseley served up heapings of farce.[51] Moseley's interest in flying saucers was piqued in early 1948 by a radio report about Thomas Mantell's death chasing a UFO. Over the next few years, he immersed himself in the books of Keyhoe, Heard, Scully, and other early ufologists. By November 1953, he had become convinced that perhaps a quarter of all sightings could best be explained by extraterrestrial visitation. In a notebook he kept at the time, he mused:

> To many, the outer-space conclusion may indeed seem . . . fantastic. . . . However, it is my opinion that there is neither anything absurd nor frightening about the idea that we are being watched by creatures from another world. There are millions of planets in this vast universe. It seems to me that the probability of ours not being the only one capable of supporting intelligent life is far greater than the probability that our planet is the only one on which such life can be sustained. . . . [T]he only sensible course for one to follow is to keep an open mind in regard to the various conflicting theories in this fascinating field.[52]

Deciding to work on a book about flying saucers, Moseley began touring the United States to interview some of the major players in what he referred to as "The Field," including Donald Keyhoe ("I wasn't impressed. I felt . . . that Keyhoe routinely made too much of too little, at least in part just to sell books"), Albert Bender ("I thought it more likely then, and still do, that he cooked the whole thing up"), and Leonard Stringfield ("he always struck me as more of an 'I want to believer' and collector of saucer stories than as a careful investigator").[53] He met others, striking up friendships with Gray Barker and two men who had been involved in Bender's IFSB organization, August Roberts and Dominick Lucchesi. In May 1954, together with Roberts and Lucchesi, Moseley decided to found his own club and newsletter.

Moseley's Saucer and Unexplained Celestial Events Research Society (S.A.U.C.E.R.S.) never really aspired to be an organization in the strict sense of the term. Instead, it gave him a banner under which he could publish his own mimeographed bulletin starting in July 1954. First dubbed *Nexus*, its name was changed a year later to *Saucer News* to better capture its content. While the publication began by stating "that flying saucers exist and are probably interplanetary," Moseley made it clear that the bulletin also would be donating space for "poking fun at our fellow saucer-enthusiasts," with humor that would "be a little biting and sarcastic."[54]

Spoof, satire, scuttlebutt, and silliness became the hallmarks of Moseley, *Nexus/Saucer News* (1954–1970), and his bulletins *Confidential Newsletter* (1955–1968) and *Saucer Smear* (1976–1997). Friends and colleagues were jokingly pilloried. Theories were pursued, then picked apart. Alien encounters were debunked. Pranks were perpetrated. And gossip about the UFO community was shared. All this reflected Moseley's view at the time that saucerists were "one big (usually) happy family." As he later recalled,

> we had our eccentric uncles, quite loony aunts, and naughty cousins, but we *were* family, after all, and we were on to something those of the mundane world didn't—and maybe couldn't—get. We were *certain* the answer to the flying saucer enigma was just around the corner, and each of us was playing a part in cracking the case.[55]

THE LODESTARS: APRO AND NICAP

Local flying saucer groups and their newsletters quickly came and went, some lasting no more than a few months. This instability, in fact, would go on to characterize local UFO organizations for decades. Since almost all club officers and members were pursuing their interests in unidentified flying objects as a pastime, consistent commitment to the work involved was hard to maintain. Groups chronically found it hard to make ends meet, with bulletin editors regularly pleading with subscribers to mail in their fees to keep afloat. Although James Moseley painted a picture of early flying saucer enthusiasts as one big, happy family, his portrait belied a growing volatility within the ranks of organizations. Personality conflicts, differences of opinion about flying saucers, and resentment over the group's pecking order only added to the challenges facing UFO circles.

Despite this, two American UFO organizations emerged that thrived over the course of the fifties and sixties. Both were headed by charismatic figures who alternately inspired devotion and rancor and became torchbearers in international ufology. In the UFO world, the groups were known by their acronyms: APRO (pronounced Æ-pro) and NICAP (pronounced NĪ-cap).

APRO, the Aerial Phenomena Research Organization, was founded in January 1952 by the couple Coral and Jim Lorenzen in Sturgeon Bay, Wisconsin.[56] Jim's job as a design engineer in computing and telemetry took them to New Mexico in 1954 and then to Tucson, Arizona, where they settled for good in 1960. While the Lorenzens shared an interest in the flying saucer phenomenon, Jim's work meant he had only a limited amount of time to devote to the task. Coral therefore was and remained the driving force behind APRO and its newsletter *APRO Bulletin*.

Coral Lorenzen's interest in the paranormal began in her childhood. Born to a Jewish father and raised Baptist, she abandoned organized religion at age twelve. It was then that she began reading the works of paranormal writer Charles Fort. After hearing of reports of flying saucers ten years later, she began her own collection of newspaper clippings. By the end of 1951, she decided to start a group to record and track sightings and contacted friends and acquaintances to see if they might be interested in joining. Around fifty people did. A portable typewriter atop a claw-foot table in the corner of the Lorenzen's living room served as APRO's first office, which later moved into a garage. Coral served as president of the organization as well as editor of its bi-monthly newsletter.

The work kept Lorenzen busy, only getting to it after leaving her clerical job at a nearby air force base for the day. "When I was a little girl," her daughter told an interviewer in 1976, "one of the last things I remembered after bedtime stories and before dropping off to sleep was the sound of the typewriter. Mother was hard at work at her desk answering mail or writing copy for the bulletin."

In a community dominated by men, Coral Lorenzen cut an uncommon figure. "I am definitely the independent type; I must be easy to spot," she

Fig. 4.3 Coral and Jim Lorenzen in Tucson, Arizona in the late-1960s. AFU.

told her Swedish friend and colleague Gösta Rehn in December 1959. "I am also independent enough not to give in and hide behind the pants of some idiotic man who knows nothing of UAO [unidentified aerial object] research." She rarely minced words. "I hate tradition, hypocrisy, short-sightedness, etc, etc, with a purple passion," she declared to Rehn.[57] She bemoaned the fact that "few men like to work with a woman if she is ca-pable of meeting their standards of performance in their field," but she insisted, "I am one of those rebels who will bear children, manage a house, but demand my intellectual rights as a human being, without the 'woman' designation to drag me down."[58]

Lorenzen was well aware that the ufology men she encountered often dismissed her, considering her effete, uppity, or simply an object of sexual attraction. She developed what many found to be an abrasive interpersonal style, berating those who provoked her ire. Her outspokenness and temper were legendary.[59] Even admirers have acknowledged the perils of getting on her bad side. "She knew the ins, the outs, the dirt and the depths of UFO research and investigators everywhere," one man recalls, "and if anybody inspired her wrath she felt obligated to tell those whom she trusted about the indiscretions, always with a sound moral attitude."[60]

Under Coral Lorenzen's direction, APRO grew, by the early 1960s be-coming one of the premier UFO organizations on the world stage. Both the group and its *Bulletin* benefited from the attention paid to the flap over Washington, DC, during the summer of 1952, and membership rose to about 750 in 1955. A tireless letter writer, Lorenzen followed up on mail received and developed a growing number of contacts whom she recruited to serve as correspondents for the newsletter.

One of APRO's distinguishing features was its international reach, par-ticularly into South America. When a flurry of sightings popped up there in 1954, two Venezuelans—José Rolas and Horacio González Ganteaume, the latter the author of the 1961 book *Platillos voladores sobre Venezuela* (Flying Saucers over Venezuela)—began reporting on activities. Three years later, Dr. Olavo Fontes, a gastroenterologist based in Rio de Janeiro, joined APRO and began to report extensively on flying saucer sightings in Brazil. Coral and Fontes became fast friends, and he and his family visited the Lorenzens several times during the early 1960s. And in the fall of 1967, Jim and Coral traveled to South America to meet up with Rolas, González, and Fontes and conduct interviews in Lima, Santiago, Buenos Aires, Rio de Janeiro, and Caracas. By that time, APRO boasted representatives from thirteen different countries across Europe, South America, Australia, and Asia.[61]

Lorenzen was keen on establishing APRO's legitimacy as a serious re-search organization. To that end, she sought out professional scientists to get involved in the group's work. She succeeded in 1962, after reaching out to Colorado State University biologist Frank Salisbury, who shared an interest in UFOs. Salisbury, in turn, helped recruit James Harder, a professor of civil engineering at Berkeley. While Harder remained a close adviser to Lorenzen until her death, Salisbury—a Mormon and creationist— eventually resigned his position as a consultant to APRO in 1977, citing his growing fear that UFOs were possibly the work of demons, his uneasiness with what he called the "fringe types" and "obvious nuts" in ufology, and the fact that his dean and department decided he "should no longer conduct UFO research on university time."[62] Nevertheless, over the course of two and a half decades, a number of academics and PhD recipients agreed to serve as APRO consultants in psychology, linguistic, physics, chemistry, aeronautics, history, and electronics.

As APRO established a name for itself, another group of saucerists were discussing the need for some kind of national UFO reporting service outside of the military.[63] Donald Keyhoe had been approached to take on the task in 1953, but he declined, citing other commitments. In 1956, however, a circle based in Washington, DC, called the Flying Saucer Discussion Group entertained the prospect more seriously after one of its members, T. Townshend Brown, an inventor with an interest in anti-gravity, filed the paperwork for incorporation in August.

Brown's organization was dubbed the National Investigations Committee on Aerial Phenomena (NICAP). From the start, his aim was to lend the enterprise an air of sobriety and credibility by naming Donald Keyhoe, clergymen, retired military officers, and scientists to its board of governors. Within two months, however, Keyhoe was accusing Brown of mismanaging funds and prioritizing his own, peculiar obsession with anti-gravity. Brown was forced to resign, and Keyhoe took over as NICAP's new director, a position he held through 1969.

Under Keyhoe, NICAP worked to enhance its public profile. The group recruited for its board of governors, among others, the first director of the CIA, the president of the Aircraft Owners and Pilots Association, a retired rear admiral, some university professors, and radio personality Frank Edwards. Membership fees were reduced, and the organization began publishing its own newsletter, *The U.F.O. Investigator*, starting in July 1957. By 1958, membership in NICAP grew to around five thousand, eventually reaching its peak in 1966 at about fourteen thousand, making it the most prominent UFO organization in the United States.

Keyhoe brought not only star power to NICAP, but also an aggressive agenda. In addition to investigating and reporting on UFO sightings, the organization pressed the Air Force to disclose what it knew about unidentified flying objects. Keyhoe was convinced that the US military knew that UFOs were extraterrestrial in origin, but that officials were engaged in an elaborate ruse. So, he used NICAP's members, publications, and press coverage to push the government to come clean and to lobby Congress to open hearings on the Air Force's UFO program.

In the first of its newsletters in 1957, NICAP offered the US Air Force an olive branch. It laid out an "8 Point Plan" of "cooperation to end the controversy over flying saucers." The proposal recommended NICAP and the Air Force exchange their records, establish a shared liaison to go over past and recent cases, and grant NICAP's advisers and board members the opportunity to independently evaluate those cases officially deemed "solved."[64] The Air Force rejected the proposition with the familiar refrain that classified UFO reports could not be shared due to their containing sensitive information about radar and weapons systems. NICAP refused to relent, and it continued its campaign for full disclosure by the military into the next decade.

From the second half of the 1950s until the end of the 1960s, NICAP and APRO were the two leading American UFO organizations. While they were competitors of a sort, initially their two headstrong leaders were mutually cordial and supportive. Coral Lorenzen and Donald Keyhoe had two different visions for their groups, and the work they did reflected their leaders' outlooks. APRO investigated and publicized cases from across the globe, including accounts of encounters with aliens. NICAP also studied and reported on UFO sightings, but it spurned talk of confrontations with extraterrestrials and used its platform instead to demand an end to government secrecy on the subject of flying saucers. Pressured by some members of APRO for the group to "throw [its] support to NICAP" and help it "press for congression [sic] hearings," Coral Lorenzen in July 1962 pushed aside the suggestion. "APRO is primarily concerned with research" and gaining the support of scientists, she wrote in *APRO Bulletin*, not with lobbying. "It is our feeling that the Air Force UFO program is a public relations program. It's an advertising scheme which explains UFOs as conventional objects because that's what it's designed to do. Why dispute them?"[65]

A WORLD OF FLYING SAUCERISTS

As the Lorenzens had discovered, American saucerists were hardly alone in their desire to chase down the mystery of unidentified flying objects. Within a decade of the founding of APRO, dedicated sleuths and intrigued aficionados in different parts of the world began setting up their own flying saucer groups.

Ufology in Spain began to take off after two Catalan writers with a mutual interest in unidentified flying objects and science—Antonio Ribera and Màrius Lleget—met in a bar outside Barcelona in 1951. Four years later, they became aware of a newly published booklet, *Astronaves sobre la Tierra* (Spaceships on Earth). It was the first to use the American acronym UFO, translated into Spanish as *objeto volante no identificado* or OVNI for short. Ribera and Lleget invited its author, Eduardo Buelta, to join their group. Buelta brought with him a rich collection of materials on flying saucers, deep knowledge of the American literature on the subject, and a network of contacts with whom he corresponded. He also had definite opinions about the UFO phenomenon: flying saucers were surveillance spacecrafts from Mars, the flurry of postwar sightings reflecting an escalation of Martian reconnaissance sparked by atomic bomb explosions.

In short order, Buelta took on a leading role in the group. Members met at his home, often working late into the evening. Together they decided to establish their own UFO research center, and in 1958 they founded the Centro de Estudios Interplanetarios (the Center for Interplanetary Studies or CEI). At their first meeting in October—attended by a police officer to ensure that the group's intentions were not seditious—Buelta was named its president and Ribera vice president. By January 1959, CEI was publishing its own mimeographed bulletin and pushing Buelta's pet theories.[66]

In Australia, the first UFO investigation groups also began operating in the early fifties. In Sydney, Edgar Jarrold started things off with his Australia Flying Saucer Bureau in July 1952. Like others, he began publishing a bulletin in May the following year, but the venture and Jarrold's general interest in UFOs only lasted six issues. Soon, however, other organizations popped up in Victoria, South Australia, and Queensland.

The most ambitious of these was the Australian Flying Saucer Research Society, established by Frederick Stone in Adelaide in early 1955. Stone's plan was to create an association with a national and international reach. The Society partly succeeded, publishing the periodical *Australian Saucer Record* from 1955 to 1963 and holding Australia's first UFO conference in 1959 with some two hundred attendees. Still, there remained relatively little effort at coordination among independent UFO groups in the country until the mid-1960s.[67]

Meanwhile, in German-speaking Europe, it was devout occultists and mystics who initiated the first organized forays into ufology starting in the mid-1950s. In Zürich, Switzerland, J. Heinrich Ragaz began publishing *Weltraumbote* (Outer Space Messenger) in November 1955, with an initial run of 2,500 copies. Ragaz was an acolyte of the American occult lecturer and writer Gilbert Holloway, who began in 1953 publishing pamphlets with titles like *Coming of the Space People*, *Communion between Worlds*, *Messages from the Space People*, and *Flying Saucers: Vanguard of the New Age*. Ragaz was taken by Holloway's idea that flying saucers were built spiritually out of astral "ether," traveling between planets at the speed of thought. In its first issue, he announced the purpose of the monthly periodical to be "spreading the truth about the extraterrestrial spaceships named 'flying saucers,' fighting against splitting the atom, and preparing for the new, spiritual age."[68]

As did many others during the 1950s, Ragaz drew on the esoteric tradition in seeing flying saucers as harbingers of a promising, new epoch in human history. Combining his knowledge of occult literature with the writings of prominent American and European ufologists, he used *Weltraumbote* not only to report on worldwide UFO sightings and speculate on the nature of the crafts but also link the appearance of flying saucers to the precarious situation in which the world found itself at the time. Citing the catastrophic impacts atomic bombs and Cold War tensions were having on weather, the oceans, and the physical and mental health of human beings, Ragaz believed that the space messengers behind UFOs offered renewed hope of an enlightened, peaceful future.[69]

In West Germany, a similar development was taking place. Media coverage of sightings and Donald Keyhoe's writings led Siegfried Schöpfer, a teacher with a background in meteorology and astronomy, to write a pamphlet about the subject in 1955, in which he dismissed "the entire phenomenon" as a phantasm "to be explained solely psychologically and that will not last very long."[70] Schöpfer's contribution was soon eclipsed, however, by a Christian mystic, Karl Veit.

In the 1920s, Veit became fascinated with the work of Jakob Lorber, a nineteenth-century Christian mystic who had claimed an "inner voice" spoke through him as the voice of Jesus Christ, believing that heavenly bodies were organic creatures and that human beings would achieve perfection through a series of reincarnations. By the early-1930s, Veit had become convinced that he too had a calling to serve as a "proclaimer, spiritual teacher, and emissary and messenger of love." In 1933, he and his father set up a small press called Urgemeinde, intending to spread news of the return of the heavenly father for the German people. The press, however, was shut down by the Nazis in 1934.[71] After a spell as a Soviet POW during World War II, Veit returned to Germany, and he reestablished the Urgemeinde Press. In 1950, he met his wife Anny, who shared his religious views, and the two married in 1954, vowing to one another "We want to get things done with God!"

Fig. 4.4 The cover of the sixth issue of *Weltraumbote* in 1956. The flying saucer pictured is accompanied with the caption "Peace!" AFU.

It was at this time that Veit had his introduction to UFO reports and claims of contact with aliens that were coming from the United States. He considered these events to be momentous and the fulfillment of the prophecies of Jakob Lorber about life in the universe. His views were confirmed when, as one report has it, he witnessed spaceships hovering over the Rhine River in 1956.[72]

The sighting spurred Karl and Anny to become actively involved in the study of UFOs. Together, they founded the Deutsche UFO/IFO-Studiengesellschaft or DUIST (German UFO/IFO Studies Society), the periodical *UFO-Nachrichten* (UFO-News), and a new press called Ventla, the name coming from what Veit claimed was an extraterrestrial term for "beamships" (*Strahlschiffe*).

Under the Veits' leadership, DUIST became the leading UFO organization in West Germany through the 1970s, eventually disbanding in 1988. The group's legitimacy was bolstered by naming rocket and aeronautic pioneer Hermann Oberth its first honorary president, who himself firmly believed that unidentified flying objects "originate exclusively from outside the earth" owing to the fact that they don't crash and defy gravity.[73] In its original charter from 1956, Veit emphasized that the organization's purpose was not only to support research about UFOs, but also to fulfill a moral mission. DUIST, the by-laws stated, "serves world peace and mutual understanding among peoples as well as the expansion of natural scientific and ethical consciousness at the start of the cosmic age."[74]

THE LUMINARIES OF EUROPE

By the second half of the 1950s, flying saucer clubs, UFO research organizations, and crusading ufologists had independently taken hold all over the globe. Groups sprang up in Argentina and Brazil. In Canada, after several government offices closed their investigations into flying saucers, electrical engineer Wilbert Smith set up the Ottawa Flying Saucer Club in 1957, where members met each month in the basement of his house.[75] In the Soviet Union, astronomer Felix Zigel, science fiction writer Alexander Kazantsev, and engineer Yuri Fomin gave public lectures and collected reports on unidentified flying objects.[76] In Sweden, the driving forces behind the earliest organizations came largely out of theosophical circles. Everywhere the pattern was largely the same, however. A few highly motivated enthusiasts— whose interest more often than not was sparked by the books of Donald Keyhoe and press coverage of American sightings—dedicated themselves to organizing fellow aficionados into more formal communities, collecting and interpreting reports, publishing bulletins, and offering public talks on flying saucers and their importance.

That said, the number of practicing ufologists remained small, and they often found convincing others of their views to be an uphill battle. Europeans were not altogether receptive to the notion of visitors from outer space. In October 1952, for instance, a survey conducted by the Netherlands Institute of Public Opinion revealed that while 92 percent of the Dutch public had heard of flying saucers (*vliegende schotels*), a majority believed there was a natural explanation for them. The idea that unidentified flying objects might be extraterrestrial in origin had little support to speak of. Nevertheless, the fact that 43 percent of those polled said they had no idea whatsoever what flying saucers might be showed a great many remained decidedly undecided.[77]

Although American voices continued to be the predominant ones globally, during the second half of the 1950s champions of ufology from two European countries established themselves as torchbearers with a worldwide following. One of these places was France, where a survey of one hundred thousand French residents conducted in February 1956 found that 53 percent of those polled thought flying saucers were extraterrestrial in origin.[78] It was here that a vibrant network of often highly original ufologists appeared on the scene.[79] The first organized community activities in France took shape during the years 1951–1958. Early French *soucoupistes* were drawn to the subject through their overlapping interests in a heady mix of the occult, science fiction, anti-nuclear activism, and dispatches about UFOs from the United States.

In the summer of 1951, Marc Thirouin, a lawyer with a passion for esoterica and the search for Atlantis, and Henri-René Guieu (pen name "Jimmy Guieu"), an anti-communist and occult writer, founded the first French UFO study group in Paris, the Commission Ouranos. By 1954, its name had been changed to Commission Internationale d'Enquête "Ouranos" or CIE Ouranos, and it was publishing its own bulletin, *Ouranos*, touted as an "international journal for the study of flying saucers and related problems."

Ambitious and determined, Thirouin and Guieu set out to both investigate reports and gain new members. By 1949, Thirouin was corresponding with people having connections to the US Air Force. Despite battling tuberculosis, he rode around on his moped carrying out his own local investigations. Guieu, for his part, served as the public face of Ouranos. Through his monthly column for a science fiction magazine and regular broadcasts on Radio Monte Carlo, he promoted the organization and nurtured a network of correspondents, some of whom would go on to become investigators in their own right.

The two men were joined by others. Graphologist Alfred Nahon took on duties as the group's Swiss representative. The author of several books himself, Nahon took the position that flying saucers were manned by benevolent extraterrestrials visiting earth in order to warn governments to give up testing atomic weapons. The specter of atomic warfare so haunted Nahon that he and Thirouin started one of the first anti-nuclear campaigns in France in 1956.

Nahon, in turn, helped inspire amateur astronomer Raymond Veillith to establish his own magazine in February 1958, *Lumières dans la nuit* (Lights in the Night) or *LDLN*. Though in the 1960s and 1970s it would go on to become the lodestar in Francophone ufology with a network of two thousand investigators and a circulation in the thousands, *Lights in the Night* began with a broader set of interests. Veillith believed that humanity faced a host of existential threats, so the publication dedicated itself to discussions of topics such as population explosion, sustainable agriculture, vegetarianism, the dangers of radioactive materials, and the arms race. The simultaneous, worldwide appearance of UFOs played a prominent role in this human drama, according to Veillith, signaling that the destiny of planet earth lay in the balance. *Lights in the Night* might not have held the answers to the intractable problems facing the human race, but it at least planned to serve as a herald to those willing to listen.[80]

France's most internationally renowned ufologist of the 1950s was only tangentially connected to the Ouranos milieu in Paris. Polio in childhood left Aimé Michel small in size, but he proved to be a towering presence in ufology for a time. Ever curious, he studied philosophy, psychology, classics, and sound engineering in his youth, eventually working for French radio and television after the war. In the early fifties, he grew interested in the flying saucer phenomenon, becoming what he dubbed a "parallel researcher"—someone who conducted conventional, "orthodox" research in public, while simultaneously working on what many would consider scandalous research in private.

Initially Michel believed the mystery of flying saucers would be cleared up quickly one way or the other. But one day an official working at the French national meteorological office presented him with a file filled with odd aerial phenomena, from halos to sun dogs to inexplicable luminous disks. From this point on, he thoroughly committed himself to investigating flying saucers. He was at first convinced that Donald Keyhoe was right in believing that the military knew more than it was letting on. After a conversation with an Air Force intelligence officer, however, Michel came away persuaded that "in this strange story, no one knew. Neither the French army, nor any army in the world."[81]

Michel published two books on flying saucers that put sightings in France at the center of civilian UFO research. *Lueurs sur les soucoupes volantes* appeared in 1954, translated into English two years later as *The Truth about Flying Saucers*. It begins, as so many books did at the time, with the familiar recital of American events and characters: the Arnold, Mantell, and Chiles-Whitted cases, the US Air Force's investigations, and Keyhoe and Menzel. It then turned to sightings of UFOs over Africa and France by an array of academics, scientists, pilots, military personnel, and clergymen (by now, citing the professional status of witnesses had become a common way in ufology to highlight the credibility of witnesses). The book ends with Michel posing the question, if aliens have been observing us, "why have they never established contact?" His answer was simple—out of fear. "Considering our bloody past, would they not be justified in thinking that their best protection is an 'iron curtain?'"[82]

The Truth about Flying Saucers was not terribly original, though it did draw attention to the frequency of sightings over France and North Africa. By contrast, Michel's second book, *Mystérieux objets célestes* (1958), was inspiringly novel. Translated into English the same year, *Flying Saucers and the Straight-Line Mystery* would have an impact on international ufology for at least a decade.

In it, Michel explored a wave of UFO sightings that took place in France and North Africa during the autumn of 1954. Up until then, Michel wrote, "the flying saucer was essentially an isolated phenomenon"—it would appear for a brief moment, then vanish. Its "sudden, fleeting, and vague" nature made it immune to "planned observation and experiment."[83] There seemed to be something different in the high concentration of reports in the fall, but the ufologist was flummoxed. He mentioned the cases to poet and artist Jean Cocteau, himself a devout follower of the UFO phenomenon. Cocteau suggested that Michel "see whether the objects move along certain lines, whether they are tracing out designs, or something like that."[84] When Michel plotted the locations and dates on a map, lo and behold, he spotted a pattern.

Michel dubbed the pattern "orthoteny" (from the Greek *orthoteneis*, meaning "stretched in a straight line"). During the 1954 wave, he argued, flying saucers appeared over the course of any given day along straight lines crisscrossing French territory. This was not to say that UFOs were flying in straight lines, but rather that disparate sightings were aligned "as though some kind of plan had assigned to these mysterious objects certain rectilinear travel routes in preference to others."[85] If true, these alignments were almost certainly deliberate, a clear sign of there being intention and intelligence behind flying saucers.

Orthoteny struck many saucerists as a promising avenue for research. During the first half of the 1960s, ufologists presented evidence of the phenomenon not only in France, but also in Brazil, Spain, and Africa. Michel himself announced that orthotenic patterns could be seen on a global scale.[86] Naysayers appeared on the scene almost as quickly. Donald Menzel judged orthoteny "a lost cause," attacking Michel's understanding of statistics.[87] Other critics questioned how precise the locations and directions of the objects observed were, given how variable witness reports could be. By 1970 orthoteny was largely considered a dead end. But for a time, it brought fame to Aimé Michel and helped establish France as an important hub in civilian UFO investigation.

In Great Britain, the first flying saucer clubs began forming in 1952 and 1953.[88] Richard Hughes's Flying Saucer Club in Hove appears to have been the first, mailing out its quarterly bulletin *Flying Saucer News* to some two thousand annual subscribers for twenty-five shillings. In November 1953, Edgar Plunkett, a navy veteran with an interest in the occult, set up the British Flying Saucer Bureau in Bristol. The Bureau thrived, organizing local lectures, exhibitions, and evening classes, answering letters from overseas correspondents, and conducting "sky-watches" in hopes of tracking UFOs. At one point, the group boasted a membership of 1,500. In February 1954 Hughes's *Flying Saucer News* merged with Plunkett's Bureau.

By 1954, saucer clubs were dotting Britain's landscape. Most were small-scale, short-lived affairs, but they testified to the British public's growing curiosity about reports of flying saucers. Admittedly, a survey conducted at the time by the *Daily Express* found that only 16.5 percent of Britons believed flying saucers were real, but the fact that 43 percent also thought nuclear weapons were adversely affecting the weather showed that there were serious concerns about what was going on in the skies overhead.

In fact, interest in UFOs reached some of the highest levels of the British government during the fifties. Both Lord Mountbatten and his nephew, the Queen's husband Prince Philip, were fascinated with the topic. In private, the men subscribed to a leading UFO magazine and delighted in discussing the subject, to the point of even inviting a number of witnesses to the Buckingham Palace to describe their encounters. In public, however, they took pains to downplay their interest.[89]

When Prime Minister Winston Churchill asked officials from the Air Ministry in 1952 to brief him on what was known about flying saucers, he was informed that the matter had already been investigated. At the instigation of its chief scientific advisor, the Ministry of Defence in August 1950 set up what was called the Flying Saucer Working Party, a team of intelligence officers tasked with reviewing the evidence for flying saucer sightings in the United Kingdom and the United States. Like its American counterparts, the panel a year later concluded that all sightings were due to mistaken identification or hoaxes and that "no progress will be made by attempting further investigation of uncoordinated and subjective evidence."[90] Several UFO reports during a NATO exercise in September 1952—particularly one by a Royal Air Force (RAF) crew describing a silver disk that followed a jet, rotated on its axis, and whizzed away at lightning speed—moved the Air Ministry to permanently track UFO reports, however. Although the Air Minister declared in May 1955 that his officers could account for 90 percent of reports filed (the other 10 percent lacking sufficient information), the Ministry continued monitoring the situation on the off chance of catching wind of some innovative foreign aircraft.[91]

Meanwhile, an eclectic group of civilian saucerists based in London began a venture that would go on to have a profound impact on ufology.[92] Well educated and linked by a common interest in the paranormal, they came from different social backgrounds and held different political worldviews. There was Derek Dempster, who had served in the RAF during the war and afterward earned a law degree yet continued working as a test pilot and writing articles on air travel for the *Daily Times*. Waveney Girvan was a trained accountant, with an interest in literature and Forteana. When World War II broke out, he joined an anti-war organization that argued for a negotiated peace with Hitler. After the war, he worked for a London publishing house and became involved with fascist, nationalist, and right-wing leaning individuals and groups. Brinsley Le Poer Trench, Lord Clancarty, was an aristocrat with a broad interest in the supernatural and flying saucers. During the 1960s and 1970s, he was a prominent champion of the idea that UFOs were extraterrestrial visitors and assumed leading positions in a number of national UFO organizations in the United Kingdom, including Contact International and the Ancient Astronauts Society. Finally, Denis Montgomery, the youngest in the circle, was working at the time as a librarian.

All the men shared a driving fascination with the flying saucer phenomenon. Montgomery in particular later recalled that at the time he was intrigued by "interplanetary travel and the new idealism of a universal brotherhood of intelligent life." Thinking that there should be some kind of institute and library to collect and catalogue all the information coming in from reports and speculation about flying saucers, Montgomery contacted Girvan to discuss the prospect.[93] Girvan, who as editor had overseen the publication of Gerald Heard's *Is Another World Watching?* in 1950, was enthused. The two of them reached out to Dempster, Trench, and several others. After meeting in December 1954, they decided to publish a bimonthly magazine, with each founder contributing £100 to get the periodical off the ground. Montgomery's institute and library never materialized, but the small UFO fraternity succeeded in launching *Flying Saucer Review*.

From the start, *Flying Saucer Review* sought to lend the study of unidentified flying objects and alien visitation an aura of highbrow learning and sobriety. "We believed these things were coming in from outer space," Derek Dempster recalled in a 2007 interview, "and we were trying to prove this with science."[94] Dempster served as the periodical's first editor, and from

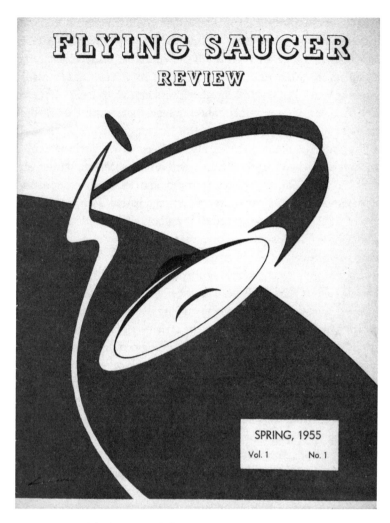

Fig. 4.5 The cover of the first issue of *Flying Saucer Review* in 1955. AFU.

the first issue appearing in January 1955, *FSR*—as it came to be referred to—assumed an air of being consummately business-like in unlocking the mystery of unidentified flying objects. Professionals from various walks of life were recruited to serve as consultants and foreign correspondents.

An especially important collaborator was former diplomat and civil servant Gordon Creighton. Creighton spent years as an intelligence officer in the Ministry of Defence and studied some twenty languages. His linguistic proficiencies allowed him to translate a multitude of foreign reports and articles, and he maintained contact with ufologists in numerous countries.

Like the vast majority of early UFO organizations and periodicals during the fifties and sixties, *Flying Saucer Review* was a decidedly male enterprise. Its air of urbane respectability was reflected in its early advertisements: antique dealers, estate agents, public relations services, and life insurance companies. Articles during its first five years appear to have been written exclusively by professional men, and published letters to the editors featured writers of a similar standing.

In addition, *Flying Saucer Review* also stressed its scholastic, ecumenical, and cosmopolitan bent. Under its first two editors—Dempster and Brinsley Le Poer Trench—the magazine featured articles by astronomers and physicists on outer space, dedicated a section entitled "World Roundup" to reports of UFO sightings from across the globe, and included essays on occult and mystical philosophy. In one instance, the staff took it upon themselves to play the role of world guardian, speaking out after high-profile US and British atomic tests from May through July 1956. "We are worried," the *Review* told its readers, "because it seems that our scientists have gone quite beserk (sic) over nuclear power and are losing all sense of proportion over the magnitude of the explosion the structure of this world can take."[95]

Flying Saucer Review's standing in the ufology community continued to grow in subsequent years. Waveney Girvan took over editorial duties in 1959, but his untimely death in 1964 led to the appointment of former boys' magazine writer Charles Bowen as editor. During his tenure from 1965 to 1982, Bowen worked closely with Gordon Creighton, and the magazine opened up its pages beyond UFO sightings to broad encounters with the bizarre and uncanny. From the mid-sixties through the seventies, the periodical gained the reputation for being the flagship in international ufology. As a veteran European ufologist once reminisced to me, when he saw his name listed under the *Flying Saucer Review* banner as a contributor for the first time he felt a special sense of accomplishment. "I was," he said, "so proud."[96]

———

Over the course of the 1950s, flying saucers went from being an American curiosity and diversion to an international mystery and obsession. It can be difficult, if not downright impossible, to discern whether the decade witnessed an increase in the number of sightings of flying saucers or instead a rise in the number of reports classified as flying saucers. Either way, flying saucers quickly spawned ancillary stories that became as captivating as the UFOs themselves. There were tales of the supposed inventors of the eerie crafts—unacknowledged geniuses, eccentric tinkerers, Nazi technicians.

There was the government cover-up, a conspiracy of silence perpetrated by military and civilian officials to fend off public hysteria. And then there were ominous figures, men in black, who menaced anyone getting too close to the truth about unidentified flying objects. All these stories contributed to the making of the flying saucer saga and created an opportunity for the ambitious to assume the role of heroic investigator.

Wherever flying saucers turned up, so too did the controversy over their meaning. Skeptics and debunkers appeared on the scene to dismiss witness observations and speculation about alien visitors. Saucer enthusiasts were not deterred, however. They leafed through press clippings, shared their pet theories, and set about organizing themselves.

The formation of civilian flying saucer groups was never centrally directed nor even particularly coordinated. But once set in motion, the trend was infectious. Flying saucer clubs offered a way to indulge one's interest in UFOs and to do so in the company of like-minded people—a safe haven, free of the ridicule often piled on those publicly expressing their fascination with the topic. Soon, individual groups took it upon themselves to publish newsletters and bulletins for eager subscribers, conduct their own investigations, keep up to date with saucer news, and openly muse about the meaning of reports.

The leaders of early flying saucer organizations were overwhelmingly drawn from a similar demographic: well-educated white males, many often coming from a science, engineering, and/or military background. The field was open to big personalities and big ideas, and there were characters aplenty, some humorous, some stern and serious, others deliberately outlandish. With no central authority policing the growth of the UFO movement, there was room at the table for materialists, mystics, and everything in between. The writings of this first cohort of saucerists show they derived inspiration from a number of different sources: the development of advanced rockets and aircraft, concerns over the arms race and the dangers of radioactivity, occult and mystical traditions, and, to a lesser extent, science fiction.

In this new marketplace of ideas, enthusiasm and conviction also fed disagreement and acrimony. The mystery of the flying saucers invited no easy solutions, at least none capable of gaining general acceptance. Thus, debate was protracted and often fractious. In fact, if anything, mystery and debate defined the UFO phenomenon. American ufologist Morris Jessup reflected at the end of the fifties:

> This embryonic science is as full of cults, feuds, and dogmas as a dog is of fleas. There are probably more opinions about the nature and purpose of UFO's as

there are Ufologers. The sky visitors are believed to come from Russia, the U.S. Air Force, open space, the moon, Venus, Mars, Jupiter, Saturn, Alpha Centauri, the outer Galaxy, distant galaxies millions of light years away, from the fourth dimension, from etheric space (whatever that may be), from the fifth dimension, from the second, third, fourth, fifth, sixth, seventh, or other spheres of intelligence and existence, from etheric planets, an invisible planet behind the moon, the spirit world, and perhaps even from a galactic Shangri-la'.[97]

If flying saucers really were the handiwork of some kind of intelligence, then who were they, what did they want, and how could we find out? "The next logical step obviously is to attempt contact, communication," as one saucerist insisted.[98] Some had already done so. Throughout the 1950s and early 1960s, numerous figures came forward to announce they had had encounters with the beings behind the flying saucers. What they had to say about their experiences inspired some, alarmed others, and drove a wedge between members of the UFO community that has lasted to this very day.

5

Journeys

In the summer of 1954, retirees Bryant and Helen Reeve sold their Detroit, Michigan home, bought a new car, and set out for Mexico. The couple had no destination in mind. "We had no particular program in mind other than going places and seeing things," they later recalled.[1] But this was no ordinary trip. Two years and 23,000 miles later, the pair had completed a journey they dubbed their "flying saucer pilgrimage."

Little information is available about Helen Reeve's background, but Bryant had been a mechanical engineer, educated at Yale University and MIT. Growing up, his family had lived in both England and Germany for a time and had traveled extensively throughout Europe. He served overseas during World War I, and afterward held both technical and executive positions in several American companies before his retirement.

By 1950, then, the Reeves appear to have been enjoying the model life of postwar America's white middle class. One thing, though, did make them stand out from their peers. For some time, they had become interested in what they called "metaphysical studies." This included psychical research, the paranormal, and esoteric religions from the Far East.

When reports of flying saucers first made headlines, the couple saw nothing to link them with their philosophical pursuits. But in November 1953, a friend showed up at a house party of theirs with a book, *Flying Saucers Have Landed*, in which one of its authors claimed to have talked to a man from Venus. Bryant thought it preposterous, but the friend insisted it was worth finding out more. "There's only one thing to do," he said. "Call the man up and get him to Detroit." They weren't able to reach the author, George Adamski, that day, but after sending him a letter and assurances of covering his expenses, he agreed.

Fig. 5.1 Helen and Bryant Reeve. Topfoto/Fortean.

GEORGE ADAMSKI AND THE MAN FROM VENUS

The son of Polish immigrants, George Adamski was steeped in Western esotericism and theosophy.[2] Working as a handyman at a diner near Mount Palomar in California, Adamski was already known in the local area in the 1920s as a self-styled spiritual leader. He had founded the Royal Academy of Tibet, and over the course of the 1930s and 1940s spoke and taught courses on what he called the "Cosmic Law," a moral and cosmological philosophy emphasizing the principles of love, humility, and the rejection of materialism. In two pieces written in 1937, entitled "The Kingdom of Heaven on Earth" and "Satan, Man of the Hour," he portrayed materialism and militarism as the two great threats to the modern world. Salvation, however, was possible by embracing the Christ-like values of love, peace, and cooperation.

Near the end of World War II, Adamski began to direct his attention to outer space, setting up his own personal observatory with a fifteen-inch telescope. He then published a pamphlet in 1946 on "The Possibility of Life on Other Planets" and in 1949 a science fiction novel *Pioneers of Space: A Trip to the Moon, Mars, and Venus*. Here he continued his theme of the need to achieve higher levels of consciousness and morality in order to avoid the destruction of human civilization. In the novel, Adamski portrays the residents of the moon, Venus, and Mars as Caucasian humanoids who once lived on earth but since have learned to embrace the Cosmic Law and to live in prosperity and peace. They also had a message for humanity: civilization on earth was still in its infancy, and its people must be careful in their use of weapons of mass destruction.

Adamski's attention soon turned to flying saucers. In 1950, he co-authored an article in *Fate* magazine—titling himself as Prof. George Adamski—on how astronomers were seeing unidentified flying objects. Then, on November 24, 1952, the *Phoenix Gazette* reported that a few days earlier and in front of a number of witnesses Adamski had had an encounter with an actual extraterrestrial in the Colorado Desert in California. According to Adamski, he had photographed the spacecraft, and a conversation with its occupant revealed that the aliens were visiting earth out of concern over the testing of atomic bombs.[3]

Shortly thereafter, Adamski wrote British occult writer Desmond Leslie to tell him that he was in the process of writing about his remarkable experience in the desert. Leslie was intrigued. He was just about to publish his own book on flying saucers in which he argued that beings from other worlds had been visiting earth since ancient times. Leslie invited Adamski to publish his piece as part of Leslie's book. He did, and *Flying Saucers Have Landed* hit bookstores in October 1953 in the United States, the United Kingdom, and Canada.

In the book, Adamski explained that he himself had his first sighting of a giant, hovering spacecraft near his home in October 1946.[4] Curious, he kept looking for more with his telescope and caught sight of more than 180 unidentified flying objects, taking some 500 photographs of them. He eventually sent his photos to a Navy lab for analysis, but never heard back from them.

Then on November 20, 1952, he went out to the desert with friends in hopes of spotting flying saucer activity. After doing some roaming, the group spotted what appeared to be a ship circling above them and following their car. Hoping to make contact with the ship's crew, Adamski told his companions to inconspicuously wait a mile or so away, while he went on foot with his camera and telescope.

Suddenly, after Adamski took some photographs, a man approached him. Almost immediately, Adamski realized he was in the presence of a genuine alien. The man, dressed in what looked like ski pants, appeared to be in his late twenties. He had long flowing hair "glistening more beautifully than any women's I have ever seen," delicate skin like a baby, "slightly higher cheek bones than an Occidental, but not so high as an Indian or an Oriental," and white teeth that sparkled when he smiled.[5] Adamski was overcome with emotions.

The beauty of his form surpassed anything I had ever seen. And the pleasantness of his face freed me of all thought of my personal self. I felt like a child in the presence of one with great wisdom and much love, and I became very humble within myself . . . for from him was radiating a feeling of infinite understanding and kindness, with supreme humility.[6]

The two men communicated with one another through what Adamski described as "feelings, signs, and above all, by means of telepathy."[7] As he came to learn, this otherworldly being's name was Orthon, and he came from the planet Venus. He told Adamski that all the planets in the solar system were inhabited and that, while there had been previous visitations in which spacecraft crashed and crews were killed, other outer space visitors would soon be coming.

Adamski asked whether Venusians believed in God and what their purpose was in coming to earth. Orthon revealed that his people indeed followed the law of the "Creator." He was here, he said, to warn us that the uninhibited testing and use of atomic bombs were creating radioactive clouds that were damaging to both earth and outer space.

Orthon provided Adamski with few details beyond this, but the longtime believer in prophetic knowledge took inspiration from his encounter. "Let us be friendly. Let us recognize and welcome the men from other worlds!" he concluded. "THEY ARE HERE AMONG US. Let us be wise enough to learn from those who can teach us much—who will be our friends if we will but let them!"[8]

GETTING THE WORD OUT

When George Adamski arrived in Detroit in March 1954, he was greeted at the railway station by the Reeves and an organizing committee. Adamski first fielded questions at a news conference, then did a live radio interview, followed by a pair of lectures for a select audience held in the auditorium at the Detroit Institute of Arts. To the disappointment of many, Adamski spent more time discussing his spiritual beliefs than his experience in the desert.

The big event was a public talk at the Detroit Masonic Temple. A crowd of 4,700 packed the hall, eagerly waiting to hear about and see images of flying saucers and the man from Venus. However, many were unable to see Adamski's slides, he appeared nervous and rambled on, and the question-and-answer period proved unwieldy, given the size of the audience. At the end, Adamski dashed off to catch a train to New York City, but it wouldn't be the last time the Reeves would spend time with "The Professor," as many came to call him.

Flying Saucers Have Landed went through eleven printings over its first two years of publication and made George Adamski famous among UFO enthusiasts worldwide. He would go on to publish two more books on flying saucers and extraterrestrials. In *Inside the Space Ships* (1955), he described new encounters he had with aliens from Venus and Saturn. In it, he provided more details about the customs and lifestyles of people on other worlds. He also related his conversations with someone he referred to as the "Great Master," a figure supposedly over a thousand years old and who preached that before earthlings travel in outer space they first would need to embrace the values of peace and brotherhood. Adamski's final book, *Flying Saucers Farewell* (1961), echoed most of the same themes he had been writing about for years, this time mixed with responses to critics, attempts to explain gravity propulsion, and references to the Bible and other ancient texts demonstrating their compatibility with the Cosmic Law.[9]

Unlike the many UFO witnesses who chose not to report their sighting or to remain anonymous, George Adamski came away from his experience emboldened to share his adventure and thoughts. From 1953 until his death in 1965, he regularly lectured to audiences and gave interviews to newspapers, magazines, and radio and television broadcasters. He also followed the lead of ufologists and began in October 1957 publishing a regular bulletin for subscribers, entitled *Cosmic Science for the Promotion of Cosmic Principles and Truths, Questions and Answers*.

Around the same time, Adamski began an outreach project he called the "Get Acquainted Program." He decided to use a network of correspondents from across the globe he had cultivated by the summer of 1957 to pass on messages from "our interplanetary visitors" to those interested. "Information of the Brothers of other worlds, with whom I continue having more or less regular meetings, will be sent regularly to each national leader [in the community], who in turn will forward it to all of his assistants," he told followers.[10] Local groups were encouraged to then meet to discuss content and nurture closer bonds of friendship. Within two years, Adamski's contact list for the program consisted of twenty-two contacts from seventeen countries, including Australia, Brazil, Japan, and Rhodesia.

The Get Acquainted Program provided Adamski with the resources to organize a 1959 worldwide speaking tour that included Asia, Australia, New Zealand, Europe, Africa, and South America. Attendance at his talks was generally good, and avid devotees repeatedly hosted and escorted him as he set down in places like Auckland, Darwin, Calcutta, Rome, Athens, and London. Arguably the high point of the tour was a private visit he was granted with Queen Juliana of the Netherlands in May.

But the trip proved to be a mixed bag. Due to poor health, he had to cut it short in June. Most vexing for Adamski was the disparaging—and at times, outright derisive—reception he got from the media and some audience members. In New Zealand, his remarks were sometimes met with chuckles, and his claims left the UFO community there deeply divided between Adamski believers and Adamski nonbelievers.[11] In Zurich, a dismissive crowd laughed him off stage. Adamski responded by speaking of there being an "organized resistance" to his message orchestrated by what he called the "Silence Group," a term that had been circulating in UFO circles since the early fifties. During the last five years of his life, Adamski went on to associate this Silence Group with a host of ugly and longstanding anti-Semitic epithets, linking it to international finance and a secret conspiracy and likening its members to "the money-changers Christ drove out of the temple."[12]

Despite recurring health issues, Adamski stayed busy during the years 1960–1965. He set up a curriculum, established the Science of Life school, and claimed to have attended an "interplanetary counsel" on Saturn in March 1962, held to discuss increasing tensions between the United States and the USSR. He also continued traveling. He embarked on another European tour during the spring and summer of 1963, during which he may have had a private audience with Pope John XXIII,[13] and went on the lecture circuit throughout the United States in both 1964 and 1965 before his death in April 1965.

CRITICS

Adamski's story of making contact with the Venusian Orthon was fantastic. To some, he was a visionary and a trailblazer. To many others, his tale was preposterous, the work of a shameless fraud.

There were critics aplenty. A notable one was writer Arthur C. Clarke, who pilloried *Flying Saucer Have Landed* and its two authors in March 1954. He found Leslie's use of ancient religious texts to prove the existence of flying saucers in antiquity ridiculous. "No doubt some diligent reader in two or three thousand years' time," Clarke wrote in the *Journal of the British Interplanetary Society*, "will employ Mr. Leslie's technique to prove, from ancient files of *Amazing Stories*, that the early twentieth century had spaceships, heat rays, antigravity and robots." Leslie may have been simply naïve, but Clarke considered Adamski a charlatan. His close-up photos of the Venusian "spaceship," he said, bore an "uncanny resemblance to electric-light fittings with table-tennis balls fixed underneath." But the notion that "he succeeds in meeting the representative of saucerian civilization, when he lands his vehicle in the—presumably— totally uninhabited State of California" beggared belief. The account was "as ludicrous as the idea that for years saucers have been flitting round Palomar—of all places!—invisible to everyone except Mr. Adamski and his friend."[14]

Jim Moseley—the gadfly ufologist who trekked across the US interviewing all the big players in the UFO scene at the time—paid a visit to the "Professor" at his home just a few months after publication of the book. Moseley was skeptical of Adamski's claims but remained open to the possibilities. In response to Moseley's questions, Adamski provided ever more elaborate details: a Venusian posing as an earthling visited him at work one day; another Venusian had worked for the Los Angeles district attorney; he had watched film showing extraterrestrial life on other planets, likely taken by earthmen during a visit. Moseley must have appeared dubious, since at one point, Adamski told him, "If you don't believe in the spaceships and the Space Brothers, as I don't think you do, young man, wait until 1968 and you will find more understanding—or at the most until 1969." Moseley came away from the conversation convinced of the Californian's sincerity, or at least for a while.[15]

Over the next twelve months, Moseley pored over *Flying Saucers Have Landed* and phoned and wrote some of the principals in the case. As he did, he encountered holes, biases, and contradictions in Adamski's stories and evidence. Some people were falsely cited as witnesses or collaborators; others went on record saying that Adamski had seriously misquoted them. The six witnesses accompanying Adamski in the desert weren't strangers, but either worked with him or shared his occult beliefs. One of the witnesses even denied ever seeing the Venusian spaceship or spaceman in question. And Moseley wondered, why couldn't anyone at the scene take a good photo of events, and why did Adamski tell his companions to keep a good half mile to a mile away?

In January 1955, Moseley published an eleven-page expose in his newsletter *Nexus* on Adamski's alleged contact with an alien. He laid out his findings and concluded that the "Professor's" account contained "enough flaws to place in very serious doubt both his veracity and his sincerity." Moseley conceded that, if the book was indeed fraudulent, it was likely out of a misguided desire on Adamski's part to dramatize his devout philosophical beliefs. "But I sincerely feel," he added, "that if the truth concerning these mysterious flying saucers is ever to be arrived at, someone must now and then perform the rather thankless task of sifting away the 'saucer fiction' from the 'saucer facts.'"[16]

Adamski never responded to Moseley's points. Perhaps he knew this was unnecessary since he already had his following. He did go on to accuse Moseley of being "an agent of Wall Street." Reflecting on this later, Moseley acknowledged, "I took this as a disguised way of saying 'agent of the Jewish conspiracy,' and I think that's the way most of Adamski's followers understood the accusation."[17]

To this day, the man who claimed to have met a being from Venus and attended a meeting on Saturn has had as many, if not more, detractors than supporters among UFO enthusiasts. He did, however, achieve something noteworthy. What Donald Keyhoe had done for flying saucer investigation, George Adamski did for alien contact. More than simply popularize the topic by telling a compelling story, he helped create a new public career, what quickly became known as the "contactee." The contactee was someone claiming to have not only witnessed a flying saucer but also actually interacted with the alien life forms piloting the crafts. In so doing, the contactee came away with remarkable information about the appearance, customs, and intentions of the extraterrestrial visitors, an experience that left a sense of obligation to share it with the world.

George Adamski was arguably the most successful contactee of his time, but just one of many during the 1950s and early-1960s. Following Adamski's visit to Detroit, Helen and Bryant Reeve were determined to meet some of them as well.

TRUMAN BETHURUM AND GEORGE HUNT WILLIAMSON

Following Adamski's stay in their hometown, the Reeves entertained saucer followers in their basement recreation room. Conversation was lively and the group mixed. There were people drawn to the topic out of love for astronomy, some with an interest in technology and engineering, and others sharing the Reeves' philosophical leanings. Some were science fiction fans, while others were what the Reeves deemed to be "a sort of fringe of fanatics." They all were driven by a common desire to get to the bottom of things, and Helen and Bryant believed the best way to do this was to personally meet witnesses and decide if there was a pattern in their experiences.

When a new book arrived by yet another contactee, the group was eager to meet him. Arrangements were made for Truman Bethurum and his wife Mary to visit Detroit.

Truman Bethurum was tall, burly, bald, and in his mid-fifties and had spent his life working as a laborer in California and Nevada. A soft-spoken man, he tended to talk in simple, straightforward terms, unencumbered by philosophical ruminations.

In early 1953, Bethurum published a two-page piece in the newsletter *Saucers* entitled "I Was Inside a Flying Saucer."[18] In it, he described working the night shift as a construction site mechanic on a highway in Nevada in July 1952. At some point, he fell asleep, only to be awakened by a group of eight small men—whom he described as appearing to be of "Latin extraction"—standing around his vehicle in a semicircle. One of the men spoke to Bethurum in English, explaining they were fluent in any language. Bethurum got out of his truck to shake hands with the man, at which point he spotted a large flying saucer hovering a few feet off the ground.

Bethurum asked to meet the captain of the ship and was escorted inside. There he was introduced to the captain. "I think my eyes fairly popped," Bethurum recalled, "as I saw their captain was a gorgeous woman, shorter than any of the men, neatly attired, and also having a Latin appearance: coal black hair and olive complexion." She explained to the dumbfounded Bethurum that her name was Aura Rhanes and that she and her crew were from the planet Clarion. The visit was brief, but upon his departure from the vessel, Rhanes told Bethurum they would come again. All told they visited him eleven times in 1952.

Bethurum told his story again at the Flying Saucers International Convention held in Los Angeles in August 1953. Then, with the help of ghostwriter Mary Kay Tennison, he published *Aboard a Flying Saucer* in early 1954. In it, Bethurum offered more details about his meetings with the extraterrestrials. They told him they had achieved the ability to read minds and had conquered the limits of space and time. Clarion itself was free of illness, poverty, crime, and worry. Unlike our world, its inhabitants had organized their lives around cooperation, education, and religious devotion. If earth only emulated their way of life, the ship's captain explained, "you'd have a very paradise in which to build your homes and rear your children and see your sons blossom into manhood in peace, without the nagging horror and fear of bloody death and maimed and crazed young bodies."[19]

Aboard a Flying Saucer is unusual in donating considerable space to three melodramatic aspects of his story: Bethurum's romantic obsession with Capt. Aura Rhanes, the ridicule he faced from peers, and tensions with his wife. The Reeves believed Mary Kay Tennison played up the apparent amorous nature of the relationship between contactee and alien. To be sure, a great deal of attention is paid to Aura Rhanes's appearance in the book. "I told her how impressed I was that a woman was captain of such a piece of equipment; how the males of our earth would rate her as tops in shape-liness and beauty," Bethurum wrote. And after sharing a particularly emotional moment, he recalled, "I stared at her face, trying to imprint it on my mind. I liked what I saw, the large lucid brown eyes, the straight nose, the high intelligent forehead, the firm sweet lips."[20]

Such descriptions drew sneers and jibes. At work, guys called Bethurum "Saucers" and complimented him on finding "a good lookin' dame in the middle of the desert." Neighbors wondered whether he actually might have met with Russian spies. His exasperated wife Mary questioned her husband's sanity and insisted he stop talking about "those weird things." One morning as he raised the topic at the breakfast table, she finally snapped. "That's enough, Truman! I don't want to hear another word! The very idea!" she yelled. "You'll have my friends not only laughing at me but thinking I'm living with a maniac."[21]

According to Bethurum, Mary eventually came around when the couple visited George Adamski in the summer of 1953. Perhaps Adamski's faith in Truman's account won her over temporarily, but Mary eventually filed for divorce in 1956. According to Coral Lorenzen, Mary cited Truman's relationship with Aura Rhanes as the reason for neglecting his marriage.

A short time after meeting Truman Bethurum, in June 1954, Bryant and Helen Reeve had the opportunity to meet yet another contactee. In his late twenties, George Hunt Williamson was considerably younger than Adamski and Bethurum. Claiming to be a student of anthropology who had done some fieldwork among Native Americans, Williamson went by the title of "Dr.," though it appears he never earned a doctorate and may never have studied the field at all.

Williamson shared with Adamski a deep interest in theosophy and the occult. In fact, he and his wife visited Adamski in November 1952, and the two were among those claiming to have witnessed his original encounter with Orthon. Months before, however, the Williamsons had apparently established their own contact with aliens.

During some fieldwork in 1951, Williamson had been struck by how Native American tribes told tales of "little people," "flying wheels," and "flying boats" arriving in antiquity and teaching their members how best to live. After reading the books of Keyhoe, Scully, and Heard, and then following coverage of UFOs over the nation's capital, he became convinced that interplanetary visitors were behind all these reports.

Williamson and his wife settled in Arizona, where they befriended another couple—railway conductor Alfred Bailey and his wife—who lived nearby. The couples shared an interest in alternative religions and the possibility of extraterrestrial life. One summer day in 1952, when the Baileys were visiting the Williamsons, they decided to try their hand at automatic writing, the communication skill associated with spiritual mediums. Using supplies at hand, they created their own Ouija board and attempted to make contact with aliens.

As Williamson and Bailey later described it, they began receiving messages almost immediately from contact leaders based on Mars and Jupiter. These spokesmen—they all claimed to be male—explained that earth was known throughout the solar system as Saras and was in danger of destruction at the hands of evil forces. "Great destruction can be caused by your H-bomb. It could all come too soon. Some destruction will come for sure!" They urged, "it is most important that you organize."[22]

Soon, they were receiving message from other planets as well, at one point being asked by their alien liaison to boil water on the stove in order to help facilitate contact. Then on August 17, 1952, the foursome were instructed to seek out a ham radio operator, Lyman Streeter Jr. Streeter, they said, would help them communicate via radio. A few days later, Streeter, Williamson, and Bailey began receiving messages from outer space through a series of dashes and dots similar to Morse code.

The name of their extraterrestrial contact was Zo, the head of a contact group based on Mars, but whose home was on Neptune. Zo explained that the rest of the planets in the solar system were concerned about the fate of Earth/Saras:

> The movie, "The Day the Earth Stood Still" was for a purpose and was more fact than fiction. Watch all nature for signs of catastrophe. These signs, such as tornados, earthquakes, floods, and so on will come to Saras soon. . . . USSR is aware of us, too. Earth's last mile, we sad [sic]. It is impossible to reason with the people of earth. Soon all could end here.[23]

And one missive in particular stayed with Williamson. "RADIOMAN HAS DEEP SECRET IN HIS MIND," Zo relayed. "WILL NOT REVEAL. WE ARE ALARMED."[24]

Williamson and Bailey published their chronicle of these events in early 1954. Four years later, Williamson expanded on the tale. By then, however, he had moved to Indiana and began working with William Dudley Pelley, a successful Hollywood screenwriter with a deep interest in mysticism, theosophy, and race theory. A supporter of Adolf Hitler's takeover in Germany, Pelley founded the Silver Legion, a Christian militia whose purpose was to help create a Nazi state in the United States, one that would exclude Jews and re-enslave Blacks. Eventually imprisoned for his activities, he was released in 1950 and began publishing arguments about how visiting aliens had bred with our evolutionary ancestors and eventually saved humanity from its fallen, moral state.[25]

In 1958, Williamson published *UFOs Confidential*, in which he revealed that the radioman Lyman Streeter was actually a so-called Wanderer by the name of Kanet, born on earth to serve as a conduit for the solar system's Space Confederation. More importantly, Williamson shed light on the flying saucer mystery, voicing sentiments similar to those of George Adamski.

The outer space visitors had arrived, he insisted, to "wake us up," to "prepare us for a new technology and age of our world so that we might be ready for the eventual journey through space that defies description!"[26] But some on earth were bent on foiling these plans. Behind the scenes, members of "The Silence Group" were operating as henchmen of "International Bankers," who were in league with the Soviet Union. The conspiracy supposedly included financier Bernard Baruch, US Supreme Court Associate Justice Felix Frankfurter, US Senator Herbert Lehman, the Warburg family, and accused spy Alger Hiss. They controlled all the wealth in the world and could spark economic booms and depressions. These schemers, he said, "serve an ancient, hideous conspiracy that is nothing but the spirit of Anti-Christ," and they knew full well that, if the Space Brothers succeeded in shepherding earth to the New Age, their days were numbered. Thus, the conspirators were intent on undermining America's spiritual fortitude through "movies, radio, TV, magazines, etc., touting the great merits of body-destroying liquor, tobacco immorality" and using the United Nations to create a one world government.[27]

Williamson went on to publish three more books over the years 1957–1959 in which he presented archaeological, folklore, cosmological, and contactee evidence to support the notion that aliens had been interacting with humanity since ancient times. Almost as soon as his star had risen, Williamson receded into the background. In 1960, he changed his name to Michel d'Obrenovic and left the UFO scene.

THE "MEXICAN ADAMSKI"

In August 1954, the Reeves headed off on their "flying saucer pilgrimage," eventually crossing the border into Mexico, where they socialized with fellow saucer enthusiasts. Mexico had begun to develop its own homegrown UFO groups. When a newspaper editor organized a UFO symposium in Mexico City in January 1955, Bryant was asked to present. At one point during his talk, he asked the audience if anyone had ever seen a space man. After a long pause, a man in the back row raised his hand. The crowd became boisterous, demanding to hear his story, and he was whisked to the podium.

His name was Salvador Villanueva Medina, and sometime later, he agreed to tell the Reeves his story. A chauffeur by trade, Medina was driving two American passengers, when his car broke down. The Americans headed on foot to town to find a mechanic, while Medina worked on the automobile into the night. As he tried fixing it, a man about four feet tall with long blonde hair, dressed in a uniform, and carrying a helmet spoke to him in Spanish. The man left, only to return with another odd-looking fellow.

They told him they were from the planet Venus and over several hours described its wonders to him. The planet's inhabitants were much more advanced than ours: solar energy was used for power, streets were metallic, sidewalks moved on automated belts, and food came from gardens and wells inside homes. The Venusians' technological achievements were matched by their moral accomplishments. Having overcome warfare and strife thousands of years earlier, they had established a universal brotherhood ruled over by a council of wise men and guided by the principles of wisdom and love. They also explained that aliens were living on earth, in the guise of humans, in order to monitor the situation. When offered a ride in their flying saucer, Medina balked, and they flew off into the distance.

Medina's simple tale had much in common with Bethurum's; both lacked George Adamski's metaphysical meditations. Nevertheless, when Adamski visited Mexico soon after, the Reeves were among a small group to attend a get-together between the "Professor" and the man now being called the "Mexican Adamski." The meeting had more the air of an interrogation than a meeting of the minds, as a skeptical Adamski directed pointed questions at the man to determine whether he was a genuine contactee or not. How did the saucer look inside? What happened when the ship took off? Why were the spacemen here? When it was all over, the Reeves recalled, "Salvador passed his examination at the hands of a man, who having seen a saucer himself, knew how to ask about certain things which no mere imaginary contact could give the answers to."[28]

Later expanding on his original story, Medina related his five-day trip with visitors to Venus in a published account in 1958. Nonetheless, he drew little attention outside of Mexico. In the end, US contactees dominated the scene.

Fig. 5.2 George Adamski (left) meeting with Mexican contactee Salvador Villanueva Medina. TopFoto/Fortean.

THE SAGE OF GIANT ROCK

In April 1955, the Reeves drove back to the United States, stopping in Arizona to visit George Hunt Williamson and his family. They went on to reach Giant Rock, California, to meet George Van Tassel, the author of a book they had read during their time in Mexico, *I Rode a Flying Saucer* (1952).

Van Tassel had long been involved in aeronautics. At age seventeen, he was already working as an airplane mechanic. Throughout the thirties and forties, he worked for some of the country's most prestigious aviation companies—Douglas Aircraft, Hughes, Lockheed. At Hughes, he became involved in flight-testing near Barstow, California, where he discovered his love of outdoor living in the desert. It was there that he became acquainted with a German American loner named Frank Critzer.

Critzer had created a home for himself by carving out a cave from a natural landmark known as Giant Rock in the Mojave Desert near Landers, California. During the early days of the Second World War, the US government became interested in Critzer's activities, likely due to his storage and use of dynamite. When local police came to Giant Rock to question him in

July 1942, the ensuing confrontation led to an explosion, and Critzer was killed.[29]

In 1947, George Van Tassel purchased the land around Giant Rock, moved there with his wife, Dorris, and three daughters, and operated a small airport. Like so many other contactees at the time, "Van"—as friends called him—was drawn to esoteric philosophy, and he began to hold meditation readings for groups of twenty-five to forty-five people, at which he reported hearing disembodied voices. It soon became clear to him that these were coming from outer space.

Van Tassel kept notes on his communications with the "unseen intelligence," transmissions that took place over the course of 1952 and were especially frequent around the time of the UFO flap over Washington, DC. The voices told him that they were commanders from various space stations and planets, their chief being an alien named Ashtar. Ashtar and the others explained that they greeted us in love and peace, but they expressed worries about earth's future. They warned that "this folly in the use of atomic power for destruction will rebound upon the users" and that the presence of flying saucers was intended as a warning against employing hydrogen bombs. In addition, Van Tassel was told other planets were also visiting earth—the reason for there being differently shaped flying objects in the skies—and that those utilizing cigar-shaped vessels were "not investigating with peaceful intent."[30]

During their visit to Giant Rock in 1955, the Reeves were invited to take part in one of Van's contact sessions. They and Van Tassel's family were seated in a circle in a room many feet below the great Rock itself. Van sat in a corner, assuming the role of a medium, while an assistant recorded everything on tape. The family then began singing songs: some were popular, others were hymns, including one relayed to them by the space contacts. George then began receiving both "sight and sound rays" from the extraterrestrials, allowing him to both hear and see the spacemen with whom he was communicating. At times, the energy being transmitted got so strong, parts of his body were wracked by pain. All this showed, Van Tassel insisted, that aliens and their flying saucers could be alternately material and immaterial, visible and invisible, going a long way to explaining their peculiar properties.[31]

Van Tassel was not content with simply relaying the apocalyptic messages of Ashtar. He went on to publish a monthly bulletin, wrote books and pamphlets about his cosmic philosophy, appeared on radio and television, and established his own College of Universal Wisdom. After receiving instructions from an extraterrestrial named Solganda, he began pursuing the goal of constructing a building that supposedly had the ability to reverse the aging process. Christened the "Integratron," the project consumed Van Tassel for the rest of his life. It was never completed.[32]

One of Van Tassel's most important contributions was organizing an annual Interplanetary Space Convention at Giant Rock. From 1954 until 1977, UFO enthusiasts—by some accounts, in the thousands—camped out there for two or three days to mingle with and hear talks by contactees and to purchase literature and artifacts. Apostles and agnostics, confirmed occultists and curious onlookers, mystics and ministers, high-spirited free thinkers of all sorts were drawn to the event at its height in the 1950s. Ufology's traveling gossipmonger Jim Moseley attended the convention in May 1960 and delighted in its unconventionality.

> For every serious person, there were perhaps ten True Believers of all types and descriptions. I doubt if any two people in the whole assemblage could have been found to agree entirely on any issue. Yet there was a prevailing tolerance, as strangers went around introducing themselves to each other and trying to outdo everyone else in spouting their own views and theories.[33]

When the Reeves left Giant Rock, they reflected on George Van Tassel and his work. "He is an advanced apostle in the 'new age' if there ever was one!" Bryant said. Helen agreed. "I will always think of him as the sage of Giant Rock and will always be grateful for the privilege of knowing him. He reminds me of a veritable modern 'John the Baptist' crying in the wilderness, 'Prepare ye for a new cosmic age.'"[34]

TWO MORE DESERT FATHERS

From Giant Rock, the Reeves headed west toward Los Angeles to pay visits to two other prominent contactees, both frequent speakers at the Giant Rock conventions. The first was Daniel Fry, an aviation technician. In the summer of 1950, he was working at the White Sands Proving Grounds in New Mexico (now the White Sands Missile Range), the site of the first atomic bomb test in 1945. On the evening of July 4, he was alone in an army camp when he saw an odd-looking light in the sky and felt a strong, prickling sensation up and down his spine. It soon became apparent that the light was an object, and when it landed near him, he saw it to be a silver-colored craft with a violet glow. One of its occupants spoke to Fry and invited him on board for a ride.

Fry learned that the extraterrestrial's name was A-Lan and that his people were originally from the empire of Lemuria here on earth, only to be

Fig. 5.3 People gathering at Giant Rock in the California desert in 1957 to attend George Van Tassel's annual Flying Saucer Convention. Ralph Crane/The LIFE Picture Collection/Shutterstock.

destroyed in a conflict with its enemy Atlantis. Some survivors succeeded in flying to Mars. They returned in order to help promote the earth's scientific progress and thereby bring about the end of war between nations. Fry had been chosen for contact, A-Lan explained, because his brain was far more receptive and open to alien knowledge than any scientist's.[35]

In subsequent contacts with Fry in 1954, A-Lan urged him to tell their story "through your newspapers, your radio and television stations, and if necessary, shout it from the house-tops, but let the people know." Fry countered that he would only draw scorn and ridicule if he went public, but A-Lan insisted. The earth's people would only find peace if they received the simple message: understand God and one another.[36]

After visiting two guiding figures in the esoteric study of UFOs at the time—Meade Layne and Mark Probert—Bryant and Helen Reeve made their way in September 1955 to the Los Angeles home of the final contactee in their pilgrimage. Like Bethurum and Fry, Orfeo Angelucci was employed in the aviation industry. Though he later learned, he said, that he had been under alien observation since 1946, he first came across flying saucers while driving home from work late one night in May 1952. Two striking figures, a male and a female, suddenly appeared before him. "There was an impressive nobility about them; their eyes were larger and much more expressive, and they emanated a seeming radiance that filled me with wonder," he later recalled.[37]

Angelucci had the chance to see earth from outer space in a remote-controlled saucer and went on to have several encounters with one extraterrestrial in particular, whom he named "Neptune." Like the other humanoids described by contactees, Neptune sounded the alarm of a looming "bloody holocaust of Armageddon." It was a fate, he added, that could be avoided, and the aliens were willing to help. The flying disks reported by witnesses were intended as messengers, "harbingers of mankind's coming resurrection from the living death." And Orfeo was given a charge. "For the present you are our emissary, Orfeo, and you must act! Even though people of Earth laugh derisively and mock you as a lunatic, tell them about us!" Moved, he could only reply, "I will . . . I will . . ."[38]

Angelucci made frequent public appearances and became one of the more beloved contactees of the 1950s, widely praised for his sincerity and humility. The Reeves similarly found the "trim slender man with fine clean-cut features and deep expressive eyes" decidedly affable and generous. As their "conversation turned to the higher aspects of the flying saucer phenomena," they noted, "we discovered that we were indeed talking with an individual of great spiritual advancement, discernment, and experience." Like the other contactees whom Helen and Bryant met on their travels,

Angelucci confirmed to them that "our advanced space brothers and sisters in the space-ships" were "coming in love and brotherhood to help us avoid mistakes and to help usher us into a great new age."[39]

THE NEW AGE

The Reeves didn't use the term "new age" lightly. "Everywhere we found people in all walks of life talking about the 'New Age,'" they emphasized. "Among the humble and inarticulate it took the form of a feeling rather than words, a feeling of great expectancy—an expectancy of mighty changes ahead in the world." The flying saucer community was, in their words, "alive with enthusiasm for new age concepts."[40]

By the early 1950s, a movement had begun taking shape within occult circles oriented around the promise of a momentous New Age that was supposedly just around the corner. Inspired in part by the teachings of British theosophist Alice A. Bailey, advocates of New Age thinking swore off mainstream Western religious institutions in favor of pursuing the path of individual spiritual evolution. This spiritual journey, it was thought, required opening oneself up to the wisdom of "ascended masters."[41]

New Age philosophy was about more than simply seeking a higher consciousness and attaining personal transformation. Leading voices in the movement argued that the present world was corrupt, captive to an empty materialism. As a result, a new cycle of cosmic evolution was underway, one by which the old world would be destroyed and replaced by a new age of enlightenment, peace, plenty, justice, and contentment. That process could either be accelerated or hindered by the relative commitment earth's inhabitants showed toward their own spiritual growth. Borrowing elements from transcendentalism, spiritualism, and theosophy, New Agers commonly saw the universe as a web of interconnected consciousnesses. This allowed them to cross the barriers of time and space by serving as mediums through which higher beings could communicate, a process called "channeling."[42]

Most of the flying saucer contactees embraced these ideas either explicitly or implicitly. Indeed, it's fair to say that during the 1950s and early 1960s, the contactee movement was the cutting edge of the New Age movement. Publishing houses like New Age in California, Ventla in West Germany, and Parthenon in Sweden gave eager readers access to the latest works of contactees as well as to metaphysical interpretations about the meanings of flying saucers. Through their public appearances at lectures and in radio and television interviews, the contactees spread their New Age beliefs to the uninitiated.

In the postwar era and later, New Age was less a rigorous philosophy or even an organized religion than it was a broad spiritual vision encompassing a range of beliefs and practices. But its merging with the UFO phenomenon in the 1950s brought a number of prominent themes to the ongoing conversation about flying saucers: fears about nuclear war, concern for the fate of the planet, and the prospects for solving the world's most pressing social problems.[43]

THE GATECRASHERS

The famous contactees the Reeves met during their pilgrimage—with one exception—shared some conspicuous characteristics. They were white. They were male. And they made their homes or had their experiences in the southwestern part of the United States.

Other contactees had similar backgrounds and stories. Texan Dan Martin claimed that while driving in August 1955, he came across a "very pleasant appearing" and "rather short though well proportioned" female from Mercury wearing a gas mask, who eventually took him on her ship and claimed the craft itself had been responsible for many of the miracles described in the Bible.[44] Californian businessman Reinhold Schmidt was on the road in Nebraska in November 1957 when, he said, "a pencil-like stream of light shot out" from a large silvery vessel and hit him in the chest, leaving him temporarily paralyzed. This began one of several contacts he had with visiting aliens who warned him about the impact atomic explosions were having on earth's atmosphere, at one point flying Schmidt to the Arctic Circle to show him how the ice there was melting at an alarming rate.[45] In 1961, however, Schmidt was put on trial for swindling money from a pair of widows who had believed his stories about his encounters with spacemen. After young astronomer Carl Sagan testified about the scientific dubiousness of his claims, Schmidt was convicted and sentenced to one to ten years in prison.[46]

To be sure, there were contactees from elsewhere. Missouri farmer Buck Nelson spoke in a disarmingly folksy way about being flown to Venus, the moon, and Mars by aliens who struck the familiar themes of abandoning atomic weapons and embracing the laws of God.[47] World War II veteran Howard Menger told of having regular contact with extraterrestrials since he was a boy in New Jersey, when he was introduced to his space sister. The aliens were here, he said, in order to rouse us to our need to seek higher understanding and avoid catastrophe.[48]

Europe, too, had its contactees. In England, George King began receiving telepathic messages from a Venusian master named Aetherium who told him he was to be the "voice of Interplanetary Parliament." The knowledge King gained from his psychical travels to Venus and Mars inspired him to found the Aetherius Society, whose worldwide mission has been to spread the teachings of Aetherius and Jesus and prepare the way for the next Master.[49]

All these contactees were white American and English men. Admittedly, their claims and beliefs set them apart from mainstream society at the time. Despite this, their social status afforded them access to resources often unavailable to others: publishing books, giving paid public lectures, and interviewing with radio and tv broadcasters. The stories they related about their contact experiences often featured thinly veiled erotic descriptions of their alien guides, who indulged the questions and insecurities of their human guests and left the men with a renewed sense of self-importance.[50]

That said, there were other contactees in the fifties and sixties who were of a different ilk from the ones the Reeves visited. Brazil, for instance, was home to Aladino Félix (pen name Dino Kraspedon), who published his account of five meetings he had in 1952 with a being from one of the moons of Jupiter. Speaking to Félix in multiple languages, the visitor supposedly warned of the devastating impact radiation from atomic bombs would have on the environment and rebuked earthlings for spending their wealth on novelties and luxury goods instead of research, infrastructure, and curing diseases like cancer, leprosy, and tuberculosis. A little over ten years later, however, Félix announced on television that his claims were a fabrication. Shortly thereafter he was arrested and imprisoned for his involvement in a right-wing paramilitary group that carried out a series of terrorist attacks in 1967 and 1968.[51]

Spain had its own, slightly more theatrical version of George Adamski in Fernando Sesma, a former postal worker and amateur journalist. Since the mid-1950s, Sesma served as the spokesman for a group that gathered in the basement of a Madrid café, the Asociación de Amigos de los Visitantes del Espacio (Association of the Friends of the Space Visitors). The assembly included a priest who had authored a small treatise on flying saucers, arguing that earth had been visited by aliens interested in exploring God's creations.[52] Taking place as it did in the restrictive environment of Franco's authoritarian Spain, meetings like these were inherently suspect. The seemingly apolitical topic of UFOs, however, offered participants a measure of freedom to associate and share opinions.[53]

One day in 1962, Sesma received a phone call from someone saying he was Saliano from the planet Auco. He also began receiving letters from the spaceman, who presented his people as peaceful and interested only in studying earth. Within a few years, direct contact with the aliens had been established, and in 1965, Sesma said he was flown out of the solar system via a fourth dimension. Sesma suddenly became a celebrity, appearing regularly on Spanish television from 1966 to 1969. It all came to an end in 1970, when Saliano supposedly claimed he would appear in the flesh at the Pakistani Embassy. When Sesma fans gathered outside the building, police broke up the assembly.[54]

Despite the dominant whiteness of American writers, speakers, and audiences, there were some voices within the African American community who drew inspiration from reports of UFOs and alien contact. Nation of Islam leader Elijah Muhammad preached that there were Black inhabitants on Mars and other planets, a feat that remained out of reach for the white man. In addition, he told followers a giant wheel-shaped object, the Mother Plane, rested in outer space and was equipped with 1,500 military vehicles. "The small circular-made planes called flying saucers, which are so much talked of being seen, could be from this Mother Plane," and when the right time arrived, they would smash white dominion over the earth.[55] Later, in 1989, Minister Louis Farrakhan announced that he himself had the experience of being carried into the Mother Wheel craft by a beam of light, where he received a message from Elijah Muhammad warning that United States was preparing for war.[56]

Arguably the most colorful and creative American contactee was Sun Ra. Born Herman Poole Blount, he was an accomplished musician and autodidact who spent much of the 1930s and 1940s reading scripture, histories of ancient Egypt, and stories about space travel and rocketry. By the early-1950s, Blount changed his name to Le Sony'r Ra, abbreviated as Sun Ra, in honor of his commitment to cosmology and the legacy of the Egyptian sun god, Ra.

In 1953, Sun Ra began telling his friends of a remarkable event that happened to him around 1936. He was contacted, he said, by space men, who beamed his body to Saturn through a process of energy transformation he called "transmolecularization." He suddenly found himself listening to a lecture in an arena by beings with antennas over their eyes and ears. They told him, "they would teach me some things that when it looked like the world was going into complete chaos, when there was no hope for nothing, then I could speak, but not until then. I would speak, and the world would listen." Back on earth, Sun Ra soon found himself on a bench in New York City, when he looked up and saw thousands of spaceships. "You can order us to land. Are conditions right for landing?" a voice asked him. Yes, he replied, and they landed, shooting bullet-like pellets that stuck onlookers to the ground.[57]

A few years after recounting his contact experience, Sun Ra formed a band called the Arkestra. He considered the band a "space orchestra," one that traveled through space just as the earth did and that offered a cosmic perspective on the boundlessness of the imagination through its music. Instruments were often given celestial names like the space harp, solar bells, and cosmic side drum, and a growing number of songs made reference to outer space. By the early 1960s, Sun Ra began dressing in elaborate gold outfits, and the stage featured a flying saucer with flashing lights. For the next three decades, he continued his mission to remind people that "space is the place," including teaching a course at the University of California Berkeley in 1971 on "The Black Man in the Cosmos."[58]

A small number of women were also among those claiming to have made contact with aliens. For example, the medium Dana Howard authored nine books between 1954 and 1964 in which she described her esoteric philosophy and her contact with inhabitants from Venus. She told of flying in a small plane that crashed around Arizona's Superstition Mountains. As she came to on the ground, she recalled feeling a "tingling glow" and "the door to my mind opening and closing." A rocket ship suddenly appeared above her, and a female figure named Diane escorted Howard into the aircraft. She, along with a Native American named Blue Cloud and a prospector named Cactus Jeff, were then taken to Venus, where Howard met the planet's Queen Zo-na and fell in love with and married a male called LeLando. She then was returned to earth in August 1952.[59]

Howard acknowledged that she didn't know whether her trip to Venus was made in her physical body or not, since its inhabitants had mastered the art of "transmutation." Her story, however, included many of the same elements as other contactees': Venusian society was advanced and beautiful, its people comely, its governing creed based on love. On the earth, a New Age was dawning, and "the lovely lady from Venus" whom she had met after her plane crash was coming to usher in a world free of disease, poverty, and conflict. Howard's account was different from most others, however, in that this grand regeneration was explicitly framed in gendered terms. As one of her alien guides told her, "The male is ever power-seeking. . . . It is the male being who makes our wars, my dear. Never the female. Under feminine rule the seeds of violence have little opportunity to find fertile soil."[60]

Venus made its appearance in tales from other female contactees as well. In South Africa, Elizabeth Klarer said she was invited onto the flying saucer of two Venusian crew members in April 1956 while walking on a hill at the foot of the Drakensberg Mountain range. Speaking in impeccable English, they informed her they had been studying earth for a while and were saddened to see its "mode of existence, precarious and always with the threat of war." Klarer heard as well about life on Venus ("civilised and cultured"), and she spoke with her hosts "about music, real and beautiful music. Not about the primitive jungle noise that is so popular throughout this world."[61] Klarer eventually went on to write a book about her experience in the late 1970s, in which she elaborated on her original story, claiming to have given birth to the child of an alien lover.[62]

Perhaps the most tragic instance of a contactee was the case of Gloria Lee. A flight attendant with an interest in theosophy, Lee claimed to have begun receiving messages from outer space via automatic writing and telepathy beginning in 1953. She discovered, she said, she was "The Instrument" for telepathic communications from J. W., a being from Jupiter. J. W. preached a message of "freedom to love" and offered humanity urgent advice to avoid the nuclear destruction of earth by taking the next evolutionary steps in the developments of higher consciousness.[63] In 1959, Lee founded the Cosmon Research Foundation, as a way to further spread J. W.'s teachings.

Three years later, in September 1962, J. W. provided Lee with blueprints for a spaceship and instructed her to give them to officials in Washington, DC. She tried to follow through on the request, but no one in power responded. According to one source, Lee then reported that the aliens were "disturbed up there because of fighting in the world and the fact the nuclear bombs might upset their planets. . . . J. W. has ordered me to go on a fast for peace until he sends a 'light elevator' down to take me to Jupiter."[64] The elevator never appeared. After two months of fasting in a Washington hotel room, Lee was rushed to a hospital, where she died a few days later. Sadly, Gloria Lee proved not to be the only casualty in the quest to make contact with extraterrestrials.

SKEPTICS

While many were fascinated by the stories of the contactees, many more dismissed them and their claims. There was no lack of critics within the UFO community itself, where prominent ufologists and organizations disparaged the contactees, seeing them as being, at best, deluded and, at worst, con artists. Even some who shared the metaphysical leanings of people like Adamski and Lee acknowledged the tales at times were difficult to reconcile with one another.

Writing in 1955, South African ufologist Edgar Sievers was buoyed by the testimony of the contactees revealing that our space brothers and sisters "have offered tidings, pronouncements, and explanations, whose content is of absolute, signal importance for the salvation of humanity." But he was also mindful of the fact that the alien declarations came with an added twist. "At closer inspection, we find that the logic in these pronouncements leaves much to be desired. Instead of conceptual clarity and genuine meaning, we encounter obscurity and meaningless nonsense." If the extraterrestrial visitors were heralds, they were being frustratingly opaque and mystifying.[65]

British writer Gavin Gibbons interviewed a family living in central England that claimed to have seen UFOs hovering over their farmhouse in 1954, even catching a glimpse of some their crew. Gibbons considered them quite credible, since they were not seeking publicity and appeared to be genuinely frightened by the experience. He held contactee George King in much lower regard, finding him bombastic. Gibbons particularly disliked King's reliance on spiritualism and trance, which he thought opened up the alien contact phenomenon to fraud.[66]

APRO's Coral Lorenzen wanted nothing to do with the contactees. After Daniel Fry visited Sweden in July 1970, Lorenzen wrote her friend Gösta Rehn, "I don't know what to do about Fry—we generally ignore characters of his ilk. They like attention of any kind, good or bad, and we don't want to get drawn into any kind of debate or verbal exchange. I can tell you one thing; he was not any kind of scientist at White Sands . . . Fry was a lousy electrician, and that was all."[67]

To those who held themselves up to be "serious UFO investigators," the contactees were an outright embarrassment, their ridiculous testimonials serving only to cast the entire UFO movement in a dubious light. In 1957, UFO researcher Isabel Davis—a founding member of the Civilian Saucer Intelligence group based in New York City—published a scathing critique of the claims of the contactees in the science fiction magazine *Fantastic Universe*. In it, Davis highlighted the convenient and seemingly contrived patterns found in the stories told by the likes of Adamski, Bethurum, Williamson, Angelucci, and Fry. In-person contacts were "usually private, usually at night, in an isolated spot, without witnesses." Female aliens were described in overtly sexualized terms. The spacemen all resembled "human beings of European-American descent," and their home worlds were all utopian. The contactees experienced no serious communication problems with their guides. And yet, the extraterrestrials spoke in prophetically cryptic terms, always refusing to provide details about crucial topics. In the end, the substance of their claims revealed more about the mindset of the contactees than it did about alien civilizations. "What is unquestionably revealed to the reader, with painful clarity, are the intense, the tragic *fears* that haunt the apostles and disciples of the contact-communication stories," Davis wrote. "Many passages are an almost rhythmic seesaw between terrors—of war, of soil sterility, of strange weather, of the atom—and feverish reassurances that the space beings will somehow give protection from these dooms."

To Davis, the reports of the contactees were riddled with implausible contradictions. The space beings supposedly had awesome abilities, and yet there were key discrepancies between the spacemen's "claim to great powers and what they are able to *do*." In Adamski's case, for example, they were able to build interplanetary vessels and communicate telepathically, but somehow when Adamski wanted to take photographs, their own photographic equipment didn't work. Time and again, the aliens kept demanding to be recognized by earth's inhabitants but did little to make that happen. "They blow hot and cold," Davis bluntly put it, "it is all inconsistent." The only consistency among the contactees was their lack of any solid proof. "There is not a line that stamps the stories as 'unearthly.' The alleged spacemen are not noble intelligences, but boastful braggarts, gifted chiefly at making excuses. The authors make egregious blunders; they contradict themselves and the spacemen contradict each other."[68]

Donald Keyhoe shared Davis's reservations. In August 1958, he discovered that NICAP membership cards had been mistakenly mailed out to George Adamski, Orfeo Angelucci, Truman Bethurum, Howard Menger, Buck Nelson, Reinhold Schmidt, and George Van Tassel. Keyhoe responded by telegramming each of the contactees to return the unauthorized card immediately. "No contactee has ever received, or will receive," NICAP announced, "favored attention, public or private, from this Committee, since all such claims are still under NICAP investigation."[69]

Over the course of the 1960s, the contactees lost the public attention and visibility they had enjoyed during the previous decade. No doubt this was related to their repudiation by prominent ufologists and organizations, but the likely finishing blow to their popularity came at the hands of US and USSR space agencies. Soviet spacecrafts Luna 3 and Zond 3 in 1959 and 1965 sent back images of millions of square miles of the moon's surface. In December 1962, the robotic probe Mariner 2 successfully flew within 21,000 miles of the planet Venus and revealed the temperature of its atmosphere to be around 900 degrees Fahrenheit. A similar probe, Mariner 4, flew to within around 6,000 miles of the surface of Mars in July 1965 and took the first close range photos of the planet. And in December 1968, the crew of Apollo 8 orbited the moon, helping pave the way for the first moon landing in July 1969. Together, these ventures in space exploration dispelled any notion of there being intelligent life on the moon, Venus, Mars, or for that matter any other planet in our solar system.

While ufologist Isabel Davis scoffed at the uplifting stories contactees told about their conversations and friendships with extraterrestrials, she was far more accepting of another set of alien encounter reports that were circulating at the time. She referred to them as "reports of 'little men' who come out of flying saucers," and they differed from the contactee accounts in three conspicuous ways. First, witnesses described the appearance of the beings as near-human, not superhuman. Second, the spacemen and their behavior were incomprehensible: they offered "no lofty messages, no explanations of ancient riddles, no admonitions, warnings, reassurances, prophecies, or esoteric doctrine." Finally, the witnesses themselves often found the experience unsettling and more often than not remained content to stay out of the limelight.[70]

Davis was on to something. While the contactees and their tales enjoyed a certain fame and notoriety from the early 1950s through the mid-1960s, a few voices in the UFO milieu were noting a growing number of freakishly puzzling alien sightings. Some of the witnesses in these cases went on to garner their share of public attention—fleeting though it often was—but few if any made a career out of their experiences. Whereas the hub for contactee reports was in the United States, Europe and South America appeared to be the focal point for these baffling encounters.

Tales of run-ins with supernatural little people—such as fairies, elves, leprechauns—abound in world folklore. Communities have associated such sprites with impishness, passing on knowledge, and an ability to travel great distances in an instant. Already by the 1960s, comparisons were being made with claims of alien contact, and enterprising ufologists uncovered accounts of brushes with peculiarly small men—described as being shorter than four feet tall—working around unusual airships dating as far back as 1914.[71]

Coral Lorenzen and her *APRO Bulletin* were among the first to track contemporary cases beginning in 1954. "APRO was the first and only UFO research organization to place any credence in these incidents. Not because we are gullible people—but rather because we had excellent sources and investigators and found a thread of continuity which lent much to the authenticity of the reports," she wrote a colleague in early 1959. "If people reporting such incidents were to conform their experiences to a particular description, I would be exceedingly doubtful, but inasmuch as interpretations have been quite varied (and quite possibly the creatures were varied), I am inclined to accept as fact that *they did see some strange creatures*" (italics in original).[72]

An early example of one of these incidents came from the Spanish press in 1953. That July, the local newspaper *Ofensiva* featured a series of articles about the claims of a fourteen-year-old herdsman named Máximo Muñoz Hernáiz. Hernáiz lived in the village of Villares del Saz, about eighty miles southeast of Madrid. In an interview with the paper's editor, the boy described how earlier that month he had been tending to some cows one afternoon when he heard a hissing sound and saw what looked like a large, gray, glowing balloon on the ground. When he went over to it, three little men about two feet tall emerged from the object. "Their faces were yellow, and their eyes narrow," Máximo recalled, and they wore hats with visors and blue uniforms with badges on the arm. One of the men began speaking to him, but "when I didn't understand what he said to me, the one standing in front of me smacked my face." After that, they got back into their machine and it flew off "very fast, like a rocket."[73]

The next year, 1954, proved to be a momentous one for stories about encounters with little spacemen. One of the most publicized and influential of these took place in France, which, like many parts of Europe, experienced a wave of UFO sightings as well as reports of UFOs landing. A little over a decade later, famed French ufologist Jacques Vallee examined 200 such reports, 156 of which occurred in France and included 42 instances where individuals caught sight of the operators of the unidentified flying object. Vallee found some variation in how witnesses described the beings they saw, but their appearance was always talked about as human-like. Ufologists at the time borrowed a term science fiction writers had made popular in the 1940s and 1950s to refer to these physical features: "humanoid."[74]

The French case drawing the most attention that year involved Marius Dewilde, a metalworker in Quarouble. Known in his neighborhood as something of a misfit, Dewilde was said to have made little effort assimilating into the local community. He made his home in an abandoned railway station with no electricity or running water.

At around 10:30 p.m. on September 10, 1954, Dewilde heard his dog barking and went outside to investigate. He saw the vague shape of a domed object and could also make out two figures. Aiming his flashlight at them, he could see they wore some kind of dark suit made of soft material and were short. Without warning, a beam of light from the object came at him. His felt a tingling sensation and was briefly paralyzed. The object became luminous, noiselessly rose in the air, and flew away. He then rushed to report the incident to the police, and soon, journalists and officials from the Air Ministry were on the scene.

Dewilde later told French UFO investigator Marc Thirouin about a second encounter with the beings. Around noon on October 10, 1954, he,

Fig. 5.4 The front page of *Radar* magazine from September 1954 depicting Marius Dewilde's encounter with strange beings. Mary Evans Picture Library.

along with his three-year-old son, saw the same machine reappear. This time, he was able to peer through a porthole and could see "human-looking beings" (*des êtres d'apperence humaine*) moving around inside. One eventually came out, wearing what looked like a rubber diving suit and helmet. He spoke to Dewilde in a language he couldn't understand, but he smiled and was friendly and several times caressed his son's head. Soon thereafter, the man headed back into the craft, and the vehicle darted off.[75]

Dewilde's descriptions of the men weren't always consistent. At one point, he said the beings were about two-and-a-half feet tall, had no arms, and wore what looked like diving suits. On another occasion, he reportedly said they wore jumpsuits, were over three feet in height, and were "Mongol" in appearance.[76]

Within days, the national and international press proclaimed France was "in the grip of flying saucer fever."[77] A young Jacques Vallee at the time was riveted. "I believed his story at the time. I still do," he wrote in his diary four years later. "During the three months the wave lasted I carefully gathered such clippings and glued them into a fat copybook."[78]

Other cases popped up in Europe, and at times, the little men seemed to get downright rascally. On the morning of November 1, 1954, forty-year-old Rosa Lotti Dainelli left her farmhouse near Cennina, Italy, carrying carnations for the local church.[79] As she walked, she came across a small clearing and was surprised to see a large, shiny spindle-shaped object about six feet high and three feet wide resting on the ground. Glass casing around one part of the gadget showed there to be two small seats inside.

Then, from around the object two figures—"almost like men, but of the size of children"—approached her in a welcoming manner. They wore helmets and grey jumpsuits adorned with capes. Though they looked old, they were quite energetic, talking animatedly, she said, "as though they were Chinese. They kept saying: 'liu,' 'lai,' 'loi,' 'lau,' 'loi,' 'lai,' 'liu.'" At one point, one of them snatched the carnations and a stocking she was carrying out of her hands. He inspected them, laughed, wrapped the flowers in the stocking he had taken, and threw them into the machine. When the two men went back to the object to retrieve something, Dainelli took the opportunity to run away, leaving the little men at work around their spindle.

Like Dewilde, Dainelli reported the incident to local police and, later, ufologists. It was said that officers and neighbors inspecting the site found a deep cavity in the ground, but little else. The Italian press immediately took to the story and reported that several witnesses in the area described seeing an odd luminous flying object around the same time and place.

South America was also replete with little spacemen stories. One evening in February 1966, sisters aged twenty and seventeen and a friend were walking on their way home in Quipapá in northeastern Brazil. At one point, they came across a strange, disk-like object hovering in the air. Next to it lay a large man, who wasn't moving, along with several little figures gesticulating wildly. They all wore jumpsuits and odd hats, both of which were equipped with bright lights that changed color. When a jeep suddenly drove by, the girls took the opportunity to leave the area. They returned a few minutes later to the site with their mother, at which point the group saw the disk fly off, spiraling along the way. The experience left one of the sisters in a state of anxiety that persisted for some time.[80]

While some little men were either unaware of or outright friendly to the humans who crossed their paths, a goodly number recoiled from encounters. In October 1965, fifty-seven-year-old Jose Camilo Filho, a mechanic in Canhotinho, Brazil, was walking home, when he came across two small men under three feet sitting on a tree branch. Around their chests they had what looked like an electric arc that emitted a strong light. One of the men wore a cap with an emblem on it. While they both had white hair and white hands, Filho said, they looked "like Japanese, their faces tan and wrinkled as though they were old." When the figures noticed the mechanic, they became so frantic that they ran into one another. One of the men leaped backward, grabbed a nearby piece of piping and aimed it at the mechanic. Filho began running off, but then thought better of it and returned to take a closer look, but by then the men had disappeared.[81]

One of the most famous encounters along these lines took place in Socorro, New Mexico, a short drive from the White Sands Missile Range— the same proving ground made famous by contactee Daniel Fry. On April 24, 1964, policeman Lonnie Zamora was driving his patrol car in pursuit of a reckless driver just before 6 p.m., when he glanced to his left and saw a white object on the ground. Fearing it might be an overturned car, he stopped to investigate and saw what he described as an "egg-shaped looking object," about the size of an automobile, standing on four supports and stamped with an insignia. Zamora called his colleague Sgt. M. S. Chavez of the New Mexico State Police for assistance. The object then began making a roaring noise and spit out a blue flame. Fearing for his safety, Zamora moved away, and the vehicle soon rose in the air and silently flew away low to the ground.

State police and the FBI arrived on the scene. So too did the media. Overnight, the unassuming policeman became something of a celebrity. As Zamora shared his recollections, elements of his story sometimes changed. In an interview with a representative from Donald Keyhoe's NICAP several days later, for instance, he said what first drew his attention to the side of the road had been the sound of a roar, not the sight of the egg-shaped object.[82] At other times, Zamora fumbled for the right words. An important detail was the fact that he initially told reporters that he had also noticed little men near the aircraft. When local radio broadcaster Walter Shrode asked him the day after the event whether the men wore helmets like spacemen, however, Zamora replied, "No, sir, I wouldn't say they were people, I just . . . I saw something white, white coveralls, that's all I can say." He added, "I would say that . . . that, that the white object turned and saw me" shortly before the craft took off. Shrode pressed the issue. Witnesses in the area, he said, claimed to have seen some unidentified flying objects at the time, and he wondered what the police officer thought about the possibility of this being something from outer space. Zamora balked at the notion. "Well, I didn't think it would be an object from outer space because I don't believe in things like this, from outer space."[83]

When Air Force and FBI officers arrived in Socorro, they cordoned off the supposed landing area and saw signs that "something" in fact had been there.[84] Project Blue Book also took an immediate interest in the case, and scientific consultant J. Allen Hynek made his way to Socorro four days after the sighting. He interviewed Zamora and Sgt. Chavez over dinner, questioned local reporters, and inspected the site. Afterward, he reported back to the Air Force that "Zamora, although not overly bright or articulate, is basically sincere, honest, and reliable," a man incapable of perpetrating an elaborate hoax. Instead, he was struck by how genuine Zamora's fear was, and "his feeling that he had seen something truly unusual is attested by the fact that he asked whether he should speak to the priest first before saying anything about it." In the end, Hynek believed the policeman had seen an actual flying object and "that NICAP and APRO, and possibly others, would consider this the best authenticated landing sighting on record. They will use it, very likely as a lever for a congressional investigation."[85]

On hearing about the sighting, ufologists indeed took notice, and several arrived within days. An investigator from NICAP, Ray Stanford, stumbled across a rock that seemed to have been disturbed by the UFO. Thinking it might contain metal traces, Stanford sent it to headquarters for analysis, but lab technicians only detected silica, a substance commonly found in the earth's crust.[86]

Coral and Jim Lorenzen from APRO made the seven-hour drive to Socorro from Tucson on April 25. The next morning, they arranged an interview with Zamora, with a deputy sheriff and a reporter sitting in. Zamora at first denied seeing any "little men," but when Coral reminded him that he had said as much earlier to reporters, the policeman admitted he had in fact caught sight of them. Asked to describe the figures, he said they looked like "young boys" or "small adults," but he couldn't make out any definite features. He also acknowledged he saw markings on the craft, but that government intelligence officers had insisted he not discuss the matter in public.

Meanwhile, Jim Lorenzen was asking questions of the police and military on site. Sgt. David Moody from Project Blue Book, unaware of Jim's relationship to Coral, blurted out, "there's a woman who heads a research group out in this area—in Tucson, I believe. Her name is Coral Lorenzen. She's a nut." Jim shot back, "She's my wife." Moody giggled, turned to another military man, said "She's his wife," and then added to Jim, "She's sincere."[87]

By the end of May, Project Blue Book investigators had explored possible candidates for the object Zamora had seen: a helicopter, a classified project at White Sands, an experimental vertical take-off and landing craft, a model of the lunar module that NASA was developing. None of them panned out, and the case remained open.[88]

CLASSIFYING ALIENS

Tales of encounters with little men and their unidentified flying objects complicated the picture of alien contact. These diminutive figures were nothing like the prophetic philanthropists that featured so prominently in the claims of the contactees. The witnesses themselves also stood out from their contactee counterparts, offering next to no insight into the motivations of the extraterrestrials and remaining comparatively unaffected by their experiences.

To anyone playing close attention, there was in fact a lot more going on than stories of conversations with handsome Venusians and brushes with celestial imps. In 1966, British ufologist Gordon Creighton combed through news articles about "alleged meetings with denizens of other worlds" in Latin American newspapers dating back to 1950. He found a veritable medley of descriptions of the creatures. There were giants, tall men, medium-sized men, and small men. Some were said to be hairy, others green. There were reports of beings with one eye, beings with three eyes, and, in one instance, an entity with eyes running up and down its body.[89]

The variations led some investigators to search for patterns in alien contact accounts. A common approach was to focus on the physical attributes of the beings encountered. In 1970, jurist and secretary of a São Paulo–based UFO research organization Jader Pereira published the results of a two-year study he conducted analyzing alien contact reports. Pereira examined 333 cases from across the globe over the previous twenty years, relying on books, bulletins, newsletters, newspapers, and magazines for his sources.

Adopting a kind of zoological scheme, he categorized the entities in terms of body type and size, skin color, hair, and attire. In the end, Pereira found a good deal of variation, but reported that in almost 96 percent of cases, creatures were described as basically human in form.[90]

Eleven years earlier in 1959, Brazilian lawyer and ufologist José Escobar Faria had pursued a similar path in one of the earliest analyses of alien contact reports. In classifying cases, he also considered the behavior of the spacemen. All told, Faria believed there to be three groups whose actions seemed tied to their racial features: peaceful beings who were white, hostile beings who were black, and an undifferentiated category of beings who were only observed from afar.[91]

The focus on race was hardly unique to Faria and Pereira. Contactees and witnesses of little men frequently turned to existing racial stereotypes in recounting their experiences. George Adamski's Orthon, for example, possessed a mix of what followers called Nordic and Oriental features. In fact, ufology after 1980 began openly referring to aliens like him as "Nordics." At the same time, witnesses of the fifties and sixties often made references to the "Oriental"—a term that could refer to South Asian, East Asian, or Semitic peoples—attributes of some extraterrestrials.[92] Their skins were described alternately as yellow, dark, or tanned, their bodies as small, their language and faces as Chinese, Japanese, or simply "Oriental."

The presumed racial features of aliens would become an enduring topic of discussion in some ufology circles.[93] Others preferred focusing on the conduct of the outer space visitors, seeing in it a possible window into their intentions. Coral Lorenzen, for one, came around to this way of thinking already in the late 1950s. And by the mid-1970s, the Brazilian Society for the Study of Flying Saucers classified alien contact experiences into four groups: extraterrestrials viewed at a distance; extraterrestrials approaching in a friendly manner; anxious and fleeing extraterrestrials; and extraterrestrials using force in making contact.[94]

These last set of cases were relatively rare among alien contact reports of the fifties and sixties. Some observers, like Donald Keyhoe, put little stock in them. Others took the stories deadly serious. To them, the harrowing actions of some aliens toward the human beings they encountered signaled an alarming change in alien visitation.

SKIRMISH IN KENTUCKY

In the spring and summer of 1955, American ufologists Gray Barker, Coral Lorenzen, and Leonard Stringfield began receiving unsettling reports from

South America and the United States of violent encounters with aliens. Witnesses provided dramatic accounts of what were often described as "little men" attacking them as they drove their cars or were going about on foot. Terrified victims often described the beings as having glowing or strangely colored eyes, hairy bodies, odd clothing, and even claws for hands.[95]

Then, in late August, newspapers and radio stations across America reported on a remarkable series of events that happened to a family in Kelly, near Hopkinsville, Kentucky, on the night of August 21. As *The Kentucky New Era* reported it the next day, around 11:00 p.m., two cars full of highly agitated adults and children pulled up to the Hopkinsville police station.[96] A man in the group told officers, "We need help. We've been fighting them for nearly four hours."

Apparently, family and friends had congregated at the farmhouse of Glennie Lankford and her son Elmer (wrongly reported as "Cecil") Sutton, when something resembling a flying saucer landed on the property. Suddenly, somewhere between twelve and fifteen men around four feet tall with bizarrely large eyes and hands and wearing metal plates got out of the ship. Elmer and his friend Billy Ray Taylor grabbed their guns, fearing the worst.

As one of the little men pressed his face against a window of the house, Elmer fired his shotgun, and the figure disappeared. Sutton and Taylor went outside to see if they had downed the creature. When they did, a big hand reached down from the low-hanging roof above the front door and grabbed Taylor by the hair. Taylor managed to wriggle away. They then spotted other little men, one in a nearby tree and another on the roof of the house. Sutton fired his shotgun, knocking one of them down. Appearing uninjured, it ran off.

The melee lasted hours, as the men fired what they estimated were around four boxes of shells, though a neighbor said he heard only about four shots all night. The bullets, in any event, appeared to have little effect on the invaders. When the household saw a chance to escape, they jumped into cars and drove to the police station for help. Officers arrived to find no trace of the little men, staying on the property for more than two hours. Two policemen returned to the Suttons' home early in the morning, when it was reported that the little men had in fact reappeared at around 3:30 a.m.

Newswires took up the story right away. "Cops Probe Spaceship Visit: Little Green Men Harass Kentucky Farm Family" was just one of many headlines appearing the next day.[97] In short order, reporters began descending on Hopkinsville.

As word spread about the apparent attack by extraterrestrials, Jacqueline Sanders, an editor at Gray Barker's bulletin, *The Saucerian*, headed to Kentucky to investigate. When she arrived, she found that the entire household had left town in response to their property being overrun by sightseers. At one point, the family put up a sign charging fifty cents to enter the grounds, a dollar for information, and ten dollars for taking pictures. It did nothing to stem the tide of tourists.

Even without an opportunity to talk to the main characters in the drama, Sanders was able to fill in more details by talking to police and others. Witnesses apparently recalled that the creatures had not just huge eyes and hands but large, pointed ears and arms that hung almost to the ground. The little men also appeared to be "nickel plated," and they seemed to float rather than walk.

Sanders was also able to confirm that police found no evidence of anything landing on the property, no footprints or tracks, and no signs of scratches on the roof. Nevertheless, local police Chief Russell Greenwell noted that when he interviewed the mother, Glennie Lankford, the morning after the incident, she was "almost petrified with fright." He, for one, believed the witnesses were sincere. "Something frightened those people," he told Sanders.[98]

While the Air Force did not carry out an official investigation, reservist Major John Albert from nearby Campbell Air Force Base was asked to drive out to Kelly to look into matters. He questioned Lankford, who told him that around 10:30 p.m. that evening, she had looked out the back door and "saw a bright silver object about two and a half feet tall appearing round. I became excited and did not look at it long enough to see if it had any eyes or move." She said the same kind of object appeared at her bedroom window later that night around 3:30 a.m. Despite the vagueness of her description, she insisted that her family and friends in the house all "saw this little man that looked like a monkey."[99]

Although press coverage of the farmhouse confrontation soon dissipated, some ufologists remained captivated by the incident. The following year, Isabel Davis from Civilian Saucer Intelligence made her way to Hopkinsville to conduct her own investigation over four days in June 1956. After inspecting the house and property and interviewing family members, policemen, and local reporters, she submitted her findings to her group in New York City.[100]

Though ten months had passed, Davis was able to add a few more pieces to the puzzle. She found that most of those involved in the incident were unwilling to speak about it, having faced months of ridicule from people in the community. Chief Greenwell, however, proved more than amenable and admitted that he himself had seen a UFO in 1952—a stationary glowing object in the sky that stayed in place for about a half hour, then flew away at high speed. Billy Ray Taylor, it turned out, was widely dismissed as a loudmouth; even members of the Sutton household believed he embellished his stories and relished the publicity.

Perhaps the most interesting evidence Davis turned up came from Andrew "Bud" Ledwith, a local engineer and radio announcer. Ledwith had gone to the farmhouse the morning and evening after the fracas, interviewed the witnesses there, and even drawn a sketch of one of the little men based on their descriptions. He found that there likely had been only two or three of the creatures at the farm, but that it had seemed like more at the time because the figures were able to disappear and reappear quickly. Their movements were especially weird. The creatures uttered no noise and made no sound moving. Every time they approached the house, they walked slowly with hands raised, exhibited no signs of hostility, and never actually tried to enter the home. When shot in a tree or on the roof, they appeared to float to the ground, but when one was knocked over on the ground, it ran away on all fours.

Among those dubious about the sensational claims made by those in the farmhouse that night, explanations were plentiful. Some suspected the group was drunk. Others wondered whether it was a case of mass hallucination. Still others noted that both Billy Taylor and Elmer Sutton regularly worked for a traveling carnival, a business often associated with trickery. Maybe, then, the whole thing was nothing more than a hoax carried out for attention, amusement, or profit. Or perhaps a monkey had escaped from a circus caravan, since rumor had it one stopped near Hopkinsville around this time.

When asked two years later to offer his recollections, the officer from Campbell Air Force Base who visited Kelly the day after chalked the incident up to rural ignorance and the family members' fevered state of mind:

Mrs. Glennie Lankford was an impoverished widow woman who had grown up in this small community just outside of Hopkinsville, with very little education. She belonged to the Holy Roller Church and the night and evening of this occurrence, had gone to a religious meeting and she indicated that the members of the congregation and her two sons and their wives and some friends of her sons' (sic) were also at this religious meeting and were worked into a frenzy, becoming very emotionally unbalanced and that after the religious meeting, they had discussed this article which she had heard about over the radio and had sent for from the Kingdom Publishers, Fort Worth 1, Texas and they had sent her this article with a picture which appeared to be a little man when it actually was a monkey, painted silver.[101]

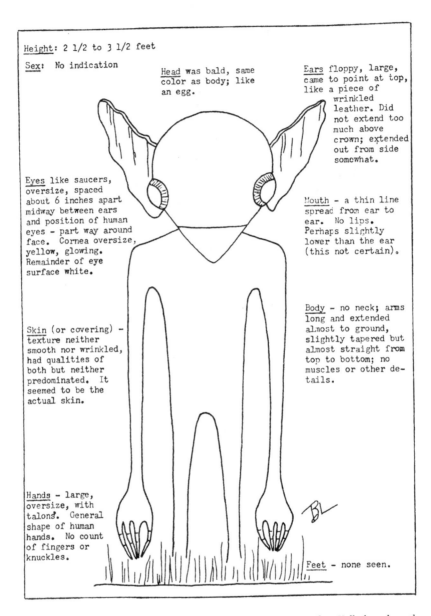

Height: 2 1/2 to 3 1/2 feet

Sex: No indication

Head was bald, same color as body; like an egg.

Ears floppy, large, came to point at top, like a piece of wrinkled leather. Did not extend too much above crown; extended out from side somewhat.

Eyes like saucers, oversize, spaced about 6 inches apart midway between ears and position of human eyes - part way around face. Cornea oversize, yellow, glowing. Remainder of eye surface white.

Mouth - a thin line spread from ear to ear. No lips. Perhaps slightly lower than the ear (this not certain).

Skin (or covering) - texture neither smooth nor wrinkled, had qualities of both but neither predominated. It seemed to be the actual skin.

Body - no neck; arms long and extended almost to ground, slightly tapered but almost straight from top to bottom; no muscles or other details.

Hands - large, oversize, with talons. General shape of human hands. No count of fingers or knuckles.

Feet - none seen.

Fig. 5.5 Drawing by Bud Ledwith of the "little man" encountered at Kelly based on the descriptions of three of the witnesses. Ledwith made the sketch the day after the incident and in the presence of the witnesses. Center for UFO Studies, Chicago, Illinois, USA.

Years later, Isabel Davis wasn't buying the military man's explanation. Lankford didn't belong to a Holy Roller Church, she said, and there was no evidence that anyone had attended services that day. Instead, Davis kept coming back to one thing that even skeptics in the local community commented on: the fear of everyone at the farmhouse. If their incredible claims were true, their reactions made perfect sense. "Their genuine, extreme terror is explained and fully justified," she concluded. "They were frightened beyond reason because what they had seen was beyond reason: weird, unearthly, invulnerable creatures."[102]

TERROR

The case of the "Hopkinsville Goblin," as it came to be known, was only one of several episodes during the first two decades following Kenneth Arnold's sighting in which witnesses claimed to have had threatening encounters with the crews of flying saucers. The stories were spectacular, the aliens menacing, the fear of eyewitnesses seemingly all too real. Indeed, the terror expressed by those reporting these incidents was often what left the deepest impression on those investigating them.

While terrifying tales like the one from Kelly remained relatively rare, during the late 1950s through the mid-1960s, they assumed a greater prominence within ufology circles. They also seemed to grow increasingly more sinister. On the international scene, people like Coral Lorenzen at APRO and Gordon Creighton at *Flying Saucer Review* took the claims seriously and tracked developments.

One incident was said to have taken place in September 1964 in the mountains northeast of Sacramento, California.[103] When rumors of it had reached members of APRO, Coral Lorenzen contacted one of her organization's advisers, Berkeley engineering professor James Harder. Harder contacted the principal witness involved, Mr. S. (who wished to remain anonymous), and taped an interview with him.

According to the man, he and two friends went out one weekend to do some bow-and-arrow hunting in the woods. One night as dusk approached, S. was heading back to camp on his own when he came to a canyon with sparse brush. He suddenly heard crashing sounds and thought it might be a bear. Concerned, he set up some signal fires to get the attention of rangers. Off on the horizon, he saw what looked like a light from a lantern. His first thought was that these belonged either to his friends or to a search party out looking for him. As the light grew nearer, he became uneasy and climbed a nearby tree.

After nightfall, the light drew close enough to circle around S's tree. He could make out some objects moving in unison with the light as well as a large dome-shaped object that fell nearby. Soon he was able to determine that there were three figures moving about. The first two were about five-and-a-half feet tall, covered in silver-grey material, with no facial features. The third, which S. called a "robot," was dark grey or black with no neck, but two reddish-orange glowing eyes and a mouth that simply dropped open.

When the things spotted him, the first two tried to help each other up the tree but failed. The "robot" then began repeated attempts to "gas" him with smoke it released from its mouth, while the other two looked on and tried again to climb the tree. S. decided to fight back. He threw down a canteen and some coins and set fire to some of his clothes, flinging those at his adversaries. At one point, he shot arrows at the robot, which set off sparks when it hit its chest. The robot then emitted more gas in his direction. This time, S. became light-headed and lost consciousness. He soon woke up, nauseous and coughing. All night, they went back and forth. Around dawn, the three entities assembled around the tree, and with their chests glowing, a cloud of gas enveloped the area. S. blacked out. When he regained his senses, they were gone, perhaps leaving him for dead. Sick, frightened, and exhausted, he made his way back to camp and told his friends.

South Americans were telling similarly bizarre stories. Back in England, Gordon Creighton used his transatlantic connections to keep tabs on them. For example, there was an incident covered by Belo Horizonte newspapers in Brazil in 1962 involving a twelve-year-old boy, who claimed floating shadowy figures visited his house one night threatening to kill his father. The next morning, the boy said, he watched as two ball-like objects with antennas and tails cover his father in a haze of smoke and dust, after which the man completely disappeared. In another instance from 1963, a truck driver from Córdoba in Argentina told newspapers about how three mysterious beings emerging out of a spacecraft used a vaporizer of some sort to shoot an abrasive liquid in his face. Doctors, he said, confirmed the burns but could not explain what the substance was.[104]

It was an earlier case, however, that caught the attention of several ufologists, first in Brazil, then in the United States, and eventually in Europe. The stunning details were unlike anything seasoned researchers had come across before. Coral Lorenzen considered it a pivotal moment in the history of UFOs but resisted talking about it publicly for years. Never one to shy away from the sensational, Gordon Creighton simply referred to it as "the most amazing case of all."

LOVER BOY AND THE BIG PLAN

In November 1957, João Martins—a Brazilian reporter who had written several articles about UFOs for the magazine *O Cruzeiro*—received two letters from twenty-three-year-old Antônio Villas Boas, who claimed to have a remarkable story that might interest him. Apparently, a month earlier he had had a disturbing encounter with a UFO and its crew at his family's farm (*fazenda*) in São Francisco de Sales in Brazil. Martins's curiosity was piqued, and he invited the man to Rio de Janeiro to discuss the matter with him and his associate, physician and ufologist Olavo Fontes, consultant to the American organization APRO. Villas Boas arrived in the city in February 1958, where he was given a physical exam and invited to tell his story.[105]

On the night of October 15, 1957, Villas Boas was out ploughing his field, something he regularly did when it was especially hot out. At around 1 a.m., he saw what looked like a red star in the sky that rapidly grew larger. The egg-shaped object was moving toward him so fast, he had no chance to react. It descended to about fifty yards above his head, engulfing him and the ground around him in its light. It soon dropped to the ground, and he saw it was actually a machine with three metal supports. When his tractor engine suddenly died, he decided to run. That's when somebody grabbed one of his arms.

Three short men dressed in strange clothes and helmets took hold of his arms and legs and dragged him into the contraption. Once inside, he was forcibly escorted into a room with silvery metal walls. While they held him, the men spoke to one another in an unintelligible language that sounded like the barking of a dog. Having finished their conversation, they began undressing Villas Boas. He resisted as best he could but to no avail. A wet sponge was rubbed over his naked body, and he was taken into yet another room.

There, one crew member applied a tube to Antônio's chin, and blood was extracted. After this, he was left alone, but after about a half hour, the room was filled with a suffocating smoke from what looked like shower heads. Nauseous, he vomited. After some time, a door opened, and a nude woman walked in.

Villas Boas described her as "beautiful." She had white hair, large, slightly slit and blue eyes, high cheekbones. Her body, he said, "was slim, with high and well separated breasts, thin waist and small stomach, wide hips and large thighs." She rubbed her head against his face. Antônio became aroused, and the two had sex. Afterward he remained "still keen," but she had no interest and tried to avoid him. It angered him. "When I noticed

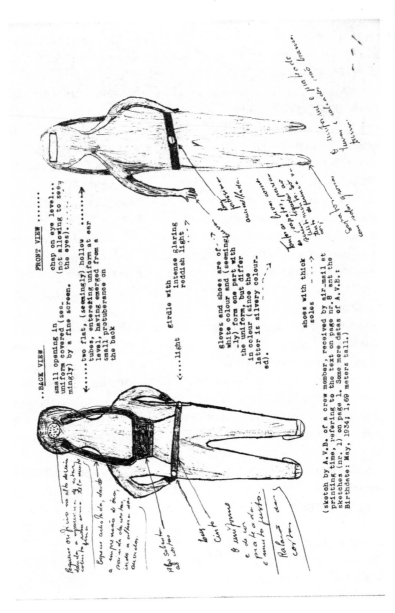

Fig. 5.6 Sketches by the Brazilian António Villas Boas of a crew member of the UFO he said had abducted him in October 1957. AFU.

this, I cooled off too. That was what they wanted of me—a good stallion to improve their stock. In the final count that was all it was."

One of the men entered the room, and she proceeded toward the door. And then she did something he found chilling.

> But, before going out, she turned to me, pointed at her belly and then pointed towards me and with a smile (or something like it), she finally pointed towards the sky—I think it was in the direction of the South. Then she went out . . . I interpreted this gesture as a warning that she was going to return to take me away with her to wherever she lived. Because of this, I am still frightened even today. If they come back to catch me again, then I'm lost.

Finally, the crew returned with his clothes, and Villas Boas was directed to get dressed. He did and was eventually escorted out of the vessel. Outside, he watched as the ship flew from sight in a matter of seconds. All told, the whole experience had lasted about four hours.

Martins and Fontes had never heard anything like it. The story seemed beyond belief, though they found Villas Boas completely sincere. A physical exam showed some signs of scarring on the man's chin. Other than that, there was only Antônio's word for what happened. Martins decided there wasn't enough to publish the man's story.

Olavo Fontes, however, told his associate Coral Lorenzen back in New Mexico about the case. The two began a feverish correspondence with one another, in which Fontes shared his ideas about the significance of what happened to "Lover Boy," as the two privately referred to Villas Boas. When it came to discussing the sexual intercourse that took place, the Brazilian was less than forthcoming, considering it inappropriate to discuss such matters with a woman. Lorenzen persisted, and eventually Fontes divulged the salacious details.

Lorenzen was torn about how to handle the incident. Privately, she believed Villas Boas and thought his experience deserved to be publicized. Fontes, on the other hand, worried that its sexual nature made it too lewd for a wider audience. Lorenzen, who described herself as holding "broad opinions of sex," personally found nothing shocking in "the Lover Boy incident." She decided, however, to keep the story in house, only mentioning it to a select few people in the APRO organization. She wouldn't raise the matter in public until the end of 1962.[106]

Nevertheless, by the fall of 1959, Lorenzen and Fontes had come to see the Villas Boas episode as crucial in piecing together the intentions of the alien visitors. It, along with other recent UFO activities, led the two to an alarming conclusion. "In short, we expect an attack of some kind in the not-too-distant future," Lorenzen wrote Swedish ufologist Gösta Rehn in October. "We think we know how they will do it and control the panicked population at the same time. We are convinced they are building bases in preparation, at the present time."[107]

In November, she filled Rehn in on the details of what she was calling "the Big Plan" of the extraterrestrials. Its full scope, she insisted, could only be seen by following the patterns in UFO activity since Kenneth Arnold's original sighting. From 1947 to 1950, the primary targets of unidentified flying objects were missile ranges and atomic bomb testing sites. In 1952, a new kind of operation was set in motion, as American and Canadian military installations experienced an uptick in flying saucer activity. This was followed by flaps in Europe during the years 1952–1954 and then South America in 1954. In both cases, Lorenzen pointed out, "Little men, usually engaged in collecting various flora and fauna and soil and rock specimens, were all over the place." A worldwide wave took place in 1956, with a heavy concentration at first in Asia, Australia, and New Zealand, culminating in a renewed focus on atomic bomb bunkers in the United States in the fall of 1957.

To Lorenzen and Fontes, all these facts taken together revealed premeditation. From 1946 through 1955, the aliens were performing reconnaissance. In 1956, reinforcements were brought in. They were on the brink of an incursion, one that would take place no sooner than 1966. The instances of electrical blackouts worldwide and the frequency of UFO sightings on roadways indicated the invaders planned to disrupt surface transportation and knock out the power supply to achieve their aims.

The Villas Boas encounter added one final piece to the puzzle. The extraterrestrials decided to send out a ship with a woman on board in order to experiment and discover if interbreeding with humans was possible. Lorenzen explained their logic.

I believe for the reason that if colonization were planned, they would want to know if cohabitation and fraternization would weaken the hold of their troops on earth. The reason a woman was used instead of a man is obvious. An earth woman (if they could find one small enough or one of their men large enough for suitable mating) would be rendered useless at the moment of kidnapping, because she would probably lose her mind from the shock. If not that, she might be rendered sterile from the shock, or, if she conceived, would miscarry from shock or loneliness. She would have to be hauled away so that scientists could observe the period of gestation and the end product. The way it was accomplished was ideal—their own woman, cued to the job at hand was ready, accomplished her task and was taken back to headquarters—wherever that is—for observation.

There, (the baby would be born en route) the product could be studied for intelligence, physical health, etc. Very neat.[108]

It was a breathtaking, if not unnerving, argument. It was also a stunning intellectual achievement—even granting that no such invasion took place. Basing their analysis on twelve years of often conflicting flying saucer reports and coverage from across the globe, Lorenzen and Fontes found a way to methodically link what seemed inconsistent strands of the UFO story into one, cohesive account. That chilling account, of course, stood in marked contrast to the hopeful message relayed by the contactees.

Back in Sweden, Gösta Rehn seemed unfazed by the prospect of an alien conquest. He wrote Lorenzen back telling her that "the idea of mass landings and attacks suits me very well." Given the state of the world, it might well bring a needed change.

> I am misanthropic enough to welcome such a solution of the messy human problem. Fake-democracies, bounderish lowdown commercialism rampant, almost everybody suffering from stress, neurotic bodily ailments due to a civilization that promotes evil and stunts biological and mental growth . . . the stupid resistance against a planned economy compared with which Sovjet (sic) becomes a hope . . . and the impossibility of total disarmament unless we get a world government with an armed police force. Perhaps the saucer catastrophy (sic) will force the nations to form that world government.[109]

When in 1962 she published her first book—*The Great Flying Saucer Hoax*—Lorenzen laid out her case to the general public for what came to be termed the "hostility thesis" about UFOs.[110] Still, she continued to keep the Villas Boas story under wraps. Others did not. That same year, two members of the Brazilian Society for the Study of Flying Saucers—Walter Bühler and Mario Prudente Aquino—published a piece on the encounter in the group's bulletin after traveling to the man's residence and interviewing him there. They chose to keep him anonymous, however, and referred to him only as "A.V.B."[111]

Bühler sent a copy of the newsletter to Gordon Creighton at *Flying Saucer Review* in London. Like Lorenzen, he sat on the story for another two years in the hope that more evidence would come to light. Then, in early 1965, Creighton relented. Apologizing "to any reader who may find this bizarre story offensive," he published the first of nine separate articles on the Villas Boas case to appear in the magazine from 1965 to 1968.[112] In making sense of the incident, Creighton suggested that folk traditions might hold the key. Lore about encounters with incubi, succubae, spirits, goblins, and ghosts, he proposed, might well be chronicles of human contact with beings from outer space. If so, what happened to Antônio Villas Boas that night in 1957 was something that had been going on for centuries.[113]

"DREAMS OR RECALL?"

The Villas Boas case has been widely seen as the first instance of a person claiming to have been abducted by aliens. To be sure, the episode contains many of the elements that later would come to stamp classic alien abduction stories in the 1980s and 1990s: coercive entities, being taken on board a spacecraft, uncommunicative extraterrestrials, a clinical setting, and a sexual dimension. But the incident must be understood on its own terms and context. Journalists and ufologists at the time generally found it weird, far-fetched, and out of step with all the other accounts circulating about contact with extraterrestrials. The sexualized nature of the encounter not only added to its strangeness, but also made it offensive to prudish sensibilities of the late 1950s and early 1960s. It was for these reasons that it took so long for the case to be publicized, and even once it reached the reading public, it mostly remained relegated to the UFO milieu.

That said, speculation about flying saucers kidnappings was not unheard of in the fifties and sixties. Pulp science fiction literature for decades had titillated male readers with images of scantily clothed damsels captured by nefarious spacemen. In a series of articles in the Forteana magazine *Magonia*, Peter Rogerson showed that starting in the mid-1950s, ufologists reported isolated incidents that hinted at kidnapping attempts by extraterrestrials.[114] Over the course of the 1960s, these kinds of stories—presented sometimes as fiction, other times as non-fiction—became more prevalent, especially in Europe and Latin America.

One American account of an alien abduction from the 1960s, however, achieved a unique status of renown. It was said to have taken place on a rural road in the state of New Hampshire the night of September 19–20, 1961. The people who reported it were a respectable, middle-class couple, Betty and Barney Hill.[115]

The Hills were no ordinary couple. Betty came from a white, church-going New England family. Growing up during the Depression, she was a supporter of Franklin Roosevelt's vision of a New Deal and remained an ardent liberal activist. After divorcing her first husband, she began seeing Barney in 1957 and became a social worker shortly thereafter. Barney came from a Black family that earlier in the century had moved from Virginia to a middle-class neighborhood of Philadelphia. Like Betty,

Barney had recently divorced his first spouse and had grown up dedicated to progressive causes and activism. When he eventually proposed to Betty, she worried how the two would navigate the challenges associated with being a biracial couple in 1960s America. After seeing a marriage therapist, they married in May 1960. They settled in Portsmouth, Barney commuted to a post office job in Boston, and they joined a local Unitarian church, attracted by its commitment to open-mindedness and social justice.

In September 1961, the Hills decided to take a car trip to Montreal. Barney later told a journalist he had had an "ominous feeling" beforehand, so he had placed a pistol in the trunk of the car. In fact, throughout the trip, Barney was on edge, and he recalled thinking to himself, "I should get a hold of myself, and not think that everyone is hostile."

After a one-night stay in Montreal, they drove home late at night on September 19. As they did, they saw an odd light in the sky. Talking about it the next day to friends and family, Betty became increasingly uneasy. She said that Barney's shoes were scuffed, and her dress was torn, and they didn't know how it had happened. They felt somehow "unclean" and worried they had been exposed to radiation. A police officer friend advised that they report the whole thing to the Air Force.

An Air Force official spoke to the couple twice over the phone on September 21 and wrote up a report. According to these interviews, Betty and Barney were driving on New Hampshire Highway 3 around midnight when they noticed a continuous band of lights in a cigar shape with extended wings. They got out of the car to look at it with their binoculars, at which point the object began to descend toward them. That's when they decided to leave. Barney sped off, but not before the UFO swooped down emitting a loud buzzing noise, a sound they heard thirty miles later down the road.

The day after talking to the Air Force, Betty picked up a copy Donald Keyhoe's book *The Flying Saucer Conspiracy* at her local public library. She found it compelling, and three days later she wrote Keyhoe and told her about the UFO sighting. This time, she introduced some new details about her husband's experience.

> As it glided closer, he was able to see inside this object, but not too closely. He did see many figures scurrying about as though they were making some hurried type of preparation. One figure was observing us from the windows . . . and [they] seemed to be dressed in some type of shiny black uniform. At this point, my husband became shocked and got back in the car, in a hysterical condition, laughing and repeating that they were going to capture us.

She added that they were searching for any clues that might help Barney recall what he saw. "His mind has completely blacked out at this point," Betty wrote. "Every attempt to recall, leaves him very frightened. We are considering the possibility of a competent psychiatrist who uses hypnotism."[116]

NICAP sent investigator Walter Webb—the same man who later wrote up the Lyndia Morel incident in 1973—to Portsmouth, and on October 21 he talked with the couple for six hours. He was impressed, especially with Barney. Once again, the Hills provided more information about the incident.

As the UFO stopped mid-air in front of the car, it hovered in a slightly tilted position. Barney stopped the car in the middle of the road, picked up his gun from underneath his seat, and put it in his pocket. He then started walking toward the craft, stopping at times to use the binoculars. As he did, he could make out eight to eleven figures watching him at the windows. They were human in form and wore "shiny black uniforms and black caps with peaks or bills on them." He likened them to the "cold precision of German officers" as they moved about. One of them in particular seemed to be the leader, and Barney was extremely afraid of him; he said he could almost feel the figure's intent to carry out some kind of plan. Barney was convinced he was going to be captured "like a bug in a net" and that there was something not human about the people inside this aircraft. Barney didn't remember anything that happened after that.[117]

While Betty did not recall seeing any of the unsettling figures inside the UFO, she did begin to share Barney's anxieties. Following a series of nightmares since the incident, she wrote down the substance of these dreams in November 1961, with the title "Dreams or Recall?" Though it came from multiple dreams over two months, Betty decided to organize the content into one single, chronological narrative, rather than in the order of the dreams themselves. This gave her written statement the feel of a seamless story, with a beginning, middle, and end. It is this document that has provided the key elements of the Hill abduction tale as it has been passed down in print and film.[118]

In this dream version of the event, Betty that night saw eight to eleven men standing in the middle of the road when they went around a turn. As Barney slowed down, the car motor died. The men then surrounded the car. "We sat there motionless and speechless, and I was terrified. At the same time, they opened the car doors on each side, reached in and took us by the arm."

The figures were about five feet tall, with grey complexions, dark hair and eyes, large chests, and long noses ("like Jimmy Durante's"). They were, Betty said, "very human in their appearance, not frightening." When communicating with her, they spoke English with a foreign accent.

The men escorted the couple through some woods. Barney seemed to be "sleep walking" and didn't respond to her. As they proceeded, one of the men told her there was no need to be afraid, that they only wanted to perform some tests. Reaching a clearing, they saw a saucer and were directed to enter it.

Once inside, a pleasant, reassuring examiner asked some questions and then began performing a physical examination on Betty. Her entire body was closely looked over and her dress removed. Some scrapings were taken from the skin of her arm. A machine with wires like an EEG was used to test her nervous system and reflexes. Next, she was given what she was told was a pregnancy test. When the examiner brought out a four-to-six-inch needle, Betty became worried. "I asked what kind of pregnancy test he planned with the needle. He did not reply but started to insert the needle in my navel with a sudden thrust." Betty immediately was in great pain. Seeing that, one of the men waved his hands in front of her eyes, and the pain subsided.

After the examination was over, Betty spent some time talking with the man she presumed to be the leader. Smiling and friendly, he apologized for giving the couple such a fright. When asked where they were from, the leader tried to show Betty on one of their maps, but it proved unintelligible to her. She did, however, ask if she might keep one of the books lying in the room as proof to others that the event had actually taken place. At first the leader agreed, but then he took it back, explaining that "it had been decided that no one should know of this experience, and that even I would not remember this." Betty was furious, insisting that she would remember. The leader laughed but said he would do his best to makes sure that was not the case. "He added that I might remember but no one would ever believe me; that Barney would have no recollection of any of this experience; in case that Barney night (sic) ever recall, which he seriously doubted, he would think of things contrary to the way I knew them to be. This would lead to confusion, doubt, disagreement."

Betty and Barney then left the ship, with the crew accompanying them to their automobile. From their car, the couple watched them leave and the disk fly off into the distance. Betty patted their dog and said, "There they go. And we are none the worse for the wear."

Despite the happy ending to Betty's dream version of the incident, both she and Barney had lingering concerns about their physical and mental health. Betty remained troubled by her nightmares, while Barney was plagued by different ailments. He had high blood pressure, found small warts around his lower abdomen, and developed ulcers so severe that at one point he had to be hospitalized. He also began drinking heavily. Though it's unclear who suggested it, someone associated with NICAP working on the case encouraged the couple to consult with a psychiatrist trained in hypnosis, as Betty had proposed. The hope was that such a technique might help overcome the amnesia that seemed to be the source of the Hills' ailments.

Using hypnosis to unlock lost memories, widely known as "hypnotic regression," was a common practice at the time. Predicated on the assumption that memory operated like a recording, the technique was believed to be capable of recovering and replaying otherwise forgotten recollections through hypnotic suggestion. From the end of World War II through the seventies, hypnotic regression enjoyed robust support among clinicians, police, and criminal courts.[119]

In retrospect, it is perhaps no surprise to find that this kind of forensic hypnosis also made its way into UFO research as well. Nevertheless, when the Hills in December 1963 began to meet with Dr. Benjamin Simon, a Boston-based psychiatrist and neurologist who worked with technique, they were embarking on a pioneering path in the study of UFOs. In looking to clinical hypnotic regression for assistance, they and the NICAP investigators involved were treating their incident not simply as emotionally troubling but as a crime scene.

By contrast, psychiatrist Benjamin Simon perceived his role and the role of clinical hypnosis quite differently. He followed the thinking of many of the leading researchers in the field at the time—University of Pennsylvania psychiatrist and psychologist Martin Orne being perhaps the most prominent—that hypnosis helped to produce confabulations, flights of fancy that could easily be folded into genuine recollections. Simon told John Fuller—the journalist to whom the Hills turned to write a book about their experience—as much in an interview in March 1966. "Hypnosis will confirm a fantasy as strongly as it will a reality," he emphasized. "In other words, the fact that they proved it under hypnosis does not prove that it was a reality. It only proves that they believed it."[120] Simon therefore did not understand his job as determining whether the alien contact actually took place; it was to help manage the anxieties that plagued the Hills.

From the end of February to the end of March 1964, Simon interviewed Betty and Barney separately under hypnosis. He taped the sessions, which he then played back for the couple to encourage more discussion. In the taped interviews, which are widely available online and transcripts of which were included Fuller's book *The Interrupted Journey* (1966), Betty mostly stuck to the story she had put together in "Dreams or Recall?" and seemed little bothered by the incident. Barney, however, presented the picture of a man overwhelmed by dread and panic. At several points, he screamed and burst into tears recalling how the UFO seemed to stalk them and how the men stood in the roadway. He also remembered the exam he was given, during which he focused on the leader's "slanted" eyes as a cup was placed around his genitals and a tube the size of a cigar inserted into his rectum.

Simon, however, was more drawn to the fact that Barney expressed being constantly on edge, living in perpetual fear of racial discrimination. During the entire Montreal trip, he had worried about how the white people he encountered would treat him. When the hotel they wanted to stay at said it had no vacancies, he suspected it was because he was Black. At various points during the trip, he was attuned to perceived slights that he believed were directed at the couple. He admitted he originally brought the gun along because "I believe in the hostility of white people, particularly when there is an interracial couple."[121] That said, he confessed he rarely shared his racial anxieties with Betty, who at times seemed oblivious to his experience as a Black man.

The Hills ended their treatment with Simon in the summer of 1964. As he explained a decade later, Simon was convinced that the Hills had had a genuine UFO sighting, but that he was "also sure that the 'abduction

Fig. 5.7 Psychiatrist Benjamin Simon treated Betty and Barney Hill from December 1963 until the summer of 1964. Although Simon used hypnosis in a number of sessions with the Hills, he and the couple interpreted the purpose and results of the technique differently. Charles Walker Collection/Alamy Stock Photo.

and examination' did not take place except as Betty's dreams."[122] The psychiatrist concluded that an anxious Barney had then assimilated Betty's nightmares into his memories of the incident. Simon's refusal to accept their recollections as reality angered the couple, and from that point on, the Hills began exclusively seeking out experts who would validate their version of events.

Barney Hill died of a cerebral hemorrhage in February 1969: he was only forty-six years old. Betty would live well into her eighties. Over time, she increasingly found inspiration in New Age thought and entertained the possibility that she and Barney had had the misfortune of meeting the "evil" aliens. She remained adamant that the abduction had taken place.

In 1975, the Hills' experience was made into an American film for television, *The UFO Incident* starring Estelle Parsons and James Earl Jones. The case eventually became the subject of countless articles, books, and broadcasts. Their story has been told and retold, dissected and debated so many times it has come to assume canonical status among readers and enthusiasts of UFO lore.

These retellings mirror what took place between the initial incident in September 1961 and publication of *The Interrupted Journey* in 1966. Barney and Betty both gave multiple statements during this period, including some based on dreams and others while in a hypnotic trance. Some details remained consistent, while others changed. Walter Webb, Benjamin Simon, and John Fuller then came along at different stages not just faithfully recording the Hills' accounts but giving them a sense and translating the information into new narratives. No one doubted that something happened to the Hills on that deserted road in New Hampshire. But as their experience was increasingly transformed into stories for and by others, that experience grew ever more elusive.

———

In 1954, Bryant and Helen Reeve got in their car and headed off on an adventure. Seven years later, Betty and Barney Hill did the same. Two very different couples. Two very different journeys, with two very different destinations. Their paths, both literally and figuratively, reveal a good deal about the early history of contact with the occupants of flying saucers.

Like UFO sightings, alien encounters and the people who claimed to have them came in all sorts of shapes and sizes. There were some patterns, however. Contact could be spectral and disembodied, something achieved through higher consciousness. It could also be a flesh-and-blood meeting, one that more often than not took place outside or in public places. Despite this, other witnesses rarely observed the event.

The aliens were always identified with superior knowledge, evident in their technological achievements and mastery of languages. The visitors were taken as confirmation of an evolutionary view of civilization, the ideal of the inexorable march of progress. The contactees, for one, believed this extended not only to the realms of knowledge, society, and politics but also to morality: our space brothers and sisters were principled, virtuous, and empathetic. These beings who epitomized beauty were here to help. On the other hand, the little men and disconcerting figures who also occasionally popped up were frequently described as cold, inaccessible, even mischievous. These figures offered no messages of hope, but instead seemed as curious about us as we were about them. We might be putting the aliens under our telescopes, but they meanwhile seemed to be putting us under their microscopes.

As for those claiming to have had an encounter, there were those who actively sought out contact (Adamski, Fry, Van Tassel) and those who didn't (Villas-Boas, the Hills). The experience trigged a variety of reactions. Some were simply left baffled. Many considered the experience to be of spiritual, even cosmic, importance. The contactees, for instance, came away feeling special; they were now messengers and prophets with a calling to announce the beginning of a New Age. Others, like the investigators at APRO and NICAP, took a forensic approach. They were detectives trying to piece together disparate facts in order to make sense of the Big Plan.

As was the case with ufology in general, men continued to occupy a privileged position in the alien contact milieu. Yet, women could be far more prominent and play a more active role in this domain—in some measure, women had historically occupied positions of authority as mediums in occult circles. Regardless of gender or background, those claiming to have met extraterrestrials regularly faced the ridicule and derision of friends, co-workers, and the general public. No wonder most witnesses sought out reassurance.

Alien contact helped promote one other form of contact: connections between like-minded people. The Reeves, the Hills, George Adamski, George Van Tassel, Marius Dewilde, and Antônio Villas-Boas all reached out to others. Some organized or attended UFO group meetings, some sought out the help of UFO investigators, some looked to reporters, and in one conspicuous case, a psychiatrist was consulted. Those claiming to have had an extraterrestrial encounter frequently made the effort to initiate contact with their fellow human beings. Contact could lead to community.

Of course, outside the contactee scene, the voices of skepticism were pronounced. The claims being made seemed ludicrous, fantastic. For many, they were so preposterous as to be utterly implausible. Surely science could easily dispatch such nonsense. At first, few scientists seemed willing to chime in about unidentified flying objects and the possibility of extraterrestrial civilizations, but that was about to change.

6

Science and UFOs in the 1960s

January 7, 1969, held the promise to bring one of the most significant announcements in modern history, perhaps even *the* defining moment in the story of humanity. In October 1966, a committee of scientific experts had begun work on an unprecedented project: a study of unidentified flying objects by some of America's most respected scientists. A little more than two years later, the panel was ready to announce its results and publish its final report.

Tight security surrounded the project from the very start, and those in charge were anxious to guard against any leaks. But when the committee's results were finally made public, it was neither the project's director nor the US Air Force's chief officer in charge of tracking UFOs who made the announcement but Associated Press science writer Frank Carey.[1]

Over the next few days, the leaked results of the study made their way into newspapers across the country. A few newspapers, such as *The New York Times*, covered the story on the front page, as did several other local papers. Most did not, as it vied for space alongside other, seemingly more pressing, items: the start of Robert Kennedy assassin Sirhan Sirhan's trial, the latest casualties of the Vietnam War, the announcement of Neil Armstrong, Buzz Aldrin, and Michael Collins as the team selected to go to the moon in July.[2] For the most part, the story was buried. *The Chicago Tribune* reported the news on page B10, *The Lawrence Daily Journal* in Kansas on page 23, and *The Phoenix Arizona Republic* on page 28.[3]

Given the momentousness of the occasion, the emphasis of the news coverage was not what one might expect. The question of whether UFOs were extraterrestrial in origin was the lede, but after that, most reports focused on the "controversy" swirling around the study itself: the fact that some members of the committee had been fired, that the impartiality of the panel was being questioned, that a Congressional House Committee had invited critics of the committee to speak at a public hearing about UFOs the previous summer.

Then there was the secrecy. Frank Carey published a follow-up piece on January 8, noting how tight-lipped the committee had been about its work and was being about its final report in a column that got picked up nationally.[4] The next day, newspapers were reporting that a blue-ribbon committee formed by the National Academy of Sciences—which was refusing to "divulge any information, even the names of committee members"—was sending a report to the Air Force agreeing with the main conclusions of the "secret report" of the scientific panel.[5]

This mix of apathy and suspicion stood in marked contrast to the buoyant mood in October 1966 when it was announced that the University of Colorado at Boulder had agreed to serve as the home for a scientific commission to investigate UFOs. Specialists in astronomy, meteorology, psychology, and psychiatry recruited from the university and elsewhere were to evaluate reports of sightings, interview witnesses, and assess forensic evidence. A $313,000 grant from the Air Force (eventually increased to $500,000, a little less than $4 million in today's currency) was to fund the project for at least fifteen months, providing the team with unrestricted access to tens of thousands of records.

The project's director, physicist Edward Condon, quickly assembled a staff. In November, he asked the military as well as renowned civilian UFO researchers to brief personnel on the history of UFO sightings.[6] It was a remarkable gesture, given the mutual disdain government officials and academics on one side and ufologists on the other had shown for one another in the past. It seemed to signal an unprecedent *rapprochement* between the skeptics and the believers in the possibility of visitors from outer space. There appeared to be reason for hope that a definitive answer could be found for the question on everyone's mind: were unidentified flying objects from another world?

But months before the committee's final report was released such optimism had given way to outrage and distrust on all sides. How did one of the most anticipated scientific investigations in modern history go from cause célèbre to mudslinging melodrama so quickly? And what does it say about the evolving role of science in society at large during the 1960s?

The decade of the sixties is rightly associated with social change and political turbulence. Cold War tensions remained high in the wake of America's military intervention in Vietnam, the construction of the Berlin Wall in 1961, the Cuban missile crisis in 1962, and the Soviet crackdown on reforms in Czechoslovakia in 1968. Young people across the globe questioned traditional cultural values and authorities and embraced political activism, protesting war, colonialism, and violations of human rights. Reformers called for radical new approaches to institutions like prisons, mental hospitals, and schools.[7]

In many ways, those active in the UFO world appeared to be oblivious or even indifferent to the developments of the day. The topics that had come to dominate their discussions and debates seemed, on the surface at least, not terribly relevant to the pressing issues facing the world. Saucer group newsletters and bulletins often expressly insisted that they were non-political. Ufology seemingly inhabited its own "ivory tower."

Yet, the changing times did have an impact within UFO circles. Some of this was due to a generational shift, as more younger people took on leading roles in flying saucer groups. At the same time, the manned space programs of the Soviet Union and the United States captured the imaginations of people all over the world and kept the theme of space exploration in the news.[8] In addition, the New Age philosophy that had been so important to the contactee movement in the fifties had already experienced a revival by the early 1960s. New Age ideas and practices increasingly were repurposed for therapeutic interventions like small-scale "encounter groups" and to legitimate the use of psychedelic drugs to help promote mystical enlightenment.[9] All these things helped ensure that UFOs and alien contact retained a foot in earthly affairs.

Across civilian UFO organizations, the biggest trend involved nationwide efforts aimed at consolidating local groups. Even by the midpoint of the decade, almost no one could boast of having anything like the national reach of American associations like NICAP and APRO. In Australia, for instance, what was billed as the first national convention of civilian UFO researchers there was held in February 1965 and a fledgling organization was founded: the Commonwealth Aerial Phenomena Investigation Organisation. Attempts were made to get groups in individual states to cooperate and collaborate under its umbrella, but these ultimately faltered.[10]

In central Europe, the leading voices in ufology continued to be those schooled in the esoteric tradition and preaching the gospel of what one observer called the new "star religions." According to one estimate, there had already been two thousand to five thousand contacts between humans and visitors from outer space by the mid-sixties. So, perhaps it's no surprise that when a UFO Convention was held in Wiesbaden, West Germany, in 1960, the one thousand participants from fourteen different countries in attendance were primarily regaled with stories by a host of contactees.[11]

In many countries, however, grassroots growth of saucer groups mostly took place during the second half of the decade. In South America, publications about unidentified flying objects and extraterrestrials regularly appeared in Spanish and Portuguese, with an increasing number by authors from the continent. Argentina proved to be a major hotspot. The country experienced a UFO wave in May 1962, a string of sightings over subsequent years, and a blackout in the city of Tigre in July 1968 that was attributed to flying saucer activity. These helped feed the founding of numerous UFO groups—including the country's first skeptics organization—in cities like Buenos Aires, Córdoba, and Rosario.[12]

In other countries, UFO enthusiasts faced hurdles. In Spain, the Center for Interplanetary Studies had been founded in 1958, and three years later, one of its co-founders Antonio Ribera published *Objetos desconocidos en el cielo* (Unknown Objects in the Sky), the country's first successful ufology book.[13] More homegrown works followed, but translated French- and English-language works predominated in bookstores. At the same time, the dictatorship of Gen. Francisco Franco had a chilling effect on the formation of private clubs like saucer groups. As one veteran Spanish UFO researcher put it, "Men in Black and such were relegated to a minor role when compared to the agents of the Direccion General de Seguridad [the General Directorate of Security], who represented a very real threat."[14]

Beginning in 1965, however, flying saucer stories made their way more consistently into Spanish news coverage, and alien-themed television shows gained popularity. Reported UFO sightings from within Spain had always been few in number, but during the last half of the decade they became more numerous, culminating in a wave in the years 1968–1969. These developments helped encourage a generation of young people—many in high school—with interests in astronautics and science fiction to enter the UFO scene starting in 1967. Often motivated by a desire to see a more science-oriented ufology, they formed their own groups. In 1968, Vicente-Juan Ballester Olmos set up the Círculo de Estudios sobre Objetos no Identificados (Study Circle on Unidentified Objects) in Valencia, and the following year he tried forming a nationwide team of researchers. In 1969, Red Nacional de Corresponsales (National Network of Correspondents) was created in Seville, an initiative focusing on data collection in the

Andalusian region, with over a hundred correspondents collecting information from multiple news sources. More organizations popped up in Barcelona, Algorta, and Tarragona, but meetings between groups would have to wait until the 1970s.[15]

At the beginning of the decade, ufology in Great Britain was still organized in a patchwork of local clubs. *Flying Saucer Review* did emerge, however, as the international flagship periodical in UFO studies after it changed editors in 1964. That year a group of London enthusiasts under the leadership of Nigel Stephenson established the British UFO Research Association or BUFORA. In its constitution, the association stated its purpose was to "encourage and promote unbiased scientific investigation and research" into UFOs, "collect and disseminate evidence and data," and coordinate UFO research on a national scale.[16] Attempts were made to try to standardize research into British reports and to catalogue worldwide cases of saucer landings.[17] Funding and membership retention were perpetual problems. In 1964, BUFORA had 300 paying members; by the end of the decade, 319 individuals and 8 local groups had paid their dues, while some 500 members and 9 associations had not.[18]

Those running BUFORA saw it as an organization zooming in on the nuts-and-bolts of unidentified flying objects and anchored in rigorous, empirical investigation. What monies were on hand were used for publications, conferences, a slide collection for lectures, UFO detectors, an infrared camera, and binoculars.[19] Nigel Stephenson even had some ideas for how to go about selecting and training skillful investigators. Get a prospective investigator to listen to a member tell two stories, one true, the other false, and then decide which was which. "With practice and study of eye movements," Stephenson argued, "it may be possible for investigators to become adept."[20]

While BUFORA branded itself as the organization taking a forensic approach to the study of UFOs, the Sky Scouts embraced the esoteric. In 1964, former *Flying Saucer Review* editor Brinsley Le Poer Trench was asked to head up a new UFO group geared toward young people. International Sky Scouts was intended to foster interest in astronomy and train people to make contact with extraterrestrials, who Trench considered to be friendly and benevolent.[21] After he was told that the organization's name might infringe on the Boy Scout movement, Trench changed the name of the English branch of the group to Contact UK in 1967 and then finally to Contact International in 1969. A decade later it had two thousand members worldwide.[22]

A glance at the activities of one chapter of the organization located in Durban, South Africa, reveals that members combined fieldwork with

Fig. 6.1 Two BUFORA investigators take part in a sky watch in June 1968, supplied with maps, astrocompass, telescope, and refreshments. The van served as a mobile headquarters for field research. Omar Fowler, *Spacelink* 5 (July 1968).

mediumship and telepathy. On International Sky Scouts Day—celebrated every June 24 in commemoration of Kenneth Arnold's sighting—in 1967, for example, a group of thirty members got into cars and set off for a location considered ideal for saucer watching. Finding a spot despite rainy and misty weather, they proceeded to collectively concentrate to establish "a possible telepathic link with our space friends." No spacecraft showed up. Undeterred, they reconvened in two groups that evening to make some observations using telescopes. The dreary weather made it impossible, so they simply hung out and talked about UFOs until about 11:30 p.m.[23] A year later, the group took part in an international event called "Invitation by Telepathy," during which everyone in the Contact community throughout the world was encouraged to simultaneously sit still and "send out the thought of Contact with the Visitors and mentally concentrate on a space ship."[24]

PALEOVISITOLOGY

In the 1960s, an idea that had been percolating within the UFO community for some time developed into its own branch of ufology. It proved so successful that by 1970 it had become a worldwide phenomenon and made its chief spokesman a household name. The idea was the notion that extraterrestrials might have left traces of previous visits to earth thousands of years in the past, and the field was named paleovisitology.

The prospect of ancient aliens—or "ancient astronauts," as they were commonly referred to beginning in the seventies—was something that had a history dating back to the nineteenth century. In 1865, French aristocrat Antoine Bernard Alfred, Baron d'Espiard de Colonge conjectured that an advanced extraterrestrial race had settled on earth long ago and had passed on its knowledge to certain human civilizations. Around the same time, theosophist Helena Blavatsky contended wise masters had shared their superior knowledge with ancient cultures, many of which had disappeared. Then, in the early twentieth century, Charles Fort raised the possibility that beings from other worlds may have landed on earth in the past and conquered the planet. By the 1940s, science fiction and fantasy writers were penning yarns that featured prehistoric spacemen, forgotten civilizations, and sunken continents.[25]

The notion of ancient aliens first made its way into international ufology in the mid-1950s. Morris Jessup, Desmond Leslie, Brinsley Le Poer Trench, Harold Wilkins, and George Hunt Williamson were among the first to speculate that beings from outer space had been interacting with humanity for thousands, if not millions, of years, conveying their knowledge and technologies and, in some cases, settling here on earth. Beginning in 1959, several European writers set about making more extensive arguments and citing sacred texts and archaeological finds to support their claims.

In Italy, Peter Kolosimo published four books between 1959 and 1968 in which he considered the notion that aliens visited earth centuries ago.[26] Largely unknown outside of Italy, he proved to be a successful popularizer of space science. Kolosimo drew on ideas from the likes of horror writer H.P. Lovecraft, Flash Gordon creator Alex Raymond, and missile engineer Wernher von Braun to speculate about not only ancient astronauts but also the future of human space travel and interactions with extraterrestrial civilizations. For Kolosimo, science fiction was a tool for imagining possibilities and for reinterpreting things like Mayan astronomy, the Nazca lines, and the legend of the phoenix in Hellenic culture.

At the same time Kolosimo first began publishing his thoughts, Soviet mathematician Matest Agrest was formulating a similar thesis in the USSR.[27] The success of the Sputnik missions had sparked his interest in the possibility of interplanetary travel and alien civilizations, and it got him wondering whether there were any indications that extraterrestrials had come to earth earlier in history. In 1959, he began combing through the book of Genesis in the Bible and was struck by references to beings falling to earth and Enoch being taken up into the heavens. Sites like the Baalbeck temple in Lebanon and objects like tektites, in turn, could be interpreted as artifacts confirming the presence of ancient visitors.

Agrest was fully aware that invoking the Bible and denying Yuri Gagarin was the first man in outer space were potentially career-ending ideas in the Soviet Union. Nevertheless, he forged ahead. After giving a lecture about his thesis at the Sukhumi Institute of Physics and Technology, colleagues were surprisingly supportive. This emboldened Agrest to seek out an academic journal where he could publish his findings. Unbeknownst to him, his typist decided to make extra copies, which she distributed illegally. Within weeks, the *samizdat* piece was known all over Moscow. In February 1960, a summary of Agrest's article was published in *Literaturnaya Gazeta* under the title "Does the Trail Lead into Space?" and newspapers and radio stations across the globe reported his hypothesis.

That fall, the Russian newspaper *Komsomolskaya Pravda* published an article by two engineers entitled "The Trail Leads into Ignorance." They decried Agrest's use of biblical texts and deemed his hypothesis to be harmful "because it is diverting our youth's interests from the unsolved problems of modern science, from the secrets of Nature." By December, the case had become a scientific hot potato, with internationally renowned astronomer I. S. Shlovskii defending Agrest's right to advance his thesis and I. F. Shevlyakov of the Moscow Planetarium organizing a campaign to denounce the ancient alien argument as "anti-scientific." In the end, Agrest was never able to find a scientific periodical willing to publish his paper; instead, it found its way into a travel and adventure magazine in 1961.

Meanwhile in France, others were toying with these same ideas. In 1960, journalist Louis Pauwels and writer Jacques Bergier published the esoteric and Fortean book *Le Matin des Magiciens* (The Morning of the Magicians). A hodgepodge of declarations and conjectures about occult sciences, lost civilizations, and Nazi mysticism, the book became something of a cult classic among French youth during the seventies and eighties. Among other things, the authors pointed to evidence of remarkable historical achievements found in Central and South America and the Middle East that seemed hardly possible for such ancient societies: the irrigation works of the pre-Inca peoples, the pyramids of Egypt, the Nazca plain and its strange figures only visible by plane or balloon. One couldn't say for sure how these were accomplished, Pauwels and Bergier surmised, but "we do not reject the possibility of visits from the inhabitants of another world."[28]

The Morning of the Magicians struck a chord with writer Robert Charroux, the pen name of Robert Grugeau. In in a series of books published between 1963 and 1967, Charroux put forward the idea that extraterrestrial travelers had come to earth, created humanity, and bestowed on it its art, science, and architecture. Citing archaeological finds and religious references to a Great Flood, he argued that no advanced civilization like our own ever could have emerged from the apocalypse without the support of alien benefactors. The extraterrestrial origin of humanity was, in his view, the most probable and most logical conclusion.[29]

Then in 1966, a thirty-one-year-old hotelier in Davos, Switzerland, began working on his own version of the ancient alien story. Erich von Däniken's *Erinnerungen an die Zukunft* (Memories of the Future) came out in February 1968, with a print run of six thousand copies. After one month, sales reached twenty thousand, and by end of the year it had become a bestseller in Germany. The next year, the first English (*Chariots of the Gods?*) and French (*Les Souvenirs du Futur*) translations were published. When Bantam Press released its paperback version in 1971, it had a first print run of over two hundred thousand. After the book was adapted for American television in 1973, a quarter million copies were sold in the United States within forty-eight hours. Pirated versions made their way into Iran, it was sold on the black market in Eastern Europe, and Indian publishers offered three different translations.[30] All in all, it was a remarkable feat for a man with no advanced training in archaeology and who was sentenced to three-and-a-half years in prison by a Swiss court on charges of embezzlement, fraud, and forgery.[31]

Chariots of the Gods? opens with a salvo worthy of Charles Fort. "It took courage to write this book, and it will take courage to read it," von Däniken wrote. "Because its theories and proofs do not fit into the mosaic of traditional archaeology, constructed so laboriously and firmly cemented down, scholars will call it nonsense and put it on the Index of those books which are better left unmentioned."[32] From there, von Däniken walked his readers through a litany of seemingly impossible archaeological artifacts: huge structures made of tons of rock in South America, Sumerian mathematics thousands of years ahead of its time, ancient electric batteries found in Baghdad, a crypt in Mexico depicting what looks like an astronaut in a command module. Of course, he didn't fail to bring up what by 1968 already had become canonical among ufologists: the Nazca lines, the Baalbeck terrace, and the pyramids of Egypt.

Von Däniken then made the argument that has become a familiar refrain among paleovisitologists. Evidence reveals that these societies either attributed such feats to or constructed them in honor of perceived gods from the heavens, but observers from the flying saucer era of the twentieth century know better.

Some parts of earth are still inhabited by primitive peoples to whom a machine gun is a weapon of the devil. In that case a jet aircraft may well be an angelic vehicle to them. And a voice coming from a radio set might seem to be the voice of a god. These last primitive peoples, too, naively hand down from generation to generation in their sagas their impression of technical achievements that we take for granted. They still scratch their divine figures and their wonderful ships coming from heaven on cliffs and cave walls. In this way these savage peoples have actually preserved for us what we are seeking today.[33]

Von Däniken would go on to publish books about ancient astronauts virtually every other year throughout the 1970s, 1980s, and 1990s, selling an estimated forty million copies of his works by century's end. His popularity with the reading public was balanced by scholars and journalists publicly criticizing the book for its shoddy representation of the historical and archaeological record, its reliance on wild speculation, and its racist assumption that non-Western civilizations were invariably backward, unsophisticated, and incapable of innovation.[34] At the same time, a Swiss magazine and a West German publisher accused von Däniken of plagiarism, pointing out clear similarities between his ideas and examples and those of Robert Charroux. Eventually the matter was dropped when Charroux's publisher abandoned the case.[35]

Erich von Däniken and arguments about ancient aliens became a staple of paranormal literature, UFO conventions, and American cable television up to the present. In the context of the 1960s, paleovisitology offered another variation on the alien contact theme. The claims were not about extraterrestrials landing in the present, nor was there any reason to expect them any time soon; interestingly enough, Charroux, Pauwels, Bergier, and von Däniken all dismissed the contactees as either fools or hoaxers.[36] Instead, earth's "space brothers" and "space sisters" were actually space fathers and mothers, giving the argument a thinly veiled religious tenor. At the same time, judged against the backdrop of the first manned missions to space and the moon, it hardly seemed a leap of faith to consider the idea of ancient astronauts exploring earth a legitimate prospect. In this way, as sociologist Jean-Bruno Renard and anthropologist Wiktor Stoczkowksi have observed, paleovisitology's mix of concepts and artifacts taken from archaeology, science fiction, theology, cosmogony, and theosophy allowed it to seem both decidedly scientific and deeply religious.[37]

Nevertheless, paleovisitology remained outside academia, dismissed as a pseudoscience. Lacking scientific credentials and scholarly professional status, Erich von Däniken and his counterparts gained no traction among scholars. When it came to the topic of UFOs and aliens in general, most mainstream intellectuals remained stonily silent, leaving the impression they considered the matter unworthy of their attention. There were, however, a few exceptions already in the 1950s.

ON THE OUTSIDE LOOKING IN

Flying saucers were not alone in provoking questions about the possibility of contact with extraterrestrials. Some observers believed the development of intercontinental ballistic missiles and the start of earth-orbit satellites and human space exploration also made the prospect of alien encounters likely in the not-so-distant future. Among those considering the implications was the first generation of space lawyers. Throughout the 1950s and early 1960s, jurists from Europe and South and North America began spelling out what was referred to as metalaw or intergent law. Metalaw was envisioned as a "science of universal jurisprudence" aimed at setting down legal principles for human interaction with aliens in outer space. Renouncing colonization, space lawyers like American Andrew Haley and Brazilian Haroldo Valladão argued that humanity's behavior toward extraterrestrials should be governed by the golden rule: treat those on other planets as we would like to be treated.[38]

When asked whether the appearance of flying saucers might mean the aliens had already reached earth, space lawyers generally scoffed at the suggestion. Theologians, on the other hand, took the notion more seriously. A 1954 survey of Protestant and Catholic theologians in West Germany found that neither tended to rule out the possibility that intelligent beings from another world were behind the UFO phenomenon. Prompted to speculate about the spiritual status of any visitors, one American theologian surmised they might enjoy a certain special, supernatural grace from God; or perhaps they had sinned and had fallen out of grace with the Lord; or maybe they were pure and innocent like children or they ruled over paradise on other planets.[39]

Some leading scientists also went on record in response to reports of flying saucers and alien encounters. In most instances, they did so to soundly criticize claims about extraterrestrial visitors. French astrophysicist Évry Schatzman and American astronomer Donald Menzel were among the first to embrace this role, but they were joined by André-Louis Danjon, director of the Paris Observatory from 1945 to 1963 and V-2 rocket engineer and American space program developer Wernher von Braun. "I am convinced that in our era, which is so proud of its scientific enlightenment," von Braun was quoted in 1954, "it should be completely absurd to call upon medieval methods of magic, when one does not fully understand a natural phenomenon."[40]

While they didn't share diehard enthusiasts' uncritical acceptance of UFOs as otherworldly vessels, other scholars nonetheless thought such beliefs and perceptions warranted closer examination. Regardless of whether flying saucers existed or not and whether they were alien or not, so this line of thinking went, UFOs were a social reality having an impact on a wide range of perceptions and attitudes.

Specialists in psychiatry and psychology were among the first to tackle the issue in this way. In 1954, physician Georges Heuyer—a key figure in French child psychiatry—became one of the first clinicians to publicly argue for there being a psychopathology at work in the phenomenon. Calling on the concept of "collective psychosis," Heuyer contended that the contemporary world was witnessing the emergence of a "flying saucer psychosis," a kind of *folie à deux* or shared psychosis on a global scale. Fueled by fears and anxieties about things like nuclear destruction, highly impressionable individuals were susceptible to the "false ideas" surrounding UFOs that were being circulated by mass media.[41] New York–based psychiatrist Joost Meerloo went on to make a similar argument in 1967 about the role rumor and Cold War media coverage had in triggering what he called a "flying saucer syndrome" in anxiety-prone individuals.[42]

Social psychologists Leon Festinger, Henry W. Riecken, and Stanley Schachter approached the subject of belief in spacemen from a less clinical angle. In 1956, they published *When Prophecy Fails*, a study that chronicled the emergence of a small group of zealous followers called the "Seekers" around the figure of Dorothy Martin (referred to in the book as "Mrs. Keech"). Martin at the time claimed to have communicated with beings from the planet Clarion, who had informed her that large parts of North and South America would be destroyed on December 21, 1954, but that her followers would be saved by the aliens that very day. The day came and went without incident. Following the failure of her prediction, Festinger and his associates sought to explain why some of Martin's followers abandoned the movement, while others remained steadfast. The conclusion they reached was that a person's response to the failure of the prophecy was contingent on whether the opinions of their friends and family clashed with those of the UFO cult. Those "surrounded by people with opinions openly opposed to their own heard arguments that could serve only to maintain or to increase their strong dissonance," while those in the constant presence of true believers were able to find rationalizations allowing them to regain "confidence in their original beliefs."[43]

While Festinger and his team didn't reduce belief in flying saucers to a form of mental illness, they did continue the pattern of viewing such convictions as inherently irrational. One figure who did not think of UFOs in this same way was Swiss psychologist Carl Jung, one of the founding fathers of psychoanalysis. Jung had been keeping news clippings about flying saucers since the late forties, fascinated by their sudden and persistent appearance. In 1958, he published *Ein moderner Mythus: Von Dingen, die am Himmel gesehen werden*, released in English translation a year later with the title *Flying Saucers: A Modern Myth of Things Seen in the Skies*.[44] As he explained to a Swiss newspaper in July 1954, he himself never personally saw a UFO, but he was convinced by that time that "it is not just a rumor, *something* is *seen*."[45] In a subsequent letter Jung wrote in August 1958 to Donald Keyhoe, he expanded on this point. "As I am a scientist," he explained, "I only say what I can prove and reserve any judgment in any case where I doubt my competence. Thus I said: 'Things are seen, but one does not know what.'"[46]

For Jung, the fact that flying saucer sightings were frequent, strange, indeterminate, and contradictory made them ideal objects for fantasy and conjecture. The rumors, visions, dreams, and graphic representations of these "things seen in the skies" were all instances of these flights of speculation. In this way, they provided insight into the state of mind of the contemporary world.

Like so many others, Jung linked the flying saucer phenomenon to American faddishness and the Cold War. Nevertheless, relying on published reports, conversations with witnesses, historical texts, and interviews with patients about their dreams, he found certain elements repeated in reports about unidentified flying objects. They were said to move in a superhuman fashion, they refrained from doing harm, and they frequently appeared near airfields and nuclear installations. Together, these components helped give shape to the standard contactee story about intelligent beings from another world, who, having witnessed the carnage of World War II and the proliferation of nuclear weapons, were poised to benevolently intervene in human affairs.

Such speculation, according to Jung, represented nothing less than the making of a modern myth or legend. The fact that this "living myth" revolved around a promise of redemption was no accident, Jung contended, given the dire state of the world at the time. Contemporary individuals sought metaphysical hope in the face of the prospect of nuclear catastrophe, yet secular modernity was ultimately resistant to occult and mystical forms of religious reassurance. The flying saucer phenomenon, then, provided a relatively rational and necessarily scientific cover to express hope for a rescue from God.

Jung's book was greeted positively by the mainstream press, especially in West Germany, where he was esteemed as the elder statesman of psychology.[47] It has also stood the test of time. His "psychosocial theory" of UFOs, as it has come to be called, went on to influence three generations of social scientists, folklorists, religious scholars, and ufologists.

THE ARCH-DEMON OF SAUCERDOM

Astronomers, of course, were more interested in the physical existence of unidentified flying objects rather than their social significance. On that count at least, most appeared to consider the claims of ufologists and contactees somewhere between implausible and absurd. Their most vocal critic in the United States remained Harvard astronomer Donald Menzel, whose debunking classic *Flying Saucers* had made him a reviled figure within the UFO community. Wearing the stigma like a badge of honor, in the spring of 1959 he began working on a second UFO book. This time he collaborated with Lyle Gifford Boyd, a writer of science and science fiction books and editor for the Smithsonian and Harvard College observatories during the fifties and sixties.

In 1963, the two published *The World of Flying Saucers*, largely based on US Air Force records to which they were given access.[48] In it, Menzel and Boyd examined a range of the most common types of UFO sightings and claims and dissected some of the most famous cases associated with them. They demonstrated how a combination of balloons, planets, stars, meteors, weather, animals, shortcomings of radar and cameras, and hoaxes could account for what was being reported. While conceding that most scientists agreed "that life of some kind probably does exist in other parts of our galaxy and in other galaxies," they concluded, "No fact so far determined suggests that a single unidentified flying object has originated outside our planet."

Menzel did not confine his work as a UFO debunker to reading Project Blue Book reports and publishing. During his extensive domestic and international travels, he often took the opportunity to interview fellow scientists and witnesses about UFOs. Along the way, he gave frequent public talks, though the kind of reception he received could differ wildly. During a trip to Latin America in early 1965, he lectured in Spanish to enthusiastic crowds that numbered as many as four thousand, while one of his well-attended public talks at Harvard two years later included a dozen or so NICAP audience members who heckled throughout.[49]

Like his counterparts in ufology, Menzel was a dedicated letter writer. He clearly believed that part of his mission as a debunker was to actively engage with the general public. He received countless letters on a regular basis from a medley of readers: curious inquisitors asking his opinion about something they had heard or read; schoolchildren requesting more information about UFOs for homework assignments; supportive skeptics congratulating him on his fight against irrationality; and disparaging saucer enthusiasts criticizing him for his narrow-mindedness. Menzel tried to respond to them all.

One correspondent in the mid-1960s was Irma De Bruycker, a candy store owner and avid amateur astronomer living in Mishawaka, Indiana, outside South Bend. De Bruycker acquired passions for astronomy and agnosticism from her father and was well known in her town for organizing a local astronomy club and inviting neighborhood kids to look at the evening sky through her personal telescope. By her own admission, she made a nuisance of herself since at least the early 1950s, writing letters to the editor, complaining to tv broadcasters about their coverage, and speaking out against people's "need to believe in the bizarre," sometimes ending her letters with the closing "Yours For More Realism In The Space Age."[50]

She also reached out to academic astronomers, including Project Blue Book's J. Allen Hynek. But it was Donald Menzel whom she found truly inspiring. In 1967, De Bruycker wrote him in part to tell him about her campaign to get *The World of Flying Saucers* into the hands of local librarians and journalists. She also wrote him to find some small measure of consolation from the man some had nicknamed "The Arch-Demon of Saucerdom." She was especially disheartened, De Bruycker said, by the way the Bible was used by contactees and others to support their claims and how anyone with a different view of religion was branded a communist. "We are battling windmills, aren't we?" she wrote the astronomer in May of that year. "Will the minds of men always cling to the comfort of the unreal? I would far rather know truth—however bleak."[51] Menzel could only acknowledge that they would never win over some of the saucerists, but he invited her to stay in touch and send him material she thought he might use for his next book. Debunking too brought with it its own form of exile.

COMMUNICATION WITH EXTRATERRESTRIAL INTELLIGENCE

While Donald Menzel played the doyen of skepticism and most other astronomers gave the debate over unidentified flying objects a wide berth, a small group of scientists sought to steer a different, somewhat precarious path. In 1959, physicists Giuseppe Cocconi and Philip Morrison published a paper in the journal *Nature* in which they attempted to establish a credible way to detect radio communications from extraterrestrials.[52] The idea itself seemed to Cocconi and Morrison to be the logical extension of a revolutionary new technology in astronomy: radio telescopes. In the 1930s and 1940s scientists in the United States, England, Australia, the Netherlands, France, and the USSR began using radio antennas—instead of optical telescopes—to detect radiated energy along the electromagnetic spectrum from objects in outer space. Spurred by a ready supply of technicians trained in radar and by governments willing to invest in the necessary technology, large radio telescopes with huge dishes were built in the fifties and sixties, and radio astronomy established itself as an exciting new subfield.[53]

Cocconi and Morrison's paper was really a thought piece. If earth was not the only planet in the universe with advanced civilizations, then it might be that one or another of these alien worlds was beaming out signals and awaiting a reply. The two offered a recommendation on what radio region and what sun-like stars to focus on as potential candidates for detecting such communication.

Meanwhile, at the National Radio Astronomy Observatory in Green Bank, West Virginia, astronomer Frank Drake had reached a similar conclusion about extraterrestrial communications.[54] After an eighty-five-foot radio telescope at the observatory became operational in early 1959, Drake was given the go-ahead to put together an initiative he dubbed Project Ozma, whose name was a tip of the hat to the fantastic world in *The Wizard of Oz*. In April 1960, Ozma conducted its first search for a signal from an alien civilization but had no luck finding one.

A year and a half later, in November 1961, Green Bank was the site for an informal conference on "Extraterrestrial Intelligent Life." Among others, Drake and the observatory's director Otto Struve invited a number of receptive researchers: Cocconi and Morrison; astrophysicist Su-Shu Huang, coiner of the term "habitable zone" to refer to regions around a star where a planet might support liquid water; John C. Lilly, designer of the first sensory deprivation tank and researcher on dolphin intelligence; and planetary scientist Carl Sagan. In retrospect, more notable than the event itself was something Frank Drake drafted beforehand. It was an equation that he thought could be used to guide conversation about the factors determining just how many alien civilizations could be transmitting signals:

$$N = R^* f_p n_e f_l f_i f_c L$$

N = number of radio-communicating civilizations in the Milky Way galaxy

R* = rate of formation of stars suitable for development of intelligent life

f_p = fraction of those stars with a planetary system

n_e = number of planets per solar system with environment suitable for life

f_l = fraction of suitable planets on which life appears

f_i = fraction of life-bearing planets on which intelligent life appears

f_c = fraction of civilizations developing a technology capable of producing detectable signs of their existence

L = average length of time such civilizations produce such signals

The equation became known as the Drake Equation, and it has remained a foundational part of scientific discussions about intelligent life in the universe.

The responses to these early forays into what was first called Communication with Extraterrestrial Intelligence (CETI) but by the early 1970s the Search for Extraterrestrial Intelligence (SETI) were a mixed bag. When it came to fellow scientists, Drake remembers colleagues being positive, though not terribly enthusiastic, while Morrison noted that "most felt it was not a good idea, probably foolish, certainly completely speculative, and hardly worth discussing." By contrast, the general public's reaction was effusive. "It got huge newspaper and media coverage, which we didn't anticipate," Morrison recalled. "The media kept chasing me because I was going around the world. In every city I visited there would be messages from reporters wanting to talk to me."[55]

The search for extraterrestrial intelligence gathered steam. In the Soviet Union, astrophysicist Iosef Shklovskii familiarized himself with the work of Cocconi, Morrison, and Drake and was convinced of the potential for interstellar communication. In 1962, he published *Universe, Life, Intelligence* in Russian—later translated and co-authored in English with Carl Sagan—in which he touted the use of radio to search for signals from alien intelligences.[56] Shklovskii's ideas inspired his student and colleague Nikolai Kardashev at Moscow University, who cast himself in the role of the Russian Frank Drake and launched the first search in the USSR in 1963. A year later, Soviet radio astronomers held their first meeting on extraterrestrial civilizations; unlike their American counterparts, they focused on addressing the technical and linguistic challenges that would be involved in effectively communicating with beings from another world.[57]

Science editor at *The New York Times* Walter Sullivan had become aware of all these developments and decided to write about them. In 1964, he published *We are Not Alone*, a title that could well have graced the cover of one of Donald Keyhoe's books.[58] In it, Sullivan took his readers on a guided tour of the science of SETI: habitable zones, life on Mars, space biology, Project Ozma, the Green Bank conference, the Drake Equation, Soviet research, applying mathematics and symbolic logic to the problem of communication. Astronomers and physicists could now present to the world their alternative to ufology's stories of earthly encounters with alien visitors.

Early results were at times surprisingly promising. In 1964, Kardashev announced he had detected a pair of radio emissions that might have been beacons from extraterrestrials (they were not). Then, in late 1967, Jocelyn Bell and a group of radio astronomers at Cambridge University discovered an extraterrestrial source that emitted a flickering pattern that was unlike any other astronomical sources and was not a form of interference coming from earth. Further observations confirmed the finding.

Bell and the others pondered whether this was the kind of signal for which Project Ozma had been searching. For about three weeks, the team entertained the real possibility that they had stumbled across "other intelligent beings [who] were trying to establish contact with us," nicknaming the signal "the Little Green Men star." As Christmas approached, individual members debated among themselves what to do if this were in fact the case. It was agreed that for the time being secrecy should be the order of the day. The announcement of such a find seemed too momentous for them, and it was suggested they contact the Royal Society. The team's leader half-jokingly questioned announcing it at all, concerned that once they did, others would be sending out signals toward the source and, in the process, possibly invite an alien invasion. In the end, there was no cause for worry; what had been discovered was in fact the existence of a rotating neutron star called a pulsar—an achievement eventually rewarded with a Nobel Prize.[59]

Researchers interested in finding evidence of extraterrestrial intelligences remained undeterred. In 1971, over fifty scientists convened at the Byurakan Astrophysical Observatory in Yerevan, Armenia, for the first Soviet-American Conference on Communication with Extraterrestrial Intelligence. After meeting for almost a week, the group concluded that recent discoveries in astronomy, biology, computer science, and radio physics had moved the question of detecting extraterrestrial civilization "from the realm of speculation to a new realm of experiment and observation." It also recommended that the focus of future research be placed on a "search for signals and for evidence of astroengineering activities" around some nearby stars and objects. "If extraterrestrial civilizations are ever discovered," the organizers summed up, "the effect on human scientific and technological capabilities will be immense, and the discovery can positively influence the whole future of Man."[60]

Such lofty sentiments about finding evidence of alien civilizations were common among that first generation of SETI promoters. The refrain that such a discovery would alter human history was rooted in their devout belief that theirs represented a pure, altruistic vision of science and progress motivated by the selfless desire to know. Here was an undertaking with no ulterior motives, they thought, uncorrupted by the political interests that had come to warp scientific research since the Second World War. As nuclear physicist Freeman Dyson expressed it in 1966, "The maximum contact between alien societies is a slow and benign exchange of messages, a contact carrying only information and wisdom around the galaxy, not conflict and turmoil." Reflecting on the significance of the 1971 conference in Armenia, Frank Drake spoke in high-minded terms. "Our unanimity of purpose gave us the courage to plot together for the future of all humankind. We were even considering the construction of a radio telescope that spanned the Israeli-Egyptian border, to search for extraterrestrial intelligence while promoting peace in the Middle East."[61]

World peace through communication, human solidarity through common cause, progress through wisdom, self-knowledge through encountering the Other. The values driving the early SETI pioneers seemed to have been lifted straight from the counterculture of the sixties and early seventies. In this sense, SETI was an example of what's been called "groovy science," a blend of "earnestness and playfulness, an unsteady mix often fueled by a sense that society was on the brink of some new revolution."[62]

SETI researchers shared much with their counterparts in ufology, beyond just a mutual interest in believing in extraterrestrial civilizations and the prospect of communicating with them. There was also their common fascination with discovery and space, a faith in technoscientific progress, their joy in speculation, belief that they were living at the dawn of a new age, fear of nuclear catastrophe, unease with the military, and an abiding desire for peaceful coexistence.[63] Over the years, SETI scholars would go to great lengths to distance themselves from all the talk about UFOs, saying theirs was a sober investigation of signals well beyond our solar system. Nonetheless, the existence of SETI signaled that academic science was starting to take aliens seriously.

THE INVISIBLE COLLEGE

There were in fact other signs that at least some in the academic world were giving UFOs a second look. Organizations like APRO and NICAP, of course, had had some success in recruiting a few university professors to serve as consultants and advisors. At Wesleyan University, astronomy professor Thornton Page—one of the members of the Robertson Panel on UFOs back in 1953—had taught a course on UFOs since the late fifties. Page by no means considered flying saucers to be ships from outer space and found the term "UFO" to describe anything in the sky one couldn't understand to be hopelessly inexact. His course "Science 101: Flying Saucers," however, was designed to introduce freshmen in fields outside the sciences to the logic, methods, and findings of astronomy and physics.[64]

Northwestern University became the home of J. Allen Hynek, the astronomer who had been serving as scientific consultant on UFOs to the US Air Force since the early days of flying saucers. For much of that time, he saw little reason to consider flying saucers anything other than natural phenomena, though he did argue for adopting a more scientific approach to sightings.[65] After moving to Evanston in 1960, Hynek began reconsidering his take on unidentified flying objects—and he found some receptive confederates. Among them was William Powers, a systems engineer who designed equipment for the astronomy department at the university and who worked alongside Hynek investigating cases for Project Blue Book. In 1963, Hynek recruited to campus an ambitious Frenchman with an interest in computer programming, Jacques Vallee, who brought with him his deep interest in unidentified flying objects.[66]

Vallee had moved to the United States in the fall of 1962. It was a year before he made the trek to Illinois to meet the astronomer but the two hit it off right away. "It is hard not to be impressed by his sharp ideas and his eagerness for action," Vallee wrote in his journal in the fall of 1963. "He has a lively face where piercing eyes are softened by a little goatee that makes it hard to take him completely seriously." Hynek, almost thirty years Vallee's senior, encouraged his protégé to finish a book he was writing on UFOs and invited him to apply for a computer programming job opening at Northwestern. A month later, he was already settled in, auditing Hynek's astronomy class and developing computer programs for the Biomedical Department.

In early November, Hynek invited Vallee and another student, Nancy Van Etten, to serve as research assistants in his investigations for Project Blue Book. A couple of weeks later, Hynek and his wife Mimi began hosting meetings of what they called the UFO Committee to discuss cases. Hynek asked Vallee to be "the driving force" of the group, claiming his ties with the military meant he himself needed to step gingerly when it came to the topic of unidentified flying objects. Vallee agreed. "My objective is to pull the problem out of the quagmire where it is stuck," he wrote in his journal on the eve of the group's first meeting. "I want to try and convince the

Fig. 6.2 J. Allen Hynek speaking to the press in 1966 about a string of sightings in Dexter, Michigan. Hynek told reporters that the photo, taken by a police officer, was in fact a time exposure of the moon and Venus. Bettmann/Getty Images.

Air Force that this is a serious scientific question, that isn't limited to the United States, and that isn't necessarily just the business of the military to investigate it."

Vallee soon began working almost full-time on what he called "the saucer problem." As he familiarized himself with Project Blue Book records and spoke with the program's chief Major Hector Quintanilla, he arrived at the conclusion that the Air Force had little interest in or experience with studying unidentified flying objects scientifically. Hynek pointed out that even the National Academy of Sciences insisted that only a piece of hard evidence—a photograph or artifact—would lead it to take the matter seriously.

In June 1964, Vallee admitted to Hynek and William Powers that the UFO Committee they had formed had outlived its usefulness. It was agreed that they needed "a new study group, a real working team, staffed by scientists rather than by students." A meeting was held, this time with an engineer, a mathematician, and a couple of astronomers.

Over the next several years, the informal assembly grew to include engineers and natural and social scientists from throughout the United States and France. Besides Hynek, Vallee, and Powers, there was Fred Beckman, an EEG specialist at the University of Chicago Argonne Cancer

Research Lab; Douglas Price-Williams, a UCLA anthropologist and expert in psychological anthropology; Ted Phillips, an engineer and photographer, who went on to specialize in physical trace research; planetary astronomer Pierre Guérin; biologist and parapsychologist Rémy Chauvin; and astronomer Claude Poher, who would later direct France's government-sponsored research group on UFOs. Half-jokingly, Hynek named the loose network the "Invisible College," a reference to a secretive group of natural philosophers in the mid-seventeenth century who fought against church dogma in defense of empirical investigation. The name stuck.

By the mid-1970s, Vallee claimed the Invisible College of UFO researchers had around one hundred members from five or six different countries working on the saucer phenomenon. Together, he wrote, they were "challenging accepted ideas in claiming that these strange observations deserve to be investigated and that no theory about them—no matter how fantastic by ordinary human standards—should be rejected without study." Theirs was a "revolutionary" new perspective on the mysterious UFO phenomenon, a phenomenon, as he put it, "still largely ignored by science."[67] In 1966, however, science appeared ready to tackle the issue once and for all.

FORMING A RESEARCH TEAM

By 1965, the Air Force's Project Blue Book had over nine thousand reports of sightings in its files, with all but around 7 percent considered "explained." Since the project's inception, the consensus within the Air Force was that UFOs posed no threat to national security. But officials recognized that government secrecy combined with continued public speculation about the origins of flying saucers had created a public relations problem for the military. So, the Office of Information of the Secretary of the Air Force formed a commission of scientific and technical experts—headed by physicist Brian O'Brien and including astronomer Carl Sagan—to review the work and mandate of Project Blue Book. The commission's final report, submitted in March 1966, confirmed that UFOs were not a threat, but that the program could be strengthened by more intensive scientific investigation of selected sightings. It was this recommendation that provided one of the inspirations for eventually forming a larger scientific committee.

By this time, pressure to take UFOs more seriously was coming from a number of directions. The same month the final report of the O'Brien group was released, witnesses in Dexter, Michigan, reported seeing a brightly lit, car-sized object flying over a swamp at high speeds. Project Blue Book sent Allen Hynek to investigate. Hynek at first appeared to be baffled, but after phoning Air Force officials he returned a verdict, which he announced at a press conference a few days later: witnesses had seen nothing more than marsh gas. Local residents were outraged by what they took to be an insult to their intelligence; they knew what marsh gas looked like and this, they insisted, was not marsh gas. The press enjoyed poking fun at Hynek's "swamp gas" explanation. Hynek phoned Vallee and admitted he probably spoke too fast. "There was so much confusion, Jacques, you can't imagine what a pandemonium we had. This just wasn't a strong enough case to base a real offensive on it. I would have found myself in a fragile position."[68]

The politicians then decided to step in. Michigan Congressman and House Minority Leader Gerald Ford was having none of the marsh gas explanation and publicly demanded a congressional investigation of UFOs "to get to the bottom of this thing." A few weeks later, the House Armed Services Committee held a hearing on UFOs. Testifying before its members, Air Force Secretary Harold Brown was pressed on the issue. In response, Brown publicly declared he was inclined to support the O'Brien panel's earlier recommendation to form a committee of academic experts to study the problem in greater depth.[69] All that was left to do was find a host for the research.

Finding a university for this first civilian scientific study of UFOs was harder than first imagined. Harvard, MIT, the University of North Carolina, and Berkeley all balked when asked. Researchers there were unwilling to put off their own projects to undertake a new one about a topic most considered suspect.[70] In July 1966, the Air Force Office of Scientific Research approached nuclear physicist Edward Condon of the University of Colorado in Boulder to consider serving as director of the venture.

Condon was a bold choice. Having earned his Ph.D. in physics at Berkeley in 1926, Condon became associate director of Westinghouse Laboratory in 1937, where he worked on finding industrial applications for nuclear physics. During the war, J. Robert Oppenheimer hired him to work on the Manhattan Project, but he left Los Alamos after only a few weeks, exasperated by the compartmentalized secrecy surrounding the work. In 1945, he became director of the National Bureau of Standards.

On a personal level, Condon was generally known as a cheerful fellow, with a sometimes-biting sense of humor and strong political views. A self-professed liberal, he became a leading postwar voice insisting that the public be informed about the dangers of atomic energy and that civilian authorities—not the military—be put in control of the new technology.[71] All this helps explain how he became a target of the House Un-American Activities Committee (HUAC). In 1947, Condon was accused of having ties with communist groups, and in 1948, a sub-committee report deemed him

Fig. 6.3 Edward Condon with a copy of his committee's final report on UFOs, January 1969. Photo by Carl Iwasaki/Getty Images.

to be "one of the weakest links in our atomic security." Condon resolutely defended himself, and an array of prominent politicians and scientific organization came to his defense. When the Atomic Energy Commission cleared him for access to restricted information, the attacks subsided for a time. But a new round of accusations a few years later led to his being subpoenaed before HUAC in August 1952. Once again, Condon prevailed and three days later he was installed as president of the American Association for the Advancement of Science. When his clearance was taken away again in the fall of 1954, however, Condon refused to fight the decision, later stating that he did so because he "decided the situation was hopeless."

In choosing Condon, the Air Force was taking into account the public relations dilemma it had been facing all along in its investigation of UFOs. Condon was not just an esteemed scientist with a history of leading collaborative government-sponsored projects. A man unafraid to stand up to authority and speak freely, he had a history of combating military secrecy and promoting open science. If anyone could convince UFO conspiracy theorists of the integrity of the study, surely it would be Edward Condon.

At first reluctant to take on the directorship, Condon discussed the Air Force's offer with others at the Joint Institute for Laboratory Astrophysics in Boulder. His colleagues were adamantly opposed to taking on the project, deeming it "outrageously silly." "Of course, that kind of a—in a certain sense, kind of pushed me into it even more," Condon later recalled, "because I'm the kind of guy that doesn't like opposition of that sort."[72] He pressed the issue, eventually finding the Physics Department at the university amenable to housing the first independent scientific study of UFOs.

With some fanfare, the *New York Times* dubbed Condon "an outspoken scientist," quoting him as saying, "I raise a little hell when I run things."[73] That said, Condon understood his mandate to be a narrow one. Having concluded there was nothing in the UFO phenomenon of military significance, the Air Force viewed the Colorado study as a way for it to "get out from under this program."[74] As Condon explained it in an interview several years later, by 1966 the Air Force had clearly determined that UFOs weren't "a defense problem," that "there was no sense doing anything more on as defense, their specialty." After the O'Brien Committee report, some recommended placing the UFO phenomenon under the jurisdiction of civilian science, but others considered it unworthy of scientific investigation. This was the context in which the project was born. "So, the question that was really put to us was kind of lost sight of in most public discussion of this thing," Condon recollected. "It was just that now our question was, ought they or ought they not to be willing to support projects in this field?"[75] In his estimation, this charge strictly limited the scope of the committee's work. Its purpose was not to examine every UFO report and determine whether aliens were behind them but rather to decide whether scientific study of UFOs was worth funding. Condon was quite right: the distinction was by and large lost on the public.

After agreeing to take on the job, Condon's next move was to assemble a team of researchers. Chair of the Department of Psychology Stuart Cook and specialist in atmospheric physics Franklin Roach were designated principal investigators. Assistant Dean of the Graduate School Robert J. Low, who held an MBA, was appointed project coordinator, and along with Low's assistant Mary Lou Armstrong, he set up a staff of twelve in Boulder.

"The UFO Project," as it was referred to at the time, consisted of three circles of experts. First, there was a small group of academic researchers, most based at the University of Colorado, who were the core investigators and who Low referred to as the "UFO Study Group." This included engineers Norman Levine and Roy Craig and psychologists Michael Wertheimer and David Saunders, who was unusual in also being a member of Donald Keyhoe's NICAP organization. A geographically wider circle of sub-contracted "consultants" were brought in, including astronomer William Hartmann at the University of Arizona and researchers at institutions like the National Center for Atmospheric Research and the Environmental Science Services Administration. Finally, a more loosely connected network of individuals were occasionally invited to consult with the UFO Study Group at times about specific cases or issues. This included people like Hynek, Keyhoe, NICAP's assistant director Richard Hall, and the Lorenzens, as well as UFO debunkers Donald Menzel and aviation writer Philip Klass.[76] It soon became apparent strong differences of opinion existed both within and across these groupings.

From the start, it was agreed that the project would work independent of the Air Force and that researchers would have full access to all government records. In order to preempt any later allegations of impropriety, it was agreed that a final report would be written, submitted first to the National Academy of Sciences for its independent assessment, then made public.

THE COMMITTEE GETS TO WORK

Just two days into its work, the Condon Committee faced its first crisis. The *Denver Post* interviewed Project Coordinator Robert Low about the study and how it began. Low was quoted as saying that the study came "pretty close" to not meeting the normal criteria for appropriate research at the university. Instead, he said, it represented a form of public service, adding, "When you're asked to do something (as opposed to applying for it) you don't say no—not to the Air Force." Angered by the insinuation that the university had no choice in the matter and that the study was of questionable legitimacy, Condon wrote a letter to the editor in which he defended the project as an "extraordinarily powerful way of learning about natural phenomena." This early public relations snafu stung, and Condon's response was swift. He informed staff that all future press requests for information should be referred to him and that "no other staff member will speak to the representatives of the mass media . . . unless he does so in the company of Dr. Condon."[77]

With everyone in place, staff set to work in October. The first order of business was organizing a library of literature about unidentified flying objects by leading ufologists. Then, in succession, UFO experts were invited to give presentations to the team: Allen Hynek, Jacques Vallee, Donald Keyhoe, and his assistant Richard Hall.

Hynek was upbeat about the Condon Committee's prospects for success. Returning from a dinner in Colorado with the entire team in late October, he told Jacques Vallee, "My first impression? They will approach the subject very serious." He conceded that most of the wives "thought the whole project was ridiculous . . . Especially Mrs. Condon." But the leadership in place was strong. "Roach and Condon feel they have a real scientific responsibility here."[78]

Right away it became clear to Low and the investigators that the UFO Project had been set up before any clear methodology had been established. Moreover, unidentified flying objects presented some vexing challenges for investigators. Chief among them was the fact that sightings by their very nature were fleeting and unpredictable and thus almost impossible to directly observe. Condon summed up the situation by contrasting their dilemma with what a medical team faced when called in to assess an epidemic. "An epidemic stays there until you get there," he noted. "Most of these [UFO] things are so transient and evanescent that you are not likely to be able to get the guys there with equipment you would like to have."[79]

For the first few months, internal discussions took place among members of the core Study Group, with an eye toward agreeing on a suitable approach. It was clear to almost everyone that, since the Air Force had already decided that national security was no concern, the primary question at hand was determining the plausibility of the notion that an extraterrestrial intelligence (ETI) was behind the UFOs. As Low put it in a memo to the Colorado team shortly before Christmas, the group needed to identify "what it would take to convince us that a given sighting, any sighting, was an ETI. What evidence would we accept as conclusive?"[80]

Despite some disagreements, by February 1967 the Condon Committee had decided on a method of operation. Both the Air Force and NICAP generally agreed that anywhere between 80 percent and 95 percent of UFO reports were explainable in terms of natural phenomena.[81] So, the team was instructed to focus only on those cases considered to be the most ideal for proving the extraterrestrial intelligence thesis. These then would be subject to further scrutiny.

Using files and documents forwarded by Project Blue Book, NICAP, and APRO, the UFO Study Group began identifying promising cases. Investigators armed with a questionnaire then interviewed witnesses (usually by telephone) about their sightings as well as their background, values, beliefs, and their exposure to media coverage about flying saucers. Three teams of two researchers then carried out field work—lasting anywhere from one to four days per case—in those instances warranting follow-up. At the same time, the group hoped that reports of live sightings could be studied in real time. So, quick-response teams were prepared to conduct field research at a moment's notice. Finally, in order to aid in forensic analysis, instruments like diffraction gratings, Geiger counters, and tape recorders were procured, a database for statistical computer analysis was set up, and arrangements were made for laboratory inspection of photographs and film.[82]

Meanwhile, team member David Saunders set out on a different path. The psychologist wondered if it might be possible to come up with measurable criteria for evaluating the credibility of observations and evidence. It turned out that Allen Hynek had already been developing a classification scheme for this very thing. Hynek's idea was to award any given UFO report two ratings on a scale of 0 to 10: a "Strangeness Rating," based on how many "odd-ball" elements popped up in the account; and a "Probability Rating," based on the consistency of the account and witness dependability.[83]

Saunders adapted Hynek's schema. He created a matrix with two axes: one measuring more or less strangeness, the other measuring more or less objectivity. UFO reports were then assigned coordinates. In principle then, the UFO Study Group could focus its attention on those sightings associated with high reliability but whose high strangeness made them more likely to be the result of something unconventional.[84]

RIFTS

By spring 1967 a picture Condon's leadership style was becoming apparent. In daily affairs, he proved to be a remote presence, involving himself very little in the nuts and bolts of the study. Many found him aloof, and some questioned his general interest in the subject altogether in light of the fact that he was prone to falling asleep whenever a consultant came in to brief the team.[85] Others, like coordinator Robert Low and NICAP representative Richard Hall were more concerned with what was catching Condon's attention. Despite coming to the project with a reputation for being a "UFO agnostic," word had it that Condon was "bending over backward" to listen to any and all alien contact stories—the more bizarre, the more he seemed to take an interest in them.[86] A worried Hall reported back to Keyhoe that Condon remained poorly informed about UFOs and was spending his time reading the books of APRO founders Coral and Jim Lorenzen about a possible alien invasion. Condon was routinely getting letters asking him to look into the most sensational cases, and he indulged them because, as Hall noted, he "feels that reasonable letters deserve answers, so that he is somewhat preoccupied with, and seeing too much of, the kooks . . . he is so 'open-minded,' feeling that everyone should have his say, that he is tending to give too much weight to the frivolous side of the UFO subject at present."[87]

As a result, Low increasingly directed the daily business of running meetings, boiling down messy conversations into concrete actions, communicating with staff, and laying out a clear division of labor.[88] In contrast to Condon, Low at first was well liked and trusted by seemingly everyone, including the consulting ufologists. Richard Hall, for instance, found Low to be affable and open and was encouraged by the fact that the coordinator was insisting that the hypothesis of alien visitors needed to be tackled head on in order for the project to be meaningful.[89]

Over the course of 1967, however, the mutual good will quickly began to erode. Those associated with NICAP wondered whether Low and Condon were being entirely honest with them. The previous December, NICAP had expressed concerns that "the overbalance of psychologists" in the Study Group was creating a "PR problem" for the UFO organization; members wondered whether it was a sign that the Condon Committee was determined to chalk the whole matter up to optical illusions and mental illness.[90] Their apprehensiveness was not without merit. In June 1967, Low told the team, "As I read them (the psychologists), they are telling us that we are faced with a situation in which, no matter how much study may be made of the observers, there remains uncertainty about how accurate their reports are. The question we have to deal with, therefore, is how do we make judgments on the UFO problem if we don't know whether the facts that are reported to us are correctly reported or not."[91]

Making matters worse, Edward Condon was in the habit of saying that he was intent on debunking UFOs. In an interview in 2006 with filmmaker David Cherniack, project consultant William Hartmann explained Condon meant something quite specific when he used the term. Hartmann recalled one day when the study's director invited him and some others to his home to talk informally. At one point, Condon said he didn't understand why people got upset when he talked about trying to debunk the UFO phenomenon. As Hartmann explained:

Well, you know, that to most people sounds like somebody that's already got his mind made up on how we can discredit it. They interpret debunk as meaning discredit. And he's saying, I don't understand why people are unhappy that I used the word debunk because, what does it mean? It means to remove the bunk from. And so that's what we want to do on your committee. You know the bunk is what we need to get out of there to see if there's any real scientific signal left. Take the noise out and see if there's a signal. Let's debunk it. So that was his claim of what debunk meant to him.[92]

Meanwhile the Project Blue Book consultant who had been pilloried for dismissing sightings in Michigan as "swamp gas," seemed to be publicly changing his tune. Already at the start of the Colorado study, Allen Hynek had publicly stated that the growing number of unexplained cases had led him to the conclusion that unidentified flying objects warranted serious scientific investigation.[93] "It has just been, you might say a growing concern," he told the Detroit News in October 1966, "a growing concern with my own scientific responsibility—at what point should I press the panic button?"[94] By the summer of 1967, he was following this up with statements in which he called for the creation of UFO task forces all over the country.[95]

For almost two decades, Hynek had worked mostly behind the scenes for Project Blue Book. With the media focus on the Colorado Study, he seized the opportunity to do countless interviews and publish opinion pieces in newspapers and popular periodicals. In the December 1967 issue of the men's magazine Playboy, he published an article in which he acknowledged that even reputable witnesses could easily err.[96] But he also admitted that the number of cases that remained unexplained were piling up, and if the United States remained dismissive of UFO reports, scientists in the Soviet Union appeared ready to tackle the problem.

When Hynek's associate Jacques Vallee heard that the astronomer was working on something for Playboy, he was dumbfounded. "That's certainly not the right way to place the subject on the map of respectable science," he wrote in his journal.[97] Hynek was undeterred and seemed to relish being in the spotlight, something that increasingly rubbed Vallee the wrong way.

Fellow astronomers and ufologists were suspicious about Hynek's true thoughts and motivations. Left off the UFO Study Group due to his ties with the Air Force, Hynek instead played the role of whistleblower, albeit a fairly subdued one. There was, however, another academic—one the Condon Committee had also kept at arm's length—who proved to be far less restrained in his criticisms of what was going on in Colorado.

A professor at the Institute of Atmospheric Physics at the University of Arizona and a member of the National Academy of Sciences, James McDonald was an internationally respected specialist in cloud physics, weather modification, and micrometeorology. Widely acknowledged to be accomplished and eloquent, he did not suffer fools (at least in his estimation) lightly.

As a doctoral student in 1954, McDonald himself actually had reported seeing an unidentified flying object over Arizona. He first began looking into sightings in the late fifties but kept his interest in the topic mostly private until shortly before the Colorado Study began. By then, he had reached the conclusion that UFOs represented "the greatest scientific problem of our times" and was spending a considerable amount of time on the phenomenon and consulting with NICAP.

McDonald publicly burst onto the UFO scene in the summer of 1966. He visited with Project Blue Book officials in Ohio and contacted major ufologists. He also arranged a meeting with Allen Hynek and Jacques Vallee in Chicago. He didn't mince words, berating Hynek for being too timid over the years in his dealings with the Air Force. "How could you remain silent so long?" McDonald demanded. Hynek, he said, should have said something already in 1953. "Public opinion was ready for a serious scientific study." Hynek tried to explain he had little choice in the matter, but it made no difference. Within a matter of a few weeks, McDonald was attacking Hynek, the Air Force, and the scientific establishment and attempted to lure Vallee into joining his campaign. Vallee wasn't having it, writing in his journal, "I don't see what good McDonald's approach will do, if he keeps behaving like a bull in a china shop."[98]

By the time the Condon Committee was being formed, McDonald already had some strong opinions about unidentified flying objects. Project Blue Book was scientifically incompetent, he thought, and the Air Force was engaged in a program of public deception. The number of unexplained cases far exceeded what was being reported. Technological and psychological error could not account for most of these cases. There was no alternative in his mind, then. "I find from my study of the problem that the most acceptable hypothesis appears to be that of the extraterrestrial nature of the UFOs," he wrote a friend in 1966. One could only speculate on what was motivating the alien visitors, but McDonald subscribed "to the view that certain parts of the total UFO pattern suggest something in the nature of a reconnaissance operation."[99]

Fig. 6.4 Atmospheric physicist James E. McDonald. SUFOI/AFU.

Intelligent, driven, and dogged, McDonald was revered by many UFO enthusiasts as an inspiring paragon of courage. He struck many of his skeptical colleagues, however, as dogmatic, abrasive, and pompous. Regardless, for anyone following the UFO story during the second half of the 1960s, he was impossible to ignore. In press conferences, public lectures, and tv and radio interviews, McDonald railed against the Air Force's ineptitude and secrecy and demanded intensive scientific study of what he constantly referred to as "the UFO problem."

The relationship between the Condon Committee and McDonald was unsurprisingly fraught. Edward Condon and Robert Low asked the Arizona physicist to Boulder a few times to brief them on his views, but they did not invite him to serve as a consulting staff member for the project. For his part, McDonald volunteered his services to the committee and initially found both Condon and Low to be open to his views. But he also expressed unease with the fact that the Air Force was funding the initiative. From the start, he was determined to use his influence to press Condon and his team to take seriously the prospect of alien travelers.

Once the UFO Project got underway, McDonald took it upon himself to use his connections to keep tabs on developments in Boulder. As a respected academic and a highly regarded advisor to NICAP, McDonald had direct access to some of the members of the core UFO Study Group as well as to several project consultants. Many of these people reported back to him on a regular, sometimes even weekly, basis.

McDonald's most constant informant was Richard Hall from NICAP. The two men were close, and McDonald often stayed at Hall's home when he visited Washington, DC. Until Hall suddenly resigned from NICAP in September 1967 for personal reasons, he provided McDonald with detailed descriptions of the project's progress as well as gossip about relations within the study group. In letters and conversations, they discussed the pros and cons of Low's decisions, poked fun at the spectacular claims of the Lorenzens and the prevarications of Hynek, and speculated about who on the Condon Committee seemed sympathetic to their views about UFOs. In short order, however, their discussions took on the character of strategy sessions.

INTRIGUES

Already in the early months of 1967, many observers both inside and outside the Condon Committee who believed UFOs worthy of serious study were expressing growing reservations about Condon's commitment to the project. In public talks, he often took great delight in regaling audiences with humorous anecdotes about the kinds of bizarre letters he received from people claiming to have ridden on a flying saucer.[100] An especially pivotal moment came in late January, regarding an article in the *Elmira Star-Gazette* about a talk Condon gave the previous night. The piece quoted Condon as saying about unidentified flying objects, "My attitude right now is that there's nothing to it," and that it was his "inclination right now to recommend that the government get out of this business."[101] He quickly condemned the piece for misrepresenting him, but the damage was done.[102] UFO enthusiasts openly questioned whether the project director already had made up his mind.

By fall of that year, Condon's leadership style and public pronouncements were impacting morale within the UFO Project. Privately, some investigators complained of there being chronic communication problems and a growing disconnect between Condon and team members. Consultant William Hartmann at the University of Arizona reported back to his colleague James McDonald that everyone in the UFO Study Group tacitly understood that Condon had a negative attitude about the extraterrestrial hypothesis and that "everybody on the project is more or less forced to go along with that."[103]

Meanwhile, pressured by its membership, NICAP stopped sending information on sightings to the project. Robert Low met personally with Donald Keyhoe, but the latter was not reassured by the answer he received when he asked about Condon's views at the time. "If he were to write a report today," Low replied, "it would be negative." In mid-November, Keyhoe made clear to Condon that he had little confidence in his impartiality.[104]

By this time, two core members of the UFO Study Group, engineer Norman Levine and psychologist David Saunders, along with Robert Low's assistant Mary Lou Armstrong, had concluded that the project had become hopelessly corrupted. They believed Condon and Low were biased against the mere suggestion of extraterrestrial visitation, and through a combination of intimidation and gross mismanagement, the two men undermined any chance of conducting a proper scientific study. So, the three dissidents began coordinating with James McDonald to decide on a common strategy.

Toward the end of November 1967, Saunders and McDonald mapped out a game plan.[105] The group would meet to discuss writing an alternative final report—one suggesting that the extraterrestrial hypothesis was vindicated—and creating a new organization for the scientific study of UFOs. Before that meeting took place, however, McDonald was let in on something that had been an open secret for months.

BOMBSHELL

While rummaging around old files in July 1967, field investigator Roy Craig had discovered a startling memo. Written by Robert Low to the University of Colorado's dean of the graduate school and its vice-president for academic affairs, the letter was dated August 9, 1966—a month before the university and the Air Force had reached an agreement to undertake the study. In the memo, Low weighed the possible costs and benefits of taking on the project. He admitted that some scholars at the university worried that to even entertain the possibility of flying saucers might result in a significant loss "in prestige in the scientific community," similar to what occurred when Duke University housed J. B. Rhine's parapsychology laboratory until 1965. But in a paragraph that has since become a canonical part of UFO lore, Low recommended a path forward:

> The analogy with ESP, Rhine, and Duke is only partially valid. The Duke study was done by believers who, after they had finished, convinced almost no one. Our study would be conducted almost exclusively by nonbelievers who, although they couldn't possibly *prove* a negative result, could and probably would add an impressive body of evidence that there is no reality to the observations. The trick would be, I think, to describe the project so that, to the public, it would appear a totally objective study but, to the scientific community, would present the image of a group of nonbelievers trying their best to be objective but having an almost zero expectation of finding a saucer. One way to do this would be to stress investigation, not of the physical phenomena, but rather of the people who do the observing—the psychology and sociology of persons and groups who report seeing UFO's. If the emphasis were put here, rather than on examination of the old question of the physical reality of the saucer, I think the scientific community would quickly get the message.[106]

For those who had questioned the integrity of the UFO Project, here was the proverbial smoking gun. To all appearances, what would become known as "the trick memo" seemed to offer conclusive proof that the Condon Committee never intended to treat the claims of witnesses seriously and that Condon, Low, and the University of Colorado had conspired to deceive the public about their real purpose. Interestingly, the memo had hardly been veiled in secrecy. Roy Craig later said that following his initial discovery in the summer, "the contents of the Low memo became common knowledge around the office."[107] Keyhoe and McDonald, however, only learned of its existence in late 1967, both agreeing, as Keyhoe put it in a conversation the two had on December 3, "There's no hope for any change with that man [Condon]." They then considered whether to leak the memo to the press.[108]

About two weeks later, McDonald traveled to Denver to meet with the three UFO Study Group dissenters, Saunders, Levine, and Armstrong. They were joined by Allen Hynek, who had been invited to be part of the group. Together, they decided to found a new scientific organization, the Committee for Research on UFOs (CRU), whose purpose would be to soberly study the UFO problem as well as publish a scholarly periodical.[109]

After the holidays, things quickly came to a head. On January 19, 1968, Robert Low and James McDonald had a heated phone conversation.

McDonald raised his usual litany of complaints: Condon was not actively engaged in the project; he was too preoccupied with "crackpots"; and there was a lack of communication across team members. Low blew up, asking McDonald to just wait until the report came out to lodge criticisms against it. A few days later, Saunders and Levine convinced their CRU associates that Condon and Low not be confronted with "the trick memo" through a media outlet, but rather that "it should be made public from inside the project."[110]

That job fell to James McDonald. In a long letter to Low dated January 31, 1968, he laid out all his criticisms about the Condon Committee and included a reference to the famous "trick memo." When Low read the letter on February 6, he was livid. That evening, he and Condon met to discuss what to do.

The next day, Condon and Low confronted Levine and Saunders and demanded to know how McDonald got his hands on the memo.[111] Condon said that the memo was an administrative file from before the project started and thus was not a public document. His chief worry was the damage done to the image of the university, and he accused Saunders in particular of disloyalty, angrily telling him, "For an act like that you deserve to be ruined professionally!"[112] Saunders replied that he did it for the good of solving the ultimate scientific problem. "Bullshit," Low shot back. "I was available," Condon rebuked Levine. "I'm just a telephone call away." Levine replied, "I wouldn't think it would be necessary for me to have to *invite* the Chief Scientist to come over and view the problem."[113] It was announced to the press the following day that Saunders and Levine had been fired for "incompetence."

The scandal and firings left the UFO Study Group stunned and in disarray. William Hartmann expressed shock. Roy Craig considered leaving the project but felt obligated to stay on. Mary Lou Armstrong resigned her position a few weeks later and informed Condon about her involvement in the McDonald faction. He was flabbergasted.[114]

FALLOUT

With the project left understaffed, remaining team members were assigned the work of former colleagues. On April 30, Edward Condon announced that all field investigations for the project had been completed.[115] What remained was the matter of writing the final report.

Meanwhile, the scandal further emboldened McDonald to press his case. For several years, he had become friendly with John Fuller, the writer and columnist who had written the book about the Hills' abduction, *The Interrupted Journey*. *Look* magazine agreed to publish an article by Fuller about the controversy surrounding the Condon Committee. McDonald volunteered to be one of Fuller's chief sources for the piece and was even invited to review and correct a first draft.[116] In its May 14 issue, the magazine published "Flying Saucer Fiasco," detailing the story of the mutiny within the UFO Project. Fuller's take was unreservedly sympathetic to the "rebels," concluding, "The hope that the establishment of the Colorado study brought with it has dimmed. All that seems to be left is the $500,000 trick."[117]

The *Look* article was covered by news outlets across the country, and NICAP declared it was breaking off relations with the Colorado study. Throughout May and June, Condon received numerous letters from angry citizens and critical academics, citing the article and questioning the project's integrity.[118] He even had to request police protection after a series of anonymous threatening phone calls.[119]

Edward Condon, in turn, scolded the magazine's publisher and insisted that the piece was "filled with falsehoods, misrepresentations, and distortions."[120] Robert Low for his part claimed to be a victim of a misunderstanding. "Of course, I'm appalled at what he [Fuller] has done," he told the press. "He took that staff memo out of context and made it look entirely different than I intended."[121]

Condon and Low remained on the defensive throughout the summer of 1968. When the periodical *Science*, an organ of the American Association for the Advancement of Science sent a reporter to Boulder to cover the scandal and its fallout, Condon was outraged. He contacted the editor as well as the president of AAAS, demanding the story never see the light of day, but to no avail.[122] An irked Condon sent a letter to the editors saying it was "difficult to know what to make of *Science*'s editors sending a reporter to Boulder to gather such immateria and solemnly spread it on your pages. This tittle-tattle is what now passes for scientific journalism?"[123]

On top of criticism from colleagues and the general public, some politicians publicly disparaged the work of the Colorado team. Once again, James McDonald had a hand in it. In June, he persuaded congressmen Morris Udall, George P. Miller, and J. Edward Roush of the need to pursue a congressional hearing about UFOs.[124] Roush had shared McDonald's interest in UFOs for some time, and on the floor of the House of Representatives he expressed "grave doubts as to the scientific profundity and objectivity of the [Colorado] project."[125]

The result was a one-day symposium held on a July 29, 1968, under the auspices of the House Science and Astronautics Committee. This time, believers in the notion of extraterrestrial visitors outnumbered the skeptics. Along with McDonald and Hynek, ufologists Stanton Friedman, James Harder, Frank Salisbury, and Leo Sprinkle were invited to testify. Skeptics Donald Menzel and Carl Sagan were also given the opportunity to raise doubts about the prospect of visitors from other planets. While the congressional committee offered no conclusions, the presentations and subsequent discussion gave the decided impression that unidentified flying objects warranted investigation and funding.[126]

While Condon and the Colorado team wrote their final report, they remained tight-lipped. After the leaking of the trick memo, members of the UFO Project were under strict orders to say nothing to the press. All that was publicly known was that the report was expected to be finished in the fall and that expelled study group member David Saunders was planning on publishing his own book criticizing the work of the Condon Committee.

On Halloween 1968, Edward Condon submitted the report to the Secretary of the US Air Force who, as planned, sent it on to the National Academy of Sciences for review. A panel of experts was formed in early November, chaired by Yale astronomer Gerald Clemence and including physicists, a physiologist, a psychologist, a mathematician, a geologist, a meteorologist, and an electrical engineer. They spent seven weeks considering the merits of the UFO Project, assessing three facets of the study: its scope, its methodology, and its findings. On all three counts, the panel found the study to be adequate and in keeping with prevailing standards of scientific research. It concluded, "We are unanimous in the opinion that this has been a very creditable effort to apply objectively the relevant techniques of science to the solution of the UFO problem."[127] The main results of the report were finally made public on January 7, 1969.

THE FINAL REPORT AND REACTIONS

Published in January by Bantam Books and introduced by *New York Times* science editor Walter Sullivan, the Condon Committee's Final Report was mammoth, weighing in at over 950 pages. It included a dizzying array of materials. There were chapters on field studies, physical evidence, photograph analysis, and fifty-nine case studies (many of which remained unexplained). There were essays on the history of UFOs, psychological aspects of sightings, discussions about radar, sonic booms, and atmospheric electricity. And there was a lengthy appendix that included a wide range of documents: questionnaires, field kit inventories, Air Force correspondence, and government UFO assessments.

The first chapter, offering conclusions and recommendations written by Edward Condon, drew the most attention. Blunt as ever, Condon wasted no time getting to the point. "Our general conclusion is that nothing has come from the study of UFOs in the past 21 years that has added to scientific knowledge. Careful consideration of the record as it is available to us leads us to conclude that further extensive study of UFOs probably cannot be justified in the expectation that science will be advanced thereby."[128] The study also found no evidence that unidentified flying objects posed a threat to national security nor anything indicating the Air Force was deliberately keeping the public in the dark about UFOs.

Condon went on to encourage physical scientists to turn their energies and talents to other endeavors but acknowledged that some might disagree with the UFO Project's judgment. And that was fine, in his estimation. "If they disagree it will be because our report has helped them reach a clear picture of wherein existing studies are faulty or incomplete and thereby will have stimulated ideas for more accurate studies."[129] He did, however, suggest that social and behavioral researchers might find the beliefs of individual and groups as well as media coverage about UFOs worthy of investigation. He ended by lamenting the fact that teachers across the country were assigning students readings from ufology literature. "Such study is harmful not merely because of the erroneous nature of the material itself, but also because such study retards the development of a critical faculty with regard to scientific evidence, which to some degree ought to be part of the education of every American."[130]

By the time the report was made public, of course, no one was surprised by its verdict. The open question was, how would people react?

Weeks before the final report was made public, psychologist and former UFO Study Group member David Saunders had already published his behind-the-scenes account of the project—*UFOs? Yes! Where the Condon Committee Went Wrong*. In it, he presented a picture of Condon as a distracted, out-of-touch, and stubborn director, someone who consistently thwarted attempts to look into the more plausible cases and undermined the study by making disparaging public comments. For Saunders, the "unhappy ending of the Colorado Project" taught that authorities—particularly the scientific community—needed to treat research on the UFO phenomenon as a respectable enterprise.

For its part, NICAP held a press conference and published a response shortly after the final report's release. It offered up a blistering indictment of the UFO Project. Condon drew most of the organization's ire, with the organization accusing him of not conducting field investigations, ridiculing witnesses, focusing on "kook cases," and neglecting credible ones.[131] UFO periodicals followed suit, awarding the study a failing grade and seeing the scandal surrounding it as confirmation of an Air Force conspiracy of deception.

Newspaper coverage was generally non-committal, summarizing the findings, while also mentioning the controversy surrounding the project. Op-eds and letters to the editor were another matter. Many praised the work, and some turned a critical eye on organizations like NICAP. "Leave the Keyhoes to the boob-tube, the paperback shelves, and the barbershop reading racks," one writer declared, "and keep them out of the science classroom."[132] Others took away lessons that ran contrary to Condon's findings. One paper in upstate New York applauded the UFO Project for finally bringing science to bear on the subject and added, "Certainly, whatever one's reaction to the report just made public, it could be agreed that further claimed sightings ought to be investigated."[133]

Since the study could not explain some cases and phenomena, a number of observers were left with nagging doubts about its legitimacy. The fact that much remained unresolved, as one editorial argued, indicated there was no "reason to drop systematic study of the UFOs."[134] Many conveyed their annoyance with the report's inconclusiveness and wondered aloud how the project could be considered anything other than a waste of taxpayer dollars.[135] The most common opinion on all sides was that the report was unlikely to persuade true believers to abandon their faith in extraterrestrial visitors and conspiracy theories.

Academics appear to have largely satisfied themselves with reading press coverage of the report's conclusion. Many of Condon's own colleagues told him they had not read the book, and it appears to have gotten only a few reviews in academic journals. In his review for the *Bulletin of the Atomic Scientists* in April 1969, Allen Hynek found the study to have many open-ended "puzzlers" that defied conventional explanation. Condon, in his mind, "grossly underestimated the scope and nature of the problem he was undertaking."[136] NASA's Institute for Space Studies invited James McDonald to review the report in its journal *Icarus*. Unsurprisingly, he criticized the work on multiple fronts: key witnesses were never interviewed; it analyzed only a small fraction of reports; it focused on trivial cases and one-third of the cases examined remained unexplained. Reviewing the report in the same volume, however, astrophysicist Hong-Yee Chiu found "the study procedure very thorough and without any bias." He declared the entire project demonstrated "UFOs cannot be regarded as scientific phenomena. More properly, ufology should be regarded as a pseudo-science."[137]

Edward Condon mostly avoided publicly speaking about the UFO Project. In May 1969, however, he gave a joke-filled lecture at the University of California at Irvine on the subject, a talk titled "UFO's I Have Loved and Lost" that became the basis for an article he published later that year.[138] In it, Condon justified the study's findings, but conceded that future researchers might arrive at a different answer using different methods. He went on to draw comparisons between ufology and astrology and lamented the state of science education in America. He ended:

> In conclusion, let me say that where corruption of children's minds is at stake, I do not believe in freedom of the press or freedom of speech. In my view, publishers who publish or teachers who teach any of the pseudo-sciences as established truth should, on being found guilty, be publicly horsewhipped, and forever banned from further activity in these usually honorable professions. Truth and children's minds are too precious for us to allow them to be abused by charlatans.[139]

DEBATING THE SCIENCE

It was clear that having studied the phenomenon and written an extensive final report, Condon believed the matter of UFOs was settled: unidentified flying objects simply were not worth scientists' time and energy. This is no more apparent than in his reaction to a plan to hold a symposium on UFOs at the annual meeting of the American Association for the Advancement of Science in Boston in December 1969. Carl Sagan had tried to organize such a panel the previous year, but it was thought best to wait until after the Committee's findings were public. In the summer of 1969, Sagan took up the idea again, with the endorsement of the chairman of the board of AAAS, Walter Orr Roberts.

Sagan and his co-organizer Thornton Page envisioned a symposium that would bring together in one place scientists with experience and interest in UFOs. This included former members of the Colorado Project, those involved in the search for extraterrestrial intelligence, along with Allen Hynek, James McDonald, and Donald Menzel. The organizers were especially keen on Condon's participation and assured him the event would be sober and free of vitriolic exchanges. Condon gave them an emphatic no.

Going further, Condon appealed to Roberts, Sagan, and Page to cancel the event. It was his conviction, he said, that "only harm can come from what you fellows are doing. . . . I know that you intend no harm, just as the AEC [Atomic Energy Commission] intends no harm from its tests, just as we are in Viet Nam from the noblest of motives."[140] By AAAS giving a forum to "the UFO nonsense," he wrote Roberts in September, "[t]he ignorant will be misled. The intelligent will think the AAAS is crazy."[141] Roberts replied that Hynek and McDonald were not "kooks" and that he should let "time and the slow, inexorable wisdom of the marketplace" sort the two out.[142] But Condon wouldn't back down. Hynek and McDonald, he insisted, were neither sober-minded nor virtuous, and the press coverage the symposium would receive would invariably be drawn to the distortions of the two renegades.[143]

Sagan and Page refused to give in. Getting nowhere with the symposium organizers, Condon tried to scuttle the forum by mobilizing colleagues in AAAS to write Roberts in protest and threaten to boycott the event. He even asked Vice President Spiro Agnew for his support. In the end, the symposium took place as scheduled. Though it resolved nothing, it was the first instance in which most of the prominent American scientists researching UFOs at the time met in person to discuss and debate the status of unidentified flying objects.[144]

WHAT WENT WRONG?

Was the University of Colorado UFO study a failure? In the more than fifty years since publication of its final report, it has largely been forgotten by mainstream media. In ufology circles, however, the Condon Committee is an integral part of UFO lore. There its story is often told as a tale of clashing personalities and institutional deceit. McDonald, Saunders, and Hynek are typically cast as heroic figures fighting for a noble cause, Condon, Low, and the Air Force as plotters bent on undermining any genuine study of unidentified flying objects.

This portrait of events is not altogether wrong, but it is not the full picture. Without question, McDonald, Saunders, and Hynek were sincere, and Condon seemed unprepared to manage the project with the attention to detail and diplomacy required. It remains unclear—though it seems unlikely—whether he and Low deliberately tried to scuttle the enterprise, but Condon certainly had a habit of tuning out those whose views he considered frivolous. On the other hand, McDonald and Saunders were not always acting in good faith.

What gets lost in the retellings of the Condon Committee story is the political and cultural climate of 1960s America. These events took place at a time still marked by Cold War concerns and heavy investment in space travel, but it was also a period of widespread protests over government secrecy, military intervention, and civil and human rights abuses.

The growing distrust of authority, especially among young people, also was being directed at universities and science. For decades, academic scientists had insisted the value of their work rested in its cool neutrality, in its detachment from public opinion and popular prejudices. In those instances when they directly engaged in public outreach, scientists tended to understand their task as filling in a presumed knowledge deficit: they enlightened with reason and facts, the public consumed with respect and appreciation. When in the years 1966–1967—the very moment the Colorado study got underway—college activists began adopting more radical stances, criticizing universities for being sell-outs and shouting down professors and speakers who to them represented the status quo, veteran liberal educators like Edward Condon often became defensive. The lofty vision of higher learning, science, and expertise they had helped bring to life to combat chauvinism and authoritarianism itself was being challenged.[145]

The tumult surrounding the work of the Condon Committee wasn't simply about the fighting between believers and skeptics regarding the reality of unidentified flying saucers. It also revealed the extent to which popular interest in UFOs was challenging scientists to reconsider their responsibilities to the public in general and the media in particular.

Take Edward Condon, a scientist who had earned a reputation as being a strong advocate for transparency and civilian control when it came to research involving the vital national interest. And yet, within days of the UFO Project beginning its work, he demanded full control over all communications with the press. Even when speaking to journalists, he offered few details about the project and often peppered his comments with derisive jokes about witnesses. How did it come to this?

For one thing, as Condon himself admitted, he was unprepared for the level of interest in UFOs. But for another, he stuck to a fairly traditional view of science: science was something that required slow, uninterrupted deliberation about subjects experts deemed important and whose authoritative findings could then be passed on to the public. The media was there to disseminate information; otherwise, it mostly got in the way. Science, after all, needed to be protected from intrusions. And when scientists settled a question, it should stand on its own. Having reached a decisive conclusion about UFOs, Condon saw no need to belabor the point afterward. He turned his back on openness not so much because he had changed his mind, but rather because the public had started to change its mind.

Interestingly enough, James McDonald seemed to share a similar view of science. In many ways, McDonald was more effective than Condon in making use of the press, largely out of necessity since his views were excluded from mainstream scientific discussion. Like Condon, he too expressed disdain for the media's coverage of UFOs, which he found to be plagued by ridicule and sensationalism.[146] He believed that once it became possible to set up an organization of professional scientists to study UFOs, it would unavoidably mean that lay organizations like NICAP would "rapidly diminish" and be marginalized.[147]

Thus, like the Air Force before them, the scientists recruited to study UFOs had a public relations problem they were ill-equipped to address. Of all those connected to the UFO Project, it was Carl Sagan who seemed to best recognize this. If the preoccupation with UFOs was but an example of a broader "drift away from science" at the time, he wrote Condon in September 1969, it was "a misunderstanding of these attitudes to talk about 'dignifying it by discussing it.'" Instead, scientists needed to engage these matters openly and directly. The answer, Sagan believed, lay not in avoiding conversation about and heaping scorn on UFOs, but in inspiring people, in communicating science's "power and beauty."[148]

AFTERMATH

The release of the Condon Committee's final report marked the beginning of the end for many involved in the UFO saga. In December 1969, the Air Force announced the closure of Project Blue Book, saying it could no longer be justified "either on the ground of national security or in the interest of science."[149] That same month, NICAP, riddled with financial problems and a dwindling membership, dismissed Donald Keyhoe as its chief. The organization never again enjoyed the public standing it had had during the sixties and eventually disbanded in 1980.

James McDonald continued investigating UFOs on his own. He also took on a new cause, warning the Department of Transportation in 1970 of the harmful effects supersonic transport planes would have on the ozone.[150] But already by then, friends were noting a change in the physicist's disposition, and he confessed to some that his frequent travel for fieldwork and talks about UFOs were taking a toll on his marriage. In March 1971, his wife Betsy told him she had met someone else, and she asked McDonald for a divorce. Two weeks later, he took a handgun and shot himself in the head. The bullet missed his brain, instead hitting the optic nerve. He was alive but blind. Over the coming months, McDonald began to recover and even returned to work but was still severely depressed. He openly shared with friends that he was again planning to kill himself. On June 12, 1971, McDonald bought a handgun, took a taxi to the desert, and did just that. While intimates confirm that his death was the result of suicide, over the years conspiracy-minded UFO enthusiasts have speculated that authorities had him silenced.[151]

For others, the end of Project Bluebook marked the start of new careers in the public limelight. Allen Hynek and Carl Sagan became the new face of ufology in the United States and the great popularizer of space science, respectively.

Edward Condon died in 1974. Both privately and publicly, he expressed only regrets about his decision to run the UFO Project. "I'd say it was the biggest waste of time that I ever had in my life," he told an interviewer only a few months before his death. "I'm sorry I ever had anything to do with the government." He conceded he had taken the job unaware of what it would entail. "Perhaps if I'd understood it better I would have seen the futility of trying to do this, but I didn't, and I didn't realize at first the intensity and passion and fervor of the true believers, how much they were out to push it."[152]

Still, the years immediately following publication of the Colorado Study's final report appeared to vindicate Condon's judgment that there was nothing to the UFO phenomenon. "If you think that UFO's are more academically alive than ever, again you are on the wrong track," Donald Menzel corrected a political science graduate student writing a dissertation on James McDonald's campaign. "There are a few individuals who would like to see this done: the NICAPs, the APROs, and Hynek. But I think the subject is typically dead. I can tell from my own correspondence."[153] Two years after Condon Committee had completed its work, Robert Low wrote his old friend Ed Condon, "The interesting thing to me is that I see absolutely nothing about UFOs in the daily newspapers, and I have even noted a marked decline in UFO jokes in the New Yorker and other magazines. The whole thing seems to be dead as a doornail."[154]

As the 1970s and 1980s would show, nothing could have been further from the truth.

7

Renaissance

"Whatever happened to flying saucers?" science fiction writer Arthur C. Clarke wryly asked in *The Saturday Evening Post* in the summer of 1971.[1] The author of *2001: A Space Odyssey* found himself reflecting on "this peculiar episode in our recent history," on "the rise and fall of the UFO's." Clarke was blunt. "Flying Saucers are dead" and "the hysterical credulity of the late 40s" a thing of the past. What killed them, he declared, was science. The extensive research conducted during the International Geophysical Year (1957–1958), along with the newfangled missile warning systems, the Mariner space probe, and radio astronomy had turned up no ships from outer space and no little green men. Astronomers were beginning to think intelligent life on other worlds was likely, but, as Clarke put it, we would inevitably have to "wait patiently" for answers "rather than get involved in any more of the half- and wholly-baked speculations which, for the last fifteen years, have hindered the serious scientific approach to the most important question that man can ask of the Universe."

At the time, there appeared to be ample evidence supporting Clarke's announcement of the death of the flying saucer rage. Within two or three years of the release of the Condon Committee's final report in 1969, the UFO landscape had changed considerably, especially in the United States. Project Blue Book was shut down. The voice of James McDonald was silent. Reported sightings declined, and public interest in the topic faded. Membership in the UFO group NICAP dipped to less than a third of what it had been in 1966, and the organization eventually folded in 1980. At the same time, NICAP's rival APRO found its own influence undercut when one of its regional officers, Walter Andrus Jr., left to set up a competing association called the Midwest UFO Network or MUFON (soon renamed the Mutual UFO Network). Andrus poached APRO members and consultants for the new group, and as a result he and an embittered Coral Lorenzen remained estranged from one another well into the 1980s.

The chill felt in UFO circles wasn't only the result of the cold water scientists had thrown on civilian UFO research. Social and economic changes also exposed some of the field's chronic vulnerabilities, as challenges facing ufology's international flagship periodical made clear. In late 1971 and early 1972, *Flying Saucer Review* found itself in the uncomfortable position of apologizing to its subscribers: it was being plagued by delays and was unable to keep to its publishing schedule. Like almost every UFO news bulletin, *FSR* had always suffered from a lack of sufficient funding, leaving its editors to make up the costs out of their own pockets. Staff illnesses and a move of offices compounded the problem, further aggravated by a postal worker strike halting mail deliveries and then a miners' strike leading to power cuts. One of the magazine's consultants explained its plight, barely concealing his resentment:

> If our cause was dumb animals, the Red Cross, battered babies, or the rehabilitation of criminals, we would only have to crook a finger to have secretaries and clerical assistants queueing up on the doorstep. But our cause is not a favoured charity, or one with which the ordinary man can identify himself: it is a mysterious cause, a puzzling cause, and a challenging cause. . . . So, dear subscribers, be patient with us. We could, of course, reduce our costs, and perhaps pay one assistant, by giving you an inferior journal mimeographed on lavatory paper, and filled with meaningless saucer-droppings. But we won't allow that.[2]

A few years earlier, the editors of the *Merseyside UFO Bulletin* in England had taken the opportunity of their last issue of 1969 to look back on the 1960s and predict what the new decade might hold for ufology.[3] "Ufology is a field that is over-endowed with prophets," a rather jaded John Rimmer observed. "Every year since the concept of the UFO was evolved has been heralded as the year the Great Revelation was going to take place, according to one writer or another." Looking ahead, he foresaw much of the same. "I can reveal that the Great Revelation will not take place in the seventies." There would continue to be, he said, stories about men in black, reports of local sightings, tabloid announcements of little men being spotted, the usual array of "crackpots and cranks," and rancor between factions. Even if the seventies were unlikely to bring any answers, "more new and unexpected elements will be introduced into, and emerge from, the whole

UFO problem, rendering it not only more complex, but considerably more interesting."

Rimmer proved to be prescient. To many veterans of the UFO scene the future may well have looked bleak around 1970. But over the next twenty years, a medley of new encounters, influences, voices, and speculations helped interest in unidentified flying objects and alien contact reach new heights and ushered in a veritable renaissance in ufology.

THE UFO WAVE OF 1973

Toward the end of October 1973, the *New York Times* science reporter Walter Sullivan informed readers of a remarkable turn of events. "Rarely, if ever, since Kenneth Arnold reported in 1947 seeing what came to be known as 'flying saucers' during a flight near Mount Rainier in Washington State," he wrote, "have there been such widespread reports of unidentified flying objects or UFO's, as in recent days."[4] While the Federal Aviation Administration declared it had not seen any uptick in reports from airline pilots, sightings by members of the general population were markedly on the rise.

With Project Blue Book shut down, local journalists and newspapers took on a key investigative role.[5] They often caught wind of individual sightings, interviewed witnesses, and publicized incidents. There appears to have been little, if any, coordination to the press coverage, and reporters seemed to rarely consult with UFO organizations. That said, there were some general trends in the accounts being recorded. Reports were concentrated in the southeastern part of the United States, with the state of Georgia serving as a hub. Although some witnesses could describe catching a glimpse of an actual craft, most reported spotting either bright lights or a glowing object of some kind in the night sky.

Ufologists and UFO groups were also keeping tabs on reports as they came in. Relying on data gathered by the new MUFON organization and the French periodical *Lumières dans la nuit*, Jacques Vallee concluded that the upsurge in sightings was part of a broader wave.[6] What began as a flap in the United States, he argued, reached its peak in September and October, but then moved on to Western Europe about two months later. Interestingly, he observed, the rise in sightings seemed to correlate with the ever-closer approach of the planet Mars to earth.

A year later, UFO researcher J. Bernard Delair confirmed that the wave had been global in scope.[7] Delair turned to UFO bulletins, magazines, books, and organizations from North and South America, Western Europe, Great

Britain, and South Africa to chronicle a total of 1,196 sightings throughout 1973, though he suspected there had been many thousands more. The descriptions of witnesses in other countries were like those that had come out of the United States: an orange sphere sighted over Sint Andries in Belgium, a luminous object spotted in Puerto Rico, a circular object seen in the skies over Tres Arroyos in Argentina, an "undescribed aerial object of unusual character" witnessed in Wellington, New Zealand.

Delair had few conclusions to offer, but he highlighted what appeared to be an ominous trend: an "enormous number" of reports of UFO landings and "the great increase in low level flights." In addition, witnesses had reported seeing "ufonauts" taking an interest in plants and animals. UFOs and their occupants, it seemed, were getting closer.

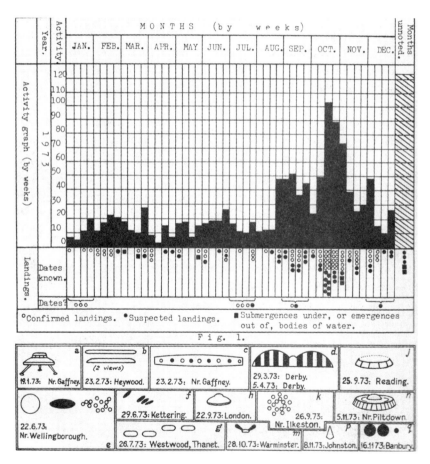

Fig. 7.1 J. B. Delair's overview of the global UFO wave of 1973. At the bottom are depictions of some of the shapes and formations of the UFOs spotted. Contact International (UK).

A year before this great wave, longstanding flying saucer debunker turned UFO exponent Allen Hynek provided a language for talking about these kinds of brushes with unidentified flying objects. In 1972, he published his first book, *The UFO Experience: A Scientific Inquiry*. In it, Hynek placed the experiences of observers at the center of investigation, remarking that in all his years talking to eyewitnesses "invariably I have had the feeling that I was talking to someone who was describing a *real event*."[8] Besides sightings of lights or vaguely disk-like objects, he pointed out, witnesses described having encounters that could be grouped into three categories. There were close encounters of the first kind in which an individual sees a UFO at close range. Then there were close encounters of the second kind involving a close-range observation leaving physical traces like scorched vegetation. Finally, there were close encounters of the third kind, where witnesses report seeing or interacting with the occupants of a UFO.

It would take time before Hynek's vocabulary would take root in ufology and popular culture. But when the astronomer founded the Center for UFO Studies (CUFOS) in 1973, the organization made clear that it would be taking close encounters seriously. In 1974, CUFOS published *1973— Year of the Humanoids*. Written by veteran ufologist David Webb, the study documented seventy encounters with humanoids recorded from August to December 1973.[9]

Like Delair, Webb used details gleaned from UFO periodicals and local newspaper articles as well as information passed on to him by fellow ufologists to gather specifics about the bizarre experiences. Some witnesses claimed to have communicated with the entities they happened upon, while many others described seeing tall, hairy creatures like Bigfoot. And there were stories of beings that flew, ones wearing silver-colored suits, others acting like robots, and still other seeming to collect samples. All told, Webb concluded, 1973 saw the largest number of cases of humanoid encounters since France in 1953.

By far, the close encounter that garnered the most media attention involved two shipyard workers in Pascagoula, Mississippi: Charles Hickson, said to be in his forties, and eighteen-year-old Calvin Parker. The two first reported the incident to authorities, then gave their first extensive interview about it to the *Mississippi Press Daily* a week later. Parker remained mostly silent during this first lengthy public conversation about their encounter, so Hickson was left to provide the details.

As Hickson told it, the two men were out fishing on the night of October 11, 1973, when Hickson heard a "zipping noise."[10] He turned around and saw a craft with bright lights hovering above the ground. Three eyeless creatures emerged from the vessel, with one making a buzzing sound. "The creatures were pale, ghost-like, about five feet high," Hickson recalled. "They were sort of light flesh-colored, or more pale gray, with crab-like claws for hands and rounded feet. . . . After I have thought about it, I believe they were more like robots."

The entities approached the men and lifted them into the craft. Parker passed out, while Hickson found himself unable to move anything but his eyes. Once aboard, Hickson said, he was taken to a room where something like a big eye painlessly moved back and forth over his body. Then the creatures carried the two men back to where they had been. "I would like to emphasize that they don't mean us any harm," Hickson told reporters. "I have always said there almost had to be some life elsewhere. Now I am a firm believer."[11]

The two quickly enjoyed some small measure of celebrity. APRO consultant James Harder arrived on the scene to try to hypnotize the men, though he was only partially successful. Allen Hynek came as well and found their testimony compelling, especially after it was divulged that a secret police tape recording of Hickson and Parker revealed the men did not deviate from their stories even in private.[12] A few months later, Hickson and Parker appeared on daytime television on the popular *Mike Douglas Show*.

Parker mostly kept a low profile until publishing two books in 2018 and 2019. Hickson, on the other hand, went on to claim the following year that he was receiving alien communications in his head and that he encountered the spaceship once again in May 1974.

WAVES AND THE MEDIA

The UFO wave of 1973 was hardly the first, nor would it be the last, but it proved especially pivotal in the history of the UFO phenomenon.[13] Coming as it did after years in which it appeared that interest in unidentified flying object was precariously waning, it injected new life into the topic and buoyed morale within the UFO scene.

Accounting for waves has proven to be much more difficult than tracking their development. One common notion is that prominent press coverage about unidentified flying objects triggers sightings. The historical record to support this is ambiguous at best, however. The July 1952 flap over Washington, DC, for example, was preceded by the appearance of *Life*'s article "Have We Visitors from Outer Space?" and a Donald Menzel piece in *Look*. But Menzel's essay was a dismissive debunking of the phenomenon, while the popular feature in *Life* was published a full fifteen weeks before the first reports came in from the District of Columbia.[14]

Another argument points to films playing a key role. Moviemakers embraced the UFO phenomenon in the early fifties and never looked back. Interestingly though, the content of films has not always matched that of reported sightings. Movies like *The War of the Worlds* (1953), *Invasion of the Body Snatchers* (1956), *The Mysterians* (1957), *The Blob* (1958), *Prince of Space* (1959), and *Day of the Triffids* (1962) portrayed extraterrestrials as menacing invaders at a time when contactees were describing them as welcoming benefactors. Hollywood films during the fifties and sixties instead took their cues from sci-fi and pulp literature. It was only in the late-1970s—starting with *The UFO Incident* in 1975—that witness reports of UFOs and extraterrestrial contact began to consistently have a direct impact on movie content in films such as *Close Encounters of the Third Kind* (1977), *Hangar 18* (1980), *Communion* (1989), *Intruders* (1992), and *Fire in the Sky* (1993).[15]

By the same merit, the evidence supporting the notion that popular films trigger surges in sightings is not compelling. No major UFO movies preceded the flurry of reports in 1952 and 1973. Even Steven Spielberg's *Close Encounters* did not generate a wave of new sightings in the United States but rather appears to have inspired more people to come forward to report old sightings they had witnessed.[16] Records of the British Ministry of Defence indicate that reported sightings actually declined following Spielberg's blockbuster *E.T. the Extraterrestrial* in 1982. And while reported sightings spiked in 1996, the year the film *Independence Day* was released, it was also the same year that the tv series *The X-Files* had reached its peak popularity.[17]

Researcher Martin Kottmeyer has noted that writers over the years have offered a range of other explanations for UFO flaps and waves, explanations that can be roughly divided into two groups.[18] Among those presuming the sightings were of actual extraterrestrial objects, arguments have raised the possibilities that such flaps represent schedules in alien reconnaissance, patterns in extraterrestrial tourism, or efforts to desensitize humans to alien contact. Others, focusing instead on social and psychological explanations, have related waves to a rise in public paranoia and mass hysteria, prominent public crises, the emergence of scientific innovations, and the news media's tendency to copycat popular stories.

Kottmeyer himself has echoed the commonly expressed hunch that "bad news generates ufos—good news or distractions from bad news about America seems to cause numbers to drop." 1973 seems to offer ample support for the claim, with its barrage of upsetting stories about the resignation of Vice President Spiro Agnew, the Watergate scandal, prominent airline crashes, American POWs returning from Vietnam, and brainwashing religious cults. As historian Andreas Killen has put it, "America in 1973 was a starkly altered place from the country of a decade earlier. Ten years of deeply unpopular war, civil unrest, assassination, and cultural transformation had produced a society that bore little resemblance to pre-Vietnam America."[19]

Yet it's fair to say that plenty of bad news makes headlines in any given year or on any given day. Linking flaps to some generic "bad news" seems destined to fall prey to confirmation bias. When trying to make sense of UFO waves, it's important to keep in mind that waves and flaps do not just happen; they are reported to happen. So, who is doing the reporting and to whom? What are people's sources of information?

Looking back at the American wave of 1973, the US Air Force had by then officially left the business of UFO investigation. Reports indicate that witnesses generally contacted local police or journalists. Local newspapers for their part received tips from either witnesses or local police departments. National news outlets appear to have taken their cues from the buzz generated by local news outlets. Some ufologists interviewed local witnesses as well, but most UFO groups, analysts, and magazines appear to have relied almost exclusively on local coverage—likely accessed via news clipping services—and reports from other UFO organizations, researchers, and publications. While some investigators did acknowledge that witness claims varied wildly in precision and credibility, most of those proclaiming that a wave had taken place offered no indication that they were differentiating between these assorted claims. Like the acronym "UFO," the term "wave" transformed a series of disparate phenomena into a uniform thing, evening out all sightings under one common rubric. Few but the most dedicated reporters and ufologists bothered to dig any deeper.

This is less an explanation of the 1973 wave than a cautionary reminder. The circulation of new information has always been crucial to sustaining interest in UFOs. Older cases may well have proved intriguing for some to pick over again and again, but enthusiasts have always looked to new incidents, developments, and stories to move discussion along. As James Moseley put it describing the UFO scene in early 1973, "(U)fology was still in the doldrums, with no dramatic new sightings or other developments to capture the public imagination and keep all but truly hard-core saucerers actively involved in The Field."[20] The wave changed that, reigniting public interest in saucers and boosting the ranks of the upstart organization MUFON.

GOVERNMENTS AND UFOS

The hubbub that year also revived the fixation on the disclosure of classified military information on UFOs.[21] Granted, it hardly accomplished this alone. Calls for greater government transparency were a part of the daily media diet of most Americans in the wake of the Watergate scandal (1972–1974) and the US Senate Church Committee's investigation of CIA abuses (1975). Among UFO enthusiasts, however, rumors swirled as individuals came forward to announce that sensational revelations were imminent, due to be revealed first in 1974, then in 1975, and then again in 1976. They never came. Still, all this breathed new life into claims of flying saucer crashes and covert retrievals, with veteran ufologist Leonard Stringfield airing a number of these stories beginning in 1977.

Such cloak-and-dagger stories were encouraged in part by the fact that the United States Air Force had officially abandoned Project Blue Book in 1969. For those prone to believing the claim that the US military knew more about the extraterrestrial origins of flying saucers than it was letting on, it seemed logical to assume that the UFO phenomena was being shrouded in greater secrecy than ever before. Closure only fueled the calls for disclosure.

While the United States left the business of investigating UFOs, several countries, including Great Britain, continued to keep their UFO desks up and running into the 1990s and 2000s. All of them, however, ran on a comparatively small budget and had few personnel dedicated solely to investigations.

Swedish Defense officials had collected sightings received from residents via mail or telephone since the 1950s, but by the seventies they concluded there was little of military value to the sightings and no evidence of alien visitation. In the mid-sixties, the Royal Australian Air Force (RAAF) acknowledged it had adopted an ad hoc approach to handling UFO reports. By and large, however, civilian interest in the subject was considered a public relations issue. Though the RAAF continued to investigate cases throughout the 1970s and 1980s, it increasingly restricted itself to those with national security implications and in 1993 announced it was no longer accepting or investigating sightings. In Spain, the Air Ministry first began requesting citizens report sightings to authorities in 1968, though these remained classified throughout the seventies. When Spanish military officials finally spoke publicly about UFOs in 1981, it was to say that they saw no reason to suspect that they were either manned or alien aircraft, and in the early 1990s they began to declassify and release their records. Subsequent research conducted by Vicente-Juan Ballester Olmos has revealed that Spanish civilians only sparingly looked to the air force to report sightings and that the high point for such reports were in 1978 and 1979.[22]

For the most part, government involvement in UFOs throughout the seventies and eighties appears to have been characterized by indifference peppered with sporadic interest. Italy serves as a good example.[23] During the 1960s, the Italian Air Force paid the subject little attention. What reports made their way to the intelligence service (SIOS) did so either directly through military and police channels or indirectly through news reports. Throughout most of the seventies, the Ministry of Defense seldomly looked into the matter—mostly those cases involving the military—and collected no statistics on UFOs. A wave of sightings in 1973–1974, however, did attract the attention of officials as well as the media, and some field investigations were conducted. The Italian carabinieri (the national gendarmerie) also were involved in collecting reports of sightings, but well into the 1980s this involved little more than taking down witness statements.

There were three notable exceptions during the seventies and eighties, countries whose governments seemed to signal a new willingness to earnestly investigate the UFO question. One was Brazil, where the military's improvised approach to the phenomenon was interrupted in 1969 when the Air Force created the Sistema de Investigação de Objetos Aéreos Não Identificados (Investigation System for Unidentified Aerial Objects or SIOANI).[24] SIOANI was unusual in that it focused on civilian sightings and conducted fieldwork investigations. The group assumed an agnostic position about unidentified flying objects and enlisted the assistance of specialists in a wide range of fields including astronomy, meteorology, sociology, and law. At the same time, it also opened up a dialogue with civilian UFO organizations in the country.

SIOANI was short-lived, shutting down in 1972. Officials closed it due to what they considered to be an inconsequential number of sightings. Archival records seem to bear this out. Despite two prominent cases of reported unusual aerial phenomena—one in 1977, the other in 1986—the number of reported sightings remained small in Brazil. From 1970 until 1976, authorities recorded less than ten sightings a year; and while those figures rose both in 1977 (85) and 1978 (63), after that the numbers remained mostly below ten until the end of the 1980s.

Another government that showed renewed interest in unidentified flying objects during this time was the Soviet Union.[25] Until the mid-1970s, communist party and state officials tolerated lectures by prominent ufologists before audiences in institutes, factories, and military units, but otherwise discouraged discussion about the subject in the media. Nevertheless, a growing number of reports began making their way to the USSR Academy of Sciences, which eventually appointed some researchers from its General Physics and Astronomy Division to collect and analyze the information being gathered.

Then, in the early morning of September 20, 1977, eyewitnesses in the northwestern city of Petrozavodsk saw what appeared to be a huge flare in the sky that pulsated shafts of light, moved toward the city, and spread above it in the shape of a massive "jellyfish." Witnessed by a broad cross-section of people—including police and airport and naval personnel—as well as observers in Finland, the phenomenon lasted around ten minutes. Newspapers and scientists afterward were inundated with queries from the general public.

The incident prompted military and civilian authorities to consider the idea of creating a government program dedicated to collecting and studying unusual aerial sightings. A state program for the study of "anomalous phenomena"—the term "UFO" wasn't used in official documents—in the Soviet Union began operation in 1978. Lasting until 1990, it was carried out jointly by the Ministry of Defense (focusing on reports from the armed services) and the Academy of Sciences (focusing on reports from research institutions). The program was exclusively centered on national security and the military implications of peculiar atmospheric and space events. Like other government UFO programs, findings were considered classified. The number of staff assigned to the work was small (four or five in both working groups), the budget was nominal, and little field-work was conducted. In the end, 90 percent of UFO reports were determined to be sightings of space rocket launches, balloons, and the testing of other aerospace technology. Not a single report of a UFO landing reached investigators during the project's existence.

The third state to take on the task of investigating UFO reports was France.[26] There, local gendarmes traditionally had handled sightings of unidentified flying objects. But starting in 1974, some French military officials began to recommend collecting and studying reports in a more organized fashion. In 1977, the French government requested that its National Center for Space Research (CNES) establish a dedicated group, and in May it founded the Unidentified Aerospace Phenomena Research Group (Group d'Etudes des Phénomènes Aérospatiaux Non-ldentifiés) or GEPAN.

The man asked to head the program was Claude Poher, a Ph.D. in astrophysics and a former pilot who directed the systems and projects division of CNES. Poher had become interested in unidentified flying saucers several years earlier, after meeting Allen Hynek in 1969. Soon he began wading through the Condon Committee Report and then began conducting his own private statistical analysis of UFOs in 1973, eventually collaborating with Jacques Vallee and Hynek's CUFOS organization.[27]

Poher envisioned GEPAN as a cooperative, interdisciplinary venture, with state stakeholders—the Air Force, gendarmerie, civil aviation, and national meteorological services—and expert researchers working together. A twelve-member scientific council was set up to which GEPAN would report at least once a year. Poher attempted to bring private ufologists on board as well, organizing a meeting of civilian investigators from more than forty UFO groups in September 1978. The initiative failed due to rancor between skeptical and conspiracy-minded investigators.

When Poher was told that GEPAN would not publish his ideas about the reality of the UFO phenomenon, he suddenly quit at the end of 1978. He was replaced by engineer Alain Esterle, who went on to conduct experiments on suspected propulsion systems in UFOs. By the time Esterle left his job and was replaced by his deputy in 1983, GEPAN consisted of little more than a director and a secretary. In 1988, the office was restructured and given a new name, the Atmospheric Re-entry Phenomena Expertise Service or SEPRA, tasked with monitoring objects entering earth's atmosphere over France.[28]

Inheriting some four hundred UFO reports from the French gendarmerie, GEPAN from the start took seriously the prospect of the extraterrestrial origins of unidentified flying objects. Already in its first year of existence, the office focused on eleven sightings "of high credibility and high strangeness" from the years 1966–1977 and found that all except one involved a physical object that couldn't be explained away as a natural phenomenon or man-made technology. The phenomenon was, in the team's estimation, a "flying machine . . . whose mode of sustenance and propulsion are beyond our knowledge."[29] In 2007, however, skeptical researchers looked over records from GEPAN and determined that its studies had been replete with shortcomings: commonsense explanations were arbitrarily ruled out; clear cases of mistaken identity by witnesses were misattributed; and there were consistent delays in the examination of physical evidence and witnesses, along with a lack of long-term follow-up.[30]

UFOLOGY IN ASIA

Where government-sponsored UFO programs struggled to find resources and respectability, civilian enthusiasts proved ready to fill the void. The 1970s and 1980s experienced a boom in the rise and spread of UFO groups and periodicals worldwide. As they had done in the United States in the fifties, those with a serious interest in the mystery of the flying saucers took it upon themselves to keep the topic alive and investigate cases. New UFO groups and publications popped up in Australia, Canada, Colombia,

Denmark, Mexico, the Netherlands, New Zealand, Peru, Turkey, Uruguay, and Yugoslavia, among other places.

But the newest front in the campaign to draw attention to the UFO phenomenon was in Asia. Japan led the way. Already in 1957, the self-professed contactee Yusuke Matsumura founded the Cosmic Brotherhood Association, a group spreading the message of an imminent global cataclysm and possible escape through the aid of benevolent extraterrestrials. Over time, the group's focus shifted to speculations about ancient astronauts and the construction of UFO stations in Japan, publishing several periodicals over the course of the 1960s.[31] Other groups soon followed, including the Japan UFO Research Association in Kobe and the Japanese Space Phenomena Society, at the same time that the 1970s saw the appearance of new publications like *UFO Information* and *UFOs & Space*.

Japan proved to be especially fertile ground for some of the more esoteric strains of ufology. The bulletin *UFO Contactee*, for example, first appeared in 1985. Edited and published by Hachiro Kubota, it was envisioned as an extension of George Adamski's Get Acquainted Program in Japan. Kubota himself had launched the program back in 1961 and had taken on the job of translating all of Adamski's works into Japanese. By the mid-eighties, the Get Acquainted Program was still operating in the country, claiming 18 local branches with 1,000 members and a newsletter circulation up to 2,500. At its headquarters in Tokyo, it held monthly meetings in which an average of seventy students explored Adamski's philosophy. Every summer, an organized group tour took interested members to visit mysterious ruins in places like Egypt, Israel, Mexico, and South America.[32]

The groups emerging in Asia at the time took their cues from American and European ufologists, while also turning their gaze toward developments in the region. In 1979, Ananda Sirisena and others began publishing the newsletter *The Sri Lanka U.F.O. Register*, later changing its name to *Kalpanava*, meaning contemplation or deep in thought in Sinhala. Sirisena was committed and attended the First London International Congress on UFOs in August 1979, interviewing prominent British ufologists during the visit. As it reported on sightings from the Philippines, India, and elsewhere, *Kalpanava* was increasingly drawn to the more esoteric strains of ufology and berated mainstream scientists for their narrow-mindedness, insisting "they must either broaden their horizons considerably or they must start removing the boundaries placed by scientists in the past and search beyond these arbitrarily placed barriers."[33]

Meanwhile in Kuantan, Pahang in Malaysia, Ahmad Jamaludin began publishing the *Malaysian UFO Bulletin* twice a year for anyone interested in "UFO reports from Malaysia and the region of Southeast Asia." His reporting included sightings from India, Indonesia, Thailand, Madagascar, Nepal, and Japan as well as an apparent wave in the Philippines that took place in April and May of 1979.[34] Admittedly, the number of cases annually reported in Malaysia was small (only four in 1981), but Jamaludin—who compiled a summary of UFO and strange entity encounters in the country between 1950 and 1980—did note the unusual fact that in "all the Malaysian entity cases," the beings "came in a standard size of 6 inches or less."[35] Despite the fact that many of the witnesses involved were schoolchildren, he was inclined to believe in the existence of such diminutive creatures. "Based on the teaching of Islam, there seem (sic) to be no other form of life similar to humans in this physical universe. If parallel universes do exist, then it is teeming with intelligent life known as Jinn. It is our conclusion that the Jinn and the UFO entities are the same."[36]

By far, however, the biggest newcomer on the scene was China.[37] For decades, news about flying saucers and alien encounters in the Americas and Europe had never reached the Chinese reading public. But public discussion of the subject surfaced starting in 1978 and 1979, when professor of meteorology Weng Shida published two critical articles about unidentified flying objects. Following in the footsteps of Donald Menzel, Shida argued that UFOs were nothing more than man-made objects and atmospheric phenomena, and he deemed reports of flying saucers "fairy tales" presented to a gullible public. In September 1979, science editor at Chinese central radio Zhou Xingyian published a response entitled "Do UFOs Exist?" in which he made the case that witnesses were too numerous and believable to be ignored. Over the next couple of years, editors of a number of prominent scientific and educational series published articles sympathetically exploring the topic. In short order, UFO investigators, groups, and publications began to pop up throughout the country.

Like elsewhere in Asia, the first Chinese ufologists were introduced to the study of unidentified flying objects through the works of American and European writers. Their accounts of encounters from across the world raised an obvious question. Since UFOs demonstrated no regard for national boundaries, shouldn't a country the size of China have visitors from outer space too? It soon became apparent that this was the case, and examining such instances became a principal task for early civilian investigators.

The first UFO group of its kind was the China UFO Research Organization (CURO), founded in May 1979 and headquartered in Wuhan. Within four years, CURO had five hundred followers and thirty regional chapters, three of which were publishing their own newsletters. Another group, the Chinese Organization for Research on Natural Mysteries, began operations soon after in Peking. Though it had few members, it published its own magazine

(*Natural Mysteries*) covering UFOs, humanoid sightings, and extrasensory phenomena, while its editors included prominent figures like science fiction author Jin Tao, English-speaking journalist Huang Tianxiang, and the science editor for central radio Zhou Xingyian.

Achieving something of an international reputation was the UFO Research Group whose work focused on publishing *The Journal of UFO Research* beginning in 1981. The brainchild of Shi Bo and Zhu Fuzheng in Peking and Paul Dong in Oakland, California, the forty-eight-page bimonthly featured articles on unidentified flying objects over China and elsewhere, aerospace, cosmogony, evolution, ancient Chinese civilizations, psychic powers, and religion, all of which were seen as related phenomena. By 1983, it claimed a circulation of over three hundred thousand, making it easily the most widely distributed UFO journal in the world.[38]

1983 also saw publication of the first book by a Chinese ufologist, Paul Dong's *Questions and Answers on UFOs*.[39] In it, Dong discussed findings into investigations on some three thousand Chinese cases, most from the 1970s and early 1980s. Incidents were generally similar to those in the West—there was the usual array of sightings by pilots, interference with electrical power, and radar tracings—but there were a few peculiarities. For one, reports of close encounters and UFO landings were comparably rare. That said, the Gobi Desert in the north appeared to be a site favored by UFOs, with around three hundred sightings made there alone. Some leading some Chinese ufologists therefore believed "that the Gobi Desert may possibly be one of the places on Earth where bases have been established by the UFOs."[40]

A NEW GENERATION IN EUROPE

The rise of ufology across Asia starting in the 1970s reflected a broader trend of growth in UFO groups and publications across the world, most apparent in Europe. There a new cohort of budding ufologists began seeing a need to open up the conversation about flying saucers, which they increasingly found stale.

Already on New Year's Day 1970, John Rimmer published a piece in the *Merseyside UFO Bulletin* in which he criticized ufology for relying too heavily on the extraterrestrial hypothesis (ETH) about the origins of UFOs.[41] He outlined instead three sets of theories—physical craft, natural phenomena, and subjective phenomena—that could also be considered. These ranged from the wild (beings from within a doughnut-shaped earth) to the Menzelian (normal atmospheric changes). "It is vital that the

Fig. 7.2 The first issue of the *Journal of UFO Research*, 1981. AFU.

alternative explanations should be given adequate consideration," Rimmer insisted. "The ETH must not be considered as the only explanation, with the assumption that if it is not the UFO subject then becomes something else of less intrinsic interest."

Other agreed. Over the course of the seventies and eighties, fresh voices emerged, bringing variety and a new vitality to the UFO scene. In Spain, for instance, UFO research centers opened up across the country. In Valencia the focus was on case and statistical analysis; centers in the north were drawn to parapsychology, esotericism, and Forteana; and near Seville there were specialists working on field interviews with witnesses. In 1970,

Barcelona's Centre d'Estudis Interplanetaris (Center for Interplanetary Studies) began publishing *Stendek*, a periodical with a decidedly scientific orientation. All the while, popular interest grew. The number of Spanish books published on the subject rose from seventeen during the years 1970–1974 to seventy-four between 1975 and 1980. At the same time, the topic became prominent in film, radio, and television, most notably in the late seventies and early eighties with the live evening radio show *Medianoche*, which took calls from listeners about their sightings.[42]

Throughout Europe and elsewhere, young people fueled the revival. Ufologists at the time estimated that anywhere between one-half to a quarter of all ufozines were being published by someone under the age of twenty.[43] As Swedish ufologist Håkan Blomqvist points out, "The UFO movement during the 1970s was certainly very much a teenage underground movement. In Sweden, hundreds of young people became involved in UFO-Sweden, often starting their own local groups. It was the Golden Era of UFO societies."[44]

Blomqvist lived the experience himself.[45] Like so many others, his interest in UFOs began when he was a child. Growing up in the sixties in Södertälje, he was fascinated by the stars and moon, read avidly about astronomy, and spent nights peering through his small telescope. He actively followed the manned spaceflights of the time, collecting press clippings and tape-recording radio and tv coverage. At the same time, his mother—whom he describes as a "spiritual seeker"—introduced the young Håkan to her personal library of books on spiritualism, theosophy, and ancient mysteries as well as translations of the works by contactees like George Adamski and Daniel Fry. He and his mother would spend evenings at the kitchen table talking about the mysteries of life and the universe.

As a teenager, Blomqvist met Kjell Jonsson, whom he introduced to UFO literature in early 1970. The two soon immersed themselves in the study of the "UFO enigma." They contacted UFO groups throughout Sweden and subscribed to UFO periodicals (including *Flying Saucer Review*) and wrote their editors. In November, the boys were invited to Stockholm to meet with Swedish contactee Sten Lindgren, who encouraged them to set up their own local UFO group and affiliate it with the larger organization UFO-Sweden.

In late November, Blomqvist and Jonsson founded UFO-Södertälje. Within a few months, they were contacting local newspapers, writing letters to the editor, and even had an UFO exhibit featured at the municipal library. As others joined them, the circle rented a small basement for their meetings and conducted skywatch outings in hopes of catching sight of a UFO. By year's end, UFO-Södertälje had sixteen members. Over the course

Fig. 7.3 Håkan Blomqvist in January 1971. Courtesy of Håkan Blomqvist.

of 1972, membership grew to fifty and the group began to conduct field investigations, invite speakers, and meet with other ufologists. Then, in 1973, Anders Liljegren joined Blomqvist and Jonsson in establishing the Arbetsgruppen för ufologi (Working Team for Ufology or AFU), publishing a newsletter and creating lending library for investigators. By 1980, as ufologists began donating books and magazines to the library and their international contacts grew, the group changed its name to the Archives for UFO Research and moved its operation to Norrköping.[46]

As he reflects on his half-century involvement in ufology, Blomqvist points out that the work brought many rewards. "The UFO movement has been homebase for me. Almost all my close friends I have found in the movement," he notes. "For me as for many colleagues, UFO research hasn't been only a purely scientific problem but also involved a deeper spiritual quest. Trying to understand the mystery of our existence on this strange planet and the mystery of our consciousness."

From the start, Blomqvist had been drawn to the esoteric branches of the UFO movement. Others came to it from a decidedly different perspective. In West Germany around the same time, two teenage boys from Mannheim working in a local department store discovered they shared a mutual interest in unidentified flying objects.[47] Werner Walter and Hansjürgen Köhler both had had their own UFO experiences and had been collecting UFO literature independently. In November 1973, they decided to found their own UFO group. Familiar with esotericist Karl Veit's national association DUIST, they successfully applied to DUIST to organize a local chapter. Over time, however, Walter and Köhler became increasingly disenchanted with the organization, particularly with its uncritical acceptance of the stories of the contactees. Over several years, Walter wrote Veit expressing his reservations and asking him follow-up questions—the response was almost always silence.

In March 1975, Walter attended a conference sponsored by DUIST, in hopes that he could finally speak with Veit personally. Walter was disappointed from the start. The room, he later reported, was "filled with old people." Veit then proceeded to give a "boring" talk about Apollo 11, after which Walter asked for the source of the photos he had used in his presentation. Veit bristled, "I can't give it to you, I don't have it any longer!"

The youngsters decided to break out on their own. In early 1976, they founded the group Centrales Erforschungsnetz außergewöhnlicher Phänomene (Central Research Network for Extraordinary Phenomena or CENAP) and began publishing their own newsletter. From the very first issues, Walter and Köhler made it clear that their organization would be challenging Karl Veit and his followers. They made their intentions clear under a banner that had all the markings of a manifesto, "What Does CENAP Want?"

> There is unfortunately in the West German UFO scene a tendency toward backwardness, secretiveness, and the use of pseudo-religious or outright occult-spiritualist intrigue, all under the pretense of serious UFO research. . . . CENAP sees itself here as a putty knife and, based on its own information (CENAP-Report), as a mouthpiece for those who no longer wish to put up with conducting "sham research" at the expense of other kinds and with doing nothing more than giving big speeches using the same empty phrases and content.[48]

Walter sent Veit a personal copy of the first issue; this time, it didn't take long for him to reply. In a letter, the patriarch of German ufology informed Walter that the board at DUIST had kicked him out of the organization and insisted that "all young people—including those who supposedly follow my special path—draw on the over twenty years of DUIST's global work." Veit didn't stop there. In a subsequent issue of *UFO-Nachrichten*, he referred to the pair as "smart-aleck youngsters." And at the 11th DUIST Congress in Wiesbaden, Veit warned his audience, "Young people and their work in UFO research can only gain significance, if [the work] is done under the protection of a large central, umbrella organization (DUIST). . . . Different groups may not form within the UFO Studies Society—to do so will only lead to a dead end."

The Mannheim boys clearly relished playing the role of underdog, but in truth their small group had nothing like the resources Veit had. Mimeographed, with pages often left illegible and handmade drawings used in lieu of photographs, the *CENAP-Report* lacked the professional flare of *UFO-Nachrichten*. At its founding, an annual subscription was DM 7.50. By the end of summer 1977, Köhler and Walter had to raise the price to DM 18, complaining that with only eighteen subscriptions, they were paying DM 100 out of pocket, and the whole venture could well go under. Still, by the early 1980s CENAP was able to host a meeting with two other UFO groups, carry out fieldwork investigations, and establish ties with fellow enthusiasts in the United States, United Kingdom, and Scandinavia.

TEARING DOWN THE WALL BETWEEN SCIENCE AND UFOLOGY

The determination of Werner Walter and Hansjürgen Köhler to move German ufology away from its occult roots and toward more materialist and natural explanations reflected a growing trend within the UFO milieu. Throughout the seventies and eighties, calls for a more scientifically grounded approach to unidentified flying objects became common. No longer was mutual antagonism between the academic world and ufology a given.

A key figure in this was astronomer Allen Hynek. Hynek's 1972 book *The UFO Experience* appeared to many to offer a blueprint for serious study of the phenomenon, and it was widely hailed as "a turning point in UFO investigation."[49] His Center for UFO Studies in Evanston, Illinois—with a board that included professionals working in physics, astronomy, biology, psychology, meteorology, physiology, and engineering—worked with a computer database of cases, conducted field investigations, and wrote up

Peiniger/GEP+Geörge/CENAP

Gastgeber Rettenberger/CENAP

Redakteur/AugsburgerAllgemeine+GEP

Fig. 7.4 CENAP hosting a meeting of UFO groups in the summer of 1980. CENAP.

technical reports on sightings.[50] By 1976, *Flying Saucer Review* was regularly featuring findings from these reports and using Hynek's "close encounter" categories in its articles.[51]

For many interested in setting ufology on a more scientific footing, it meant making its collection and storage of information more systematic. In Austria, Luis Schönherr made this the focus of his UFO research. He kept a scrapbook with news clippings about unidentified flying objects from mainstream media between the years 1947 and 1981. Using these as his foundation and then consulting ufological literature, he created a chronological catalogue of cases dating back to 1500 BCE. Each case was given its own index card, with notes, bibliographical information, and cross-references duly recorded. In this way, he catalogued somewhere around two thousand to three thousand UFO cases. Inspired by American David Saunders's UFOCAT database, adopted by Hynek's new UFO center, Schönherr hoped to find an effective way to exploit new computer technology to analyze the information gathered.[52]

Others shared Schönherr's methodical bent. Ivor Grattan-Guinness, professor of mathematics at Middlesex Polytechnic and the editor of *Annals of Science*, was one.[53] In 1976, he published a piece in *Flying Saucer Review* in which he argued that what was holding ufology back was not simply the hostility of scientists. It was also "the unending effluent of trashy UFO books in sub-English with sensationalist claims amidst the inaccurate reportage. If ever a subject needed rescuing from its advocates, then ufology is one." In an essay published in the *New Scientist* magazine in 1979, writer James Oberg agreed that the enterprise was too reliant on spurious rumors and unfalsifiable claims. And sociologist Shirley McIver criticized the field for a lack uniformity in both its recruitment of researchers and its gathering and distribution of information.[54]

In many ways, it was in the Soviet Union that the wall separating the academic establishment and UFO groups seemed promisingly porous. During the seventies and eighties, scientists from various backgrounds—many of them members of the USSR Academy of Sciences—openly expressed their interest in the subject. Felix Zigel set up a group to study unidentified flying objects at the Moscow Institute of Aviation in 1970, though his interests increasingly turned to landings and witness observations of alien beings. At the same time, Vladimir Azhazha was among the leading figures in Soviet ufology, giving regular lectures on the topic and becoming president in early 1979 of a new department at the Popov Scientific and Technical Society dubbed the "Search for Extraterrestrial Civilizations in the Neighborhood of the Earth by Means of Electronics." Though the department was disbanded later that year, members published articles in several scientific journals and newspapers. By the second half of the 1980s, new UFO study groups had popped up to study anomalous "atmospheric phenomena"—the accepted pseudonym for UFOs in the USSR at the time—joined by a host of scientists working privately on the subject, including geologist Vladimir Avinskii, philosopher of science Vladimir Rubtsov, and researcher at the Institute of Chemical and Experimental Medicine Valerii Sanarov.[55]

In circumstances where academic researchers did not take the lead, some sought to introduce an air of sober professionalism to UFO investigation. In the spring of 1977, a group of British ufologists believing more needed to be done to put collaborative research at the center of their activities formed a national network of investigators.[56] The UFO Investigators Network or UFOIN was expressly not intended to be "another social club." Driven in part by energetic ufologist Jenny Randles, the working group aimed at bringing on board investigators with proven experience and deemed to be capable of producing "a detailed and unbiased report on a case." By the end of 1979, UFOIN had collected information on around one hundred cases, adopted a standardized reporting format, and was storing the data in an office in Nottingham, where researchers could access it for study.

By the 1980s, a new attitude was apparent among civilian researchers. Surveys of practicing ufologists showed that a surprising number of them were not operating under the presumption that aliens were visiting earth. In fact, according to a 1984 study of 102 ufologists, only 39 percent believed UFOs were extraterrestrial in origin.[57] Many were on record expressing what the Italian Center for UFO Studies in 1987 referred to as an "agnostic" stance on the UFO question, reflecting a "growing 'skepticism' of ufologists, who no longer identify themselves as flying saucer believers but comprise a full range of different opinions."[58]

THE SCIENCE OF UFO WITNESSES AND BELIEVERS

While segments of the ufology community were being drawn to the example of mainstream science, the academic sciences were themselves beginning to show a newfound interest in UFOs and ufology. One prominent example in the mid-1970s was Canadian neuroscientist Michael Persinger, who explored the possibility that paranormal experiences might be attributable to any number of natural phenomena, including electro-magnetic field waves and high voltage static electricity fields.[59] He became convinced that one phenomenon in particular offered the best prospect for explaining UFO sightings: "earthquake lights," luminous phenomena (flashes, balls, and streamers) in the sky sometimes accompanying earthquakes and first studied by Japanese seismologists in the 1930s.[60] Close-proximity exposure to this "natural phenomenon that appears correlated with geophysical processes involved with tectonic strain and strain release," Persinger argued, could help explain not only the visual perceptions of witnesses, but also a variety of other experiences: tingling sensations, feelings of apprehension, amnesia, shock-induced alterations in consciousness, and post-event temporary blindness, nausea, malaise, and sleep difficulties.[61]

Persinger's idea quickly became known as "the tectonic strain theory" of UFOs. Over the course of the 1980s and early 1990s, Persinger, along with his occasional collaborator John Derr, collected and analyzed historical data to see whether in fact UFO sightings correlated with geophysical variables. To do so, he needed to find historical sources of information on unidentified flying objects sightings. For this, he turned to an unusual set of sources that included those from ufologists and paranormal specialists: the database of the Center for UFO Studies, report files from various UFO organizations, the works of writer Charles Fort, issues of *Fate* magazine, and newspaper accounts. In all, Persinger concluded geomagnetic or seismic activities could account for anywhere between 50 percent and 80 percent of the variance in UFO reports, including experiences of alien encounters.[62] While some, like British writer Paul Devereux, were generally won over by Persinger's explanation, French journalist Claude Maugé found it too reliant on unreliable data.[63]

Persinger's interest was drawn to the experiences of witnesses, whereas social scientists at the time were directing their attention instead to the beliefs of UFO enthusiasts. Some looked to explain their attitudes as the effect of exposure to paranormal media, others as responses to the social and political crises of the time.[64] By far, the lion's share of social scientific research focused on surveys. Social psychologist Aldora Lee appears to have conducted the first university-based survey in the United States during the spring of 1968 for the Condon Committee. Her findings confirmed what many had long suspected: younger people were much more receptive to the notion of alien visitation than older people, and fear of ridicule led many observing a UFO to not report it to authorities.[65]

Over the next two decades, pollsters surveyed an array of individuals about their views on unidentified flying objects. Witnesses, buffs, ufologists, academics, and the public at large were all queried about their opinions, as well as their social values and backgrounds. The results sometimes proved surprising.[66]

In 1973 and 1975, Stanford University physicist Peter Sturrock mailed out two separate questionnaires about UFOs to colleagues. The first sent to

1,175 members of the American Institute of Aeronautics and Astronautics based in San Francisco and the second to more than 2,600 members of the American Astronomical Society.[67] Results revealed that 40 percent of aeronautical engineers believed UFOs to be a significant scientific problem, while 53 percent of astronomers thought they either certainly or probably warranted scientific study.

Surveys of the public during the seventies and eighties found relative consistency in the percentage of people who reported seeing and believing in the reality of unidentified flying objects. A Gallup poll in 1973 learned that 95 percent of Americans had either heard or read something about UFOs. At the same time, 11 percent of men and 12 percent of women in the United States said they had seen a UFO, while 51 percent said they thought UFOs were real, and 28 percent thought them to be imaginary.

A Roper poll one year later elicited a somewhat more skeptical response, with only 40 percent expressing the view that the UFO phenomenon was genuine. Perhaps its most surprising finding was that belief in the reality of UFOs was more prevalent the more education people had: 51 percent of university-educated respondents declared their belief in the phenomenon, while 21 percent with only an elementary education did so. A 1978 poll of Americans confirmed this finding. In that study, 66 percent of those with a college education considered unidentified flying objects to be real, while 57 percent with only a high school education and 36 percent with only an elementary level education thought so. The disparaging stereotype of believers as backward and the less educated as gullible proved to be wildly inaccurate.

Social scientists in the seventies also saw little reason to conclude believers were more mentally unstable than others. They reported finding no evidence that belief in the existence of UFOs and alien visitors was related to certain psychopathologies. Instead, belief appeared to be influenced by a variety of cultural factors: a wider belief in the possibility of extraterrestrial civilizations, having a circle of friends and relatives receptive to the notion, and exposure to UFO literature, science fiction, news reports about flying saucers, Christian fundamentalism, and New Age philosophy.[68]

Polling throughout the eighties revealed little change in American public opinion. By 1986, a survey conducted by the Public Opinion Laboratory found that 43 percent thought it likely that UFOs were extraterrestrial space vehicles, while 50 percent considered the prospect improbable. A year later, a Gallup poll found that around half of respondents thought unidentified flying objects were something real, and that there was no significant difference in how men and women thought about the issue. Similar to findings in the 1970s, education level remained a factor in how skeptical people were about the subject. Regional differences appeared as well, with 62 percent of those living in the West believing in their reality in contrast to only 39 percent in the South.

Surveys conducted outside the United States, however, showed there to be greater reserve about the subject in other countries. In a poll of Canadians in 1974, 67 percent said they had heard or read about UFOs, and only 36 percent thought they were actual objects. Skepticism ran even deeper in Western Europe. A West German survey in the summer of 1976 found that only 22 percent of residents believed UFOs were alien vessels, despite the fact that 77 percent believed in the existence of extraterrestrial intelligences in the universe. Tracking changes in public opinion in Great Britain between the years 1978 and 1981, *The Daily Telegraph* reported that belief in unidentified flying objects actually declined during that time from 27 percent to 24 percent of those polled, even while belief in both an after-life (from 36 percent to 40 percent) and ghosts (from 20 percent to 24 percent) rose. The Swiss appeared to be mostly dubious about the topic, with a 1988 study revealing that only 22.8 percent of those polled there believed UFOs were alien artifacts.

Results in southern Europe mirrored those found elsewhere on the continent. Surveys conducted in Spain during the years 1976–1979 showed that around 40 percent–46 percent believed UFOs were real, and of those, more than 80 percent thought they were likely extraterrestrial in origin. Those expressing the most interest in the subject tended to be younger, less devout in their attachment to Catholic Church, and overwhelmingly middle or upper class.[69]

In Italy, two surveys conducted by Doxa—one in 1979, the other in 1987—showed a marked decline in confidence about the reality of UFOs over the course of the eighties. Those expressing belief in UFOs went from 35 percent to 19 percent over that time, while those espousing a skeptical outlook rose from 32 percent to 53 percent. (A big UFO wave in the country in 1978 may well account for the difference). Similar to American findings, the 1987 poll indicated that those younger and more educated were more likely to believe in the physical reality of unidentified flying objects. Regional differences also were evident, with belief more common in the central regions of Italy and less common in the south and north.[70]

While pollsters were tracking public opinion, university social scientists were increasingly drawn to the community of those who saw and studied flying saucers. In 1970, sociologist Donald Warren, who wrote extensively about social alienation, relied on what was called "status inconsistency theory" to interpret recent Gallup survey results.[71] Status inconsistency referred to a situation in which one or two factors out of three in a person's career—income, occupation, education—were out of sync with the other(s). The evidence showed, he argued, that sightings were primarily associated with white males, and that "low income with moderate to high education or occupational status . . . produces a high level of saucer reporting." He concluded that those reporting UFO sightings tended to be individuals frustrated with their relative status in society and suspicious of conventional authority. By opening their lives to an experience that brought them into new social relationships, they found recognition and a renewed sense of security.

Warren refined his views a few years later, arguing that overall status and not inconsistencies in status held the key to those experiencing UFOs. Fellow sociologist Ron Westrum, however, considered Warren's analyses to be inadequate largely due to the fact that existing surveys failed to consider other factors that might be equally, if not more, significant. One example he pointed out was age, with the rate of sightings highest among eighteen-to-twenty-one-year-olds and lowest among those sixty and over.[72] In 1977, Westrum instead proposed paying attention to the ways in which the experiences of witnesses were translated into reports by officials and UFO groups and, in turn, how those reports were selectively transmitted to scientists and others.[73]

RESEARCHERS, SEEKERS, AND CULTS

If interest among social scientists in the background of UFO witnesses and believers was something new in the seventies and eighties, their curiosity about UFO groups was not. Since the 1956 study *When Prophecy Fails*, university-based researchers had shown a sustained, albeit modest, interest in the communities of saucer enthusiasts. A new generation of researchers came onto the scene, providing a more three-dimensional picture of the organizational landscape.

Two doctoral dissertations in sociology in particular stand out. For his 1973 study, Michael Kelly Schutz observed the meetings and interviewed members of four UFO groups centered around the Chicago metropolitan area to see how they went about gaining and maintaining support.[74] His findings revealed the relative diversity and precariousness of saucer circles in the early 1970s. While some offered a spiritual message of personal enlightenment and interplanetary brotherhood, others sought merely to provide a public platform for prominent ufologists to speak (for a fee that might well rise to the hundreds of dollars), while still others envisioned themselves as investigative bodies. Some were comfortably self-sustaining, but others had to rely on the largesse of one or two people to do the work and pay the bills. What all the groups shared was a commitment to providing a steady and pleasant setting for like-minded individuals to socialize.

Groups and their members also shared a desire to have their perspectives on unidentified flying objects recognized as legitimate. Groups and members looked for this respectability by tying their work to the authority of science. This often took the form of highlighting their connections to credentialed scientists. As famed ufologist Stanton Friedman told Schutz in an interview, "[S]trange as this may sound, the kook groups love me. To some extent, not because I'm saying anything they're saying, but because they want the legitimacy to rub off. See, a Nuclear Physicist says Flying Saucers are real. I say Flying Saucers are real. He's legitimate, so I must be legitimate. It's kind of okay by association."

Ten years later, University of York doctoral student Shirley McIver explored the beliefs of British followers in her dissertation, "The UFO Movement."[75] She examined organizations, newsletters, and publications, surveyed the membership—more than five hundred—of the British UFO Research Association (BUFORA), interviewed members of local saucer groups, and corresponded with lapsed members. Like Schutz, McIver was warmly welcomed by those with whom she met, who affectionately referred to her as the "sociological ufologist" and "accepted [her] as a participant with yet another point of view." Her results provide the most detailed snapshot of the UFO scene in the United Kingdom during the early 1980s.

McIver divided UFO enthusiasts into two categories: "researchers," who sought to learn about, investigate, and discuss sightings, and "seekers," who dedicated themselves to searching for transcendental meaning through contact with aliens. In both cases, she found two things that tended to rouse people to join a group: some kind of personal experience—be it a direct or indirect—involving UFOs or aliens and enjoyment in the speculative nature of studying the UFO mystery. Neither expressed antipathy toward conventional science per se but rather believed it merely needed to expand its horizons.

BUFORA by and large attracted "researchers." McIver's survey found 80 percent to be male, the majority between the ages of twenty-one and forty, employed in white-collar work, possessing a relatively high level of education, and supporters of either a minority political party or none at all. Reading played a pivotal role in most of their lives, with 56 percent saying it was an article or book that first drew their attention to UFOs. In fact, when it came to the kinds of topics they liked to read about, heading the list was space science (60 percent), psychic research (49 percent), astronomy (43 percent), science fiction (32 percent), and Fortean phenomena (31 percent).

Although 61 percent thought they had seen something that was a UFO, only 6 percent claimed to have had a close encounter of the second kind and 44 percent chose aliens as their first guess at what might be behind the UFO phenomenon. As for why some left a group they had joined, the two most frequent reasons they gave was a change of circumstances, like lack of time, and distaste for where the group was heading.

"Seekers," on the other hand, were drawn to organizations oriented around either spiritual or physical contact with extraterrestrial brothers and sisters. Membership in these instances appears to have been more diverse compared to BUFORA. For instance, some consisted mainly of elderly women or housewives, while others formed around young men. Reading also played a pivotal role for most of those involved, but they tended to find their inspiration in psychic and paranormal experiences. The term most often used to refer to their activities was "metaphysics," meant to imply the exercise of studying the ultimate nature of reality beyond the five senses. The group operated as a welcoming place to learn techniques in higher spiritual development and to commune with others. It's not surprising, then, that members tended to come from the wider esoteric, mystical, and New Age subcultures of the time, and it was common for newcomers to cite someone significant in their lives as responsible for first recruiting them.

The seventies and eighties provided fertile ground for the growth of new spiritually oriented UFO communities. Holding to beliefs similar to those of the contactees of the 1950s, many of these groups took the shape of millenarian religious movements preaching imminent salvation through the intervention of wise extraterrestrials. Two in particular garnered a great deal of international publicity, not all of it good.

In December 1973, Claude Vorilhon was a French sports car journalist living in small town in central France when he was telepathically induced to go to the volcano Puy de Lassola and there observed an unidentified flying object descending.[76] As he explained it afterward, an extraterrestrial *Eloha*—singular of *Elohim*, in Hebrew meaning "one who comes from the sky"—revealed that Vorilhon was in fact Raël ("the light of the Elohim"), the final prophet sent by a race of highly advanced scientists from another planet to bring a message to the people of earth. Over six days, the small black-haired and bearded alien with greenish skin and almond-shaped eyes instructed him in the true meaning of the Bible and explained that alien scientists had created all life in laboratories and that humans were the product of alien genetic engineering. By 1979, Raël went on to claim that he was not simply a prophet, but the son of an alien named Yahweh, directly related to Jesus, Moses, and Buddha, and that he was the Messiah of the Age of Apocalypse.

So began what became known as Raëlism, a religious movement preaching a coming technological utopia realized through prophetic teachings understood as messages from an advanced race of extraterrestrials. Holding the first meeting of The Movement to Welcome the Elohim, Creators of Humanity (MADECH) in December 1974 to a crowd of 170 members, Raël moved on to spread his gospel to Japan and Quebec. By the start of the twenty-first century he could boast of having sixty-five thousand followers in eighty-four countries. From the mid-seventies on, Raël added successive elements to the movement: initiation rituals like raëlian baptism, meditation practices, congregational gatherings, a code of ethical behavior, tithing, missionary work, and even a museum called UFOland. Like many of his contactee predecessors, Raël advocated for human improvement through scientific progress and enlightenment, world peace, and an end to nuclear weapon testing (in 1977 the movement went so far as to adopt A.H., After Hiroshima, in its calendar, in lieu of A.D.).

In the United States, another group made headlines in the fall of 1975, when around thirty-five people in Oregon attending a lecture about flying saucers suddenly disappeared.[77] The meeting's hosts were a man and woman who called themselves Bo and Peep (also referred to as "The Two") who had been recently holding small meetings on the West Coast proclaiming themselves to be members of the kingdom of heaven in human form. They offered their followers a path to the "next evolutionary kingdom," one that required they abandon family, friends, jobs, and material possessions and overcome their emotions, sexual desires, and worldly attachments in a strict process called Human Individual Metamorphosis. If successfully completed, Bo and Peep assured them, they would be taken up to heaven in UFOs at some future date.

Peep was nurse Bonnie Lu Nettles, while Bo was Marshall Herff Applewhite, a music teacher from Texas. The two met in 1972 and shared an immediate spiritual connection with one another. Soon they began developing and promoting their unique mixture of metaphysics and Christian thought that integrated flying saucer mythology, reincarnation, Biblical revelation, and resurrection. Besides its emphasis on a process of transcendent human metamorphosis with the aid of UFOs, Bo and Peep's endeavor was initially marked by their lack of contact with adherents and the stark lifestyle they insisted their followers adopt: members were first divided into pairs, then later divided into families of about fourteen, and instructed to rigorously control contact with the outside world as well as all affectionate and erotic feelings. Evidence gathered by sociologists Robert Balch and David Taylor, who spent seven months as "hidden observers" in the group, showed that belief in the basic message of Bo and Peep remained tenuous, and the strict code of conduct limited the size of the community to around 150.

In 1976, Nettles and Applewhite revamped the organization and created an isolated residential community. This helped solidify the group, but only for a while. In 1985, Nettles died of liver cancer. Applewhite was personally devastated, but her death proved momentous for the group. The fact that she physically died before she underwent the transformation from human being to alien and boarded the UFO forced radical alteration of the movement's direction. Nettles was now celebrated as a God-like figure, Applewhite became the sole leader, and talk began about perhaps there being a need to first "abandon the vehicle" of the body before one could advance to the Next Level and join the extraterrestrials.

All this ultimately led Applewhite and the group—eventually renamed Heaven's Gate—down a ruinous path by the mid-1990s. When in 1997 rumors circulated that a flying saucer was following the nearby comet Hale-Bopp, Applewhite and thirty-eight followers determined that this was the much-anticipated rapture. Convinced they must leave their physical bodies in preparation for the aliens' arrival, the group donned black track suits, swallowed barbiturates, put bags over their heads, and killed themselves.

The mass suicides received international media attention, in part owing to the members' extensive use of the internet to post apocalyptic messages.[78] Ridicule was heaped on not just Heaven's Gate but the wider UFO community, targeting especially those who found spiritual meaning in the UFO phenomenon. Such derisive attitudes, however, were hardly new.

Beginning the late 1960s and early 1970s, organized religious institutions, conservative activists, and even lawmakers on both sides of the North Atlantic noted with alarm the rise of a host of new, unconventional religious communities. Groups like the Hare Krishna, the Peoples Temple, the Unification Church, and Scientology were condemned as "cults" in North America and as "sects" in France and Germany, accused of kidnapping recruits, brainwashing followers, and engaging in deviant (mostly sexual) practices. Distraught families soon sought out self-proclaimed experts in "deprogramming" who promised to liberate and undo the "mind control" the cults supposedly had over loved ones. Some went so far as to pursue civil lawsuits against group leaders.[79]

The anti-cult movement began to wane by the late 1990s, but not before its impact was felt in the UFO scene. Groups like Ashtar Command and Human Individual Metamorphosis were widely cited and decried as cults, even while academics debated the usefulness of the label. Raël especially drew the ire of anti-cult activists in France, Switzerland, Belgium, and Quebec. There, some journalists took up the task of "exposing" the

Raëlians, accusing them of "mental manipulation" and sexual misconduct. The organization responded with lawsuits of their own. By the 1990s, lawyers, judges, and juries would have their say about unidentified flying objects and aliens.

UFOS FROM INNER SPACE

As historian Alexander Geppert has rightly noted, speculation about space exploration got swept up in two currents during the seventies and eighties.[80] On the one hand, changing political, economic, and technological realities were a stark reminder of the limits of human ingenuity. The energy crisis, rising inflation, unemployment, budget deficits, the retrenchment of welfare states, the end of manned space flights to the moon, increasing awareness of environmental pollution, the American and Soviet fiascos in Vietnam and Afghanistan, and the Three Mile Island (1979), Bhopal (1984), and Chernobyl (1986) accidents raised questions about just how far civilizations could go in solving problems and mastering new frontiers. At the same time, the emergence of new UFO religious movements signaled a broader change in the outlook of many who were finding adventure and hope in the untapped powers of the human spirit. New Age philosophy, transcendental meditation, extrasensory perception, exorcism, reincarnation, telekinesis, astrology, channeling, psychic healing, and cryonics all enjoyed a robust following and became staples of television and magazines.[81]

Inner space, not outer space, suddenly seemed a likelier place to unlock the mystery of unidentified flying objects. As British ufologist Roger Sandell observed in the spring of 1978, the "nuts and bolts" view of flying saucers piloted by aliens from another planet seemed to be giving way to speculation about "a malignant, supernatural, anti-human force" or perhaps a phenomenon akin to religious "visions, ghostly experiences, and similar events."[82] At the suggestion in 1970 that ufology be subsumed under the umbrella of parapsychology, editor of *Flying Saucer Review* Charles Bowen didn't demur. It is, he wrote, "of paramount importance that *everything* be considered."

> Nothing should be discarded just because it doesn't *seem* right. Even the weirdest of contactee claims should be closely scrutinized, not forgetting the contactee himself—what is *his* history? Is he clairvoyant? Is he a deep-trance subject?—for who knows, the poor, derided contactee may be saying what something somewhere wants him to say.[83]

Under Bowen's and his successor Gordon Creighton's direction, the flag-ship publication of international ufology took that advice to heart. For two decades, *FSR* published articles on all sorts of paranormal phenomena and their possible connections to UFOs: healing through electromagnetic radiation, the Loch Ness monster and Bigfoot, psychic abilities and me-diumship, teleportation, levitation, spoon-bender Uri Geller, time travel, psychic projection. As new stories appeared in the 1970s—mysterious crop circles, the deadly Bermuda Triangle, suspicious black helicopters, bizarre cattle mutilations—these were easily folded into the riotous Fortean mix of supernaturalia.

When it came to explaining this turn of events, ufologists who took these reports seriously generally fell into one of two camps. One ap-proach, associated with France and its expatriate ufologist Jacques Vallee, suggested looking more closely at the stories being told. The other was in-spired by the works of an itinerant American investigator of the uncanny who proposed that beings far more sinister than aliens were behind the UFO phenomenon.

In 1969, Jacques Vallee published *Passport to Magonia*, a work that many ufologists consider his greatest.[84] The title referred to a tale told by the ninth-century Archbishop Agobard of Lyon, who decried a belief among some in his region of there being a land called Magonia, whose dwellers traveled in ships in the clouds causing storms and stealing crops. In the book, Vallee highlights striking parallels between historical descriptions of odd celestial phenomena and encounters with magical beings and contem-porary reports about flying saucers. Vallee dashes across time and place, at one moment lighting on depictions of a "little blue man" by schoolchildren in England in 1967, then swooping down to talk about how similar fairy people in Gaelic folklore are to the "little men" of UFO encounters.

What's to be made of these common features, Vallee asked? He offered no easy answers. Perhaps they point to a shared reality, a realm beyond modern science's understanding; or maybe they reveal something about the human imagination. What could be said, however, was "the modern, global belief in flying saucers and their occupants is identical to an earlier belief in the fairy-faith. The entities described as the pilots of the craft are indistinguishable from the elves, sylphs, and lutins of the Middle Ages." The UFO phenomenon was "a resurgence of a deep stream in human cul-ture known in older times under various other names."

To be sure, others had drawn comparable observations. Proponents of the "ancient astronauts" theory had noted the same kinds of similarities. Where Vallee parted ways with paleovisitologists like Kolosimo, Charroux, and especially von Däniken was that he proposed that it was not our ancestors but rather we in the modern day who are the ignorant ones. We mistook flying saucers for something futuristic when in fact they are part of something age-old and enduring.

To many, Vallee's latest take on the UFO phenomenon was a fresh and promising new avenue for study. Nowhere was his impact felt more than in France, where a few prominent UFO researchers ran with the notion that ufology was neglecting the cultural facets of unidentified flying objects and aliens.

The first salvo came from Michel Monnerie, an editorial board member of the French-language periodical *Lumières dans la Nuit*. In 1977, he published *Et si les ovnis n'existaient pas?* (What If UFOs Didn't Exist?), followed in 1979 by *Le naufrage des extra-terrestres* (The Shipwreck of the Extraterrestrials).[85] Monnerie sparked controversy within French ranks by arguing that ufologists were all-too-conveniently ignoring the fact that the descriptions and stories told by witnesses of unidentified flying objects didn't substantially differ from those told by witnesses of identified flying objects. To him, this made it clear that what accounted for consistency across reported sightings came from witnesses unconsciously turning to rumors and myth in making sense of foggy or bizarre experiences. This response was neither intentional nor pathological but simply human—certainly not extraterrestrial.

The following year, Bertrand Méheust, a trained sociologist and scholar of parapsychology, published *Science-fiction et soucoupes volantes: une réalité mythico-physique* (Science Fiction and Flying Saucers: A Mythico-Physical Reality).[86] In it, he challenged the argument that descriptions of flying saucers and aliens were unique to the postwar world. On the contrary, he showed virtually every element in the flying saucer phenomenon appeared in science fiction literature dating back to the nineteenth century. In a subsequent book released seven years later, Méheust demonstrated parallels between stories of hostile encounters with aliens and stories in folklore about brushes between humans and creatures from other worlds.

In short order, others in Francophone Europe began taking up the ideas of Monnerie and Méheust, helping to establish what was soon being called "the socio-psychological hypothesis" or simply "the new ufology." Belgian Jacques Scornaux defended Monnerie in some of the prominent French-language UFO periodicals, and Thierry Pinvidic, a key figure in Parisian ufology, co-organized with Scornaux two important international European ufology meetings in 1981 and 1988. Journalist Claude Maugé went on to refine the definition of unidentified flying objects and pointed to the ways in which information about sightings got distorted as it circulated.[87]

The new ufology was soon winning over others outside of France. In England, where the outlook became known as the "psychosocial hypothesis," some of the organizers behind the *Merseyside UFO Bulletin* had been moving in a similar direction over the course of the seventies. In the fall of 1979, they formally changed the name of their periodical to *Magonia*, and the magazine became a prominent outlet for introducing English speakers to the views of French writers.[88] In a series of books he published during the 1980s, librarian and writer Hilary Evans added his voice to the choir of those seeing the lore of sprites, elves, and imps haunting the talk about visitors from outer space.[89]

By the end of the decade, change was palpable—at least on one side of the Atlantic. Taking stock at the First European Congress on Anomalous Phenomena in Brussels in November 1988, veteran researchers Edoardo Russo and Gian Paolo Grassino from the Italian Center for UFO Studies summarized the state of affairs bluntly.[90] European and American ufologists seemed to be parting ways. While their American counterparts largely remained committed to looking for flesh-and-blood aliens behind nuts-and-bolts flying disks, Europeans had come to embrace uncertainty and skepticism. For many of them, identified flying objects were as interesting to study as the unidentified variety, and psychological and historical explanations only added to their fascination.

It's not that Americans were deaf to the new developments. Researchers—many with links to Allen Hynek's Center for UFO Studies—such as Jerome Clark, Allan Hendry, Mark Rodeghier, and Michael Swords—took seriously the need to adopt an informed, skeptical perspective toward reported sightings. At the same time, the renaissance of interest in supernatural phenomena seemed to offer an alternative way to investigate and explain the UFO experience.

THINGS GET STRANGE

In the fall of 1970, Gordon Creighton, one of the leading figures at *Flying Saucer Review*, wrote one of his correspondents in Hong Kong about what he believed lay behind the UFO mystery. He explained that he had come to the view that "other, non-human agencies" were nefariously interfering in human affairs, "busy at present misleading, bedevilling, and fooling the human race." Underscoring his message, he resorted to capital letters. "THE UFOS ARE <u>NOT</u> FROM OUTER SPACE. PROBABLY NONE OF THEM ARE. ALL ARE FROM OTHER LEVELS OR OTHER DIMENSIONS OR OTHER TIME/SPACE FRAMEWORKS RIGHT HERE. THEY ARE

PROBABLY RESPONSIBLE FOR ALL 'PSYCHIC PHENOMENA.'"[91] Almost a decade and a half later, he related to another correspondent in India, "I don't believe that anything of this that I see around me is REAL. REALITY THEREFORE HAS TO BE SOMETHING ELSE, SOMEWHERE ELSE."[92]

Creighton was not alone in thinking that UFOs were the product of neither human nor extraterrestrial ingenuity. Some sought their origins in spirits and ghosts, others in the intrigues of Satan.[93] At a time when mysteries, miracles, and marvels seemed to abound, there were those who suspected that ufologists might be as narrow-minded as the academic scientists they criticized.

No one better epitomized this audacious—and, at times, dark— perspective than American writer John Keel. Keel made his living as an author of adventure and sensational tales for pulp magazines like *True*, *Saga*, *Male*, and *Men* as well as for syndicated newspaper features. He had already published a book about the "mysteries of the Orient," when in 1966 *Playboy* commissioned him to write an article about UFOs. Though the men's magazine rejected the article, Keel was hooked and began immersing himself in the world of ufology. He pored over back issues of APRO's news bulletin and *Flying Saucer Review*, spoke with police, local officials, and journalists about reported sightings, and interviewed hundreds of what he called "silent contactees," the ones not seeking publicity.

Soon Keel began publishing articles and his own newsletter about what he referred to as "the phenomenon."[94] His stories had an aura of peril about them, depicting a world of unlikely coincidences, ominous encounters, and dark, forbidding figures who could materialize and vanish in the blink of an eye. There were flying saucer eyewitnesses who described being visited by unnerving, dark-skinned figures demanding they change their stories and reports of meetings with "ufonauts" warning about imminent threats to the people of earth. There were sightings of large, hairy monsters in the very places where UFOs had been spotted. And distressed women reported seeing black-cloaked figures loitering in backyards, leering in windows, and standing over them in bedrooms, as well as getting phone calls from someone speaking in a "bizarre metallic voice speaking in an incomprehensible language."

Such happenings would become Keel's stock and trade throughout the seventies. He is best known today for his 1975 book *The Mothman Prophecies* in which he linked a series of baleful and puzzling events to a large, winged creature in West Virginia dubbed "Mothman."[95] During 1970 and 1971, Keel published four books in which he offered more than just a litany of monsters, creepers, and UFOs.[96] He presented an overarching explanation—one he admittedly altered time and again—that he believed accounted for all sorts of uncanny experiences, including the flying saucer mystery.

Keel was an avid reader of the works of ufologist Morris Jessup, Coral and Jim Lorenzen, the writers at *Flying Saucer Review*, and esotericist Meade Layne, who already in 1950 had suggested that flying saucers were the work of interdimensional beings. His greatest influence, however, was Charles Fort. Keel modeled his own style on Fort's, winding his way from one freak event or anomalous encounter to the next. These tales then were punctuated by elaborate paranormal speculations. He combined all this with elements of what's been called "the new journalism," a style gaining popularity in which reporters presented personal observations, overheard conversations, and extracts from notes, while making their quest for information a central part of the story.[97] In this way, Keel represented an updating of Fort for the late twentieth century that placed UFOs and alien contact at the center of the Forteana universe.

Keel's proposition was that the messages of doom and salvation that contactees claimed to have received from extraterrestrials were actually "cunning techniques of deception and psychological warfare" on the part of "ultraterrestrials." These ultraterrestrials were "superior humanlike nonhumans," who walk among us and manipulate the electrical circuits of our minds, making "us see whatever they want us to see and remember only what they want us to remember."[98]

Keel argued we could only guess at the identity and cosmic plan of these superior beings. Perhaps there were different alliances of supernatural entities at war with one another, along the way exploiting humans as their pawns by using psychic means to foment hate.[99] Perhaps they were gods or some god-like force, both fickle and ruthless. "The same force that answers some prayers also causes it to rain anchovies and is behind everything from sea serpents to flying saucers," he wrote in 1971. "It distorts our reality whimsically, perhaps out of boredom, or perhaps because it is a little crazy." At times, Keel seemed to despair of any chance at making sense of things. "When a hairy monster stalks across the landscape and peers into a bathroom window, the event has no meaning, so we invent a meaning for it. We have complicated our reality by developing whole cults of unreason to define unreasonable intrusions and make them important in our lives."[100]

Keel would go on to write more articles about flying saucers for men's magazines and UFO periodicals, now and again dipping his toes in new paranormal waters like alien submarine sightings and women sexually assaulted and impregnated aboard UFOs.[101] By the mid-eighties, however, he appeared to back away from his earlier positions, insisting that he had never considered ultraterrestrials anything other than a literary device.[102]

No matter. While some ufologists dismissed him as a trickster, many others saw, and continue to see, great promise in his ultraterrestrial interpretation of the UFO phenomenon.

MOBILIZING THE DEBUNKERS

John Keel's popularity reflected the public's growing receptiveness to supernatural topics and explanations. If ufology was moving into ever stranger territory, some believed, it is because it needed to acknowledge that reality was not what it seemed and that a common thread linked UFOs to all sorts of paranormal experiences. Not everyone agreed.

Even among ufologists, some eyebrows were raised. In the early seventies, for instance, a group of British investigators conducted an experiment in Warminster to see what would happen if fake photographs of a UFO were circulated among local enthusiasts and the editors at *Flying Saucer Review*; the images were doctored to explicitly contradict what witnesses had in fact seen. The photographs were widely accepted as genuine, leading the researchers to question the commitment of leading ufologists to critical analysis and fact-checking.[103] A few years later, longtime American ufologist Allen Greenfield published his "Confessions of a Ufologist," in which he admitted he and others in the field had become increasingly skeptical about the reality of UFOs, but they nonetheless planned to stay in the field. Their conversion was not going to lead them into the arms of the debunkers.[104]

The debunkers were still out there, of course. Donald Menzel's last book on the subject was published posthumously in 1977.[105] Co-written by physician and experimental psychologist Ernest Taves, *The UFO Enigma* among other things examined the twenty-three "unexplained" cases in the Condon Report. It largely rehashed Menzel's familiar argument that natural explanations could easily account for all UFO sightings.

By the mid-seventies, Menzel may have represented UFO skepticism's past, but others were more than ready to carry on his mission. Increasingly worried about the apparent rise in paranormal and occult beliefs in the United States, a number of concerned skeptics from the worlds of academia and stage magic decided to take action. In 1976, they formed the Committee for the Scientific Investigation of Claims of the Paranormal or CSICOP (pronounced SIGH-cop).

CSICOP was the first of its kind—an organization dedicated to debunking paranormal claims and beliefs.[106] It was the creation of two separate groups. One included Martin Gardner, illusionist James Randi, psychologist Ray Hyman, and sociologist Marcello Truzzi and was interested in scientifically evaluating paranormal claims. The other centered around SUNY Buffalo professor of philosophy Paul Kurtz, who published a manifesto entitled "Objections to Astrology" in the magazine of the American Humanist Association in 1975. Kurtz and Truzzi became the co-chairmen of CSICOP, with Truzzi editing the Committee's first periodical, *The Zetetic*.

Discord over the direction and tone of the organization quickly arose. Kurtz took a polemical view of their work, favoring broadsides aimed at advocates of paranormal claims; Truzzi believed in a more measured approach rooted in academic study that would allow proponents of the supernatural a place at the table. Members sided with Kurtz, and a little over a year after the group's founding, Truzzi resigned. He went on to edit a new periodical, *Zetetic Scholar*, while CSICOP renamed its magazine *Skeptical Inquirer*.

At the organization's inaugural conference, Kurtz spoke alarmingly about the growing number of "cults of unreason and other forms of nonsense." Referencing Nazi Germany and Stalinism, he lamented the fact that "western democratic societies are being swept by other forms of irrationalism, often blatantly antiscientific and pseudoscientific in character." Skeptics needed to be decisive. "If we are to meet the growth of irrationality," he insisted, "we need to develop an appreciation for the scientific attitude as a part of culture."[107]

Over the next decade and a half, CSICOP went on to establish itself as a leading voice in debunking a wide range of paranormal claims: astrology, telekinesis, psychic and faith healing, reincarnation, ghosts, exorcism, fortune telling—and of course UFOs and ancient aliens. At first, some members of the committee dipped a toe into research. After controversy erupted in 1981 over whether some of the more uncomfortable results of one study were being swept under the carpet, however, CSICOP announced it would no longer conduct its own research. Its main focus became public relations, in particular trying to influence the media's presentation of the paranormal, from national television broadcasters to local radio stations and newspapers.

In the early 1980s, local skeptics groups began to form, eventually becoming local chapters and extending beyond the United States into over a dozen countries. And by the early nineties, a picture began to form of those involved in CSICOP. For one, they were highly educated: its leadership, fellows, and consultants often held academic posts, while 83 percent of its magazine's readers had a college degree. Like UFO research groups, both the national organization and local chapters were predominantly composed of white males, though in the case of CSICOP many identified as atheist or secular humanist.

CSICOP's leading voices brought a combative zeal to their work, one that was grounded in a confidence in the righteousness of their cause. They regularly framed Western science as modern and progressive, the very epitome of rationality, while they ridiculed paranormal belief as ludicrous, backward, and dangerous. CSICOP in many ways presented a mirror image of the New Age movement it so despised, both groups presenting themselves as the guardians of truth and morality.[108]

When it came to UFOs, CSICOP's point man was an irrepressible aviation journalist, Philip J. Klass. A trained engineer in aviation electronics, Klass began working for the magazine *Aviation Week*, going on to serve as its longtime senior editor. He came to the attention of Donald Menzel and Edward Condon during the Colorado UFO Study when he proposed that ball lightning—glowing orbs of highly charged plasma that can suddenly appear and disappear and even pass through walls—could account for many, if not all, cases of UFO sightings. From that point on, he dedicated himself to refuting the existence of flying saucers and alien visitors. Between 1968 and 1997, he wrote seven books and countless articles, published a newsletter, and regularly appeared on television making the case that every reported UFO sighting had a natural explanation.

Sarcastic and pugnacious, Klass treated debunking as a full contact sport. He pressed the Office of Naval Research (ONR), for instance, to investigate whether James McDonald was using some of his grant money to fund his UFO research; the ONR found he did and eventually ended its funding. In 1973, he looked into making the case that Allen Hynek was guilty of plagiarism.[109]

If people sensed an ad hominem flavor in his approach, he once told Carl Sagan,

> perhaps they are correct, for I always have had great trouble in disguising my contempt for those who resort to trickery and intellectual dishonesty. And I have never been one to hold back in pointing out that "The Emperor has no clothes," even though that might, in some quarters, be considered an "ad hominum (sic) attack" on the Emperor.[110]

Paranormal book dealer Robert C. Girard put it bluntly: Klass's method was "science by ridicule."[111]

At the same time, Klass could exhibit a puckish sense of humor. During the holiday season of 1968, he sent a Christmas card to leading figures in

APRO and NICAP that said, "We regret to inform you that there is no Santa Claus. Rejoice."[112] Years later when a young boy wrote him explaining his own interest in UFOs, Klass told him he would be better off investigating the existence of Santa Claus or the Tooth Fairy. After the boy responded by telling him he knew for a fact that it was his parents who left presents under the Christmas tree, Klass acknowledged that might be true in his case. "But that does not prove that all Xmas presents come from parents," he added. "UNTIL YOU HAVE INVESTIGATED [THE CASES OF] MILLIONS OF OTHERS AND HAVE PROVEN THAT ALL OF THEIR PRESENTS CAME FROM THEIR PARENTS, ONLY THEN WILL I BE PREPARED TO BELIEVE THAT THERE REALLY IS NO SANTA CLAUS."[113] Klass was perhaps most famous, however, for his standing offer of $10,000 to anyone who could provide definitive proof of alien visitors.

Klass took his correspondence seriously, considering it part of the job of being the leading UFO debunker in the United States. By the mid-1970s, he was receiving thirty to forty letters a day. Upon returning home from work, he would eat quickly, then sit at his typewriter answering his mail—some of it, downright insulting—until 3 or 4 a.m. Weekends he spent working on new UFO cases.[114]

Yet, for all his combative bravado, Klass appeared to delight in rubbing elbows with ufologists. He regularly attended UFO conferences, shared his

Fig. 7.5 Philip Klass in his study in 2005. ClasSvahn.

source material with UFO investigators, and had cordial correspondences with the likes of Allen Hynek and James Moseley. He even made a seemingly generous gesture. On learning that the UFO group NICAP was in debt and in crisis in 1969, Klass donated money to the group and volunteered to serve as a speaker for free, with all income generated going to the organization.[115]

———

As 1986 drew to a close, Philip Klass wrote Goran Bengtson, the head of cultural programming at Swedish television, "let me note that interest in UFOs in the U.S. is at an *all-time low*. Even our sensationalist tabloids rarely run UFO stories, whereas a decade ago they were featured in almost every issue." Both NICAP and APRO were now all but dead, and MUFON had fewer than 1,200 members. "Even stalwart UFO promoters here express their disappointment in the low level of interest by the news media and the public."[116] Just as there had been fifteen years earlier, there was talk that UFOs seemed to be on the verge of being relegated to the dustbin of history.

If there was any truth to Klass's assessment, it may have reflected where talk about UFOs was going, not that it disappeared. While there was continuing interest in sightings, by the mid-1980s the conversation within the UFO community had begun to take a turn. Ufologists increasingly were being drawn away from discussions about nuts-and-bolts flying saucers and toward considering the experiences witnesses were having. This invariably led them down new pathways of speculation.

There is no better example of this than a pair of influential publications by British investigator Jenny Randles in 1983 and 1984.[117] Randles criticized ufology for its either or obsession with the reality of sightings, the did-it-exist vs did-it-not-exist question. She instead called for taking more seriously the exotic, "quasi-conscious experiences" many witnesses described having in their encounters with UFOs. This "dream-like aura" that accompanied many close encounters she dubbed the "Oz factor" (a reference to *The Wizard of Oz*), and she believed it might hold the key to the mystery of unidentified atmospheric phenomena.

Putting Oz experiences at the center of UFO investigation opened up conversation instead of shutting it down. The curious could adopt the position of someone like Michel Monnerie and explore the cultural motifs behind the Oz factor; they might speculate instead along the lines of

John Keel, searching for the ways the Oz factor connected to other eerie experiences. In any event, this kind of exploration took ufology into a more subjective, a more embodied, a more intimate direction. In doing so, it took its cues from the new-found success of New Age philosophy, parapsychology, and the occult, boosted by the lively syncretism of it all. The rising paranormal tide lifted all boats.

This, of course, only raised new questions. In what new directions were UFOs taking us? And where were we taking UFOs?

8

Intruders

On July 1, 1989, William (Bill) Moore stood ready to make a much-anticipated presentation to those attending the Mutual UFO Network's convention at the Aladdin Casino in Las Vegas.[1] By this time, Moore had become something of a luminary in ufology. He was on the board of directors of Coral and Jim Lorenzen's competing organization APRO. He had co-authored two books with Charles Berlitz, who himself had achieved fame popularizing the idea of there being a so-called Bermuda Triangle where ships and planes mysteriously disappeared. Together, the two men wrote *The Philadelphia Experiment* (1979), in which they contended that in 1943 the US Navy had successfully made a destroyer escort vanish, appear hundreds of miles away, then reappear where it had first been. A year later, they followed up with *The Roswell Incident*, resuscitating the notion that a crashed UFO and its alien crew had been recovered at Roswell in 1947 and the government had been involved in an elaborate cover-up ever since. Moore subsequently became a frequent speaker at UFO conferences.

On that July evening Moore gave a two-hour talk in which he owned up to a stunning set of revelations. For the previous nine years, he had worked with military intelligence officers reporting back to them about the thoughts and activities of ufologists and prominent witnesses. In addition, he had deliberately withheld information from fellow UFO investigators, while also distributing misleading and incomplete information about the government's involvement with unidentified flying objects. All this, he claimed, he did in order to receive access to classified military documents that confirmed the existence of longstanding contact between humans and aliens.

The crowd greeted Moore's admission with a mix of disdain and disillusionment. Writer Greg Bishop was in attendance and noted that some in the audience shouted and hollered, others cried, while still others simply got up and left. There was so much to process: agents of the government were spying on UFO groups; a prominent ufologist had been recruited to help in their work; witnesses were being manipulated; lies were being spread. All the while, there was definitive proof that extraterrestrials were on earth and intervening in human affairs?

Bill Moore's speech is now legendary within the UFO scene. As he himself admitted, his involvement in this web of subterfuge had started almost a decade earlier and involved three other figures: a businessman, a contactee, and a counter-intelligence officer.

Paul Bennewitz was an engineer and physicist whose company developed equipment for the Air Force and NASA. Bennewitz and his family lived in Albuquerque, New Mexico, just north of Kirtland Air Force Base. During the second half of 1979, he began filming multicolored lights that seemed to hover and fly around the base as well as recording weird radio transmissions he believed were linked to them. By the fall, he had become convinced that malevolent extraterrestrials were behind the phenomena and decided that officials at the base needed to be notified.

Even before his sightings, Bennewitz had expressed an interest in the paranormal. He had avidly followed the development of an expert panel in New Mexico in April 1979 to consider and discuss the rash of cattle killings and mutilations that seemed to plague western states over the decade. In addition, he served as a consultant to APRO.

Bennewitz relayed his findings about the UFOs to not only officials but also Coral and Jim Lorenzen at APRO. Then, in May 1980, he was introduced to a woman by the name of Myrna Hansen, who was upset after having witnessed two hovering objects over a field.[2] Hansen wanted to know more about what she saw, but her memory remained foggy. Thinking he could help, Bennewitz asked another APRO consultant, psychologist Leo Sprinkle, to aid in hypnotizing her as a way to extract more information. Over several sessions with Sprinkle, Hansen described being lifted into a UFO along with frightened cattle. Once on board, she was undressed and given a physical examination, then taken to a base where she saw various body parts stored in vats. Before she was released, a device was implanted in her so that the aliens could track her and control her mind.

By early June, Bennewitz had begun arming himself in the conviction that the extraterrestrials would be coming for Hansen as well as himself and his family. He replaced Sprinkle with another APRO consultant and hypnotist, James Harder. Together, Bennewitz and Harder moved Hansen around from location to location and collected more information from her under hypnosis—all the while shielding her with an umbrella lined with aluminum foil, with the intent of keeping her safe from extraterrestrial surveillance.

After this Bill Moore entered the picture. He was asked to look in on Bennewitz to see how he was getting on. Exactly who asked Moore to check on him is not entirely clear. It may have been the Lorenzens at APRO, who were increasingly concerned about the bizarre nature of the reports they were getting from Bennewitz.

In September 1980, Moore was approached by Richard Doty, a counter-intelligence agent at Kirtland Air Force Base. Doty explained that officials were interested in keeping tabs on Bennewitz and his activities and sought Moore's help. In time, it became clear they wished to recruit Moore as an undercover asset. In a cloak-and-dagger scenario straight out of a John le Carré novel, the two men struck a bargain. Doty would provide Moore with revealing classified information about the Air Force's investigations into UFOs and, in exchange, Moore would offer Doty details about what was going on within ufology circles. In reality, however, Doty used Moore's information to fashion bogus documents that aligned with longstanding suspicions about government cover-ups, crashed saucers, and retrieved alien bodies.

Over the course of the next several years, Doty and Moore fed Bennewitz's appetite for ever more fantastic and startling claims about aliens and the US government with spurious information and forged documents. At one point, a set of papers emerged said to represent notes on a briefing to President Jimmy Carter revealing that a secret government agency named Majestic 12 (aka MJ-12)—a group of a dozen scientists and intelli-gence specialists brought together after the Roswell UFO crash to study its wreckage and its crew—had been in operation since the early 1950s with the purpose of collaborating with aliens and keeping their presence a se-cret. Though widely recognized as a clumsy fake, the contents of the MJ-12 document became (and remain) a subject of debate in UFO circles.

In any event, Bennewitz felt vindicated by what he was learning. Toward the end of 1981, he circulated his summary of all the information he had to UFO researchers, two US senators, and President Ronald Reagan. In what he dubbed *Project Beta: The Report*, he concluded "A) They [the aliens] cannot under <u>any</u> circumstances be trusted. B) They are totally deceptive and death-oriented and have not respect for human or human life. C) No negotiation, <u>agreement</u> nor <u>peaceful compromise</u> can be settled upon in any way."[3]

Doty's professional involvement with Bennewitz ended in 1984, when the former was transferred to Germany. Nonetheless, the obsessed UFO investigator's mental health only seemed to worsen. When Moore visited him in 1987, he found him chain-smoking, getting little sleep, and sounding incoherent. In August 1988, Bennewitz accused his wife of being controlled by aliens and barricaded himself in his home, after which he was hospitalized for a month.

Paul Bennewitz passed away in 2003. Following his famous MUFON speech in 1989, Bill Moore kept a low profile within the UFO scene. Richard Doty, however, continues to remain in the public eye, doing interviews, attending UFO conventions, and making tv and film appearances.

In the end, what were Doty and his superiors after? Doty himself has frequently changed his story. Some, of course, wonder whether Bennewitz had in fact unearthed the truth about aliens on earth. In 2005, Greg Bishop took the view that Bennewitz stumbled upon classified technologies and tests at the base, so officials wanted to throw him off track so that he didn't inadvertently reveal their existence. Writer and publisher Mark Pilkington has offered another line of speculation. Perhaps Doty's real target was the world of ufology itself, and the Air Force baited Bennewitz and Moore as part of a psychological operation aimed at wreaking havoc on the UFO community.

Whatever the case, the claims Bennewitz, Hansen, Moore, and Doty had cobbled together lived on. Beginning in 1987, John Lear—son of the inventor of the Lear jet—breathed new life into them using UFO bulletin boards and interviews to make the case that the US government was involved in an elaborate cosmic cover-up involving extraterrestrial human breeding experiments and the application of alien technology by the military.[4] Lear and others repeated many of the elements in the tales and fake documents from the foursome in New Mexico—alien kidnappings, captured UFOs, experiments on innocent human beings, surveillance implants, secret military bases, MJ-12. By the first half of the 1990s, these cast of characters and plots spilled out from the confines of the world of ufology to become the stuff of a popular television series, *The X-Files*.

When recounted, the twisted and tangled tale of the undoing of Paul Bennewitz and Bill Moore tends to be written as a cautionary tale. It's said to testify to the unscrupulous nature of the American military and government. Or it's said to show the dangers awaiting those obsessing over conspiracies. Or it's taken as an illustration of the gullibility of those taking UFOs seriously.

Viewed less as a morality play than a variation on a theme, it can also be seen a product of history. In the 1980s and 1990s, interest in UFOs and extraterrestrial visitors took a brooding, alarmist turn. Dominated by the specter of alien abduction, the focus of ufology—particularly in the United States—moved away from speculations about nuts-and-bolts spacecraft and toward analyzing the stories of individuals having unnerving encounters with entities from another world.

If a darkness was descending upon ufology, the question is, how did it come to this? How did the bulk of reports of alien encounters go from, say, a comforting meeting between George Adamski and the angelically radiant Orthon to Myrna Hansen's kidnapping by unfeeling beings engaged in horrific experiments?

HOSTILE INCIDENTS AFTER THE HILLS

Claims of hair-raising encounters with extraterrestrials were hardly new. Since at least the early 1950s, adults and children on both sides of the Atlantic reported seeing aliens pestering and assaulting people. Sometimes the culprits were described as tiny, impish men, other times as hairy beings with weird eyes and dressed in unfamiliar garb, or they might be accompanied by robot-like figures. Once in a while, an episode—like the one in Kelly, Kentucky, in August 1955—drew some mainstream media attention.

Hostility incidents, as they came to be called, rarely changed the minds of those who were skeptical about witnesses claiming to have made direct contact with beings from outer space, however. Then came Betty and Barney Hill. Their story and personalities proved far more compelling to the dubious. James McDonald and Donald Keyhoe, both dismissive of the self-professed "contactees" of the fifties and sixties, believed the Hills needed to be taken seriously. John Fuller's 1966 book about their case and the subsequent television adaptation in 1975 made Betty and Barney household names of a sort.

And yet, broad interest in alien abductions did not take off until the 1980s. Why the delay? If the interrupted journey of the Hills made such an impact, why didn't it spark a wave of similar stories during the late sixties and seventies that deluged ufology and arrested the attention of mass media?

While the general public may not have been on the lookout for confrontations with aliens, some UFO investigators were. John Keel was among them. In an article he published in February 1967 under the headline "UFO Kidnappers!" he declared that all over the world "strange flying lights and weird circular machines have been chasing" automobiles and airplanes for years, in some cases leaving no trace of the machine, passengers, or crew.[5] Relying on cases previously reported by APRO, Keel painted an unsettling picture of mostly men (but also children) in a car, on a plane, or simply out walking when they suddenly found themselves pursued by eerie beings in saucer-like crafts. "We only hear about the people who got away," he added. Compounding apprehensions was the fact that "a very active group of mysterious 'government agents' have been apparently assisting UFO pilots by trying to suppress information about their activities."

Keel was neither the first nor the last to make these kinds of claims. For some time, Coral Lorenzen and *APRO Bulletin* had been repeatedly making the case that the beings behind the flying saucers were more than likely malevolent. And in the 1970s, *Flying Saucer Review* began devoting ever greater space to the phenomenon of alien abduction.

Drawing much of the attention at the time was South America, where a great many reports originated. Brazil was a hotspot. One prominent case investigators looked into was that of a twenty-four-year-old enlisted soldier by the name of José Antônio da Silva.[6] On the afternoon of May 4, 1969, da Silva was fishing at a small lagoon in Bebedouro, north of Rio de Janeiro, when he heard some figures rustling behind him. Suddenly paralyzed by a beam of light, two figures around four feet tall and clad in silver and gray uniforms seized him, dragging him into an object that looked like two saucers connected by a cylinder. Once he had been secured, the vessel took off, and the crew spoke to one another in an incomprehensible language. Upon landing, the aliens took off their suits, and da Silva could see their hirsute appearance, as around a dozen of them surrounded him.

Observing his surroundings, da Silva saw pictures of earthly animals, vehicles, plants, and houses, but was startled when he noticed the corpses of four humans of various races. The crew and their captive eventually found a way to communicate with one another through pantomime, and it became clear they wished the soldier to go back to earth to provide information (military secrets?) that he would then pass on to them upon their return. He refused, fearing for his life, but da Silva was returned several days later. Once home, he displayed a number of symptoms: he had marks on his shoulder and stomach pains, he was gaunt and sunburnt and had difficulty walking. He later reported being revisited a few weeks later outside his home–the aliens clearly wanted to see if he had changed his mind. He sent them on their way, but their visit left him with the unmistakable impression that these were dangerous beings who posed a threat to the world.

Antônio da Silva's elaborate tale of extraterrestrial contact was only one of dozens coming out of Brazil.[7] Many conjured up a similar set of images and events: a man out driving or walking home, then carried away by extraterrestrials, given a physical examination, and finally returned far from his point of origin and left with lingering side effects. The prominence of these incidents was due in no small measure to the commitment of leading members of the Brazilian Society for the Study of Flying Saucers to investigating and publicizing hostile close encounters of the third kind.[8] Ufologist Walter Bühler in particular passed on his most intriguing cases to both APRO and *Flying Saucer Review*.

Argentina was another important site of tales of confrontation between UFO occupants and human beings. Among the most renowned

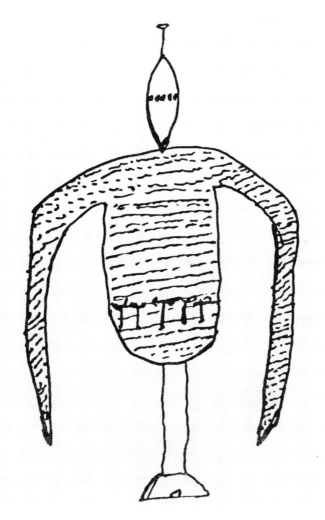

Fig. 8.1 A drawing made by Brazilian bus driver Antonio La Rubia of a robot-like entity he claimed forced him into a craft and extracted blood from him in October 1977. TopFoto/ Fortean.

involved two casino employees in Mendoza in August 1968.[9] Fernando José Villegas and Juan Carlos Peccinetti told authorities that when their car broke down, they had been seized by five aliens. Communicating with the two men through a combination of telepathy and the use of a monitor, the extraterrestrials supposedly paralyzed them both, pricked their fingertips, and showed them images of an earth made desolate by atomic bomb explosions. Though officials and later investigators concluded the whole episode was more than likely a prank, their story quickly became the subject of news coverage throughout the country.

The cases emerging from Argentina also manifested certain patterns. In 1980, UFO researchers Roberto Banchs and Richard Heiden published an analysis of fifty-four reported encounters there between UFO occupants and individuals between 1949 and 1975.[10] Focusing their attention of what were considered the twenty-two most reliable reports, they found that 47.6 percent of the witnesses were driving a vehicle at the time of contact; in only two cases were they inside their home. As for the entities, they rarely appeared alone and in most encounters were said to have been preoccupied with carrying out tasks. All told, it generally appeared—rather ominously—that the extraterrestrials were making contact in the middle of the night in relatively unpopulated areas, and that they seemed uninterested in establishing lines of communication with earthlings.

Europe too was the site of claims of disturbing encounters with the occupants of flying saucers.[11] But it was in the United States in the mid-seventies that a new pattern began to emerge, one with striking similarities to the experiences of Betty and Barney Hill.

On November 5, 1975, Travis Walton was working as part of a Forest Service crew in Arizona clearing out an area around 150 miles northeast of Phoenix. Quitting for the day, the men headed out in a truck but stopped after catching sight of some strange lights in a clearing. The team later reported that Walton got out to have a closer look. As he neared the source, a beam of light from a UFO struck him and carried him into the craft. The rest of the crew left the scene. Walton was not heard from for five days, but when he resurfaced, he said he had been held captive by short, large dome-headed beings with no eyebrows and small mouths, ears, and noses. He recalled being held for a time in a hot, wet room, then being placed on a table and having a mask placed over his face before he lost consciousness. Within days, the tabloid *National Enquirer* and APRO took over the investigation, with the latter sending one of its consultants to hypnotize Walton to retrieve more information from him. When Walton failed a polygraph test, he and his defenders argued that it was due to his state of agitation at the time.[12]

Fig. 8.2 In 1972, the tabloid *National Enquirer* formed what it called a "blue-ribbon panel" of UFO experts whose task was to examine promising reports and award prize money to anyone with evidence considered scientifically valuable. Travis Walton and his workmates were later the recipients of one of these rewards. This photo from 1974 features the panel's five members: left to right, J. Allen Hynek, Robert Creegan, Leo Sprinkle, James Harder, and Frank Salisbury. TopFoto/Fortean.

The story of Travis Walton went on to occupy a canonical place in UFO lore. It became the subject of a feature-length film in 1993, *Fire in the Sky*, and Walton himself became a constant presence at UFO conventions. Another case from a few months later has not achieved the same level of renown as Walton's, but it too presented many of the same elements that were coming to define the American experience of alien abduction.

On January 6, 1976, three women—Mary Louise Smith, Mona Stafford, and Elaine Thomas—were driving home when, according to them, a UFO took control of their automobile.[13] The next thing they remembered was entering a town eight miles from where they had originally spotted the unidentified flying object. Both the *National Enquirer* and MUFON arrived on the scene to investigate. APRO sent one of its consultants to hypnotize the trio—at first, three months after the incident and then another four months later. Under hypnosis, the women recalled a chilling series of events. Smith was said to have "suffered much as she relived the experience," moaning, crying, shuddering, and tossing her head. A tearful Stafford told of being examined by a large eye after being placed on a table, and with a bright white light overhead, humanoids wearing "surgical garments" tested her physiological reactions to stimuli. Thomas, too, was described as highly emotional during her trance and told of being placed in a separate chamber. There, humanoids with dark eyes and grey skin placed some kind of "covering" around her neck so that when she tried to speak or even think, it tightened and choked her. The odd contraption was never explained to her, but Thomas believed it to be some kind of experiment the aliens were conducting to study human intellectual and emotional abilities.

By the middle of 1976, then, a UFO kidnapping scenario was starting to take shape, one involving an increasingly common set of features. Ufologist Scott Rogo summarized its main points four years later, in 1980:

> The witness will be driving along some lonely and deserted area when he becomes aware of a UFO, either following his car or hovering at the side of the road. This is usually all the witness will consciously remember. After making his initial observation, he will often "black out" and will only come to about an hour or so later with no conscious memory of what has taken place during the interim. In the following weeks, though, he may begin to realize that something extraordinary has happened to him. He may start having dreams of a UFO abduction or develop odd obsessions and compulsions. These stressful developments will eventually encourage him to seek help from a ufologist, or perhaps a psychiatrist; and these professionals will usually suggest that hypnotic regression back to the scene of the encounter would help the witness remember exactly what happened to him. Under hypnosis, the victim will invariably recall how he stopped his car after seeing the UFO and watched helplessly as alien beings came out of the craft and forced him into it. He will go on to describe how he was subjected to a medical examination or shown a series of visions before being returned to his car—with the admonition that he forget all that had transpired.[14]

Admittedly, not every case revolved around all these elements, but their growing ubiquity made some ufologists at the time take note. Was the consistency in the witnesses' stories testimony to the reality of their claims? If so, what were the extraterrestrials up to?

A CLOSER LOOK AT A UFO ABDUCTION SCENARIO

As had been the case with the contactees during the fifties and sixties, observers would debate the veracity of these remarkable assertions of coercive experiences with extraterrestrials. Regardless of whether these events really happened as described, the context in which these claims were made

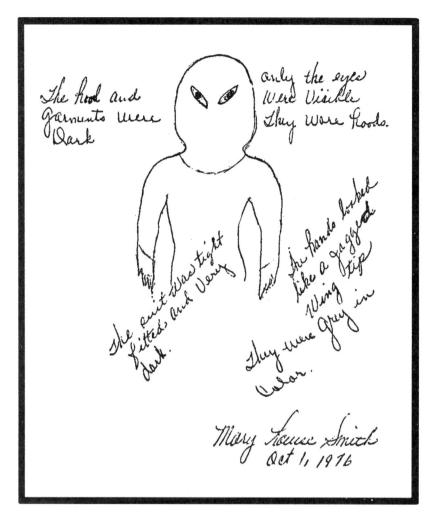

The hood and Garments were Dark

only the eyes were Visible They were Hoods.

the suit was tight fitted and Very dark.

the hands looked like a jagged Wing Tip

They were Grey in Color.

Mary Louise Smith
Oct 1, 1976

Fig. 8.3 Mary Louise Smith, Mona Stafford, and Elaine Thomas worked with UFO investigators at reconstructing what happened to them. This included drawing sketches of what they came to recall, like this one by Smith of one of the UFO occupants she said abducted her and her friends. Photo courtesy of MUFON (www.mufon.com)/Mary Louise Smith.

deserves closer inspection. UFO abduction scenarios did not spring forth as ready-made, finished products presented by isolated individuals—far from it. They arose over the course of time and after numerous individuals and groups intervened in very specific and substantial ways.

One particular case involving events taking place between the fall of 1973 and the summer of 1975 is worth looking into for several reasons. It is representative in that it shares most of the characteristics found in alien abduction scenarios of the 1970s. And the case was considered by some ufologists to be a landmark incident, revealing a new arrogance in the tactics of the extraterrestrial visitors.

On the night of October 16, 1973, Patty Price (a pseudonym), a divorced mother, had just moved into a new home and had put six of her children to bed.[15] Shortly after midnight, she asked a neighbor to call the police because she thought an intruder might be in the house. There in fact had been reports of a prowler in the neighborhood recently. Not wanting to take any chances, Patty and the kids went and stayed at a friend's home the rest of the night. The next morning the family were discussing what had happened the previous evening when the seven-year-old daughter said, "It wasn't a prowler, mama, it was a spaceman."

Patty gave the event little thought until the spring of 1975, when she happened upon a copy of the men's magazine *SAGA* containing an article about people's encounters with UFOs. She thought back to the incident in 1973 and wrote the magazine. Staff there put her in touch with a consultant at APRO, Kevin Randle. Randle initiated an investigation and interviewed the family. The children confirmed that there was a good deal of commotion that night, with one of them saying he saw a skeleton in the corner of the living room, while the pets made a ruckus. Meanwhile, the daughter who had claimed to have seen a spaceman expanded on her story, insisting she had seen a spaceship and creatures in the home.

Patty's memory, however, remained foggy. Randle therefore asked APRO's senior researcher James Harder to join him, since Harder had been using hypnosis with witnesses since the early 1960s. When Harder arrived on July 8, he put Patty into a trance. Under his questioning, Patty hesitatingly began to call to mind seeing skinny people in uniforms in the house and was worried about the children's welfare. Frightened, she told Harder she couldn't remember anything more, but he insisted. "You can remember," he said. "You can tell us what happened. Were you told that you wouldn't remember?" His prompting led Patty to recall the aliens—about four feet tall, thin, with large, slanted eyes, and claw-like hands—grabbing her and the children. Despite trying to fight off their captors, the family floated above the ground and was taken to a room where Patty was examined.

The extraterrestrials were, she volunteered, "coldblooded" in going about their work. "They treated me like a guinea pig," Patty added. When Harder pressed her again to remember details, she was reluctant. To calm her, he explained that remembering the events would enable her to reassure the children. Then came the following exchange:

"They'll want to know, and you should remember so that you can tell them. What kind of information do you think they [the beings] wanted?" he asked.

"They wanted to know how our minds work. They want it [sic] to give them certain information that they don't have yet."

"It would be very helpful for me to know, as a scientist, what kinds of things they are looking for," Harder said.

"How we think. How we feel. Our emotions."

Harder remarked, "That's interesting. Do you think that it makes them . . ."

Mrs. Price became angry. "No, I don't like what they want."

"You thought you were being intruded upon?" Harder asked.

"Yes." Her voice was angry. "They didn't care because they don't have an understanding of emotions like ours."

Harder went on to hypnotize some of the children as well but they produced little worthwhile information. The next day, he hypnotized Patty for a second time, once again urging her to remember details about the examination. She went on to describe being put on a table and hooked up to machines. Harder asked if she was given a gynecological exam, and she answered yes (under subsequent hypnosis with her mother, daughter Betty recalled seeing her mom nude on the table). But what most disturbed Patty was the aliens' insertion of a needle into her body through which, as she put it, "they took my mind, my thoughts." She also noticed a bald human male with glasses assisting in the examination. Finally, her examiners questioned her about the things she loved, the things she hated, what animals she liked, her family background and relations.

Looking back on this series of events, it is clear that a lot of people played a role in the drama. Besides the aliens, there were seven family members, two UFO investigators, a UFO organization, and a magazine and its staff who all contributed at one point or another in bringing details to light. Moreover, what was involved was not someone directly and immediately relating an experience. Rather, an effort was being made to cobble together a story whose elements were presented in a fragmented, inchoate manner. Added to this was the fact that the full tale was only revealed two years after the incident. So, behind Patty Price's story was an evolving process involving multiple figures, with delays and hesitations along the way.

Stories about experiences do not just present themselves fully formed; they are made, and they change. This is not to say that Patty was lying, but circumstances invariably shape the stories that she and all of us tell. Keeping this in mind, it is evident that several people and things had a hand in the making of Patty's alien abduction tale.

First, there was her daughter's original remark about spacemen that at the very least offered a way to reframe the night in question away from either a lurking prowler or a spooked family scenario. Patty only began to explore the possibility of alien intruders when she happened upon the magazine that inspired her to not only reconsider events but also to contact APRO, inviting its consultants to come to her home and interrogate the family. Investigators were far from passive: as one of the leading UFO groups looking into alien abductions as flesh-and-blood events, its team had a clear sense of what to expect and what it sought to know.

This emerges clearly from James Harder's relentless questioning about Patty's examination at the hands of the extraterrestrials. Time and again, she either expressed the wish to not discuss the subject or insisted that it was not terribly disturbing to her. Yet Harder pressed again and again for details. At one point, he even suggested to her that it involved a gynecological examination. She agreed but did not dwell on the subject, explaining that she felt far more violated by the aliens' mind-reading.

"They took my mind, my thoughts." When Patty angrily mentioned she felt treated like a "guinea pig," she seemed to be referring to this. Here is something that is rarely acknowledged in the UFO literature but speaks to a key moment in the evolution of the alien abduction scenario.

Coral and Jim Lorenzen—APRO's lead investigators and the presenters of Patty Price's story—regarded human states of mind and feelings as a crucial part of alien abductions as well as their own investigations. In their 1977 assessment of the phenomenon they concluded, "In the few abduction cases which have come to our attention, we have learned that UFOnauts are curious about our psyches. The Patty Price incident indicates an interest in our emotions and our likes and dislikes." The extraterrestrials were, it seemed, "obtaining psychological profiles" of their captives.[16] At the same time, the Lorenzens took note of the lasting psychological toll these encounters were having on their victims. APRO considered Patty's tempestuous reactions to the memories she conjured both evidence of the truth and a barrier to the truth. Somehow, these responses needed to be addressed, navigated, vanquished.

APRO's consultants did so by mirroring the aliens. While the extraterrestrials attempted to prevail over Patty's resistance by taking her thoughts and experiences to gain the information they sought, James Harder used his own version of mind-control—hypnosis—to overcome Patty's memory loss and her aversion to remembering to find out what the aliens were up to. The content and context of Patty Price's alien abduction echoed one another. Once again, she seemed to find herself being used as a guinea pig.

The invasive tactics of the aliens triggered a reciprocally invasive response by investigators. Research into UFOs had come a long way from the days of tracking the flight paths or comparing the shapes of unidentified flying objects. How did UFO investigation get to this point? Who exactly were these consultants? And why were they resorting to hypnosis?

THE COUNSELING INVESTIGATOR AND MIND CONTROL

By the time reports mushroomed in the 1980s and 1990s, the alien abduction phenomenon had already given birth to a new kind of UFO investigator with a new method of investigation. Back in the fifties and sixties, virtually all self-professed contactees spoke for themselves. They saw no need for intermediaries to help them understand what had happened to them, and they tended to embrace the limelight, prophetically bringing the messages of our extraterrestrial superiors to all willing to listen. Their encounters with space brothers and sisters may have been awe-inspiring, but they were generally accompanied by a comforting sense of personal warmth and reassurance. As a result, few UFO investigators bothered to do much more than dig into the backgrounds of some of the contactees or pick apart their claims. There was no market for a consulting outsider in their cases.

As more ufologists began to engage in fieldwork research over the course of the 1950s, some began to take a more directive approach with timid witnesses, some of whom wished to remain anonymous. This might involve prodding them to meet in person, interviewing them in their homes, and speaking with family, neighbors, and local authorities. Those claiming to have had a close encounter with a flying saucer or its occupants also tended to have more detailed and elaborate stories to tell than those who only caught a fleeting glance of something in the sky—an additional draw for inquisitive ufologists. At times, the information investigators teased out of witnesses could get quite intimate, as in the case of the sexual revelations of Antônio Villas Boas in 1958.

By the time Betty and Barney Hill wrote Donald Keyhoe and NICAP for help in the fall of 1961, it had become a common enough practice for witnesses to initiate contact with UFO organizations. NICAP investigators quickly arrived on the scene and worked closely with the couple. Their investigation, however, took an unusual turn. It was suggested that the Hills seek out a psychiatrist or psychologist to hypnotize them to aid in the inquiry.

This was not the first time hypnosis was used in a close encounter case. After two men in Sweden in 1959 claimed to have come across four lead-gray creatures about four feet tall near their spacecraft, they subsequently were put into a drug-induced hypnotic state—administered sodium amytal or pentothal, at the time commonly referred to as "truth serums"—to see if their story would change.[17] The Hills' case was different. While Betty, Barney, and NICAP investigators believed hypnosis could potentially recover the couple's lost memories, the hypnotist was a psychiatrist who instead saw the technique as a tool to aid in overcoming their anxieties. For him, hypnosis was intended to serve a therapeutic purpose.

Most UFO researchers during the first three and a half decades of the flying saucer era, showed no interest in playing therapist to their informants. They saw themselves as investigators. So, when some began to get trained in hypnotic regression, it was solely with the intent of forensically using it to uncover the truth about alien activities here on earth.

James Harder, the hypnotist in the Patty Price case, was one of the first to do so. Serving as Director of Research at APRO from 1969 to 1982, he personally interviewed up to one hundred contactees. Harder was no clinician, however.[18] He had a PhD in mechanical engineering, specializing in fluid mechanics, and he worked as a professor of engineering at the University of California at Berkeley from 1957 until his retirement in 1991.

Harder's interest in unidentified flying objects developed in 1952. By the mid-sixties, he had become active in APRO, working as a consultant. Around this time that he trained in hypnotic regression, which he believed provided investigators with access to the suppressed memories of those having close encounters with UFOs and their occupants. He would go on to use the technique on a number of high-profile abductees, including Betty Hill, Calvin Parker, Charles Hickson, and Travis Walton.

Harder was convinced that the memories witnesses recovered under hypnosis were so detailed and so consistent with one another that they had to be accepted as accurate. He rejected both the dismissive attitude of the US government toward UFOs as well as the extravagant tales told by famous contactees. Instead, he concluded that the recalled memories of abductees suggested there were various extraterrestrial species visiting earth, some likely benevolent, others not. In any event, they appeared to be interested in studying human beings to suss out their capabilities and frailties.[19] By 1980, the growing number of reports with a sexual dimension led Harder to wonder privately whether an alien group was embarking on a "eugenic program to create more intelligent and compassionate humans via genetic manipulation."[20]

Alien abductees and their investigators at first did not tend to describe their encounters in spiritual, let alone New Age, terms, unlike the early contactees. What made their encounters different was the presence of coercion. Sometimes this involved physical intimidation, but more often than not what victims reported was the aliens' ability to read and control the minds of their captives.

Belief in and concern over the possibility of seeing into and directing another person's mental state was hardly unique to the world of ufology. Interest in the possibility dates back to at least the late eighteenth century, when hypnotism first emerged as a technique. Clinicians and academic researchers debated the extent to which hypnosis could make people perform acts against their will. By the late nineteenth century, some drew inspiration from new technologies such as cable telegraphy, spiritualist seances, and X-rays to argue that "thought reading" and "thought transference"—otherwise known as telepathy—were possible.[21]

With the Cold War, the prospect of mind control took on a more menacing tone.[22] Both sides of the Iron Curtain were militant about the need to shield their citizens from what they considered the subversive intellectual influences of their opponent. In the United States during the 1950s and 1960s, that worry was embodied in the popular notion of "brainwashing." Widely talked about as a form of "mind murder" or "menticide," it was portrayed as a hijacking of an individual's free will so that, as journalist Edward Hunter put it in 1956, they "can be trusted to never revolt, always to be amenable to orders, like an insect to its instincts." Most of the general public became familiar with the idea of brainwashing through the highly publicized cases of American POWs during the Korean War who "turned" while in custody. Some made false confessions and denounced their homeland, and twenty-three went so far as to decide to resettle in communist China. Techniques like sleep deprivation, drug injections, and relentless indoctrination were believed responsible for poisoning the minds of men who eventually reached their breaking point. It soon entered popular culture, reaching a wide audience through Richard Condon's 1959 novel *The Manchurian Candidate* and the subsequent acclaimed Hollywood adaptation in 1962.

Seen against this backdrop, James Harder's brand of hypnotic regression was a kind of psychological combat, a tactic to break through the mental roadblocks aliens were putting up in the minds of those they kidnapped. Indeed, in 1977 Harder helped develop a technique designed to uncover "hidden UFO experiences" in those who never reported or recalled having a close encounter. Holding a small pendulum, the person was to answer a series of carefully selected questions about their unconscious memories. Swings in the direction of the pendulum would indicate "yes" or "no," as muscle memories bypassed the conscious mind.[23]

The use of hypnotic regression in UFO encounters during the sixties and seventies was also advocated by psychologist Leo Sprinkle. Sprinkle earned his Ph.D. in counseling and guidance at the University of Missouri in 1961 and spent decades working as Counseling Psychologist and Associate Professor of Psychology at the University of Wyoming's Counseling and Testing Center.

Sprinkle estimated that he conducted more than five hundred hypnotic regression sessions with people who claimed to have had a close encounter. His interest in UFOs began after he himself had two sightings, one in 1949 and another seven years later. Encouraged by his wife, Marilyn, he joined both APRO and NICAP. In 1963, he started conducting survey research on UFO contactees, and after getting trained in hypnosis in 1965, he applied his clinical skills with alien abductees both as a consultant for APRO and as a private practitioner. Sprinkle was quickly asked to tackle high-profile cases, eventually serving on the *National Enquirer*'s Blue Ribbon UFO Panel. By the early eighties, administrators at the University of Wyoming had become increasingly impatient with Sprinkle's UFO activities, and he tendered his resignation as director of the counseling center there in 1983.[24]

Sprinkle was interested in a broad range of paranormal phenomena besides UFOs, especially reincarnation, near-death experiences, parapsychology, and prophecy. These interests helped inform his evolving views on alien abduction. In 1970, for instance, he told one of his many correspondents he considered it possible that "UFO contactees may be under surveillance in some form of post-hypnotic remote control." His perspective was always expansive. A few months later he added, "It seems to me that it is possible for one to accept the extra-terrestrial hypothesis and the ultra-terrestrial hypothesis."[25] In fact, in 1980 at the age fifty, Sprinkle underwent hypnotic regression and discovered that he too had had an alien encounter as a child.[26]

Like James Harder, Leo Sprinkle considered hypnotism a key tool in unlocking the truth about alien visitations. As a psychologist and clinician, however, he considered its use in UFO research to be fraught. For one thing, he began to see it as a procedure that could enhance a person's imaginative involvement in their experiences, not necessarily something that recovered the "whole" truth.[27] In addition, he saw two sets of potentially conflicting interests at work in the interviews conducted under hypnosis: the interest of UFO researchers to maximize the amount of information revealed and the counseling consultant's interest in relieving distress. In his estimation, hypnotism needed to be handled not just as a way of gathering information but "as a method of providing emotional support and psychotherapeutic assistance to the UFO witness."[28]

It was Sprinkle's insistence on caring for alien abductees that made his a distinctive voice in the field of ufology research in this area.[29] Given his reputation for listening and offering soft-spoken comfort, his demeanor resonated with those who worked with him. Myriad letters from former clients confirm that most found him to be, as one former Ph.D. student expressed it in 1986, "a caring, sincere human being who involves himself much more deeply in his clients' problems and growth than the typical psychologist."[30] Sprinkle was not beyond scolding fellow abductee researchers using hypnosis whom he thought were being overly "argumentative and demanding" in their sessions. As he told two investigators in Seattle in 1981, "we UFO contactees are a sensitive bunch and we need kind reassurance and tender loving care as well as assistance to help us explore our UFO experiences."[31]

Sprinkle went on to encourage the formation of self-help support groups among abductees, and in 1980 he co-founded the annual Rocky Mountain Conferences on UFO Investigation in Laramie, Wyoming, that welcomed contactees to gather and share their experiences and ideas with one another.[32] Over time, he came to view close encounters with aliens as initiations in a collective spiritual journey of growth. As Sprinkle explained to me, he tried to "get [clients] to see the ET experiences as a test" toward "getting ready for cosmic citizenship." His role, as he saw it, was to provide abductees with the training to arrive at some kind of "completion or acceptance of their experience" in place of the attitude of "those goddamn SOBs."[33]

THE INTIMATE INVESTIGATOR

By the beginning of the 1980s, James Harder, Leo Sprinkle, and Coral and Jim Lorenzen together had fashioned a new kind of UFO investigation, along with a new kind of investigator for cases involving alien abduction. The shape, features, and tensions inherent in both would mold the investigation of close encounters for decades to come, especially in the United States. Built around a clinical approach that encouraged storytelling (by the witness) and story making (by the investigator), some who suspected they might have had a close encounter invited outside consultants with links to UFO organizations to help recover buried, troubling memories of their encounters with the help of hypnosis. The results often led to the emergence of elaborate, grippingly dramatic tales that entered the ufology canon.

As the seventies came to a close, other American investigators began exploring cases in a similar fashion. For example, Ann Druffel had been investigating UFO sightings for NICAP in southern California since 1957. After 1970, she joined the Mutual UFO Network as well as Allen Hynek's Center for UFO Studies and became a trained hypnotherapist in 1977.

In August 1975, Druffel started delving into a case involving multiple women in California.[34] It all started when Sara Shaw contacted MUFON after watching a tv documentary about UFOs that made her wonder about a bizarre evening in 1953 when she and a friend were sharing a cabin and suddenly were surrounded by strange lights and caught sight of a "vaporous" figure. She and her friend could recall little else about the event, however. With the assistance of parapsychologist Scott Rogo, Druffel used hypnotic regression with Sara and others to reveal what appeared to be a series of close encounters in the area over several decades with eerily similar features: victims being taken from their home or car, being led by humanoids with elongated heads into a craft, then returned with no memory of events.

In another celebrated case, Raymond E. Fowler—like Druffel, a leading investigator for both CUFOS and MUFON—helped direct a group of researchers in interrogating Betty Andreasson in 1977.[35] Andreasson, a devout Christian and divorced mother of seven children, first reached out to the Center for UFO Studies in 1975 about a strange incident in her home a decade earlier. Enlisting the help of New England Institute of Hypnosis director Harold Edelstein, a team of investigators conducted and recorded more than a dozen hypnotic regression sessions over several months with Betty and her daughter Becky about the evening in question.[36]

Under hypnosis, Betty and Becky (who was eleven at the time) recalled being in the house with the other children when strange entities with an ability to pass through solid objects like walls entered the house. Betty described being taken on board a vessel, forced to change into a white examination garment, and subjected to a series of invasive procedures. She eventually recounted a frightful experience of having a needle placed up her nose and then again through her navel. She later would take solace in the fact that the beings said they were here to offer the inspirational message to live simply and renounce arrogance, one that she believed was a reaffirmation of Christ's teachings. Nevertheless, going through the experience of being prodded with a needle seemed to shake her deeply. At one point, hypnotist Harold Edelstein felt compelled to release her from her trance.

"I didn't experience this when we first went through it," [Betty] said. "Why am I more shaky (sic)?"

"Because you went through a trauma now," Dr. Edelstein explained. "That's why I cut it short."

"But before when it came out, it . . ."

"Because you weren't reliving it," Harold said. "It was just something you were talking about."

Druffel, Rogo, and Fowler shared the details about their investigations in books they published in 1979 and 1980. These display some familiar figures, events, and themes in alien abduction cases: suspecting witnesses with memory lapses contacting ufologists, UFO investigators using hypnotism to recover unconscious recollections, terrifying experiences involving clinical examinations and experiments, aliens with parapsychological powers. But new elements also were present: the emergence of women as principal targets, home invasions with entire households taken captive, and serial abductions over time.

In hindsight, it's evident that investigators and those investigated were taking part in a kind of improvised dance. Neither partner quite knew where the other would lead them, but the alien abduction scenarios that emerged required both sides. The pointed questions of ufologists elicited ever more details about mesmerizing and harrowing events. In turn, the memories that came flooding to the minds of abductees spurred ever deeper questioning on the part of investigators.

Admittedly confused and vulnerable witnesses were spending extended periods of time sharing moving stories with curious and attentive interviewers. Such rapport made it possible for the relationship between factfinder and informant to become one accompanied by deep, mutual affection. Leo Sprinkle enjoyed just such a relationship with his clients. But in the 1980s, a new man came onto the scene who epitomized the figure of the intimate and caring investigator of alien abductions.

Budd Hopkins was a renowned New York abstract artist. His interest in unidentified flying objects dated back to a sighting of his own in 1964. Inspired to join NICAP, he read John Fuller's book about the abduction of Betty and Barney Hill years later and was persuaded that the events recounted were true. After a neighborhood liquor store owner told him about a close encounter with a UFO and its occupants he had had in January 1975, Hopkins began investigating the incident with local ufologist Ted Bloecher. Hopkins would publish an article about the case in *The Village Voice*, and he and Bloecher became good friends.[37]

Over the next few years, Hopkins received letters from individuals claiming to have had experiences of time having gone by for which they could not account. With Bloecher's assistance, he decided to study the phenomenon. As he was talking with one witness, Hopkins had a déjà vu experience, so he arranged to have two hypnosis sessions with a psychiatrist during which he experienced a sense of paralysis. In February 1978, he sought Leo Sprinkle's counsel. Sprinkle urged him to take seriously the hypothesis developed by James Harder and Corel Lorenzen of "hidden UFO experiences," in other words, that many people were living their lives wholly unaware that they had been victims of an alien abduction.[38]

Hopkins's investigations culminated in the summer of 1981 with his book *Missing Time*, in which he detailed seven cases involving people who observed a UFO, then found themselves having no memory of the events that followed.[39] In it, Hopkins declared alien abduction an "epidemic," a global phenomenon that may well affect "tens of thousands of Americans." Like his predecessors, he believed the key to uncovering the truth about encounters lay in hypnotic regression, so he enlisted the help of several clinicians trained in hypnosis, including Robert Naiman, George Fisher, and Aphrodite Clamar. They carried out sessions with abductees over several days, while Hopkins and Bloecher observed and sometimes posed questions themselves.

One of the most arresting cases involved a young writer, artist, and performer, Michael Bershad (aka "Steven Kilburn"), with whom Hopkins began working in 1978. At first, Bershad had only a vague feeling that something had happened to him back in 1973 when he was driving along a Maryland highway. Under hypnosis, he recalled being taken by white, hairless beings with putty-like skin and fingers like tubes who communicated with one another through telepathy. He went on to describe how he was fastened to a table by metal loops and forced "into a posture not unlike that which results from obstetrical stirrups." It made him, he said, "feel like a frog." Paralyzed and dazed, naked save for a diaper, he had a needle inserted into his back.

Hopkins ended his book by inviting others who had similar experiences to write him. At the same time, he insisted it was time for the public to accept that the recovered memories of abductees accurately reflected a harrowing reality. After all, there were precedents for such a thing. One need look no further, he noted, than the recent case of a young woman so traumatized by a sexual assault she had suffered in 1978, she couldn't remember details about it. By undergoing hypnosis, however, she was able to recall the assailant was a former babysitter.

In 1982, Hopkins met David Jacobs, a historian at Temple University, who had published the first academic monograph on the history of the UFO controversy in the United States in 1975. Hopkins soon convinced Jacobs about the authenticity of alien abduction claims. The two men struck up a lasting friendship and collaboration. Jacobs decided to get trained in hypnosis, and by mid-1986 he and Hopkins began working together with witnesses.

Late in 1983, Hopkins received a letter from a woman he referred to as Kathie or Kathy Davis.[40] She had read his book *Missing Time* and wondered if she too might be a victim of the phenomenon. Over the course of several interviews and hypnosis sessions, Davis recounted how extraterrestrials had taken her (and others in her family), removed her clothes, set her on a gynecological examination table, and inserted instruments into her body through her vagina and navel. The pain was extreme. At one point during a regression, she recalled revealingly yelling at her captors, "It's not fair! It's mine! It's mine!" Hearing more stories like this, Hopkins and Jacobs became convinced they had unlocked the key to the strangely clinical nature of alien abductions: they were taking humans for the purpose of a hybrid breeding project.

In 1987, Hopkins published the results of his investigation of Davis's encounter in his book *Intruders*. In his conclusion, he was resolute that there

Fig. 8.4 Budd Hopkins speaking at the MUFON UFO Symposium in San Antonio, Texas in 1984. TopFoto/Fortean.

were only two explanations for what was going on. Either the claims of witnesses "represent some new and heretofore unrecognized and nearly universal psychological phenomenon," or they were real events. The fact that those affected suffered from long-term feelings of "fear, dread, help-lessness, profound maternal confusion and loss, the sense of physical— and even sexual—vulnerability" only added credence to their memories. It was society's obligation to respond accordingly. "[W]e must offer under-standing and heartfelt emotional support to these fellow human beings who have endured such profoundly unsettling, unfathomable, truly alien experiences. They are, in every sense of the word, victims."[41]

In 1992, Davis revealed herself to be Debra Jordan-Kauble and went on to publish her own account of events. While she admitted to having remarkable experiences and dreams, Jordan-Kauble denied ever claiming to have been impregnated or having her baby taken by aliens. In fact, she went so far as to say she herself didn't "know if they originated from out-side or inside me."[42]

CARING VS. CARE

During the second half of the 1980s, offering understanding and support became an integral part of Hopkins's work with abductees. Journalist Patrick Huyghe saw this firsthand. He had been accompanying Hopkins for some time, and the two had become friends. By the summer of 1987, however, things had taken a turn. "I was no longer welcome at regular gatherings, which were now largely comprised of abductees," he later explained. "The once informal get-togethers had become support group meetings with Hopkins acting as counselor."[43]

His books, articles, and public appearances made Hopkins the new super-star of ufology. The Mutual UFO Network offered their stamp of approval, giving him their annual award for the most outstanding contribution to UFO research in both 1986 and 1988. At the same time, his solicitous ap-proach toward abductees meant ever more individuals sought him out.

Hopkins's outlook on the alien abduction phenomenon was a bleak one, however. Both he and his associate David Jacobs categorically rejected any "kind of alien theology" that looked at UFO occupants as enlightened space brothers and at abduction encounters as blessings.[44] The experiences humans were having with extraterrestrials were terrifying, leaving their victims devastated. This was not about transcendence but abuse.

Hopkins responded by establishing the Intruders Foundation in 1989. Funded by UFO enthusiast and businessman Robert Bigelow and a prince from Liechtenstein, the organization was intended to serve two major functions. One facet focused on research, specifically compiling a data bank of information gleaned from hundreds of Hopkins's cases and publishing a quarterly bulletin on developments in the field. The other was about helping abductees deal with their disturbing encounters by setting up a network of sympathetic therapists, hypnotists, and investigators across the United States and Canada to whom anyone in need could turn.

Throughout the 1990s and early-2000s, Hopkins and Jacobs continued their own hands-on interventions, working with a seemingly endless procession of presumptive abductees. Hopkins hosted a regular support group meeting that, over the course of the evening, moved from an informal, party-like atmosphere of small talk and refreshments to a more formal, round-robin discussion of abduction experiences. The key, he said, was adopting a "supportive spirit," helping abductees cope by minimizing their fears and sense of shame and making them "feel normal, comfortable, and at home."[45]

The stories Hopkins and Jacobs brought to public attention became ever more elaborate and bizarre. In 1996, Hopkins published *Witnessed: The True Story of the Brooklyn Bridge Abductions*, which detailed the alleged alien abduction of Linda Napolitano (aka "Linda Cortile") in November 1989.[46] Over several years hypnotizing and talking with Napolitano, Hopkins uncovered details that left even some of his supporters in the UFO community dubious. According to the two, extraterrestrials floated Linda out of her twelfth-floor Manhattan apartment in the middle of the night in full view of several witnesses. Two of the witnesses were supposedly security officers working for the government and Secretary-General of the United Nations Javier Pérez de Cuéllar. Hopkins later revealed that the security guards, Pérez de Cuéllar, Linda, one of her sons, and another woman had all been abducted together at one point.

Even within Hopkins's inner circle, doubts were creeping in. In 1996, Hopkins married filmmaker Carol Rainey, who served as his research partner during their years together. As she later reflected on it, the way in which Budd was handling cases left her with nagging qualms.[47] Here was someone without clinical training, providing unsupervised guidance to vulnerable, distraught people. He seemed oblivious to the power he held over his advisees and ignored evidence when some witnesses were caught in obvious lies. In the Linda Napolitano case, Linda and Budd had shared the advance for his book about her and had agreed to share any subsequent revenue if Hollywood optioned the story. All the while, the abductee was a constant presence in their home, Rainey recalled. "Linda was simply part of our lives, a friend, sometimes at the house being interviewed by the media, sometimes

Budd's co-presenter at conferences. When the rest of Budd's people gathered in the living room for abductee support groups, Linda was always there."

Objections were also later raised about the methods of David Jacobs. Emma Woods (a pseudonym) began speaking with Jacobs about her paranormal experiences in 2002.[48] Between 2004 and 2007, when she finally broke off contact with him, Woods underwent ninety-one hypnotic regressions with the abductee researcher, all over the telephone. In revelations since that time, Woods has described a series of disturbing ethical abuses at the hands of Jacobs. These included discussing the cases of other research subjects with her in advance, failing to bring her out of a hypnotic state after a session ended, presenting his research under false pretenses, telling her to send him her unwashed underpants, and suggesting she wear a chastity belt that he would purchase for her.

The critical reflections of Carol Rainey and Emma Woods on the time they spent with Hopkins and Jacobs ultimately led some of the two men's supporters to disparage the women and their claims in UFO forums and publications. The concerns they raised, however, were hardly new. In the late eighties, another associate of Hopkins and Jacobs, Rima E. Laibow, had raised questions about whether an artist and a historian were qualified to be offering counsel to their fraught charges.

Rima Laibow was a psychiatrist who had a private practice outside of New York City.[49] After a patient of hers in 1988 happened to see an image of a large-eyed alien on a book jacket, she confessed to Laibow she had fragmentary memories of encounters with similar creatures. Laibow soon sought the advice of Budd Hopkins and David Jacobs and became convinced that the abduction phenomenon warranted serious clinical consideration. Later that year, she sought funding from the Fund for UFO Research to create a professional "crisis center" and hotline for individuals left emotionally disturbed by their close encounters.

In May 1989, she organized a conference at Fairfield University in Connecticut, "Treatment and Research of Experienced Anomalous Trauma" (TREAT). The conference brought together clinicians, social scientists, journalists, and UFO investigators to exchange views about frightening close encounters. Laibow's rebranding of "alien abduction" as "experienced anomalous trauma" reflected her growing insistence that (1) the focus be placed on the psychological impact of these experiences and (2) clinical assessment and treatment be given priority in addressing the issue.

Laibow informed the UFO community that, in her experience, a very large number of those who reveal themselves to be abductees also prove to have been victims of child abuse at the hands of human beings.[50] They were, as she put it, "dual victims." As such, they tended to exhibit behavioral patterns similar to victims of child sexual abuse, such as initially experiencing a sense of affection toward their abusers. "As with abused children in general," Laibow wrote, "as they grow older, abductees often report that these feelings of affection are replaced by other, perhaps more appropriate, reactions of fear, anger, distrust and resentment." Little wonder, since "these children are probed, violated, cut, sampled, sometimes impregnated or genitally and sexually stimulated."

Laibow didn't fully commit herself—at least in print—to accepting the reality of alien abductions, but she made it clear both publicly and privately that she considered the work being done by the likes of Hopkins and Jacobs dangerously amateurish. As she put it to journalist Patrick Huyghe, she was seeking to professionalize the field of abduction research. "There's a huge difference in being able to induce a hypnotic trance and being a clinician who knows what to do when you've got a trance, who knows how to not contaminate the material, and who knows how to facilitate recovery rather than cause retraumatization," she argued.

> And what do you do if a UFO investigator does you clinical harm by taking on clinical responsibilities? Where is his malpractice liability, and how are you going to be protected? People who are not willing to take the time and the effort to become clinicians should not be stomping around in the unconscious.[51]

Hopkins's retort was that credentials, especially when it came to the new frontier of alien abduction research, guaranteed nothing.[52]

By late 1989 and 1990, Laibow and Hopkins were exchanging barbs in letters, papers, and comments circulated among ufologists. Each accused the other of unethical behavior: she said Hopkins was not above badgering abductees into saying what he wanted them to say; he said abductees privately described Laibow as "arrogant," "divisive," and "authoritarian." When the second TREAT conference was held in January 1990 in Virginia, Hopkins and Jacobs were not invited.[53] Laibow remained prominently involved in alien abduction studies until at least the mid-nineties. Her skirmish with Hopkins helped move the conversation about the alien abduction phenomenon further into the realm of clinical work, away from supportive caring and toward health care.[54]

TRAUMA

Was it now, as psychotherapist and Hopkins associate Aphrodite Clamar asked in 1988, "time for psychology to take UFOs seriously?"[55] There did appear to be a pathway making this possible: trauma. The idea that certain feelings, thoughts, and memories could have a lasting negative impact on the mental health of a person was already a part of nineteenth- and early twentieth-century medical discussions. After World War II, psychological trauma began to be discussed in the analysis and treatment of Nazi concentration camp survivors. Their experiences of terror and abandonment, persistently upsetting dreams and memories, and emotional and attention difficulties were quickly universalized, as the Holocaust became what clinical psychologist Nathalie Zajde dubbed the "paradigm for mental trauma."[56]

In the United States, the boundaries of the concept began expanding around the late 1960s and early 1970s under two influences.[57] As some returning veterans of the Vietnam War experienced chronic adjustment and mental problems, some clinicians promoted the idea that these men should also be seen as victims of psychological trauma. More important for the alien abductee phenomenon was a parallel trend. Feminist and consciousness-raising groups—bringing political activism, self-help, and self-exploration to center stage—began putting the ordeal of rape on the public agenda. They effectively spurred the growth of local Rape Crisis Centers where victims could find assistance, leading to the establishment of some four hundred centers between 1972 and 1976. These centers, in turn, provided key data for researchers, two of whom—Ann Burgess and Lynda Holstrom—coined the term "rape trauma syndrome" to capture the acute and chronic stress reactions victims had to their assaults.[58] In short order, rape trauma syndrome was being widely applied in both therapeutic and criminal justice settings.

The broad acceptance of mental trauma as a condition eventually spurred the American Psychiatric Association in 1980 to introduce a new diagnosis, post-traumatic stress disorder (PTSD), in its revised *Diagnostic and Statistical Manual*. It declared that "the essential feature is the development of characteristic symptoms" such as feelings of estrangement, sleep disturbance, and memory impairment "following a psychologically traumatic event that is generally outside the range of usual human experience."[59]

By the time Hopkins, Jacobs, Laibow, and others were discussing alien abduction as a harrowing life-event, then, abductees and their advocates had a ready-made vocabulary and set of responses to which to turn for tackling their own experiences. Moreover, the fact that the American Psychiatric Association recognized signs of post-traumatic stress of various kinds as indicators of a genuine disorder triggered by real events seemed to open the way for the alien abduction phenomenon to gain mainstream acceptance.

Alien abduction researchers seized on the opportunity. In 1986, ufologist and sociologist Ron Westrum coined the term "post-abduction syndrome" to characterize the challenges facing abductees after the fact. He emphasized that theirs was hardly a new experience, but rather "it was simply one variant of the post-traumatic stress syndrome which afflicts some Vietnam veterans, rape victims, and those who have been through harrowing accidents, shootings, and so forth."[60] Six years later, David Jacobs refined the diagnosis further, arguing that post-abduction syndrome differed from PTSD in that "external forces" were responsible for repressing the memories in the case of the former.[61] Could it be that psychiatry and psychology—and, ironically enough, not astronomy and military intelligence—were poised to unlock the secrets of alien visitation?

THE PHENOMENON

By the nineties, there were any number of people volunteering to speak on behalf of the alien abductees and to explain what it all meant. Organizations like the Intruders Foundation were in place to help facilitate just this kind of work. And self-appointed UFO investigators often referred puzzled and distraught individuals seeking help to fellow researchers.

Take, for instance, ufologist Cynthia Hind. Based in Zimbabwe, she joined MUFON in 1974, working as a field investigator for the group. During the 1980s, Hind established herself as the leading UFO researcher in Africa and went on to publish the periodical *UFO Afrinews* from 1988 to 2000.

In June 1996, Hind was approached by an ex-Rhodesian soldier who asked for her help looking into an experience he had during his service in the late 1970s. The man explained to her that he had been abducted by aliens at that time and was subjected to violent and disturbing experiments. The two wrote one another, and during their correspondence Hind encouraged the veteran to recount more details. She asked questions about things such as any smells he noted and how the extraterrestrial communicated with him. After several months of correspondence, Hind told him:

> As usual, your letter was fascinating, with the new information. I will get this all together for you to make a story. I am sure you have many more recall events, but I would really like you to try and do some regressive hypnosis with someone of note. I have never believed in keeping my cases secret, and willingly hand them over for study to the top people in the field if I think they are worthwhile and I am sure yours is . . . I know Dr. John Mack of Harvard University who

specializes in cases like yours; also Prof. Leo Sprinkle of Laramie, in the USA; Budd Hopkins, Dr. David Jacobs, Joe Nyman, a clinical psychologist, Dr. Grey Woodman (all of the United States); John Spencer and Philip Mantle (BUFORA in the United Kingdom). These are all the top people in the world: could I pass on your case to them, not mentioning your name if you don't want me to, although they never reveal identities unless you agree.[62]

The reach of the UFO expert network, as it had for decades, still extended across oceans and continents.

Amid all the speculating and squabbling over alien abductions that characterized the 1980s and spilled over into the 1990s, it is perhaps easy to overlook one group: the abductees themselves. At times, they seemed lost in the shuffle, as self-professed specialists interpreted their experiences and presented them to the public in books and interviews. Some, however, were able to bypass the middlemen and speak for themselves.

Arguably the most famous and influential abductee has been someone who never entirely considered himself a victim of alien abduction at all. Whitley Strieber was a successful fiction writer, acclaimed for his horror novels *Wolfen* (1978) and *The Hunger* (1981), when he published *Communion: A True Story* in 1987.[63] In it, he chronicled his attempt to recall and understand several encounters he and his wife had had with uncanny phenomena. At the center stood an experience he had while staying at his cabin in upstate New York the day after Christmas 1985.

That night, he noticed several murky figures moving around in his bedroom. Suddenly, he found himself being taken from his cabin, naked and unable to move. The beings—some short and stocky, others slender with slanted dark eyes—eventually inserted a needle into his head, then transported him to an operating theater, where an object with wires was inserted into his rectum. He was outraged at the violation.

Afterward, Strieber said he exhibited various physical ailments and remained frustrated by his cloudy sense that something distressing had happened to him. He did what so many others before had done: he consulted some of the literature on UFO sightings and alien abductions. The experiences he read about seemed similar to his, so he called Budd Hopkins, who had been mentioned in one of the books. It was decided that Strieber be hypnotized by a professional. Renowned psychiatrist Donald Klein of Columbia University took on the job in March 1986, with Hopkins present.

What eventually emerged from these sessions were memories Strieber had of other strange encounters throughout his life. What most struck him was a recollection he had of one of the entities once saying to him, "You are our chosen one." This, among other things, led Strieber to wonder who these "visitors" were. Aliens? The dead? Folkore sprites? Ultraterrestrials? His own unconscious? He never could settle on any one explanation for what he has come to refer to as "the phenomenon."

Strieber's story became a bestseller, but for many the most gripping part of the book was its cover art—a contextless portrait of a so-called grey alien with a triangular-shaped head and large black eyes. Since its first appearance, the image has triggered numerous people to weigh whether they too might have had encounters with such visitors. The work was the creation of Ted Seth Jacobs, an artist with an interest in UFOs since the 1940s and who also was good friends with ufologist Ted Bloecher. Jacobs was eventually introduced to Budd Hopkins, who in turn recruited him to work with abductees on graphically reconstructing what they remembered. He described his process as akin to a police sketch artist's. Hopkins invited him to work with Whitley Strieber, and Jacobs and Strieber sat down in a New York City apartment and together fine-tuned the image.[64]

Though Strieber had consulted Hopkins for guidance and thanked him in his book's acknowledgments, the two men soon drifted apart. While there were some personal issues driving a wedge between them, at the heart of the matter were considerable differences in how the two believed the alien abduction phenomenon should be interpreted and handled. Hopkins thought the aliens were engaged in breeding experiments and that those who had encountered them required therapeutic support. Strieber, on the other hand, remained open-minded about who the "visitors" were and increasingly saw the encounter experience as a test or an opportunity for spiritual growth requiring enlightenment, not repair.[65]

THE ABDUCTEES

By the end of the summer of 1987, Strieber began forming his own referral service network of doctors and counselors—excluding UFO investigators—for others who were having paranormal experiences. Since the publication of his book, Strieber was receiving a steady stream of letters from people all over the world detailing their own inexplicable experiences. That response led him to begin publishing his own bulletin for subscribers in spring 1989, *The Communion Letter*.

In its first issue, Strieber lodged some pointed criticism at those like Budd Hopkins and David Jacobs who used hypnosis to reveal abusive scenarios. In all the letters Strieber was receiving, he said,

Fig. 8.5 The cover of Whitley Strieber's 1987 book, *Communion*. Artist Ted Seth Jacobs made the influential portrait based on Strieber's description. CBW/Alamy Stock Photo.

There are only a handful that mention anything like the "alien rape" scenario that is the main feature of books written by UFO "abduction" researchers. It almost seems that you have to be hypnotized by one of these researchers, or become convinced by their books, in order to remember something like this.

It seems important to avoid being hypnotized by "abduction" researchers. They are not helping us to overcome our fears and build our relationship with the visitors. People end up full of anger and fear, huddling together in little groups that spend most of their time alien bashing. It is beginning to seem more and more that the whole alien abduction/alien rape scenario may be a fantasy that started in the minds of the "abduction" researchers themselves.[66]

Two years later in a farewell he wrote to subscribers upon retiring his newsletter, Strieber did not hold back about those he accused of "brainwashing" unfortunate people. The "so-called 'UFO-ologists' are probably the cruellest (sic), nastiest and craziest people I have ever encountered. Their interpretation of the visitor experience is rubbish from beginning to end. The 'abduction reports' that they generate are not real. They are artifacts of hypnosis and cultural conditioning."[67]

Despite his misgivings about support groups for abductees, Strieber gave his stamp of approval to the formation of local Communion groups across the United States. By the spring and summer of 1989, these had sprung up in cities like Cleveland, San Antonio, Los Angeles, Boulder, Minneapolis, Houston, and New York City. Organizers sometimes reached out to others in their area with visitor experiences through Strieber himself, who would pass on the invitation to those who had written to him personally. The informal, self-run circles offered a space for sharing thoughts and feelings. Ranging in size from ten to thirty-five members, some met weekly at local restaurants, while others incorporated barbecues and camping trips in their activities. What all the groups shared was an environment of welcoming fellowship. "What keeps the group together is that we all like each other," the San Antonio group told Strieber. "Although our goal is information, rather than therapy, we find we've been brought closer together by being able to talk freely about such an emotionally charged subject."[68]

It is difficult to generalize about who exactly became active in such communities in the late eighties and early nineties. Sociologist Christopher Bader surveyed one abductee group around this time that tended to share Strieber's more encouraging attitude toward the phenomenon.[69] Bader found that among its membership around two-thirds were female, with an average age of forty-four; almost 89 percent self-identified as "white" (the rest as native American); 55 percent were married; and 68 percent had attended college. Members also reported being abducted on average ten times, yet 88 percent found the experience to be at least partly positive.

One of the most conspicuous aspects of the alien abduction phenomenon by the 1990s was the prominence of women. Well into the decade, males continued to dominate organized ufology. Religious studies scholar Brenda Denzler found that between the years 1995 and 1997, 80 percent of invited speakers at twenty-one UFO conferences were men, while male authors accounted for 87 percent of the articles published in major UFO periodicals around this time. Yet various surveys conducted during the first half of the decade showed that between 55 percent and 74 percent of alien abductees were women.[70] Here was one area where women's voices were consistently given a privileged place in the UFO scene.

Nevertheless, as Denzler also observed, women tended to be restricted to being abduction witnesses, and if they wrote about the subject, it was generally to chronicle their own story. Female researchers like Ann Druffel and Jenny Randles or abductee-turned-investigator Karla Turner were exceptions.[71] Far more often women were placed in the role of vulnerable informant to charismatic male figures who acted as their counselors and spokesmen.

While a good deal is known about the social background of abductees in the eighties and nineties, the scope of the phenomenon is sketchier. In 1991, Budd Hopkins, David Jacobs, and Ron Westrum helped organize a survey of 5,947 Americans conducted by the public opinion research center Roper.[72] Those polled were given a list of various unusual experiences—for example, seeing a terrifying figure in the bedroom or having the feeling of flying through the air—and asked, "how often has this occurrence happened to you?" The results led them to conclude that the alien abduction scenario was part of the experience of perhaps as many as one out of every fifty adults, or 3.7 million Americans. Skeptics heavily criticized the study and disputed the organizers' conclusions.[73]

The fact that so much of the public attention surrounding the phenomenon revolved around cases in the United States begged the question: was alien abduction somehow a peculiarly American thing? Some ufologists outside the country at the time certainly thought so and wondered aloud why their counterparts across the Atlantic were becoming so obsessed with topic.[74] There is in fact good evidence supporting the notion that its principal home was the United States. In 1988, researcher Paolo Fiorino found that out of 382 reports of close encounters of the third kind in Italian history, less than a dozen possibly fit the description of an alien abduction, and the media there showed little interest in the subject.[75] Folklorist Thomas Bullard found that by 1994 two-thirds of all alien abduction reports worldwide came from North America.[76]

There were, then, claims of coercive encounters with extraterrestrials elsewhere in the world, even if the numbers appeared to be smaller. UFO periodicals reported on cases from Brazil, France, Sweden, and the United Kingdom, among other places. In some settings, the scenarios were strikingly different from those coming out of the United States. Soviet witnesses in the eighties, for instance, sometimes described confrontations with human-looking entities, other times with creatures that seemed like small animals.[77] In 1984, researcher Antonio Ribera found that in Spain 90 percent of the abductees were young people, most of whom were male, and they tended to report being given a mysterious charge by their captors, along with a cryptic message.[78] During the second half of the 1990s, anthropologist Erik Saethre conducted fieldwork with the aboriginal Warlpiri people of central Australia.[79] Many in their community reported seeing flying saucers, though none had ever seen the occupants inside. While they believed the aliens posed no direct threat to them—although it was supposed the extraterrestrials were draining water sources—it was widely thought that they did abduct "white people" who went off on their own. As such, they recommended that non-aboriginal visitors to their community ensure they had one of the Warlpiri with them when driving home at night.

In many instances, alien abduction scenarios elsewhere in the world stuck closely to the pattern that had emerged in the United States. This was not an accident, as investigators looked to American counterparts for guidance. Abductee researcher Johannes Fiebag, for example, consulted the works of Budd Hopkins, David Jacobs, Whitley Strieber, and Ray Fowler for his 1994 examination of cases throughout central Europe.[80] He too relied on hypnosis and found many of his informants by inviting audiences in his lectures and readers of his publications to contact him about their experiences. Fiebag found virtually all the now-conventional elements of the alien abduction scenario: a sense of missing time; encountering a book or film that inspired the witness to reexamine their memories; being taken at night in one's bedroom; memories of being abducted during childhood; recollections of undergoing medical exams and experiments, often of a sexual nature; discovering strange scars. Like his predecessors, Fiebag began to organize a self-help support group for abductees to deal with the trauma, one modeled on those found in the United States.

THE DOCTOR

In 1990, a new high-profile figure entered the scene surrounding alien abduction. John Mack had been a professor of psychiatry at the Harvard Medical School since 1972. A man with eclectic interests, he published a Pulitzer Prize–winning biography of T. E. Lawrence, studied the psychological impact of the specter of nuclear war, and founded the Center for Psychological Studies in the Nuclear Age at the Cambridge Hospital. As his activism and interests expanded to include environmentalism, the center's name was changed to the Center for Psychology and Social Change.

In January 1990, Mack met Budd Hopkins, who told him about the work he had been doing. Dubious about the claims of alien abduction, Mack began reading the works of Hopkins, Whitley Strieber, and others and was intrigued. He agreed to meet with some abductees and found their stories compelling. By August of that year, he told Carl Sagan he saw no way that the experiences of such individuals could be chalked up to some version of a contagious religious fervor; their memories were unwanted, intrusive, too traumatic.[81] He decided he would explore the phenomenon in a more deliberate fashion.

By the time John Mack added his voice to the conversation about extraterrestrial encounters, the alien abduction scenario in the United States

Fig. 8.6 John Mack in 1992. © 1992 John E. Mack Archives LLC.

already had taken on medical overtones. As American Studies scholar Bridget Brown has observed, the contactee of the 1980s and 1990s was less likely to portray aliens as gods than as clinical researchers.[82] In turn, abductees responded to their experiences by embracing self-help, psychotherapy, and the language of trauma, while psychiatrists and counselors of various kinds were offering treatment and supporting the work of abduction investigators. The involvement of someone with Mack's background, then, was not altogether novel or strange.

What made Mack's association with alien abduction so noteworthy was his position as an esteemed professor at one of the world's most prestigious universities. Up until this point, the medical establishment appeared to favor the position taken by two French physicians in 1983: those claiming to have had encounters with extraterrestrials were by and large clinically delusional.[83] It was soon apparent that Mack would be lending his stature to the view that abductees were not only sincere but also of sound mind and eminently reliable.

Mack's openness to the stories the abductees were telling stemmed from more than his commitment to being a caring listener; it also sprang from his evolving understanding of human consciousness.[84] By the early nineties, he had come to embrace the perspective of transpersonal psychology. The field had emerged in the late 1960s as one of many activist movements within the American psychological sciences proposing an alternative to conventional academic psychology.[85] Transpersonal psychology was concerned with humanity's ultimate potential beyond the personal self toward understanding and achieving holistic, spiritual, and transcendent states of consciousness.[86] It "envisioned the human psyche as embedded in invisible realms, as immersed in a context that extends beyond our ordinary ken, beyond the reality presented by our sense experience."[87] Incorporating cosmic awareness, wonder, mystical encounters, and spiritual enlightenment, transpersonal psychology had strong ties to themes that had been part of the New Age movement for decades.

Mack's curiosity was thus piqued by the prospect that alien abduction might offer a unique glimpse into human contact with the transcendent. He began taking on abductees as clients, and throughout 1991 and early 1992, his caseload picked up. By the time the CBS television network broadcast in May 1992 the miniseries *Intruders*, based on Hopkins's book of that name, Mack had investigated fifty-eight cases. After that, he was in such high demand he had to turn away requests for consultations.[88]

He soon established a standard set of practices in working with abductees.[89] An assistant first screened prospective clients to ensure they showed no indications of psychopathology but had some memories of being abducted by aliens. Despite this, Mack estimated that about a quarter of those he saw turned out not to be genuine abductees. In an initial session, he spent two hours going over their personal history. No physical exam was conducted. After this, subsequent sessions generally lasted about three hours. At first he relied on hypnotic regression, using deep breathing exercises to help abductees recall details of their experiences but eventually abandoned hypnosis in favor of simple relaxation methods. Initially, Mack saw his clients in his home (sometimes in his son's bedroom), but he later used his office at Cambridge Hospital. In addition to the one-on-one work, he also organized a support group that met monthly.

Skeptical colleagues then and now have questioned why an accomplished clinician like John Mack was indulging these new clients.[90] More might be learned, however, by considering why they were seeking him out. Karin Austin, an abductee who worked closely with Mack and is the executive director of the John E. Mack Institute, recently explained her less-than-direct path to his doorstep.[91] Following her abduction experience, she first reached out to SETI and NASA, thinking they might offer helpful resources in understanding what was happening. When it was clear they couldn't, she visited a MUFON meeting, but members there showed no interest in abduction cases. Next Austin called a local hypnotherapist, who disappointingly assured her he could rid her of the spacemen by curing her insomnia.

She then visited a clinician who wrote her a prescription for antipsychotic medication, which she promptly threw in the trash.

"So where does one go after that?" Austin observed. "When 'alien' beings that don't seem to exist in our spacetime are suddenly appearing in one's home in the middle of the night? In the nineties, David Jacobs, Budd Hopkins, and John Mack were the most visible and respected researchers known to be working with [abductees]." For her at least, Mack was the ideal candidate to help, "someone who was inclined to work within the strictures of science and . . . a researcher who was reputable, highly intelligent, and not inclined to immediately psychopathologize me."

THE CONFERENCE

While he worked with his clients, Mack also consulted regularly with other abductee investigators. As he did, he was struck by the ways witnesses were describing what had happened to them. He was persuaded of their utter sincerity by the powerful, traumatic emotions their experiences elicited, the consistency in their testimony despite their isolation from one another, and the fact that even children as young as age two reported encounters. That said, he remained non-committal as to whether these were actual encounters with physical extraterrestrials or something even more ineffable. The fact that every abductee he had met had come away from the encounter with a deepened sensitivity to the environmental crisis facing the world at the end of the millennium confirmed that the experiences carried weighty moral and ontological implications. In his eyes, "the phenomenon" represented a challenge to Western materialist science and to conventional notions of reality.[92] Mack quickly dispensed with the label "abductee," which he found too confining, and redubbed those claiming such encounters "experiencers." The name stuck.

Mack then did something that made him a hero to abductee researchers while also placing himself in the crosshairs of critics. Over five days in June 1992, he and MIT physics professor David Pritchard co-chaired the first academic Abduction Study Conference. Hosted by MIT, it was financed with funds from the Robert Bigelow Foundation and the Fund for UFO Research, the latter of which had already given around a half million dollars to the study of unidentified flying objects since 1979.

The list of participants reads like a Who's Who of alien abduction researchers from the Anglophonic world over the previous three decades. Besides Budd Hopkins and David Jacobs, there were papers by Ann Druffel, Richard Hall, James Harder, Jenny Randles, and many others. In addition, several alien abductees were invited to speak. While a range of topics and perspectives were represented, the conference focused on a few themes: abductee experiences, supporting physical evidence, psychological profiles of abductees, theories on what was going on, and the ethics of investigation and therapy. Journalist C. D. B. Bryan interviewed several of the presenters and went on to publish a book about the conference—*Close Encounters of the Fourth Kind*—which received rather positive, though generally skeptical, reviews.[93]

In his opening remarks at the conference, Mack acknowledged that they were embarking on a controversial path and called his colleague David Pritchard "courageous" and "heroic" for organizing it. To Mack, what experiencers were reporting held the potential for something momentous. Did the phenomenon, he asked, demand the creation of "a new scientific paradigm" about what exists in the universe, and did it raise the possibility that our consciousness is really "the play of some divine or cosmic technology?"[94]

Those attending the conference left with renewed confidence in their ventures. For some, like veteran ufologist Richard Hall, the conference forced him to reconsider any doubts he had had about the phenomenon. For others, the meeting further cemented their convictions about the reality and importance of alien abductions. Afterward, Budd Hopkins told a few fellow researchers that it would be best in the future to exclude abductees from some sessions, so that investigators and therapists could speak more freely among themselves.[95]

The conference made Mack an instant celebrity. His measured, thoughtful tone attracted journalists across the country, and a steady stream of newspapers, magazines, and television stations interviewed or featured him. He also drew the attention of wealthy businessman Laurance Rockefeller, who shared his interest in environmental conservation and UFOs. With funds donated by Rockefeller—over the years 1993–2001 amounting to $1.2 million—Mack founded the Program for Extraordinary Experiences Research (PEER) in 1993 as a project housed within his Center for Psychology and Social Change. It was under the auspices of PEER that he continued his work with experiencers.[96]

BACKLASH

While many in ufology circles were delighted by the breath of fresh air Mack seemed to inject into alien abduction discussions, others took a dim view of developments. Most tellingly, members of his own profession were among the first to speak out critically about his methods. Director of the Ridgeview Center for Dissociative Disorders George K. Ganaway expressed the concern that Mack was "feeding into a mutual deception" by "encouraging the patient to accept such memories as truths rather than looking at all the different possibilities that may be contributing to why the person is conceptualizing his experience this way." Ganaway and others were equally critical of his reliance on hypnotic suggestion as a technique for memory enhancement, something the American Medical Association in June 1993 warned was "fraught with problems of misapplication." The testimony of vulnerable self-identified experiences was too easy to fit into the therapist's version of reality, clinical professor of psychiatry at Georgetown Medical School James S. Gordon argued. "If you're looking for false memories, you're more likely to find false memories," he pointed out, "and if you're looking to say they are absolutely true, then that's what you're going to find as well."[97]

Mack was undaunted, and he began working on a book. As he continued his work with experiencers, he searched for outlets to publish the results of his investigations. At some point in 1992 or 1993, he submitted an article to a peer-reviewed psychiatric journal. Reviewers requested extensive revisions before it could be re-evaluated for possible publication, a normal revise and resubmit stage. Mack, however, considered the suggested revisions too demanding, the importance of his research too pressing for him to wait any longer. He decided to move forward with the book, bypassing academic journals and publishers—that would have required peer evaluations before deciding to publish—and reaching an agreement with the commercial press Charles Scribner's Sons/Macmillan.[98]

In the late fall of 1993, Budd Hopkins looked over a draft of Mack's manuscript with foreboding.[99] He wrote the psychiatrist a lengthy letter outlining the reasons why "I fear that your book offers every reason the skeptic needs to reject your message, and little reason to take it seriously." Hopkins told his friend that there was too much discussion of the use of hypnosis, too many clients making unrelated, hyperbolic claims, and too great an emphasis on Mack's spiritual interpretation of things. He added, "on a more personal level, John, I'm worried about your own fine reputation. I'm worried that you will be seen as a latter-day Timothy Leary, preaching a wobbly philosophy based on a 'dangerous, even reprehensible' technique—hypnosis rather than drugs, channeling rather than tripping."

The two men went on to address these and some other criticisms Hopkins had. When the book was released a few months later, it was dedicated "To Budd Hopkins, who led the way."[100] It became a bestseller, outstripping sales of his biography of Lawrence of Arabia and leading to an appearance on Oprah Winfrey's television show. On TV, Mack related not only the stories of some of his clients but also his thoughts on how the spiritual transformation of experiencers seemed to indicate that alien abductions were part of two grand projects—"changing human consciousness to prevent the destruction of the earth's life and a joining of two species for the creation of a new evolutionary form." In contrast to Hopkins, Mack saw hope and promise in the encounters of experiencers.

Following publication of his book, media interest in John Mack and his views on alien abduction soared throughout the rest of 1994 and 1995. Not all the attention was positive, however. In late April 1994, *Time* magazine published a critical article about Mack's work, featuring Donna Bassett, who had been one of his experiencer clients.[101] Bassett had undergone several hypnotic regression sessions and had revealed, among other things, that her grandmother had seen "little people," she had had a childhood alien friend named "Jane" who exhibited healing powers, and she had once met John F. Kennedy and Nikita Khrushchev onboard a UFO during the Cuban missile crisis. Telling *Time* it had all been a sham, she revealed herself as an undercover debunker. Her investigation, she claimed, showed that Mack steered abductee testimony, observed no formal research protocols, provided no consent forms to his research subjects, and billed insurance companies for some of the work he did with experiencers.

Mack denied any wrongdoing. Within Mack's PEER community in Cambridge, Bassett was remembered as a troubled and divisive figure in the abductee self-help group, someone who had seemed determined to undermine Mack's authority. Some questioned her mental stability, and it remained an open question as to whether she ever had been working as an undercover journalist. A few months later, at the national meeting of the skeptics' organization CSICOP in June, Bassett turned up to confront an unsuspecting Mack, who had been invited to defend his work to the group. Asked afterward by one attendee why she had gone undercover and was so focused on Mack, Bassett was said to have replied, "Because that's how Hitler started."[102]

Critical comments from academics only seemed to reinforce Bassett's complaints, however. Richard Ofshe, a sociologist at Berkeley who specialized in studying coercive influence in interrogation settings, went on record saying he considered Mack's methods not simply wrong-headed but dangerous. "If this were just an example of some zany new outer limit of how foolish psychology and psychiatry can be in the wrong hands, we'd look at it, roll our eyes, and walk away," he told *Time*. "But the use of his techniques in counseling is substantially harming lots of people."

Harvard Medical School decided it was time to look into the accusations and in June appointed an ad hoc committee of three faculty members to do so. Chaired by the former editor of the *New England Journal of Medicine* Arnold Relman, the committee was not asked to investigate alleged misconduct but rather "to determine whether Dr. Mack's work met 'the standards expected of a faculty member at the Harvard Medical School.'" Over several months, the committee read Mack's publications and reviews of his book, interviewed academic psychiatrists as well as PEER staff and experiencers, and listened to twenty-five to thirty hours of audio tapes of regression sessions Mack conducted with abductees. A draft of the group's final report was sent to Mack and his lawyers in December for their comments. One of the lawyers, however, leaked some of its content to people connected to the Mutual UFO Network, an action that led to his firing; by March 1995 aspects of the report were being discussed in online forums. The final report was eventually sent to Mack and his team a few months later.

The committee, insisting that they were not calling into question his right to study and argue anything he desired, determined that Mack's work with abductees was riddled with methodological shortcomings. They singled out, for instance, his lack of peer review publications and his lack of consideration of psychological explanations for the experiences of his informants. The committee was most concerned about the fact that Mack did not make clear whether he was treating abductees as research subjects (S) or as patients (P) and that he was inappropriately steering the testimony of experiencers. Listening to the audio tapes, the committee concluded "that his choice of words, his line of questioning and his reactions to their statements reflected a persistent pressure on the S/Ps (sometimes subtle, at other times overt and aggressive) to get them to accept that they had really been abducted by aliens (or to reinforce the S/Ps' belief that they had) and to dismiss other possible explanations."[103]

That summer, the dean of the Harvard Medical School issued his final judgment voicing his agreement with the committee's findings. Although he warned Mack to be more careful in upholding the standards of conduct for clinical practice and research, there were no sanctions, and he remained a "member in good standing of the Harvard Faculty of Medicine."[104]

But the floodgates had been opened. Up until the publication of Mack's book, social scientists had rarely tackled the subject of alien abduction directly, save for the occasional comment to a journalist. Afterward, this changed.

The reason for this change of heart was not entirely due to Mack's involvement with abductees. Since 1993, a number of academics were voicing their criticisms of the idea that so-called repressed memories could be recovered. A public and acrimonious debate took place, which one critic dubbed "the memory wars."[105] What spurred skeptics to weigh in on the matter was a growing number of individuals—many, if not most, of whom were women—claiming to have recovered lost memories of sexual abuse earlier in their lives. Coupled with this was the rise of allegations against teachers and day-care centers of having engaged in the sexual abuse and murder of children as part of Satanic cult rituals. These accusations, initiated by charismatic Christian groups, were bolstered by the testimony of children whose memories of events were supposedly recovered through interrogation. Despite the absence of forensic evidence in these cases, many reputations were sullied, careers ended, and some individuals were jailed.[106]

The same year John Mack's book was released, social psychologist Elizabeth Loftus, New Yorker magazine writer Lawrence Wright, and sociologist Richard Ofshe published their own books about repressed memory and Satanic ritual abuse.[107] Together they pointed to multiple shortcomings in the assumptions, techniques, and conclusions of those engaged in helping people recover what they presumed to be lost memories. The result, they argued, was that "false memories" were being produced, feeding a moral panic that unnecessarily led to the ruin of lives and families.

The similarities between Satanic ritual abuse and alien abduction claims and the way they circulated were evident.[108] In both cases, crusading, self-appointed experts—often with little to no formal training—guided victims to recover supposedly buried memories of harrowing events and acted as their advocates. They spread the word about the phenomena through conferences, papers, and articles, and they advised the public on how to look for signs of undetected experiences. And when questions about what were admittedly spectacular allegations were raised, proponents pointed to the signs of traumatic stress in witnesses as proof of their veracity.

Starting in 1993 and 1994, skeptical social scientists began setting their sights on the alien abduction scenario. Psychologist and director of the Laboratory for Experimental Hypnosis at Carleton University Nicholas Spanos was one of those leading the charge.[109] In a number of pieces, Spanos argued that the similarities in the stories abductees told need not be attributed to accurately recovered memories of real events, but rather were more likely artifacts of a process of socialization on the part of individuals predisposed to esoteric beliefs. Since "abduction survivors frequently befriend one another and also participate in support groups where they share experiences and offer one another mutual support," he noted, it is hardly surprising that this sharing of memories is "likely to enhance the uniformity with which such 'memories' are described and understood."[110]

Spanos's criticisms were reinforced in 1995 by social psychologists Steven Clark and Elizabeth Loftus. In a review of his book *Abduction*, the two criticized John Mack for neglecting years of research confirming the unreliability of human memory and the peculiar vulnerabilities of highly suggestible individuals. Taking him to task especially for his reliance on hypnosis, Clark and Loftus noted that decades of research on the technique had shown "that although hypnosis may increase the vividness and detail of recall, as well as the sheer volume of recall, it does not increase the overall accuracy of memory."[111]

Then in 1996, the journal *Psychological Inquiry* dedicated around one hundred pages to a target article and twelve commentaries about alien abduction. Authored by psychologists Leonard Newman and Roy Baumeister, it offered a "cognitive-motivational" explanation for the apparent memories individuals were having about being abused by extraterrestrials.[112] Newman and Baumeister flagged a number of characteristics of abductees that were likely contributing to the creation of false memories: a susceptibility to sleep-induced hallucinations, high suggestibility, exposure to publicity about alien abductions, a tendency to fantasize, and a masochistic streak.

The commentators were mostly unconvinced by Newman and Baumeister's explanations but generally agreed that memories of alien abduction were not a reflection of real events. John Mack and colleagues from PEER were also invited to comment. Experiencers, they responded, did not repeat nor derive pleasure from their experiences; a third of accounts did not involve hypnosis; many events did not occur at bedtime; and abductees showed no signs of being unusually prone to fantasy.[113]

That same year, the television science documentary series *Nova* explored alien abduction. The episode featured both Budd Hopkins and John Mack, but its unflattering portrait of their work as well as the inclusion of whistleblower Donna Bassett and skeptics Elizabeth Loftus and Carl Sagan left the two men cold. Hopkins and Mack went on investigating cases, speaking to the media, writing books, and giving talks at UFO meetings, but by the end of the millennium, it was clear that alien abduction was not commanding the public's attention as it had just a half dozen years earlier. Indeed, Mack's 1994 *Abducted* remained the only book on the subject to make the *New York Times* bestseller list. When he published his second book on the topic in 1999, *Passport to the Cosmos*, it garnered far fewer readers and less media attention. Four years later, Mack's organization PEER ended its work.[114]

The alien abduction phenomenon hardly disappeared after 2000: experiencer groups continue to be a staple at most of the larger UFO conventions, and online forums have provided spaces for abductees–some now preferring to be called "witnesses"–to converse. But the landscape changed. Some of the most prominent faces in abduction research found it difficult to shake well-publicized criticisms about their handling of controversial cases involving female advisees: Budd Hopkins with Linda Napolitano, John Mack with Donna Bassett, and David Jacobs with Emma Woods.[115] These episodes may well have contributed to journalists—especially science reporters—looking elsewhere for news stories. At the same time, the internet made the figure of the abductee expert increasingly obsolete since it afforded experiencers the possibility of bypassing them completely, as they established contact with one another directly.[116] And with the deaths of Mack in 2004 and Hopkins in 2011, the abductee community lost two of its most high-profile voices.

What is to be made of the alien abduction phenomenon? How can it be explained? Abductee researchers, of course, offered their own thoughts: extraterrestrial breeding experiments and empyrean communion with visitors from other worlds were the two most popular alternatives.

By contrast, psychiatrists and clinical psychologists outside the experiencer community have more frequently looked on the experience as a clinical syndrome. There are indications that abductees may be especially prone to sleep disorders like sleep paralysis and also to certain personality dysfunctions.[117] Other studies, however, have found no evidence of higher rates of psychopathology among abductees in comparison with the general population.[118] Instead, it has been argued that abductees manifest a tendency to hold New Age beliefs and score unusually high on tests for so-called absorption, "a measure related to a vivid imagination and a rich fantasy life."[119] That said, a 2014 study found there to be something of a disagreement between practicing clinicians and researchers when it came to the phenomenon of recovered memory, the latter being more skeptical about its accuracy than the former.[120]

While it can be debated whether there is something common in the makeup of abductees, the psychological focus on individuals largely neglects something that has been true of the UFO phenomenon from the start: it has a history. Reports of close encounters changed over time, as did the responses to those claims. Regardless of whether the accounts of witnesses are true, false, or something in between, people could only make sense of these out-of-the-ordinary experiences and descriptions based on what was familiar to them. Context inevitably informed content.

Looking simply at the substance of stories emerging from the testimony of abductees, it is evident that certain themes consistently cropped up that mirrored prevailing trends in popular culture. This was no accident. Researchers of close encounters in the late sixties and seventies, for instance, openly drew inspiration from the occult revival. Their turn to parapsychology, in turn, helped feed interest in the supposed telepathic powers of extraterrestrial captors. The preoccupation of investigators like Leo Sprinkle and John Mack with the dangers posed by atomic energy, nuclear war, and environmental pollution was hardly theirs alone. The year that christened the start of the American environmental movement with "Earth Day"—1970—was the same year eschatologist Hal Lindsey published his popular book *The Late Great Planet Earth*, in which he mapped biblical prophecy onto current geopolitical calamities. The likelihood of global cataclysm appeared to lurch precariously between fact and fiction over a span of ten years. The Three Mile Island accident in 1979, the films *The Day After* (1983), *War Games* (1983), and *Threads* (1984), the disasters at Bhopal in 1984 and Chernobyl in 1986, and the Exxon Valdez oil spill in 1989, all contributed to a haunting sense of doom awaiting humanity and the planet.[121]

Nor were the kinds of anxieties expressed in alien kidnapping tales altogether unusual. This becomes evident from the location of reported abductions and how this changed over the decades. As time went on, the number of witnesses reporting being taken from a vehicle or out in the open declined, while the number saying they were taken from their bedroom rose considerably.

Certain current events and cultural trends speak to this pattern. The phenomenon that became known as carjacking, a term first coined in 1991, did not receive sustained press coverage until the 1990s and 2000s. Before that, what drew media attention was skyjacking. The hijacking of airplanes in the United States and Western world first began in 1961. Over a seven-year period, twelve separate skyjacking incidents took place, according to the US Federal Aviation Administration. Then suddenly over the years 1968–1972, the number of hijackings soared to 147, an annual average of 29. This is what has been referred to as the "golden age of hijacking," a period when television newscasts, newspapers, and magazines reported on every new dramatic development in skyjacking incidents in real time. Being taken by force in the skies had become a frighteningly tangible prospect.[122]

Hijackings declined significantly from 1973 through 1977, but there were periodic waves during the years 1978–1980 and 1982–1983. But just as skyjacking incidents rose and then gradually became more infrequent,

Table 8.1 REPORTED LOCATION OF ALIEN ABDUCTEES AT THE TIME OF THEIR CAPTURE

	1957–1977	1978–1986	1987–1996
Total Number	52	131	254
Taken from bedroom	18%	34%	59%
Taken from vehicle	49%	35%	17%
Taken from open air	33%	31%	24%

From Thomas E. Bullard, "Abduction Phenomenon," in *Cultural Studies: The UFO Encyclopedia*, by Jerome Clark. 3rd ed. Omnigraphics, Inc., 2018. http://ss360.libraries.psu.edu/cgibin/ssredirpg? D= 7F9&U=http%3A%2F%2Falias.libraries.psu.edu%2Feresources%2Fproxy%2Flogin%3Furl%3Dht tps%3A%2F%2Fsearch.credoreference.com%2Fcontent%2Fentry%2Fogiuf, accessed 10 May 2019.

popular media was helping to conjure the specter of another form of captivity on the ground: home invasion.

Truman Capote's 1966 novel *In Cold Blood* and its 1967 film adaptation, chronicling the real-life murder of a family in their rural Kansas house by two strangers, can be seen as setting this new type of dread in motion. From 1969 to 1972, the media provided extensive coverage of the horrific home invasion murders committed by Charles Manson and his followers in California. Over two decades, the American film industry regularly turned to plots involving domestic break-ins coupled with violent assaults: *Wait Until Dark* (1967), *A Clockwork Orange* (1971), *Last House on the Left* (1972), *Death Wish* (1974), *When a Stranger Calls* (1979), *Extremities* (1986), *Fatal Attraction* (1987). The trend was even more pronounced on television. In the 1980s, tv films frequently took the form of domestic melodramas in which the cozy setting of the home was disturbed by malicious trespassers.[123]

If one of the things that made the alien abductions of the 1980s and 1990s so terrifying was the sense that people weren't safe even in their own apartment or house, popular culture had already primed the public for just this very thing. The rise in the number of reports of being taken from the bedroom reflected a growing intimacy that began to characterize alien abduction scenarios. It also hinted at the unsettlingly sexual and predatory elements that were becoming a common feature in abduction accounts.

This is no more apparent than in the claims about generations of children being taken, women being impregnated, and infants being stolen from their human mothers. Was there anything more horrifying than being helpless to stop these assaults on one's own child and violations of one's parenthood? Once again, these fears were voiced against the backdrop of profound changes in attitudes.

For one thing, the 1980s witnessed an emerging public acknowledgment of child abuse. In the United States, the groundwork for this awareness was forged decades earlier as schooling was extended to adolescents and the school day was lengthened. These changes led parents to see even their older children as not-yet-adults and magnified their worries about who was looking after them in their absence. Over the last two decades of the twentieth century, as women's groups successfully called attention to the scourge of sexual and domestic assault, the problem of child abuse found its place in clinical, scientific, legal, policy, and media deliberations.[124]

The apprehension of parents about potential predators bent on harming their children rarely if ever was directed inward at members of the family. Instead, their focus was on the outside world. While parents had expressed concerns about missing and abducted children already in the 1950s, in the 1970s and 1980s the topic drew even greater public attention. The notion that strangers, whose motivations were attributed to sexual perversion, were the likeliest perpetrators became increasingly popular. In fact, surveys conducted between 1987 and 1997 showed that as many as 72 percent of parents were scared "that their child will be kidnapped by a stranger" and 76 percent of children feared "being kidnapped." All this was despite the fact that such abductions were extremely rare.[125]

Alien abduction scenarios embodied these worries over home invasions and families set upon by stalking kidnappers. Yet there was another unmistakable theme in the conventional story told by experiencers in the eighties and nineties, one that also played no major part in the tales of earlier contactees. This was the role of medicine.

Physical examinations, psychological tests, operating theaters, medical instruments and experiments, surgeries, and implants: the trappings of medicine appeared time and again in the stories abductees revealed. In fact, clinical research, devices, and operations were the centerpiece in most abductee stories by the end of the eighties.[126] As Bridget Brown, one of the most astute analysts of the alien abduction phenomenon, has observed, "This clinical facet of the abduction scenario as it emerged during the 1960s seemed to register a new set of anxieties about the personal implications of advances in technology—specifically biotechnology and the increasing technologization of the body."[127] Once again, the sixties and seventies set the scene, focusing unprecedented public attention on the ethical and legal dilemmas tied to human and animal experimentation: the trial of Adolf Eichmann (1961), announcement of the dangers of thalidomide (1961), introduction of an "informed consent" mandate in drug testing (1962), establishment of ethical review boards (1966, 1974), revelations about the Tuskegee syphilis study (1972), the Kennedy congressional committee hearings on human experimentation (1973), the founding of the animal liberation movement (1975–1976).

The medical procedures featured in the reports of abductees were usually of a specific kind, centering on human reproduction. Sperm was extracted from males, while females found themselves impregnated in vitro and their eggs and fetuses harvested. Both Budd Hopkins and David Jacobs were instrumental in publicizing this aspect of the alien abduction scenario, seeing it as evidence of a wide-scale alien-human breeding project. Here too innovations in the technology of pregnancy management and genetics— some of which sparked vigorous public debate—haunted these tales: amniocentesis became a standard procedure in obstetrics (1966–1970), the popularization of laparoscopy (1967–1976), the first baby conceived through in vitro fertilization (1978), the first magnetic resonance imaging machine built (1977), the first successful birth of a baby from a frozen embryo (1984) and frozen egg (1986), the creation of the Human Genome Project (1990–2003), and the cloning of Dolly the Sheep (1996).

Things had certainly changed since Bryant and Helen Reeve embarked on their flying saucer pilgrimage back in 1954. By the end of the twentieth century, stories of handsome sages offering comfort and salvation were all but a faded memory in many circles. Even if the likes of Leo Sprinkle, Whitley Strieber, and John Mack offered words of spiritual consolation to experiencers, the stories about run-ins with aliens that dominated much of the UFO scene mostly took on a forbidding and harrowing character. Over time, an escalating invasiveness crept into the stories of encounters with extraterrestrials. Abductions shifted from outdoors to indoors, from fields and cars to homes, from homes to bedrooms, and from bedrooms to the human body, to sexual organs and the human mind. As the reach of the aliens became more intimate, women and children became more central characters in the drama in a way that had not been the case during the golden era of the contactees.

Yet time and again the stories of abductees were shared with others through the intermediary of an abduction expert. He—after all, it was almost always a man—stepped in to counteract the spell the visitors had cast over their victims, helping retrieve lost memories, interpreting murky signs, and offering advice and solace. The abductee researchers served as modern-day mediums, each with their own gift of access to an occult wisdom. The aliens were not the only enchanters.[128]

The alien abduction experience cannot be separated from the production of its stories, from the process of how their tales got told, heard, and spread. Just like the contactee scenario of the fifties, the abduction scenario was the result of a collective effort through multiple tellings and with many authors. The avuncular expert invited to delve into the life of the vulnerable abductee came with a playbook in hand. The alien abduction scenario as such was not simply a set of common plot elements but a template for interrogation and intervention. Once consulting clients made their way into the home or office of abduction researchers—something often triggered by first encountering a book, article, or show about UFOs—it set in motion a series of choreographed suspicions, lines of questioning, follow-up questions, worries, theories, referrals, advice, and treatments.

This is not to say, as some debunkers do, that investigators and abductees just lifted characters, events, and plot twists from popular culture. Instead, the point is that both researchers and experiencers came to their meetings with one another with expectations. Even when the stories told under hypnosis grew more grotesquely elaborate and incredible, the anxieties and fears more acute, all those involved could turn to the world they knew to make sense of the unfathomable details and powerful emotions that came spilling out. They were not unprepared.

Conclusion

Where To, Where From, Wherefore?

As the century that gave birth to the moniker "flying saucer" came to a close, the UFO phenomenon entered a new phase in its history. For many veteran ufologists, the new developments have not always been welcome.

In some instances, political changes helped rekindle interest in unidentified flying objects. This was no more apparent than in the USSR and Russia, where Mikhail Gorbachev's policy of *glasnost* (openness) and the eventual dissolution of the Soviet Union enabled once-proscribed esoteric ideas and literature to flourish. Chief among these was the movement known as cosmism, an occult science of truth- and soul-searching mixing theosophy, astrology, cosmology, ecology, and science fiction that also seeks profound meaning in the UFO and alien contact phenomenon. Suppressed for years by the Communist Party, Russian cosmism experienced a revival in the eighties that has continued to this day.[1]

Cosmism's renaissance fueled and reflected the growth of a more visible ufology in the Soviet Union and Russia. Beginning in the mid-1980s and extending into the first decades of the twenty-first century, a succession of UFO-themed newspapers, magazines, bulletins, and newsletters were launched. While some—like the Moscow-based *Tonnel'* (Tunnel) and *Vestnik NLO* (UFO Messenger) and the Yaroslavl *Nevedomoye* (Unknown)—tried to establish themselves as investigative research outlets, most tended to report more speculatively on a wide range of paranormal phenomena. With titles like *Anomaliya* (Anomaly), *Anomalnye Yavleniya* (Anomalous

Phenomena), and *Dayzhest NLO i Gumanoidi* (UFO and Humanoids Digest), these publications covered not just flying saucers and contact with extraterrestrials but also Yeti encounters, threats to the environment, mind expansion, space travel, and telekinesis.[2]

Throughout much of the world, however, signs of an erosion of interest in the subject became increasingly conspicuous beginning in the 1990s. Journalists reported a noticeable decline in the public's fascination with UFOs from China to Germany.[3] The number of UFO sightings, after a steady rise, appeared to fall beginning around the years 2012–2014, at the same time reports of alien abductions all but disappeared from mainstream media.[4]

Meanwhile, ufology and the UFO social scene went through momentous changes of their own. UFO organizations that once attracted hundreds reported no longer being able to carry on business as usual. Some, like the British Flying Saucer Bureau in 2001 and the Belgian Committee for the Study of Space Phenomena in 2007, announced they were shutting down. Others, like the Fund for UFO Research, were simply no longer active by 2011. And still others, like UFO-Sweden and the Danish group SUFOI, began diverting much of their time and efforts to archiving their records.[5]

Other staples of ufology also fell away in short order. In 2011, Rod Dyke ended his longtime UFO news clipping service out of Seattle, and three years later Errol Bruce-Knapp decided to close down his discussion list UFO Updates (though a version was revived on Facebook). The British UFO Research Association had to cancel its 2014 conference in Glastonbury, explaining to members, "we all work entirely on a voluntary basis, and it was felt that it wasn't currently viable to hold this conference." UFO publications also fell under the axe. Of some three thousand known UFO-related periodicals that had once existed worldwide, only two hundred remained by the mid-1990s; by 2009, no more than sixty were still being published. One of the casualties was *Magonia*, one of Britain's oldest UFO magazines, which ceased publishing in 2009. Its editor, John Rimmer, expressed his "disappointment and frustration that the whole field of UFO research [has] seemed incapable of making any kind of progress, and that it has deteriorated into an endless scrutiny of issues that were once considered settled."[6]

Rimmer was not alone in his disenchantment with the state of ufology. Reporting a 96 percent drop in reported sightings since 1988, the chairman of the Association for the Scientific Study of Anomalous Phenomena in Britain told the *Sunday Telegraph* in 2012 that "the days of compelling eyewitness sightings seem to be over" and that on balance it appeared "that nothing is out there."[7] In the United States, James Carrion, who was named director of the Mutual UFO Network in 2006, resigned a mere four years later, declaring that ufology was plagued by bogus claims, bias, and a lack of investigative standards. In a 2014 interview with the podcast *The Paracast*, he declared, "I think the bottom line is—there are folks that are in the field that call themselves ufologists, call themselves researchers, investigative journalists—whatever they want to call themselves, it doesn't really matter—but when their modus operandi is to perpetuate the mystery instead of solving it, we have a big issue."[8] And in 2017, after Pennsylvania's state director of MUFON, John Ventre, posted a racist rant on his Facebook page, many were upset by the fact that the organization seemed to do little to distance itself from him. MUFON's tepid response led its director of research, Chris Cogswell, to resign.[9]

As ufology reeled, states appeared to signal it was time to reassess priorities when it came to UFOs. Some have stayed involved. Argentina, Chile, France, Peru, and Uruguay actively ran and still run government programs collecting UFO data.[10] But Great Britain's Ministry of Defence shut down its UFO desk in November 2009, after years trying to shed itself of the job. And perhaps the surest sign that governments were adopting a different attitude toward the UFO phenomenon was the fact that so many began declassifying their UFO records. Not only the United States but also Australia, Brazil, Canada, Denmark, Finland, Italy, New Zealand, Norway, Spain, and the United Kingdom released hundreds of thousands of pages of historical UFO documents. Great Britain proved to be an exemplar, archiving some sixty thousand pages of reports and correspondence under the steady direction of journalist and university professor David Clarke over the years 2008–2013.[11]

Arguably some of the developments taking place during the first two decades of the new century were hardly unfamiliar to the UFO scene. Groups big and small had always teetered on the brink of ruin, differences of opinion have led to defections in the past, there have been a fair share of scandals over the years, and government interest has always waxed and waned. This downturn felt like something new, however, and observers have not been short on explanations for it. Some have blamed the hype over alien abductions in the 1990s for taking all the oxygen out of the room, leaving ufologists nowhere to go after its celebrity faded. Others have pointed to a staleness in ufology, a sense that the whole venture had devolved into little more than true believers spinning their wheels. A common refrain has been, where are those convincing photographs? In an age of cellphone cameras, many have contended, the lack of any definitive film of a flying saucer or extraterrestrial perhaps signals the futility of the hunt.[12]

Some longtime UFO researchers point to one factor contributing to the changed landscape: the internet. As one veteran ufologist explained it to me, the demise of so many local UFO groups since the nineties can be traced directly to the worldwide web and social media, which have left younger people in particular seeing no need to create communities in person. And by providing an open forum for hoaxers, scammers, and rumormongers to spread misinformation, the internet has hardly made ufology more discriminating.[13] Yes, the web has allowed dedicated groups—like the Archives for the Unexplained and the Sign Historical Group—to make historical UFO documents publicly available through digitized scans. At the same time, social media like YouTube and advances in editing technology have made it possible for some self-proclaimed UFO hunters to create a kind of UFO theater and to monetize their ventures.[14]

While the internet is partly responsible for the decline in traditions that once characterized ufology before the turn of the millennium, it also gave the UFO phenomenon a new lease on life. Websites and online forums offered a new generation of enthusiasts a way to discover and exchange views about reports of unidentified flying objects. And the fact that some entrepreneurs were able to create money-making products testified to the entertainment potential of UFOs for other media outlets.

Over the past ten to fifteen years, streaming services, podcasts, and cable television have made minor stars of any number of UFO detectives, and some deep pockets have helped make this possible. Discovery, Inc., Hearst Communications, the Walt Disney Company, and Warner Brothers—mass media companies producing so-called factual televised programming for channels like Discovery, History, and Travel—have introduced a new generation of viewers to classic UFO cases and ancient alien theories. At the same time, the for-profit company To the Stars, whose co-founder was former Blink-182 guitarist Tom DeLonge, inaugurated its To the Stars Academy of Arts and Sciences in 2017. Its original purpose was to coordinate three branches of work in promoting paranormal investigation: entertainment, science, and aerospace development. To the Stars, however, soon decided to shed its R&D side, and in 2022 it became exclusively an "entertainment company that creates original content . . . told across film, television, publishing, and merchandise with the goal of turning the world on to new ideas and new possibilities."[15]

The commercialization of UFOs is only one part of their surprising revival taking place on several fronts. Besides American intelligence agencies, a new generation of spiritual and personal growth seekers are being drawn to unidentified anomalous phenomena as well. In Japan, the new religion Kōfuku no Kagaku (aka Happy Science) has embraced the ancient astronauts theory preached by paleovisitologists, and its recently deceased leader, Ōkawa Ryūhō, argued that malicious Reptilian-like aliens were conspiring with China and had a hand in the coronavirus pandemic.[16] Silicon Valley professionals also have proven to be receptive. In recent years, for instance, the Esalen Institute—a retreat center for esoteric practices and humanist psychology in Big Sur, California—has succeeded in attracting new devotees from the tech industry. The institute that once helped introduce John Mack to transpersonal psychology has sponsored at least three events since 2015 exploring the significance of UFOs.[17]

There is also evidence of a sea change happening within academia and civilian science.[18] A 2022 survey of over 1,400 American research university professors revealed that while few considered it likely the phenomenon had an extraterrestrial explanation, 37 percent considered it "very important" or "absolutely essential" for there to be more academic research about the subject. That summer, in an unprecedented move, NASA announced it was establishing a panel of scientists and industry experts to explore the need for and feasibility of studying unidentified aerial phenomena. At its first public meeting in May 2023, committee chairman David Spergel explained that the group's purpose would not be to resolve the issue but to "create a road map" for how NASA might help produce "more uniform data."

Efforts to collect this data are already underway. Scientific organizations involved in space research from China and Russia have lent their support for a plan to organize periodic international conferences on UFOs in San Marino. The University of Würzburg's Interdisciplinary Research Center for Extraterrestrial Studies has added UFO/UAP research to its portfolio, and astronomer Avi Loeb has established the Galileo Project at Harvard University that searches for evidence of extraterrestrial technological artifacts. Scholars at Stanford, the University of North Carolina at Wilmington, SUNY Albany, Durham University, NASA, and the Blue Marble Institute of Science have all published works taking the UFO phenomenon seriously. And in 2023, researchers launched both a new international society (Society for UAP Studies), a peer-reviewed journal (*Limina*), and a foundation (Sol Foundation) dedicated to the study of unidentified anomalous phenomena.[19] Once again, rumors of the death of UFOs have proven to be greatly exaggerated.

If the Cold War once played the key role in invigorating the preoccupation with flying saucers and visitors from outer space, it is fair to ask what is fueling the most recent resurgence of interest in unidentified anomalous phenomena. For one thing, the development of new sensors and sophisticated spying techniques has made it possible for militaries to detect unusual aerial activities more precisely, something that in turn heightens suspicions about foreign governments engaging in high-tech espionage. At the same time, the discovery of thousands of exoplanets since the early 1990s has made the prospect of extraterrestrial civilizations seem much more likely—a fact confirmed by recent international surveys showing that 47 percent polled believe in the existence of extraterrestrial civilizations and an average of 18 percent believed it likely that aliens would visit earth in 2023. In addition, speculation about UFOs has always thrived in environments where questions are raised about the trustworthiness of authorities. The coronavirus pandemic of 2020–2023 did just that, feeding a widespread sense of uncertainty and powerlessness that leaders across the globe exploited to call into doubt the integrity of experts, especially scientists.[20]

Now more than two decades into the twenty-first century, UFOs continue to be associated with alien travelers, conspiracy theory, rumor-mongering, demands for disclosure, the paranormal, and distrust of traditional experts. Many of those today seeking to legitimate the study of UFOs are intent on weeding out what they consider to be this unwanted "cultural baggage" from the phenomenon itself. The decision to replace the acronym UFO with the more generic UAP was done in the hope of accomplishing that. But this misses the point. The baggage is the phenomenon—or certainly as much as anything else can claim to be—and a name change will not divest it of its entanglements with politics and popular culture.[21]

The question of whether extraterrestrials have made it to earth is actually settled. They have been here for centuries, inhabiting the human imagination. In thinking about them, observers have necessarily called on the inventory of mental tools available to them. UFOs have been seen through the lens of an idiosyncratic repertoire of metaphors: crafts compared to rockets, intelligence measured in terms of technological feats, beings associated with the attributes of gods, royalty, sprites, doctors, ghosts, and demons. In return, UFOs have become metaphors of their own. Advertisers have used them as a graphic shorthand to invoke modernity, innovation, and transcendence, while the clichés of the tin foil hat and the alien probe serve as stand-ins for madness and folly.[22]

The UFO phenomenon can't be explained by tracking the popularity of certain ideas and images alone, however. What needs to be acknowledged is the extensive work that has gone into building what might be called a UFO world. It is a world populated by people and institutions who have made a point to foster habits and create protocols for talking, writing, reading, studying, speculating, and debating about unidentified flying objects and aliens.

The purpose of this trek into the history of the unidentified flying object and alien contact phenomenon has not been to arrive at some definitive answer about whether UFOs are real and are the work of extraterrestrials. Delving into the first seventy-five years of interest in flying saucers, rather than judging the likelihood of alien visitors, underscores the human side of this extraordinary effort to makes sense of a great enigma—the people, places, and things that have made UFOs make history.

Contrary to popular stereotypes, those who have seen, those who have reported seeing, and those who have studied unidentified flying objects have not been uneducated people whose minds are clouded by superstition. Far from it, all the evidence shows that most of the individuals involved in giving voice to the UFO question have been highly educated and have thought critically about the matter.

Ufologists generally have been neither anti-science nor anti-scientist. Rather, they have believed that academic scientists have not lived up to the standards, promise, and ideals of science. For most, advances in science and technology represent the future and hope. Ufology then has not tended to denigrate science but instead has venerated it (at times to a fault), while ufologists have not worked as merchants of doubt but rather as purveyors of mystery.

Conspiracy thinking and theorists have played their part in the UFO scene, but their role has often been overestimated. Yes, conspiracies of silence—especially on the part of governments—have been suspected since the very early days of flying saucer sightings. There have been any number of voices in ufology who have peddled paranoia and fear. Nevertheless, throughout most of its history, the UFO phenomenon has drawn people to it by inspiring fascination and awe. Enthusiasm, not anxiety, has been the primary motivation for those who have taken up an interest in unidentified flying objects.

That said, some familiar assumptions are largely accurate. Both the civilian and military study of UFOs has been dominated by men. In places like the United States, Britain, and Europe, members of UFO groups have been overwhelmingly white, though the fact that organizations have also flourished in Latin America and Asia would suggest that gender, education, and social class are the most decisive variables in determining who joins. Individuals who have taken part in UFO religious communities have tended to be people who already were receptive to unconventional spiritual exploration. Hoaxes and deceits have been a frustratingly persistent part of the phenomenon. Until recently academics have been mostly dismissive about the subject, and those publicly admitting to witnessing or studying UFOs have been subject to ridicule in their everyday lives.

The widespread view that UFOs and alien encounters have been a peculiarly American obsession is only partly true. Prominent sightings, reports, waves, and flaps in the United States have garnered the attention of journalists and writers throughout the rest of the world. And American ufologists and groups have often provided the inspiration for new organizations and research agendas in other countries. Without a doubt, the United States has been a central hub for producing and distributing UFO news since the 1940s. Yet it was also the case that homegrown UFO sightings and movements could be found across the globe starting in the 1950s. These, in turn, were exported to investigators and periodicals in the United States. An international network of ufologists, spiritual leaders, and devotees developed and expanded quickly, so the story of UFOs cannot be told as an exclusively American one.

With no "headquarters," no central directing institution, the study of UFOs and their meaning has always been driven by local enthusiasts and the tireless efforts of dedicated volunteers. The centrifugal force inherent in such a framework left the whole thing constantly vulnerable to falling apart, and most ventures did just that. Coordination, however, came from the work done by a small number of individuals. They historically have done the investigative work, collected and analyzed information, lectured, written articles and books, published newsletters and magazines, and organized communities. Many have fashioned themselves as crusaders or missionaries tasked with enlightening the public and solving the riddle of the flying saucers; the same can be said for the debunkers of UFOs. What has kept the UFO movement alive all these years has been a combination of charismatic personalities and compelling, canonical stories.

The trappings of the flying saucer era—the preoccupation with alien visitors, the military investigations, the groups, the meetings, the research, the magazines, the speculations, the debates, the media attention, the skeptics—developed at a particular moment in history. They carried in tow the ideals, fears, and imagined possibilities of their time. Born after the slaughter and destruction of World War II, the UFO phenomenon tapped into an array of Cold War–era values, movements, innovations, and sensitivities: space exploration; science fiction; new aeronautic, intelligence, and biomedical technologies; nuclear war and the emergence of superpowers; secularization; globalization of mass media; liberation movements; self-help; the psychotherapy boom. The UFO saga has often harkened back to ghosts of the xenophobic past, frequently reincarnating earlier stories of enchanted grounds, looming bogeymen, and menacing outsiders.[23] But it updated these, taking on some of the most pressing existential questions of the times. Are we on the verge of global annihilation?

What does it mean to be human? Are science and technology forces of good or ill?

The UFO phenomenon essentially has been asking us to think of ourselves historically: what has been our past, what is going on right now, and what does the future hold? The last question is one that has haunted the flying saucer mystery from the very beginning, and it was one that was acutely pressing during the Cold War.[24] If unidentified flying objects are the work of extraterrestrials, then what is their plan, and will we be capable of matching their achievements? The worry that humanity seemed to be on the brink of global catastrophe inflected discussions with moralizing overtones.

In the end, the unidentified flying object has been and remains many things to many people. Its resilience as a social phenomenon largely stems from its nebulous nature and its ability to be a thing and a theory at the same time.[25] Dealing with something so elusive that it's unclear whether it can even be called an object, the conversation about the UFO has been invitingly open-ended. Anything can count as evidence, and speculation knows no bounds.

From the start, flying saucers have kept much of the world in a state of suspense. It's little wonder they have elicited reactions alternating between confusion, marvel, dread, anger, and derision. For those who have found themselves unable to look away, UFOs have offered aC place to linger in strangeness.

NOTES

INTRODUCTION

1. The following narrative is based on Walter N. Webb, "Occupant Encounter in New Hampshire," *APRO Bulletin* 22 (January–February 1974): 5–7.
2. Greg Eghigian, "The Year of the UFOs," *Smithsonian Air & Space Magazine* February 2020, https://www.airspacemag.com/space/year-ufos-180973965/, accessed 30 August 2022.
3. *Ufolore* Podcast, Episode 2, "Two (Equal) Sides: Black Triangle UFOs," 17 April 2020.
4. Arnaud Esquerre, *Théorie des événements extraterrestres: Essai sur le récit fantastique* (Paris: Librairie Arthème Fayard, 2016), 228–248.
5. http://www.noufors.com/Encyclopedia_of_Terminology_and_Abbreviations. html, accessed 10 January 2020.

CHAPTER 1

1. Kenneth Arnold and Ray Palmer, *The Coming of the Saucers: A Documentary Report on Sky Objects That Have Mystified the World* (Boise, ID, and Amherst, WI: Ray Palmer, 1952), 10.
2. Though Arnold would later claim that he did coin the phrase first. Martin Shough, "Return of the Flying Saucers: A Fresh Look at the Sighting That Started it All," *Darklore* 5 (2017): 69–99.
3. Gilles Fernandez, "The Coming of the (Term) 'Flying Saucers,'" *Sceptiques vs. les Soucoupes Volantes*, 15 March 2017, http://skepticversustheflyingsaucers. blogspot.com/2017/03/the-coming-of-flying-saucers-term.html, accessed 11 July 2017.
4. Herbert Joseph Strentz, "A Survey of Press Coverage of Unidentified Flying Objects, 1947–1966" (PhD diss.: Northwestern University, 1970), 26.
5. Ted Bloecher, *Report on the UFO Wave of 1947* (self-published: 1967, reproduced by Jean Waskiewicz and Francis Ridge, 2005); Strentz, 26–28.
6. Michael Swords, Vicente-Juan Ballester Olmos, Bill Chalker, Barry Greenwood, Richard Thieme, Jan Aldrich, Steve Purcell, "Ghost Rockets," in *UFOs and Government: A Historical Inquiry* (San Antonio and Charlottesville: Anomalist Books, 2012), 12–29.
7. Michael B. Petersen, *Missiles for the Fatherland: Peenemünde, National Socialism, and the V-2 Missile* (New York: Cambridge University Press, 2009); Michael J. Neufeld, *The Rocket and the Reich: Peenemünde and the Coming of the Ballistic Missile Era* (New York: Free Press, 1995). Also, see https://airandspace.si.edu/col

lection-objects/v-1-cruise-missile/nasm_A19600341000 and https://airandsp
ace.si.edu/collection-objects/missile-surface-surface-v-2-4/nasm_A19600342
000 both of which were accessed on 20 April 2015.

8. Mats Burström, Anders Gustafsson, and Håkan Karlsson, "The Air Torpedo of
Bäckebo: Local Incident and World History," *Current Swedish Archaeology* 14
(2006): 7–24.

9. For the previous discussion of ghost rockets, see Swords et al., "Ghost Rockets."

10. Archives for the Unexplained (hereafter, AFU), Ghost Rockets Public Records
Office 1946 England (GRPROE), British Legation, Stockholm, "Projectiles," 13
July 1946; AFU, Official Ghost Rocket documents US Archives 1946 (OGRUSA/
1946), US Office of Military Attache in Stockholm, Memorandum Regarding
Light Phenomenon Over Swedish Territory, 13 August 1946.

11. AFU, OGRUSA/1946, Memorandum Regarding Light Phenomenon Over Swedish
Territory, 13 August 1946.

12. AFU, GRPROE [British Consulate in Sweden], "Reports on Suspected V-Weapons
Over the Baltic," undated (ca. July 1946).

13. AFU, OGRUSA/1946, US Naval Attache in Paris, "Report on Guided Missiles
sent from Soviet Controlled Territories over Scandinavian Territories, 13
August 1946.

14. Ibid.

15. AFU, OGRUSA/1946, U.S. Naval Attache Stockholm, "Guided Missiles: Rocket
Sightings Over Sweden," 16 August 1946.

16. AFU, OGRUSA/1946, Memorandum for the President, 22 August 1946.
Historian Michael Neufeld, an expert on the Nazi V-2 program, told me in a
personal communication that it would have been impossible for the rockets to
have been launched by the Soviets at Peenemünde after the war, since the site
had been completely stripped clean by the Red Army.

17. AFU, GRPROE, Cabinet Offices to UK Liaison Mission Tokyo, 16
September 1946.

18. AFU, Official Ghost Rockets Documents US Archives 1947–1955 (OGRUSA/
1947–1955), U.S. Naval Attaché, Helsinki, "Strange Light Phenomenon or
Rocket," 10 February 1947.

19. AFU, OGRUSA/1947–1955, U.S. Naval Attaché, Stockholm, "Guided
Missiles: Alleged Rockets Over Sweden," 15 April 1947.

20. Ibid., Chief of Naval Intelligence, "Guided Missile Intelligence," 11
September 1947.

21. Ibid., Col. Clingerman, USAF Intelligence Department to Chief of Staff, USAF, 1
October 1948.

22. Ibid., Navy Department, Chief Office of Naval Operations, Scientific and
Technical Memorandum, 4 April 1950; Brig. Gen. E. Moore, Memorandum for
Director of Intelligence and CNI, 8 December 1948; Col. Brooke E. Allen (USAF),
Memorandum for Chief, Air Intelligence Division, 11 October 1948; Lt. Gen. N. F.
Twining to Commanding General Army Air Forces, 23 September 1947.

23. Maurizio Verga, "Making the Saucers Popular: Cartoons and Comics in the 1947
Press," *Cielo Insolito* 3 (2017): 9–27.

24. "RAAF Captures Flying Saucer on Ranch in Roswell Region," *Roswell Daily
Record*, 8 July 1947. For an examination of how the story of what happened
at Roswell changed over the years, see Benson Saler, Charles A. Ziegler,
and Charles B. Moore, *UFO Crash at Roswell: The Genesis of a Modern Myth*
(Washington: Smithsonian Institution Press, 1997).

25. Sources for historical newspaper coverage from 1947 are from the Newspaper Archive database and from the website Project 1947.

26. "Starr to Reveal Data on Saucers," *Portland Oregonian*, 6 July 1947.

27. Jonathan Silberstein-Loeb, *The International Distribution of News: The Associated Press, Press Association, and Reuters, 1848–1947* (New York: Cambridge University Press, 2014).

28. For example, a story about how the Soviets reportedly believed the saucers to be connected to US army experiments attempting to find ways to knock out radar was repeated in local newspapers—with the same title and content—during the summer and fall. See, for instance, "Red Saucers: Soviets Curious," *Terril Record*, 28 August 1947, 4.

29. Maurizio Verga, *Flying Saucers in the Sky: When UFOs Came from Mars* (Self-published: Maurizio Verga, 2022), 104–121.

30. Hal Boyle, "Beer Bottle Saga of Flying Disks," *Winona Republican Herald*, 8 July 1947: 6.

31. "Harassed Saucer-Sighter Would Like to Escape Fuss," *Statesman* (Boise, Idaho), 27 June 1947, http://www.project1947.com/fig/1947b.htm, accessed 11 July 2017.

32. Kenneth Arnold to Commanding General, Wright Field, undated (ca. 11 July 1947), http://www.project1947.com/fig/1947b.htm, accessed 13 July 2017.

33. "Sidewalk Savants Squint Skyward for Solution of Soaring Saucers," *Amarillo Globe*, 7 July 1947, 2.

34. Chalyle Holt, "Flying Saucer Old Stuff to U.S. Fliers During War," *Globe* (Boston, MA), 13 July 1947; "New German Weapons Revealed," *The Day* (New London, CT), 20 August 1947.

35. "Gromyko Gives His Opinion of Flying Saucers," *Chester Times*, 10 July 1947, 2.

36. "No Takers for 'Saucer Rewards,'" *The Daily Register* (Harrisburg, IL), 8 July 1947, 12.

37. "Disc Hoax Gives Town Dizzy Day," *Joplin Globe* (Joplin, MO), 12 July 1947: 1.

CHAPTER 2

1. Jacques Vallee and Chris Aubeck, *Wonders in the Sky: Unexplained Aerial Objects from Antiquity to Modern Times and Their Impact on Human Culture, History, and Beliefs* (New York: Jeremy P. Tarcher/Penguin, 2009).

2. Richard Stothers, "Unidentified Flying Objects in Classical Antiquity," *The Classical Journal* 103 (2007): 79–92.

3. Vallee and Aubeck, *Wonders*, 149.

4. Dario Tessicini and Patrick J. Boner, eds., *Celestial Novelties on the Eve of the Scientific Revolution, 1540–1630* (Florence: Leo S. Olschki, 2013); John North, *The Norton History of Astronomy and Cosmology* (New York: W. W. Norton, 1995).

5. Sara J. Schechner, "Comets and Meteors," in *The Oxford Guide to the History of Physics and Astronomy*, ed. John L. Heilbron (Oxford: Oxford University Press, 2005), 65–66 and Sara Schechner Genuth, *Comets, Popular Culture, and the Birth of Modern Cosmology* (Princeton: Princeton University Press, 1997). See also Ken Kurihara, *Celestial Wonders in Reformation Germany* (London: Pickering & Chatto, 2014).

6. Alexandra Walsham, "Sermons in the Sky: Apparitions in Early Modern Europe," *History Today* 51 (April 2001): 56–63.

7. Chet Van Duzer, *Sea Monsters on Medieval and Renaissance Maps* (London: British Library, 2013).

8. Lorraine Daston and Katharine Park, *Wonders and the Order of Nature, 1150–1750* (New York: Zone, 1988), 52.

9. Raymond Lamont-Brown, *Phantoms, Legends, Customs, and Superstitions of the Sea* (Glasgow: Brown, Son & Ferguson, 1989).

10. Michiko Iwasaka and Barre Toelken, *Ghosts and the Japanese: Cultural Experience in Japanese Death Legends* (Logan: Utah State University, 1994), 105–106.

11. Kathryn A. Edwards, "The History of Ghosts in Early Modern Europe: Recent Research and Future Trajectories," *History Compass* 10 (2012): 353–366.

12. Robert Ford Campany, *A Garden of Marvels: Tales of Wonder from Early Medieval China* (Honolulu: University of Hawaii Press, 2015); Owen Davies, *The Haunted: A Social History of Ghosts* (Basingstoke: Palgrave Macmillan, 2007); Sarah Iles Johnston, *Restless Dead: Encounters Between the Living and the Dead in Ancient Greece* (Berkeley: University of California Press, 1999); Jean-Claude Schmitt, *Ghosts in the Middle Ages: The Living and the Dead in Medieval Society* (Chicago: University of Chicago Press, 1998); R. C. Mclagan, "Ghost Lights of the West Highlands," *Folklore* 8 (1897): 203–256.

13. Sara Horsfall, "The Experience of Marian Apparitions and the Mary Cult," *The Social Science Journal* 37 (2000): 375–384.

14. On photographing ghosts, see Daniel Wojcik, "Spirits, Apparitions, and Traditions of Supernatural Photography," *Visual Resources* 25 (2009): 109–136.

15. Daston and Park, *Wonders and the Order of Nature*, 347–348.

16. Angela Haas, "Miracles on Trial: Wonders and Their Witnesses in Eighteenth-Century France," *Proceedings of the Western Society for French History* 38 (2010): 111–128.

17. Vladimir Jankovic, *Reading the Skies: A Cultural History of English Weather, 1650–1820* (Chicago: University of Chicago Press, 2000).

18. Wolfgang Schivelbusch, *The Railway Journey: The Industrialization of Time and Space in the 19th Century* (Berkeley: University of California Press, 2014).

19. Bernhard Rieger, "'Modern Wonders': Technological Innovation and Public Ambivalence in Britain and Germany, 1890s to 1933," *History Workshop Journal* 55 (2003): 153–176.

20. Tom D. Crouch, "Dream of Aerial Navigation," in *Astride Two Worlds: Technology and the American Civil War*, ed. Barton C. Hacker (Washington, DC: Smithsonian Institution Scholarly Press, 2016), 205–244. Italics in original.

21. Ibid.

22. "A Few Years Hence," *Scandia Journal* (Kansas), 18 January 1895: 4.

23. "Will Visit the Moon," *Logansport Daily Pharos* (Indiana), 31 January 1895: 4.

24. "Ten Miles Up," *The Berkeley Gazette* (California), 16 April 1895: 3.

25. "Autobiography of John Pulsipher (1827–1891)," Book of Abraham Project, https://doctrineandcovenantscentral.org/history/john-pulsipher/, accessed 9 August 2017.

26. James Taylor, "Written in the Skies: Advertising, Technology, and Modernity in Britain since 1885," *Journal of British Studies* 55 (2016): 750–780.

27. Unless otherwise indicated, details of the 1896–1897 wave are from: Seamus Dunphy, "UFO Fever in America's Historical Newspapers: The Mysterious Airships of 1896–1897," *The Readex Blog*, http://www.readex.com/blog/ufo-fever-america's-historical-newspapers-mysterious-airships-1896-97, accessed 12 July 2017; Robert E. Bartholomew and George S. Howard, *UFOs and Alien Contact: Two Centuries of Mystery* (Amherst, MA: Prometheus, 1998), 21–79.

28. "Voices in the Sky," *The Evening Bee*, 18 November 1896, http://www.rense.com/general11/ggsd.htm, accessed 10 August 2017.

29. "Three Strange Visitors, Who Possibly Came from the Planet Mars," *Evening Mail*, 27 November 1896: 1, https://www.newspapers.com/article/the-evening-mail-col-hg-shaw-alien-en/111845204/, accessed 19 July 2017.

30. Thomas E. Bullard, *The Myth and Mystery of UFOs* (Lawrence: University Press of Kansas, 2010), 111.

31. Michel Meurger, "Zur Diskussion des Begriffs 'modern legend' am Beispiel der 'Airships' von 1896–97," *Fabula* 26 (1985): 254–273.

32. John Nerone, *The Media and Public Life: A History* (Cambridge and Malden: Polity, 2015), 125–133. Also see, Richard R. John, *Network Nation: Inventing American Telecommunications* (Cambridge: Belknap Press, 2010), 145–149.

33. Cecil D. Eby, *The Road to Armageddon: The Martial Spirit in English Popular Literature, 1870–1914* (Durham and London: Duke University Press, 1987), 11.

34. Guillaume de Syon, *Zeppelin! Germany and the Airship, 1900–1939* (Baltimore: Johns Hopkins University Press, 2002), 1–75; Robert Wohl, *A Passion for Wings: Aviation and the Western Imagination, 1908–1918* (New Haven: Yale University Press, 1994), 70–77.

35. Alfred M. Gollin, "England Is No Longer an Island: The Phantom Airship Scare of 1909," *Albion* 13 (1981): 43–57. Quote of Haldane is from p. 53.

36. David Clarke, "The Scare in the Air: The British Airship Scare of 1909," in *The Scareship Mystery: A Survey of Worldwide Phantom Airship Scares (1909–1918)*, ed. Nigel Watson (Northamptonshire: Domra, 2000), 16–28. Quote is from p. 20.

37. Bartholomew and Howard, *UFOs and Alien Contact*, 92–108; Watson, "The New Zealand Invasion," in *The Scareship Mystery*, ed. Nigel Watson (Northamptonshire: Domra, 2000), 29–38.

38. AFU, Valentin Goltz, Наблюдения аая (НЛО) в СССР: сборник сообщений No. 14 (Samizdat, Leningrad, 1985), 2.

39. Bartholomew and Howard, *UFOs and Alien Contact*, 125–137; Watson, "'Here Comes the Airship!' The British 1912–1913 Scare," in *The Scareship Mystery*, ed. Nigel Watson (Northamptonshire: Domra, 2000), 61–74.

40. Nigel Watson, *UFOs of the First World War: Phantom Airships, Balloons, Aircrafts, and Other Mysterious Aerial Phenomena* (Gloucestershire: The History Press, 2014).

41. Brett Holman, "Constructing the Enemy Within: Rumours of Secret Gun Platforms and Zeppelin Bases in Britain, August–October 1914," *British Journal for Military History* 3 (2017): 22–42.

42. Syon, *Zeppelin*, 71–109.

43. Quotes are from Watson, "The New Zealand Invasion," 34 and 36.

44. Steven J. Dick, *Plurality of Worlds: The Origins of the Extraterrestrial Life Debate from Democritus to Kant* (Cambridge: Cambridge University Press, 1982), 10.

45. Michael J. Crowe, *The Extraterrestrial Life Debate, 1750–1900: The Idea of a Plurality of Worlds from Kant to Lowell* (Cambridge: Cambridge University Press, 1986), 65. Quote from Kant is from p. 54

46. John L. Brooke, *The Refiner's Fire: The Making of Mormon Cosmology, 1644–1844* (Cambridge: Cambridge University Press, 1994).

47. Crowe, *Extraterrestrial Life Debate*, 199, 239–240.

48. Crowe, *Extraterrestrial Life Debate*, 367–393. Quote from Flammarion, p. 382.

49. Mark Bevir, "The West Turns Eastward: Madame Blavatsky and the Transformation of the Occult Tradition," *Journal of the American Academy*

of Religion 62 (1994): 747–767; Bruce F. Campbell, *Ancient Wisdom Revived: A History of the Theosophical Movement* (Berkeley: University of California Press, 1980).

50. Theodore Flournoy, *From India to the Planet Mars: A Case of Multiple Personality with Imaginary Languages* (Princeton: Princeton University Press, 2015, originally published in 1899).

51. Flournoy, *From India*, 91.

52. Victor Henry, *La Langage Martien* (Paris: J. Maisonneuve, 1901).

53. Crowe, *Extraterrestrial Life Debate*, 393–400; the Tesla quote comes from Florence Raulin Certeau, "Fraction of Civilizations That Develop a Technology That Releases Detectable Signs of Their Existence into Space, fc, pre-1961," in *The Drake Equation: Estimating the Prevalence of Extraterrestrial Life through the Ages*, ed. Douglas A. Vakoch and Matthew F. Dowd (Cambridge: Cambridge University Press, 2015), 219–220.

54. Joshua Nall, "Constructing Canals on Mars: Event Astronomy and the Transmission of International Telegraphic News," *Isis* 108 (2017): 280–306; Steven J. Dick, *Life on Other Worlds: The 20th-Century Extraterrestrial Life Debate* (Cambridge and New York: Cambridge University Press, 1998).

55. "Flash Gordon," *Revolvy*, https://www.revolvy.com/main/index.php?s=Flash%20 Gordon&item_type=topic, accessed 3 October 2017. See also, Dick, *Life on Other Worlds*, 106–136.

56. Charles Fort, *The Book of the Damned* (New York: Tarcher/Penguin, 2016), 196.

57. Robert Wohl, *The Spectacle of Flight: Aviation and the Western Imagination, 1920–1950* (New Haven: Yale University Press, 2005), 215.

58. Brett Holman, "The Air Panic of 1935: British Press Opinion between Disarmament and Rearmament," *Journal of Contemporary History* 46 (2011): 288–307.

59. Wohl, *The Spectacle of Flight*, 219–227.

60. On *The War of the Worlds* episode, see W. Joseph Campbell, *Getting It Wrong: Ten of the Greatest Misreported Stories in American Journalism* (Berkeley: University of California Press, 2010); Hadley Cantril, *The Invasion from Mars: A Study in the Psychology of Panic* (New Brunswick and London: Transaction, 2005). Quotes are from Campbell, 32–34.

61. Jefferson Pooley and Michael J. Socolow, "War of the Words: *The Invasion from Mars* and its Legacy for Mass Communication Scholarship," in *War of the Worlds to Social Media: Mediated Communication in Times of Crisis*, ed. Joy Elizabeth Hayes, Kathleen Battles, and Wendy Hilton-Morrow (New York: Peter Lang, 2013), 35–56.

62. Thomas Hippler, *Governing from the Skies* (London and New York: Verso, 2017).

63. Children of the Atomic Bomb, http://www.aasc.ucla.edu/cab/200708230009. html, accessed 30 October 2017.

64. Jeffrey A. Lindell, "The Real Foo Fighters: A Historical and Physiological Perspective on a World War II Aviation Mystery," *Skeptic Magazine* 17 (2012): 38–43. Quotes are from pp. 38 and 39.

65. "Foo-Fighter," *Time* 45 (15 January 1945): 72.

66. *Report of Scientific Advisory Panel on Unidentified Flying Objects Convened by Office of Scientific Intelligence, CIA*, 14–18 January 1953, 8.

67. Daston and Park, *Wonders*, 63.

CHAPTER 3

1. "Flier Dies Chasing a 'Flying Saucer,'" *New York Times*, 9 January 1948: 11.
2. "Chiles Whitted Sighting," in *The UFO Encyclopedia*, 3rd ed., vol. 1, ed. Jerome Clark (Detroit: Omnigraphics, 2018), 234–236.
3. Edward J. Ruppelt, *The Report on Unidentified Flying Objects: The Original 1956 Edition* (New York: Cosimo Classics, 2016), 40–41.
4. George Gallup, "9 Out of 10 Heard of Flying Saucers," *The Boston Globe*, 15 August 1947: 15.
5. "Trendex Polls Shows 1 in 4 Believes UFOs Are Real," *The UFO Investigator* 1 (August–September 1957): 6.
6. Nick A. Komons, *Bonfires to Beacons: Federal Civil Aviation Policy under the Air Commerce Act, 1926–1938* (Washington, DC: US Department of Transportation, 1978), 210–211; 125–163, 355–356; and personal communication with historian Bob van der Linden at the Smithsonian National Air and Space Museum.
7. R. E. G. Davies, *Airlines of the United States since 1914* (Washington, DC: Smithsonian Institution Press, 1998), 269–275, 325.
8. Davies, *Airlines*, 336–387. Statistics from Aircraft Industries Association of America, *The Aircraft Year Book for 1947* (New York: Lanciar, 1947), 384 and *The Aircraft Year Book 1955* (Washington, DC: Lincoln Press, 1956), 48.
9. Statistics are from Aircraft Industries Association of America, *The Aircraft Year Book 1955* (Washington, DC: Lincoln Press, 1956), 36. Quotes and Newark Airport incident are from Davies, *Airlines*, 354–355.
10. Richard Toronto, *War Over Lemuria: Richard Shaver, Ray Palmer, and the Strangest Chapter of 1940s Science Fiction* (Jefferson: McFarland, 2013).
11. Sam Moskowitz, "The Origins of Science Fiction Fandom: A Reconstruction," in *Science Fiction Fandom*, ed. Joe Sanders (Westport, CT: Greenwood, 1994), 17–36. Quote p. 28.
12. Fred Nadis, *The Man From Mars: Ray Palmer's Amazing Pulp Journey* (New York: Penguin, 2013), Kindle Edition, Loc 238–245.
13. Ibid., Loc 720.
14. Ibid., Loc 1902.
15. Quote is from Kenneth Arnold and Raymond Palmer, *The Coming of the Saucers* (London: Global Grey ebooks, 1952/2018), 30.
16. Ibid., 63.
17. "Maury Island Hoax," in *The UFO Encyclopedia*, vol. 1, Clark, 720–723.
18. John A. Keel, "The Man Who Invented Flying Saucers," 1983, http://greyfalcon.us/The%20Man%20Who%20Invented%20Flying%20Saucers.htm, accessed 31 July 2019.
19. David Halperin, "Frank R. Paul – The Man Who Created Flying Saucers,'" 17 May 2019. https://www.davidhalperin.net/frank-r-paul-the-man-who-created-flying-saucers/, accessed 4 June 2019.
20. Sidney Shalett, "What You Can Believe about Flying Saucers," *Saturday Evening Post* (30 April 1949): 20–21, 136–139 and (7 May 1949): 36, 184–186
21. Charles A. Ziegler, "UFOs and the US Intelligence Community," *Intelligence and National Security* 14 (1999): 1–25.
22. Michael D. Swords, "Project Sign and the Estimate of the Situation," *Journal of UFO Studies* 7 (2000): 27–64.
23. Edward J. Ruppelt, *The Report on Unidentified Flying Objects* (Garden City: Doubleday, 1956), 41.

24. Personal communication with Michael Swords; Kate Dorsch, "Reliable Witnesses, Crackpot Science: UFO Investigations in Cold War America, 1947–1977" (PhD diss., University of Pennsylvania, 2019), 88.

25. Michael D. Swords, "UFOs, the Military, and the Early Cold War," in *UFOs and Abductions: Challenging the Borders of Knowledge*, ed. David M. Jacobs (Lawrence: University Press of Kansas, 2000), 93.

26. Irving Langmuir, "Pathological Science," Colloquium at the Knolls Research Laboratory, 18 December 1953. https://www.cs.princeton.edu/~ken/Langmuir/langmuir.htm, accessed 7 August 2019.

27. For all quotations from and the summary of the final report, see Technical Intelligence Division, Intelligence Department, Air Material Command Wright-Patterson Air Force Base, *Unidentified Aerial Objects: Project "SIGN"* (February 1949), http://www.nicap.org/docs/SignRptFeb1949.pdf, accessed 7 August 2019.

28. Air Materiel Command HQ, Wright-Patterson Air Force Base, Technical Report Unidentified Flying Objects, Project "GRUDGE," August 1949. http://www.noufors.com/Documents/Books,%20Manuals%20and%20Published%20Papers/, accessed 14 May 2014.

29. Terence E. Hanley, "Donald E. Keyhoe (1897–1988)," *Tellers of Weird Tales*, 11 April 2012, https://tellersofweirdtales.blogspot.com/2012/04/donald-e-keyhoe-1897-1988.html, accessed 3 August 2019.

30. "Keyhoe, Donald Edward (1897–1988)," in *The UFO Encyclopedia*, vol. 1, ed. Clark, 648–651.

31. Sign Oral History Project Interview with Albert M. Chop, 7, https://sohp.us/interviews/pdf/Chop-Albert-1999.pdf, accessed 9 January 2020.

32. Ibid.

33. Donald Keyhoe, *The Flying Saucers Are Real* (New York: Fawcett, 1950). For the article, see http://www.project1947.com/fig/truejan1950.htm, accessed 27 September 2019.

34. Keyhoe, *Flying Saucers Are Real*, 111 (2011 Gutter Books edition).

35. Frank Scully, *Behind the Flying Saucers* (New York: Henry Holt & Co., 1950).

36. Frank Scully, "Scully's Scrapbook," *Variety*, 12 October 1949: 61; 23 November 1949: 24. The Singer midgets were the performers who played the munchkins in the film *The Wizard of Oz*.

37. Scully, *Behind the Flying Saucers*, xi–xii.

38. J. P. Cahn, "The Flying Saucers and the Mysterious Little Men," *True* (September 1952), https://www.saturdaynightuforia.com/html/articles/articlehtml/anatomyofahoax-part11.html, accessed 2 October 2019. Cahn later detailed their con, trial, and conviction in "Flying Saucer Swindlers," *True* (August 1956): 36–37, 69–72.

39. Gerald Heard, *The Riddle of the Flying Saucers: Is Another World Watching?* (London: Carrol & Nicholson, 1950), Foreword (no pagination).

40. Bernard Newman, *The Flying Saucer* (New York: Macmillan, 1950).

41. Robert Sheaffer, "The Trent Photos—'Best' of All Time—Finally Busted?" *Skeptical Inquirer*, 39 (2015), https://skepticalinquirer.org/2015/01/the_trent_ufo_photosbest_of_all_timefinally_busted/, accessed 12 October 2019.

42. http://www.project1947.com/fig/1950a.htm, accessed 7 January 2020.

43. "What Were the Flying Saucers? Eyewitnesses Believe They Saw Secret Aircraft," *Popular Science* 159 (August 1951): 74–75, 228.

44. H. B. Darrach Jr. and Robert Ginna, "Have We Visitors from Space?" *Life*, 7 April 1952: 80–96.

45. Jerome Clark, "Foreword," in *Flying Saucers Over the White House: The Inside Story of Captain Edward J. Ruppelt and His Official U.S. Airforce Investigation of UFOs*, ed. Colin Bennet (New York: Cosimo, 2010), 7–8.

46. Robert E. Ginna Jr., "Saucer Reactions," *Life*, 9 June 1952: 20–26.

47. Edward J. Ruppelt, *The Report on Unidentified Flying Objects* (Garden City: Doubleday, 1956), Project Gutenberg Ebook, 402, 542.

48. Harry G. Barnes, "Washington Radar Observer Relates Watching Stunts by Flying Saucers," *New York World-Telegram*, July 29, 1952, cited in Thomas Tulien, *History of the United States Air Force UFO Programs*, https://sohp.us/history-of-the-usaf-ufo-programs/6-project-blue-book.php, accessed 8 January 7, 2020.

49. "Radar Spots Air Mystery Objects Here," *Washington Post*, 22 July 1952.

50. "Jets Ready to Chase Lights," *Washington Daily News*, 28 July 1952.

51. Herbert B. Nichols, "'Flying Saucers' Whirl Between Rumour and Fact," *Christian Science Monitor*, 30 July 1952.

52. "AF Thinks 'Saucers' Friendly, Eager to Identify Them," *Washington Daily News*, 30 July 1952.

53. Loren Gross, *UFO's: A History 1952–August* (Fremont: Loren Gross, 1986).

54. Ibid., 18.

55. Bard C. Sparks, "CIA Involvement," *The Encyclopedia of UFOs*, ed. Ronald D. Story (Garden City: Doubleday, 1980), 72–73.

56. Frederick C. Durant, *Report of Meetings of Scientific Advisory Panel on Unidentified Flying Objects Convened by Office of Scientific Intelligence, CIA: 14–18 January 1953* (Washington, DC: Central Intelligence Agency, OSI Operations Staff Washington, 1953), http://www.cufon.org/cufon/robert.htm, accessed 16 January 2020. All quotes are from this report.

57. Raymond L. Garthoff, "Foreign Intelligence and the Historiography of the Cold War," *Journal of Cold War Studies* 6 (2004): 21–56.

58. Christopher Simpson, *Science of Coercion: Communication Research and Psychological Warfare 1945–1960* (New York: Oxford University Press, 1994).

59. John Scheid, "Superstitio," *Oxford Classical Dictionary*, 2020, https://oxfordre.com/classics/view/10.1093/acrefore/9780199381135.001.0001/acrefore-9780199381135-e-6150, accessed 23 January 2020.

60. Stuart Clark, *Thinking with Demons: The Idea of Witchcraft in Early Modern Europe* (Oxford: Oxford University Press, 1999).

61. Davies, *The Haunted*.

62. Richard Gordon, "*Superstitio*, Superstition, and Religious Repression in the Late Roman Republic and Principate (100 BCE–300 CE)," *Past and Present* 199 (2008): 72–94.

63. Irving Langmuir, "Pathological Science," Talk at Knolls Research Laboratory, 18 December 1953. https://www.cs.princeton.edu/~ken/Langmuir/langmuir.htm, accessed 22 May 2020.

64. Martin Gardner, *Fads and Fallacies in the Name of Science* (New York: Dover, 1957).

65. Gardner, *Fads and Fallacies*, 7.

66. Peter Lamont, *Extraordinary Beliefs: A Historical Approach to a Psychological Problem* (Cambridge: Cambridge University Press, 2013), 251.

67. Jessica Wang, "Scientists and the Problem of the Public in Cold War America, 1945–1960," *Osiris* 17 (2002): 323–347.

68. "Donald Howard Menzel," *Biographical Memoirs*, vol. 60 (National Academies Press, 1991), https://www.nap.edu/read/6061/chapter/11#149, accessed 25 May 2020.

69. David H. Levy, *The Man Who Sold the Milky Way: A Biography of Bart Bok* (Tucson: University of Arizona Press, 1993), 159. There is no evidence to support more recent claims that he was commissioned to do so by government psychological warfare agencies (like the Psychological Strategy Board).

70. Donald H. Menzel, "The Truth about Flying Saucers," *Look* 16 (17 June 1952), www.project1947.com/fig/look61752.htm, accessed 28 May 2020.

71. Donald H. Menzel, *Flying Saucers* (Cambridge, MA: Harvard University Press, 1953).

72. Stanton T. Friedman, *Top Secret/Majic: Operation Majestic-12 and the United States Government's UFO Cover-Up* (Cambridge, MA: Da Capo, 1996).

73. "Those Flying Saucers: An Astronomer's Explanation," *Time* 59 (9 June 1952): 55.

74. John Sharples, "Sky and Stardust: The Flying Saucer in American Popular Culture, 1947–1957," *Cultural and Social History* 12 (2016): 81–98.

CHAPTER 4

1. Project Blue Book Archive, 1948-05-9670225-Adapazari-Turkey-170. https://archive.org/details/project-blue-book, accessed 17 July 2020.

2. Ronald D. Story, ed., *The Encyclopedia of UFOs* (Garden City, NY: Doubleday, 1980), 274.

3. Henri Chaloupek, "Les Debuts de l'Ufologie en France: Souvenirs d'un soucoupiste," paper given 26 March 1994 in Paris at Hotel Paris-Lyon-Palace, 9.

4. Verga, *Flying Saucers in the Sky*, 347–356.

5. "Cosmos ou aéronautique?" *Le Monde*, 6 July 1947, https://ufologie.patrickgross.org/press/lemonde6jul1947f.htm; "L'affaire des 'soucoupes volantes,'" *Le Monde*, 8 July 1947, https://ufologie.patrickgross.org/press/lemonde8jul1947f.htm, accessed 24 July 2020.

6. "De mystérieuses 'soucoupes volantes,'" *La Libre Belgique*, 5 July 1947, https://ufologie.patrickgross.org/press/librebelgique5jul1947f.htm, accessed 23 July 2020.

7. Ignacio Cabria García, *Entre ufólogos, creyentes y contactados: Una historia social de los OVNIs en España* (Santander: Cuadernos de Ufología, 1993), 8.

8. "Eine 'Scheibe' landet zischend in einem Blumenbeet," *Wiener Illustrierte*, 12 July 1947: n.p.

9. Diego Zuñiga, *Los Ovnis: La prensa escrita en la difusión de creencias populares. Memoria para optar al título de periodista* (Santiago: Universidad de Chile, 2003).

10. AFU, Svenska klipp, 1949-1772-1949, Dagspress.

11. Giuseppe Stilo, *Un cielo ross scuro. 1947–1949: l'arrivo dei dischi volanti sull'Italia e sul mundo* (Turin: Edizioni UPIAR, 2017), 15–16.

12. Roberto Banchs, *Guía biográfica de la ufología argentina* (Buenos Aires: Cefai Ediciones 2000), 106.

13. Ibid., 99–117.

14. On developments in Brazil, see Rodolpho Gauthier Cardoso dos Santos, *A Invenção dos discos voardores: Guerra Fria, imprensa ciêcia no Brasil (1947–1958)* (São Paulo: Alameda, 2017).

15. Ibid., Loc 1053.

16. "Transatlantisches Sausen," *Der Spiegel* 29 (1947): 19.

17. Stilo, *Un cielo ross scuro*, 263–264.

18. See, for instance, Great Britain. Mass Observation for the Advertising Service Guild, *The Press and its Readers* (London: Art & Technics, 1949), Newspaper Reading Collection 61, 1937–1962, 61-11-C. Barbara Wace, "Killing Hunting Flying Saucer," *Daily Graphic and Daily Sketch*, Friday, 9 January 1948: 1. "The elusive 'flying saucers' have claimed their first victim." Newspaper Reading Collection 61, 1937–1962, 61-12-A *Daily Mail* and "'Hit Saucer': Plane Blew Up," *Daily Mail*, Friday, 9 January 1948: 1.

19. National Archives, Record Group 341, NAID: 28935719, Moscow Summer, 1949.

20. Ufo Museum Bagnoregio, https://www.facebook.com/ufomuseumbagnoregio/photos/a.840111563100124/1004864709958141/?type=3&theater, accessed 3 August 2020.

21. Ernie Smith, "The Long, Strange History of People Filing Flying Saucer Patents," *Atlas Obscura*, 27 October 2017, https://www.atlasobscura.com/articles/flying-saucer-patents-alexander-weygers, accessed 4 August 2020.

22. Zuñiga, *Los Ovnis*, 48–53.

23. Dos Santos, *A Invenção dos discos voardores*, Loc 2328-2473.

24. "The Tale of The Nazi Saucer," *Saturday Night Uforia*, 2011, https://www.saturdaynightuforia.com/html/articles/articlehtml/taleofthenazisaucer.html, accessed 4 August 2020.

25. Gerhard Wiechmann, *Von der deutschen Flugscheibe zum Nazi-UFO: Metamorphosen eines medialen Phantoms 1950–2020* (Paderborn: Brill/Schöningh, 2022).

26. "Tale of the Nazi Saucer."

27. "Sie fliegen aber doch," *Der Spiegel*, 30 March 1950: 33–35.

28. Eric Kurlander, *Hitler's Monsters: A Supernatural History of the Third Reich* (New Haven, CT: Yale University Press, 2018).

29. Peder Roberts, "The White (Supremacist) Continent: Antarctica and Fantasies of Nazi Survival," in *Antarctica and the Humanities*, ed. Peder Roberts et al. (London: Palgrave, 2016), 105–124; Nicholas Goodrick-Clarke, *Black Sun: Aryan Cults, Esoteric Nazism, and the Politics of Identity* (New York and London: New York University Press, 2002), 107–172.

30. Giuseppe Stilo, "1947–1949: I dischi volanti arrivano in Italia," paper presented at the 32nd National Convention of Ufology, Turin, 7 October 2017.

31. Giuseppe Stilo, "Operation Origins. 'Flying Saucers' and the Press in Italy, 1946–1954," *Italian UFO Reporter* 10 (June 1989): 10–12.

32. Dos Santos, *A Invenção dos discos voardores*, Loc 2009-2013.

33. Zuñiga, *Los Ovnis*, 66.

34. Héctor Escobar, "La oleada de 1950," *Perspectivas Ufológicas* 6 (1995): 15–22.

35. Zuñiga, *Los Ovnis*, 62.

36. García, *Entre ufólogos*, 9–11.

37. Phillip J. Hutchison and Herbert J. Strentz, "Journalism Versus the Flying Saucers: Assessing the First Generation of UFO Reportage, 1947–1967," *American Journalism* 36 (2019): 165.

38. Dos Santos, *A Invenção dos discos voardores*, Loc 3176; Chaloupek, "Les Debuts," 9.

39. Isabelle Kerr, "Flying Saucers and UFOs: An Investigation into the Impact of the Cold War on British Society, 1950–1964" (BA diss., University of Bristol, 2015), 6, 24.

40. Évry Schatzman, "Les soucoupes volantes," *La Pensée* 36 (1951): 87–90; "Les soucoupes volantes, vertes, possibilities, illusions," *Science et Vie* 403

(1951): 216–220; and "Une mystification: Les soucoupes volantes," *L'Education nationale* 7 (26 April 1951): 10.

41. Personal correspondence, 26 August 2020.

42. Richard K. Popp, "Information, Industrialization, and the Business of Press Clippings, 1880–1925," *The Journal of American History* 101 (2014): 427–453.

43. Personal communication, 28 August 2020.

44. Jan L. Aldrich, "Civilian Saucer Investigation (Los Angeles)," Sign Historical Group, http://www.project1947.com/shg/csi/csiintro.html, accessed 28 December 2020.

45. The following details and quotations regarding CSI-LA are from *Civilian Saucer Investigation Quarterly Review* 1 (September 1952).

46. *Civilian Saucer Investigation Quarterly Bulletin* 1 (Winter 1954): 1.

47. Details about Leonard Stringfield's early work in ufology comes from Leonard H. Stringfield, *Inside Saucer Post . . . 3-0 Blue* (Cincinnati: CRIFO, 1957), 6–16.

48. AFU, "Statement of Importance," *Space Review* 2 (October 1953): 1.

49. Gray Barker, *They Knew Too Much about Flying Saucers* (New York: University Books, 1956).

50. Albert K. Bender, *Flying Saucers and the Three Men* (Clarksburg, WV: Saucerian Books, 1962).

51. Details about James Moseley's early work in ufology comes from James W. Moseley and Karl T. Pflock, *Shockingly Close to the Truth: Confessions of a Grave-Robbing Ufologist* (Amherst, NY: Prometheus, 2002), 25–113.

52. Ibid., 28–29.

53. Ibid., 42, 45, 113.

54. "Greetings Fellow Saucer Fiends!" *Nexus*, July 1954: 1.

55. Moseley and Pflock, *Shockingly*, 109.

56. Unless otherwise noted, the biographical information on Coral Lorenzen in this section is from Dick Ruhl, "A History of APRO," *Official UFO* 1 (January 1976): 24.

57. AFU, Gösta Rehn korrespondens, Coral Lorenzen to Gösta Rehn, 18 December 1959.

58. AFU, Gösta Rehn korrespondens, Coral Lorenzen to Gösta Rehn, 19 November 1959.

59. James Moseley—who shared Lorenzen's reputation for being plain-spoken—remembered Coral as "opinionated, prejudiced, and just not a very nice person." Moseley and Pflock, *Shockingly Close*, 223.

60. Robert Barrow, "Remembering Coral Lorenzen," *Robert Barrow Blog*, 22 May 2007, http://robert-barrow.blogspot.com/2007/05/remembering-coral-lorenzen.html, accessed 22 January 2021.

61. *APRO Newsletter* 1 (3 July 1967).

62. University of Wyoming, American Heritage Center (hereafter UWAHC), R. Leo Sprinkle Papers, Box 29, Frank B. Salisbury to Jim and Coral Lorenzen, 20 September 1977.

63. Details about the emergence and early development of NICAP are, unless otherwise noted, from Clark, *UFO Encyclopedia*, vol. 2, 792–795 and David Michael Jacobs, *The UFO Controversy in America* (Bloomington: Indiana University Press, 1975), 132–157.

64. AFU Digital Archive, "8 Point Plan Offered Air Force," *The U.F.O. Investigator* 1 (July 1952): 1, 5, 25.

65. "Support NICAP?" *APRO Bulletin*, July 1962: 1–2.

66. García, *Entre ufólogos*, 15–21.

67. Keith Basterfield, "The South Australian UFO Story," 2007, https://ufosa.files. wordpress.com/2011/05/south_australian_ufo_story.pdf, accessed 6 February 2021; Bill Chalker, "Australian Ufology," 1998, http://www.auforn.com/Bill_Cha lker_31.htm, accessed 6 February 2021.

68. *Weltraumbote* 1 (1955): 1.

69. *Weltraumbote* 2 (1955–1956): 5–6.

70. Siegfried Schöpfer, *Fliegende Untertassen—Ja oder Nein?* (Lüneburg: Carola Von Reeken, 1980, original 1955).

71. This and the following biographical information on Veit is from http://wiki.gren zwissen.de/index.php/Karl_L._Veit, accessed 22 January 2019.

72. "Marsmenschen über Mainz," *Spiegel Online*, 5 November 2007, http://www.spie gel.de/einestages/ufologie-a-948811.html, accessed 22 January 2019.

73. Hermann Oberth, "They Come from Outer Space," *Flying Saucer Review* 1 (1955): 12–15. Quote from p. 14.

74. Werner Walter, "The German UFO Chronicles: Ein Abriß der deutschen UFO-Geschichte von den Anfängen bis Heute," http://alien.de/cenap/chronicles.htm, accessed 23 February 2019.

75. Matthew Hayes, *Search for the Unknown: Canada's UFO Files and the Rise of Conspiracy Theory* (Montreal: McGill-Queen's University Press, 2022).

76. A. V. Golubev, "НЛО над планетарием: эпистемологическая пропаганда и альтернативные формы знаний о космосе в СССР в 1940–1960-е годы," *История* 54 (2021): 5–16.

77. "Vliegende Schotels," *Het Neiuws*, 10 November 1952: 3.

78. "Le Referendum d'Europe N°1: 53% des Français croient que les soucoupes volantes viennent d'une autre planéte," *France-soir*, 25 February 1956: 8.

79. Details about developments in France are from Manuel Wiroth, *Ovnis sur la France: histoire et étude du phénomène des années 1940 à nos jours* (Agnières: Éditions Le temps présent, 2017); Thibaut Canuti, *Histoire de l'ufologie française: 1 Le temps des soucoupistes* (Agniéres: Temps présent, 2011), 21–39; Chaloupek, "Les Debuts," 9–22.

80. AFU, *Lumiéres dans lu Nuit* 1–2 (1958).

81. Aimé Michel, "Les tribulations d'un chercheur parallèle," *Planète* 20 (January–February 1965), http://www.aime-michel.fr/les-tribulations-dun-cherch eur-parallele/, accessed 25 February 2021. In 1960, Michel wrote Keyhoe to tell him that NICAP was wasting its time trying to get information out of the military—the latter being incompetent, not scheming—and instead should focus its attention on doing scientific research. "Aime Michel Correspondence with NICAP," *Journal of UFO History* 2 (May–June 2005): 11–12.

82. Aimé Michel, *The Truth about Flying Saucers* (New York: Pyramid, 1956), 240.

83. Aimé Michel, *Flying Saucers and the Straight-Line Mystery* (New York: Criterion, 1958), 13.

84. Ibid., 51.

85. Ibid., 80.

86. Peter M. Seeviour, "Foundations of Orthoteny," *Flying Saucer Review* 11 (1965): 10–12; Aimé Michel, "Global Orthoteny," *Flying Saucer Review* 9 (1963): 3–7; Jacques Vallee, "Towards a Generalisation of Orthoteny and Its Applications to the North African Sightings," *Flying Saucer Review* 8 (1962): 3–7;

Antonio Ribera, "Spanish Orthotenies in 1950," *Flying Saucer Review* 9 (1961): 9–11; Olavo T. Fontes, "Brazil—Again," *APRO Bulletin*, July 1960: 1, 3–4.

87. Donald H. Menzel, "Orthoteny—A Lost Cause, Part 1," *Flying Saucer Review* 11 (1965): 9–11; "Orthoteny—A Lost Cause, Part 2," *Flying Saucer Review* 11 (1965): 26–28.

88. On developments in the United Kingdom, unless otherwise noted, see David Clarke and Andy Roberts, *Flying Saucerers: A Social History of UFOlogy* (Loughborough: Alternative Albion, 2007), 27–32, 37, 53–61.

89. David Clarke, "Prince Philip: The Royal Flying Saucerer," *DrDavidClarke*, 11 April 2021, https://drdavidclarke.co.uk/2021/04/11/prince-philip-the-royal-flying-saucerer/, accessed 8 May 2021.

90. British National Archives, Kew, DEFE-44-119-2, Ministry of Defence, Directorate of Scientific Intelligence and Joint Technical Intelligence Committee, "Unidentified Flying Objects," June 1951.

91. David Clarke, *The National Archives Research Guide (UFOs)* (Sheffield: Sheffield Hallam University Research Archive, 2008), 5–8.

92. Unless otherwise noted, details about the formation of *Flying Saucer Review* are from Steve Holland and Roger Perry, *The Men behind the Flying Saucer Review* (UK: Bear Alley Books, 2017).

93. Denis Montgomery, "How It All Began: Founding the Flying Saucer Review," 5 May 2014, http://fsr.org.uk/fsrintroduction.html, accessed 2 March 2021.

94. http://www.fsr.org.uk/fsrintroduction.html, accessed 5 March 2021.

95. *Flying Saucer Review* 2 (July–August 1956): 1.

96. Personal communication, 23 June 2015.

97. M. K. Jessup, "Ufology: A Plea and a Warning," *Miami Saucerlore* (Spring 1958), reprinted in *Saucers* 7 (Spring/Summer 1959): 6.

98. Max B. Miller, "Editorial," *Saucers* 7 (Fall/Winter 1959/1960): 2.

CHAPTER 5

1. Bryant and Helen Reeve, *Flying Saucer Pilgrimage* (Amherst, WI: Amherst Press, 1957), 33. All information about the Reeves and their trip is from their book, unless otherwise noted.

2. On Adamski's thinking and writing before 1953, see Aaron John Gulyas, *Extraterrestrials and the American Zeitgeist* (Jefferson, NC: McFarland, 2013), 42–44, 60–86.

3. "Flying Saucer 'Passenger' Declares A-Bomb Blasts Reason for Visit," *The Phoenix Gazette*, 24 November 1952: 1.

4. All references and quotes from the book are from Desmond Leslie and George Adamski, *Flying Saucers Have Landed* (London: Panther, 1957).

5. Ibid., 140.

6. Ibid., 139–140.

7. Ibid., 141.

8. Ibid., 161.

9. George Adamski, *Inside the Space Ships* (New York: Abelard-Schuman, 1955) and *Flying Saucers Farewell* (London: Abelard-Schuman, 1961); Gulyas, *Extraterrestrials*, 74–75.

10. Gerard Aartsen, "Get Acquainted Program," *The George Adamski Case*, https://www.the-adamski-case.nl/his-mission/global-reach/gap/, accessed 24 May 2021.

11. Robert S. Ellwood, "Spiritualism and UFO Religion in New Zealand: The International Transmission of Modern Spiritual Movements," in *The Gods Have*

Landed: New Religions from Other Worlds, ed. James R. Lewis (Albany: State University of New York Press, 1995), 166–186.

12. On this part of Adamski's 1959 world tour, see Gulyas, *Extraterrestrials*, 77–78; Marc Hallet, *A Critical Appraisal of George Adamski: The Man Who Spoke to the Space Brothers* (Self-published, 2016), 115–122.

13. Gerard Aartsen, "Vatican Visit," *The George Adamski Case*, https://www.the-adam ski-case.nl/his-mission/vatican-visit/, accessed 25 May 2021.

14. Arthur C. Clarke, "Review of Desmond Leslie and George Adamski, *Flying Saucers Have Landed*," *Journal of the British Interplanetary Society* 13 (1954): 119–122.

15. Moseley, *Shockingly Close*, 64–69.

16. James Moseley, "Some New Facts about 'Flying Saucers Have Landed,'" *Nexus* (January 1955): 7–17. Quotes from p. 17.

17. Moseley, *Shockingly Close*, 69.

18. Truman Bethurum, "I Was Inside a Flying Saucer," *Saucers* 1, no. 2 (1953): 4–5.

19. Truman Bethurum, *Aboard a Flying Saucer: A True Story of Personal Experience* (Los Angeles: DeVors, 1954), 75.

20. Ibid., 69, 117.

21. Ibid., 51, 129, 183.

22. George Hunt Williamson and Alfred C. Bailey, *The Saucers Speak! A Documentary Report of Interstellar Communication by Radio Telegraphy* (Los Angeles: New Age Publishing, 1954), 45–46.

23. Ibid., 71.

24. Ibid., 95.

25. Jason Daley, "The Screenwriting Mystic Who Wanted to be the American Führer," *Smithsonian Magazine*, 3 October 2018, https://www.smithsonianmag. com/history/meet-screenwriting-mystic-who-wanted-be-american-fuhrer-180970449/, accessed 29 May 2021.

26. George Hunt Williamson and John O. McCoy, *UFOs Confidential! The Meaning Behind the Most Closely Guarded Secret of All Time* (Corpus Christi: Essene, 1958), 59–60.

27. Ibid., 40–53.

28. Reeve, *Pilgrimage*, 83.

29. George W. Van Tassel, "A Brief History of Giant Rock Covering the Last 90 Years (1887–1977)," *Integratron*, n.d., https://www.integratron.com/a-brief-history-of-giant-rock-covering-the-last-90-years-1887-1977/, accessed 3 June 2021.

30. George W. Van Tassel, *I Rode a Flying Saucer: The Mystery of Flying Saucers Revealed* (Los Angeles: New Age, 1952). Quotes are from pp. 22 and 23.

31. Reeve, *Pilgrimage*, 95–99.

32. *Calling All Earthlings*, dir. Jonathan Berman (2018).

33. Moseley, *Shockingly Close*, 164.

34. Reeve, *Pilgrimage*, 99.

35. Daniel W. Fry, *The White Sands Incident* (Los Angeles: New Age, 1954).

36. Daniel W. Fry, *Alan's Message: To Men of* Earth (Los Angeles: New Age, 1954). Quote from p. 21.

37. Orfeo Angelucci, *The Secret of the Saucers* (Stevens Point, WI: Amherst, 1955), 7.

38. Ibid., 124, 103, 30.

39. Reeve, *Pilgrimage*, 223, 258.

40. Ibid., 259.

41. Arthur Versluis, *American Gurus: From American Transcendentalism to New Religion* (New York: Oxford University Press, 2014), 162–163.

42. Wouter J. Hanegraaff, *New Age Religion and Western Culture: Esotericism in the Mirror of Secular Thought* (Leiden: Brill, 1996), 23–41, 95–103.

43. J. Gordon Melton, "A History of the New Age Movement," in *Not Necessarily the New Age: Critical Essays*, ed. Robert Basil (Buffalo: Prometheus Books, 1988), 35–53; Christof Schorsch, *Die New-Age-Bewegung: Utopie und Mythos der neuen Zeit* (Gütersloh: Gütersloher Verlag Haus Mohn, 1988).

44. Dan Martin, *The Watcher: Seven Hours Aboard a Space Ship* (Clarksburg: Saucerian Publications, 1969, original 1959).

45. Reinhold O. Schmidt, *The Kearney Incident and to the Arctic Circle in a Spacecraft* (Hollywood: Reinhold O. Schmidt, 1959).

46. Curt Collins, "The Trial of a UFO Gold Digger," *The Saucers That Time Forgot*, 27 August 2020, https://thesaucersthattimeforgot.blogspot.com/2022/04/early-accounts-of-alien-abductions.html?fbclid=IwAR0CTyWcx00bHOzGqlsK80xOU_aFyNvnwhzuFX571Ib9Xs-J_R4spCAP2Ic, accessed 7 April 2022.

47. Buck Nelson, *My Trip to Mars, the Moon, and Venus* (West Plains: Quill, 1956).

48. Howard Menger, *From Outer Space to You* (Clarksburg: Saucerian Books, 1959); "Howard Menger's Own Story," *Flying Saucer Review* 4 (March–April 1958): 14–17.

49. George King, *You are Responsible!* (London: Aetherius, 1961).

50. Angela Hague, "Before Abduction: The Contactee Narrative of the 1950s," *The Journal of Popular Culture* 44 (2011): 439–454; Gulyas, *Extraterrestrials*, 201–223.

51. Dino Kraspedon, *My Contact with Flying Saucers* (London: Neville Spearman, 1959, originally published in 1957); "Brazil Cult Leader Who 'Contacted Aliens' Backed Dictatorship with Terror Attacks, Documents Show," *The Guardian*, 3 October 2018, https://www.theguardian.com/world/2018/oct/03/brazil-cult-leader-aliens-terror-aladino-felix-dino-kraspedon, accessed 14 June 2021.

52. Severino Machado, *Los platillos volantes ante la razón y la ciencia* (Madrid: Machado, 1955).

53. Eduardo Bravo, *Ummo: Los increíble es la verdad* (Sineu, Islas Baleares: Autsaider Cómics, 2019).

54. Cabria, *Entre Ufólogos*, 37–41.

55. Elijah Muhammad, *The True History of Master Fard Muhammad* (Phoenix: Secretarius MEMPS, 1996), 167; *The Mother Plane* (Phoenix: Secretarius MEMPS, 1992). Quote from Elijah Muhammad, *Message to the Blackman in America* (Phoenix: Secretarius MEMPS, 1965, 1973), 499.

56. Stephen C. Finley, *In and Out of This World: Material and Extraterrestrial Bodies in the Nation of Islam* (Durham: Duke University Press, 2022), 131–157.

57. John F. Szwed, *Space Is the Place: The Lives and Times of Sun Ra* (New York: Pantheon, 1997), 29–30.

58. Ibid., 137–191.

59. Historian Ronald Hutton has noted the prominence in Western lore of a sacred figure referred to as "The Lady" that sounds a good deal like Diane and the queen Howard described. The terms that sources say common people used to describe her "embody the same bundle of qualities: abundance, generosity, opulence, the power of divination, and above all general goodness as a patroness and companion." Ronald Hutton, Lecture "The Wild Hunt and the Witches," *The Folklore Podcast*, 2017, https://thefolklorepodcast.weebly.com/season-5/episode-74-the-wild-hunt-the-witches-a-lecture-by-prof-ronald-hutton, accessed 21 June 2021.

60. Dana Howard, *My Flight to Venus* (San Gabriel: Willing, 1954), 61; *Diane: She Came from Venus* (London: Regency, 1955); *Over the Threshold* (Los Angeles: Llewellyn, 1957).

61. "Landing in South Africa," *Flying Saucer Review* 2 (December 1956): 2–5. Quotes from pp. 4–5.

62. Elizabeth Klarer, *Beyond the Light Barrier* (Aylesbury: Howard Timmins, 1980).

63. Gloria Lee, *Why We Are Here by J. W. A Being from Jupiter through the Instrumentation of Gloria Lee* (Los Angeles: DeVross & Co., 1959); *The Changing Conditions of Your World by J. W. of Jupiter Instrumented by Gloria Lee* (Palos Verdes Estates: Cosmon, 1962).

64. Jerome Clark, *Hidden Realms, Lost Civilizations, and Beings from Other Worlds* (Canton, MI: Visible Ink Press, 2010), 172.

65. Edgar Sievers, *Flying Saucer über Südafrika: Zur Frage der Besuche aus dem Weltenraum* (Pretoria: Sagittarius, 1955). Quotes from p. 268.

66. Gavin Gibbons, *They Rode Space Ships* (London: Neville Spearman, 1957).

67. Håkan Blomqvist, "K. Gösta Rehn and George Adamski," *Håkan Blomqvist´s Blog*, 4 September 2019, https://ufoarchives.blogspot.com/2019/09/k-gosta-rehn-and-george-adamski.html, accessed 19 June 2021.

68. Isabel L. Davis, "Meet the Extraterrestrial," *Fantastic Universe* 9 (November 1957): 31–59. Quotes from pp. 40, 48, 51–52, 56.

69. "Contactees Told to Return NICAP Cards," *The U.F.O. Investigator* 1 (August–September 1958): 4.

70. Davis, "Meet the Extraterrestrial," 44–45.

71. Michelle Cooke, "Little People and Leprechauns: Creatures of Cultural Folklore," *Journal of Chickasaw History and Culture* 15 (2013): 21–33; Jacques Vallee, *Passport to Magonia: From Folklore to Flying Saucers* (Chicago: H. Regnery, 1969); Valerii I. Sanarov, "On the Nature and Origin of Flying Saucers and Little Green Men," *Current Anthropology* 22 (1981): 163–167.

72. AFU, Gösta Rehn Papers, Coral Lorenzen to Gösta Rehn, 22 January 1959.

73. Antonio Ribera, "The Landing at Villares Del Saz," *Flying Sauer Review, Special Issue: The Humanoids* 1 (October–November 1966): 28–29.

74. Jacques Vallee, "The Pattern Behind the UFO Landings," *Flying Sauer Review, Special Issue: The Humanoids* 1 (October–November 1966): 8–27.

75. Details about the incident are from Marc Thirouin's interviews of Dewilde conducted over the course of one week in 1955. Marc Thirouin, "Marius Dewilde n' a pas menti," *Ouranos* 24 (1959): 11–13 and 25 (1959): 20–25.

76. James Miller, "Seeing the Future of Civilization in the Skies of Quarouble: UFO Encounters and the Problem of Empire in Postwar France," in *Imagining Outer Space: European Astroculture in the Twentieth Century*, ed. Alexander C.T. 7 (Basingstoke: Palgrave, 2012), 245–264.

77. For press coverage from the time, see Patrick Gross, "The 1954 French Flap: September 10, 1954, Quarouble, Nord," https://ufologie.patrickgross.org/1954/10sep1954quarouble.htm, accessed 20 June 2021.

78. Jacques Vallee, *Forbidden Science: Journals 1957–1969* (Berkeley: North Atlantic Books, 1992), 15.

79. Sergio Conti, "The Cennina Landing of 1954," *Flying Saucer Review* 18 (September–October 1972): 11–15.

80. Walter K. Bühler, *40 Begegnungen mit Außerdischen in Brasilien* (Wiesbaden: Ventla, 1975), 37–39.

81. Bühler, *40 Begegnungen*, 110–112.

82. Streeter Stuart interview of Lonnie Zamora, 29 April 1964, https://www.yout
ube.com/watch?v=Al529ZRUDrw, accessed 23 June 2021.

83. Walter Shrode interview of Lonnie Zamora, 25 April 1964, https://www.yout
ube.com/watch?v=Wu4suk4db4o, accessed 24 June 2021.

84. American Philosophical Society (hereafter APS), Edward Condon Papers, Box 4,
32-B, Summary of UFO Report Received by Phone on 25 April 1964.

85. APS, Edward Condon Papers, Box 4, 32-B, J. Allen Hynek, Report on Socorro
New Mexico Trip (undated).

86. "Socorro Analysis," *U.F.O. Investigator* 2 (September/October 1964): 4.

87. "UAO Landing in New Mexico," *APRO Bulletin* (May 1964): 1–10. Quotes are
from p. 4.

88. APS, Edward Condon Papers, Box 4, 32-B, Col. Eric T de Jonckheere, UFO
Sighting Socorro, New Mexico, 28 May 1964.

89. Gordon Creighton, "The 'Humanoids' in Latin America," *Flying Saucer Review,
Special Issue: The Humanoids* 1 (October–November 1966): 30–46.

90. Jader U. Pereira, "Les Extra-terrestres," *Phénomènes Spatiaux* 24 (June
1970): 14–20.

91. J. Escobar Faria, *Discos voadores: Contatos com sêres de outros planêtas* (São
Paulo: Melhoramentos, 1959).

92. Christopher F. Roth, "Ufology as Anthropology: Race, Extraterrestrials, and
the Occult," in *E.T. Culture: Anthropology in Outerspaces*, ed. Debbora Battaglia
(Durham, NC: Duke University Press, 2005), 38–93.

93. Craig Campobasso, *The Extraterrestrial Species Almanac: The Ultimate Guide to
Greys, Reptilians, Hybrids, and Nordics* (Newburyport: MUFON, 2021).

94. Bühler, *40 Begegnungen*, 27.

95. Stringfield first published about these cases in 1957. See his *Inside Saucer
Post*, 63–69.

96. "Story of Space-Ship, 12 Little Men Probed Today," *The Kentucky New Era*, 22
August 1955, https://www.kentuckynewera.com/eclipse/article_fecf69ce-8611-
11e7-beaf-0ffce93df895.html, accessed 30 June 2021.

97. https://www.skeptic.com/podcasts/monstertalk/17/10/04/, accessed 30
June 2021.

98. Jacqueline Sanders, "Panic in Kentucky," *The Saucerian Review* (January
1956): 19–25.

99. APS, Edward Condon Papers, Box 4, 20-B, Copy of statement made by Glennie
Lankford, 22 August 1955.

100. Isabel Davis and Ted Bloecher, *Close Encounter at Kelly and Others of 1955*
(Evanston, IL: Center for UFO Studies, 1978).

101. APS, Edward Condon Papers, Box 4, Statement of Maj. John E. Albert to 1st Lt.
Charles Kirk, 26 September 1957.

102. Davis and Bloecher, *Close Encounter*, 93.

103. Coral Lorenzen, "UFO Occupants in the United States Report," *Flying Saucer
Review, Special Issue: The Humanoids* 1 (October–November 1966): 52–64. The
case is found on pp. 61–64.

104. Gordon Creighton, "The Brazilian Abduction," *Flying Saucer Review* 8
(November–December 1962): 10–12; AFU, Gordon Creighton Papers, Círculo
Daamizade Sideral (Curitiba, Brazil), 4 (October 1963–February 1964).

105. "Deposition by Antônio Villas Boas," *Flying Saucer Review* 12 (July–August
1966): 24–27; Gordon Creighton, "Even More Amazing, Part 2," *Flying Saucer
Review* 12 (September–October 1966): 22–25; "Even More Amazing, Part 3,"

Flying Saucer Review 12 (November–December 1966): 14–16; "Even More Amazing, Part 4," *Flying Saucer Review* 13 (January–February 1967): 25–27.

106. AFU, Gösta Rehn Papers, Lorenzen to Rehn, 19 November 1959.

107. AFU, Gösta Rehn Papers, Lorenzen to Rehn, 22 October 1959.

108. AFU, Gösta Rehn Papers, Lorenzen to Rehn, 4 November 1959.

109. AFU, Gösta Rehn Papers, Rehn to Lorenzen, 17 November 1959.

110. Coral E. Lorenzen, *The Great Flying Saucer Hoax: The UFO Facts and Their Interpretation* (New York: William-Frederick Press, 1962).

111. "The A.V.B. Contact Case," *SBEDV Boletim* 26/27 (April–July 1962): 7–9, 14.

112. Gordon Creighton, "The Most Amazing Case of All, Part 1," *Flying Saucer Review* 11 (January–February 1965): 13–17. Creighton at first decided to not use Antônio's real name, calling him instead "Adhemar." But after the paper *O Cruzeiro* revealed his name, he did as well.

113. Gordon Creighton, "Postscript to the Most Amazing Case of All," *Flying Saucer Review* 11 (July–August 1965): 24–25.

114. Peter Rogerson, "Fairyland's Hunters: Notes Towards a Revisionist History of Abductions, Part One," *Magonia* 46 (June 1993); "Fairyland's Hunters: Notes Towards a Revisionist History of Abductions, Part 2," *Magonia* 47 (September 1993); "Sex, Science, and Salvation: Notes Towards a Revisionist History of Abductions, Part 3," *Magonia* 49 (June 1994); "Recovering the Forgotten Record: Notes Towards a Revisionist History of Abductions, Part 4," *Magonia* 50 (September 1994); "Abduction Updates," *Magonia* 54 (November 1995), http://magoniamagazine.blogspot.com/2013/11/notes-towards-revisionist-history-of.html, accessed 7 July 2021.

115. I am indebted to Matthew Bowman for providing me with a draft version of his book manuscript *Interrupted Journeys: The Abduction of Betty and Barney Hill and the Fragmentation of America*. I rely heavily here on his impressive research. Unless otherwise cited, details about the case are from his study.

116. Letter in Walter N. Webb, *A Dramatic UFO Encounter in the White Mountains, New Hampshire: The Hills Case—Sept. 19–20, 1961* (August 30, 1965), 38–39.

117. Ibid., 5–6.

118. "Dreams or Recall? Betty Hill's Own Account of Her Dreams Written Nov., 1961," in Webb, *A Dramatic UFO Encounter*.

119. Alison Winter, "The Rise and Fall of Forensic Hypnosis," *Studies in History and Philosophy of Biological and Biomedical Sciences* 44 (2013): 26–35. Quote from p. 33.

120. Quote is from Matthew Bowman's manuscript.

121. Ibid.

122. Benjamin Simon to Philipp J. Klass, 28 October 1975. From: http://www.debunker.com/historical/BettyHillBenjaminSimonPhilipKlass.pdf, accessed 21 May 2018.

CHAPTER 6

1. Frank Carey, "No Evidence Found That UFOs Are Alien Craft," *Sterling Daily Gazette*, 7 January 1969: 2.

2. Harold M. Schmeck, "2 Who May Land on Moon Selected," *New York Times*, 10 January 1969: 1.

3. "UFO Probe Spurns Outer Space Theory," *Chicago Tribune*, 8 January 1969: B10; "Study of Saucers Finds None Flying," *Phoenix Arizona Republic*, 8 January

1969: 28; "No Evidence of Spaceships in Secret Probing of UFO," *Lawrence Daily Journal World*, 8 January 1969: 23.

4. Frank Carey, "Secret Report Suddenly Not So Secret," *Helena Independent Record*, 8 January 1969: 20.

5. "UFOs Visitors from Another Planet?" *Bryan Daily Eagle*, 7 January 1969: 1; "Flying Objects Validity Denied by Scientists," *Jefferson City Daily Capital News*, 9 January 1969: 5.

6. David R. Saunders and R. Roger Harkins, *UFOs? Yes! Where the Condon Committee Went Wrong* (New York: Signet, 1968), 50–74.

7. Timothy Scott Brown, *Sixties Europe* (Cambridge: Cambridge University Press, 2020); Arthur Marwick, *The Sixties* (London: Bloomsbury Reader, 1998).

8. Slava Gerovitch, *Soviet Space Mythologies: Public Images, Private Memories, and the Making of a Cultural Identity* (Pittsburgh: University Pittsburgh Press, 2015); Howard E. McCurdy, *Space and the American Imagination* (Baltimore: Johns Hopkins University Press, 2011).

9. Nevill Drury, *The New Age: The History of a Movement* (New York: Thames & Hudson, 2004), 64–96.

10. Chalker, "Australian Ufology."

11. Sergius Golowin, *Götter der Atom-Zeit: Moderne Sagenbildung um Raumschiffe und Sternenmenschen* (Bern: A. Francke, 1967). Figures are from pp. 14 and 25.

12. Banchs, *Guía biográfica de la ufología argentina*.

13. Antonio Ribera, *Objetos desconocidos en el cielo* (Barcelona: Argos, 1961).

14. Scott Corrales, "Saucers in the Sixties—UFOs in Latin America and Spain," 2007, http://www.noufors.com/Documents/saucerssixties.pdf, accessed 14 May 2014.

15. Cabria, *Entre ufólogos*, 55–78.

16. AFU, BUFORA Minutes of Meetings, 1964–1970, BUFORA Constitution

17. AFU, BUFORA Minutes of Meetings, 1964–1970, BUFORA Document "B" to Researchers, 8 September 1965.

18. AFU, BUFORA Minutes of Meetings, 1964–1970, Meeting of the Executive Committee, 6 December 1969.

19. AFU, BUFORA Minutes of Meetings, 1964–1970, Meeting of the Executive Committee, 24 April 1965.

20. AFU, BUFORA Minutes of Meetings, 1964–1970, G.N.P. Stephenson, Central Research and Information Co-ordinator's Annual Programme, ca. early 1966.

21. AFU, Brinsley Le Poer Trench, "Take Higher Ground," *Skywatch: Quarterly of "Contact" (S.A.)* 4 (March–April–May 1968): 2–6.

22. Clarke and Robert, *Flying Saucerers*, 167–170.

23. AFU, "Activities in South Africa," *Skywatch: Quarterly of the International Sky Scouts (S.A.) Durban* 2 (October–December 1967): 6.

24. AFU, "Invitation by Telepathy," *Skywatch: Quarterly of "Contact" (S.A.)* 5 (June–July–August 1968): 4.

25. Chris Aubeck, *Alien Artifacts, Vol. 1: From Antiquity to 1880* (Monee: Aubeck, 2022), 255–256; Jason Colavito, *The Cult of Alien Gods: H.P. Lovecraft and Extraterrestrial Pop Culture* (Amherst: Prometheus Books, 2005).

26. Marco Ciardi, *Il mistero degli antichi astronauti* (Rome: Carocci, 2017), 143–151.

27. Matest M. Agrest, "On the Development of the Idea of Paleocontacts in the USSR at the Beginning of the 1960s," *RIAP Bulletin* 8 (2002): 4–8.

28. Louis Pauwels and Jacques Bergier, *The Morning of the Magicians* (Rochester, VT: Destiny, 2009), 148.

29. Canuti, *Histoire de l'ufologie Française*: 1, 92–95.

30. Wiktor Stoczkowski, *Des hommes, des dieux et des extraterrestres: Ethnologie d'une croyance moderne* (Paris: Flammarion, 1999), 45–47.

31. Richard R. Lingeman, "Erich von Daniken's Genesis," *New York Times*, 31 March 1974: 6.

32. Erich von Dänekin, *Chariots of the Gods? Unsolved Mysteries of the Past* (New York: G. P. Putnam's Sons, 1970), 9.

33. Ibid., 47–48.

34. Barry Thiering and Edgar W. Castle, *Some Trust in Chariots: Sixteen Views on Erich von Däniken's* Chariots of the Gods? (Folkstone: Bailey Brothers & Swinfen, 1973); John Peter White, *The Past Is Human* (Sydney: Angus & Robertson, 1974); Ronald Story, *The Space-Gods Revealed: A Close Look at the Theories of Erich von Däniken* (New York: Harper & Row, 1976).

35. Stoczkowski, *Des hommes*, 48–49, 54. Stoczkowski himself concludes 71.8 percent of the archaeological monuments von Däniken mentioned and over a third of his arguments could already be found in the earlier works of Charroux, Pauwels, and Bergier.

36. Ibid., 81.

37. Ibid., 293–294, 303; Jean-Bruno Renard, "La sacralization de la science," in *Nouvelles idoles, nouveaux cultes: Dérives de la sacralité*, ed. Claude Rivière and Albert Piette (Paris: L'Hartmann, 1990), 82–98.

38. François Rulier, "Les juristes à la rencontre d'une vie intelligente extra-terrestre: composition d'une astroculture disciplinaire dans les années 1950 et 1960," *Sociétés & Représentations* 57 (2024), in press.

39. "Theologen über Untertassen," *Hamburger Abendblatt* 182 (9 August 1954): 8; "Untertassen-Menschen: Absolute unverletzlich," *Der Spiegel* 36 (1952): 17.

40. "Braun glaubt nicht an Untertassen," *Hamburger Abendblatt* 229 (October 2–3, 1954): 10.

41. Georges Heuyer, "Note sur les psychoses collectives," *Bulletin de l'Académie Nationale de Médecine* 138 (1954): 487–490.

42. Joost A. M. Meerloo, "Le syndrome des soucoupes volantes," *Médecine et Hygiène* 794 (September 1967): 992–996.

43. Leon Festinger, Henry W. Riecken, and Stanley Schachter, *When Prophecy Fails* (Minneapolis: University of Minnesota Press, 1956), 228–229.

44. C. G. Jung, *Ein moderner Mythus: Von Dingen, die am Himmel gesehen werden* (Zürich and Stuttgart: Rascher-Verlag, 1958); C. G. Jung, *Flying Saucers: A Modern Myth of Things Seen in the Skies* (New York: MJF Books, 1978).

45. Letter to *Weltwoche*, 22 (9 July 1954), reproduced in Jung, *Flying Saucers*, 131–133.

46. Letter to Donald E. Keyhoe, 16 August 1958, reproduced in Jung, *Flying Saucers*, 137–138. According to one of his biographers, there is evidence that, despite his public comments to the contrary, Jung himself privately believed that flying saucers were extraterrestrial in nature. See Deirdre Bair, *Jung: A Biography* (Boston: Little, Brown and Company, 2003), 572–573.

47. Franz Schonauer, "Immer noch fliegende Untertassen," *Die Zeit*, 15 May 1958, www.zeit.de/1958/20/immer-noch-fliegende-untertassen, accessed 22 May 2013; "Himmlische Zeichen," *Der Spiegel* 12 (19 March 1958): 61–62.

48. Donald H. Menzel and Lyle G. Boyd, *The World of Flying Saucers: A Scientific Examination of a Major Myth of the Space Age* (Garden City: Doubleday, 1963). Quotes are from pp. 216 and 289.

49. APS, Donald H. Menzel Papers, Box 4, Menzel to De Bruycker, 15 March 1967 and 10 April 1967.

50. Ibid., De Bruycker to Voice of the People, 14 May 1967; De Bruycker to Mishawaka Times Mailbag, 23 August 1965.

51. Ibid., De Bruycker to Menzel, 6 May 1967.

52. Guiseppe Cocconi and Philip Morrison, "Searching for Interstellar Communications," *Nature* 184 (1959): 844–846.

53. Woodruff T. Sullivan III, *Cosmic Noise: A History of Early Radio Astronomy* (New York: Cambridge University Press, 2009) and "The History of Radio Telescopes, 1945–1990," *Experimental Astronomy* 25 (2009): 107–124.

54. On Project Ozma and the Drake Equation, see Steven J. Dick, "The Drake Equation in Context," in *The Drake Equation: Estimating the Prevalence of Extraterrestrial Life through the Ages*, ed. Douglas A. Vakoch and Matthew F. Dowd (Cambridge: Cambridge University Press, 2015), 1–20.

55. Kenneth I. Kellermann, Ellen N. Bouton, Sierra S. Brandt, *Open Skies: Historical & Cultural Astronomy* (Cham: Springer, 2020), 237.

56. I. S. Shklovskii and Carl Sagan, *Intelligent Life in the Universe* (San Francisco, London, and Amsterdam: Holden-Day, 1966).

57. Dick, *Life on Other Worlds*, 200–216.

58. Walter Sullivan, *We Are Not Alone: The Search for Intelligent Life on Other Worlds* (New York: McGraw-Hill, 1964).

59. Alan John Penny, "The SETI Episode in the 1967 Discovery of Pulsars," *European Physical Journal H* 38 (2013): 535–547. Quote is from p. 537.

60. "First Soviet-American Conference on Communication with Extraterrestrial Intelligence (CETI)," *Icarus* 16 (1972): 412–414. Quotes are from pp. 412 and 413.

61. Robert Poole, "ET and the Bomb: Origins of the Scientific Belief in Extra-Terrestrial Intelligence," paper for the British Society for the History of Science Conference, Exeter, 2011. Quotes are from pp. 6 and 15.

62. David Kaiser and W. Patrick McCray, "Introduction," in *Groovy Science: Knowledge, Innovation, and American Counterculture*, ed. David Kaiser and W. Patrick McCray (Chicago: University of Chicago Press, 2016), 8.

63. Rebecca Charbonneau, *Mixed Signals: Cold War Communication with Extraterrestrial Intelligence* (Cambridge: Polity Press, 2024).

64. APS, Donald H. Menzel Papers, Box 11, Page to Harnett, 1 October 1957; Course Description, Sci. 101 Flying Saucers, Fall Semester 1967.

65. Mark O'Connell, *The Close Encounters Man: How One Man Made the World Believe in UFOs* (New York: Dey St., 2017), 78.

66. On Hynek, Vallee, and the Invisible College, see Vallee, *Forbidden Science: Journals 1957–1969*. Quotes are from pp. 72, 76, 104.

67. Jacques Vallee, *The Invisible College: What a Group of Scientists Has Discovered about UFO Influence on the Human Race* (San Antonio: Anomalist, 1975), 11.

68. Vallee, *Forbidden Science: Journals 1957–1969*, 174.

69. Narrative from the preface of Roy Craig, *UFOs: An Insider's View of the Official Question for Evidence* (Denton: University of North Texas Press, 1995).

70. Saunders and Harkins, 25.

71. Jessica Wang, "Science, Security, and the Cold War: The Case of E.U. Condon," *Isis* 83 (1992): 244.

72. The quotes from Condon are from Interview of Edward Condon by Charles Weiner on 1973 September 11, Niels Bohr Library & Archives, American Institute

of Physics, College Park, MD USA, www.aip.org/history-programs/niels-bohr-library/oral-histories/4997-3.

73. "An Outspoken Scientist: Edward Uhler Condon," *New York Times*, 8 October 1966: 15.

74. Robert R. Hippler to Edward Condon, 16 January 1967, http://www.nicap.org/docs/HipplerLetters.pdf, accessed 11 August 2021,

75. Quotes are from AIP Interview with Condon, 11 September 1973.

76. APS, Box O.25, "Dramatis Personae—UFO Project."

77. Saunders and Harkins, 47–49.

78. Vallee, *Forbidden Science: Journals 1957–1969*, 224.

79. Arturo F. Gonzalez, Jr., "Marsh Gas, Moonshine or Space Men? The Flying Saucer Mystery," *Irish Times*, 22 March 1967: 8.

80. APS, Condon Papers, Box O.25, Robert Low to Investigating Group, 23 December 1966.

81. APS, Condon Papers, Box 9, Luke Frost, "A Cloak of Respectability: $313,000," UFO Reports, 1967.

82. APS, Condon Papers, Box O.8, Condon to Page, 13 February 1968; APS, Condon Papers, Box O.25, Low "Position Paper," 21 April 1967.

83. J. Allen Hynek, *The UFO Experience: A Scientific Inquiry* (New York: Ballantine, 1972), 25–30.

84. James E. McDonald Papers (hereafter, UA, McDonald Papers), University of Arizona Special Collections, MS 412 Box 3, A.J. Cote, Jr. to James McDonald, 3 July 1968.

85. UA, McDonald Papers, MS 412, Box 5, McDonald to Hall, 15 August 1967.

86. "Condon, UFO Agnostic, Should Keep Sparks Flying," *Denver Post*, 19 October 1966: 5.

87. UA, McDonald Papers, MS 412, Box 5, Hall to Keyhoe, 28 February 1967. See also MS 412, Box 3, Hartmann phone call notes, 11 October 1967.

88. UA, McDonald Papers, MS 412, Box 3, Notes on phone call with Richard Hall, 1 March 1967

89. UA, McDonald Papers, MS 412, Box 5, Hall to Keyhoe, 28 February 1967.

90. UA, McDonald Papers, MS 412, Box 5, Hall to McDonald, 12 December 1966.

91. APS, Condon Papers, Box O.25, Robert Low to UFO Study Team, 8 June 1967.

92. David Cherniack Interview with William Hartmann, 5 September 2006.

93. J. Allen Hynek, "UFOs Merit Scientific Study," *Science* 21 (1966): 329.

94. APS, Condon Papers, Box 9, Jerome Aumente, "'Possible, But Not Probable,'" *Detroit News*, 23 October 1966.

95. J. Allen Hynek, "'White Paper' on UFOs," *The Christian Science Monitor*, 23 May 1967: Section 2, 1.

96. J. Allen Hynek, "The UFO Gap," *Playboy* 12 (December 1967): 144, 146, 267–271.

97. Vallee, *Forbidden Science: Journals 1957–1969*, 300.

98. Ibid., 187, 194.

99. UA, McDonald Papers, MS 412, Box 5, McDonald to Hall, 1 October 1966.

100. UA, McDonald Papers, MS 412, Box 3, Bickel to McDonald, 20 September 1967.

101. Saunders and Harkins, 117.

102. APS, Condon Papers, Box O.17, Condon to Keyhoe, 2 February 1967.

103. UA, McDonald Papers, MS 412, Box 3, Hartmann phone call notes, 11 October 1967.

104. APS, Condon Papers, Box O.17, Keyhoe to Condon, 14 November 1967.

105. UA, McDonald Papers, MS 412, Box 3, McDonald notes on phone call with Saunders, 27 November 1967.
106. APS, Condon Papers, Box O.6, Low to K. James Archer and Thurston E. Manning, 9 August 1966.
107. Craig, *UFOs*, 197.
108. UA, McDonald Papers, Audio Recording, phone conversation between Keyhoe and McDonald, 3 December 1967.
109. UA, McDonald Papers, MS 412, Box 3, McDonald notes on meeting, 12 December 1967.
110. UA, McDonald Papers, MS 412, Box 3, Levine to McDonald, 21 January 1968.
111. Some of the details of the meeting are from UA, McDonald Papers, MS 412, Box 3, McDonald notes on phone call, 7 February 1968.
112. Saunders and Harkins, 189.
113. Saunders and Harkins, 191.
114. UA, McDonald Papers, MS 412, Box 3, McDonald notes on phone call, 23 February 1968.
115. Evert Clark, "Colorado U. Ends Saucer Study But Does Not Disclose Results," *The New York Times*, 1 May 1968: 8.
116. UA, McDonald Papers, MS 412, Box 5, John G. Fuller, "Inside the Colorado UFO Study: The $500,000 Trick," first draft, 8 March 1968.
117. John G. Fuller, "Flying Saucer Fiasco," *Look*, 14 May 1968, https://www.project1 947.com/shg/articles/fiasco.html, accessed 27 July 2021.
118. See APS, Condon Papers, Box O.8.
119. UA, McDonald Papers, MS 412, Box 3, McDonald to Saunders, 25 June 1968.
120. APS, Condon Papers, Box O.8, Low to Robert P. Gilman, 9 May 1968.
121. Bill Farr, "'Trickery' Charge Aimed at UFO Prober," *Santa Ana Register*, 1 May 1968.
122. APS, Condon Papers, Box O.6, Walter Orr Roberts to Condon, 18 July 1968.
123. E. U. Condon, "UFO Trouble in *Science*," *Science* 161 (30 August 1968): 844; Philip M. Boffey, "UFO Project: Trouble on the Ground," *Science* 161 (26 July 1968): 339–342.
124. UA, McDonald Papers, MS 412, Box 3, McDonald to Saunders, 25 June 1968.
125. Jacobs, 233.
126. *Symposium on Unidentified Flying Objects*, U.S. House of Representatives, Committee on Science and Astronautics, 29 July 1968 (Washington: U.S. Government Printing Office, 1968).
127. National Academy of Sciences, *Review of the University of Colorado Report on Unidentified Flying Objects* (National Academy of Sciences, 1969), http://www.project1947.com/shg/articles/nascu.html, accessed 1 August 2018.
128. *Final Report of the Scientific Study of Unidentified Flying Objects* (New York, Toronto, London: Bantam Books, 1969), 1.
129. Ibid., 2.
130. Ibid., 5.
131. "The Truth about the Condon Report," *The U.F.O. Investigator* 4 (January 1969): 1–5.
132. William Hines, "UFO Buffs Launch A Paperback Barb," *Dubuque Telegraph Herald*, 17 January 1969: 3.
133. "Perspective on the UFOs," *The Glens Falls Times*, 16 January 1969: 4.
134. "The Subject Is Far from Closed," *Portsmouth Herald*, 20 January 1969: 4.
135. "UFO 'Secret,'" *San Mateo Times and Daily News Leader*, 17 January 1969: 28.

136. J. Allen Hynek, "The Condon Report and UFOs," *Bulletin of the Atomic Scientists* 25 (April 1969): 39–42.

137. Their reviews can be found in the journal *Icarus* 11 (1969): 443–450.

138. UA, McDonald Papers, MS 412, Box 3, Adrian Vance to McDonald, "OOFO's I Have Known and Loved," undated.

139. E. U. Condon, "UFO's I Have Loved and Lost," *Proceedings of the American Philosophical Society* 113 (December 1969): 425–427.

140. APS, Condon Papers, Box O.6, Draft letter Condon to Sagan, ca. 24–29 September 1969.

141. APS, Condon Papers, Box O.6, Condon to Roberts, 5 September 1969.

142. APS, Condon Papers, Box O.6, Roberts to Condon, 16 September 1969.

143. APS, Condon Papers, Box O.6, Condon to Sagan, 6 October 1969; Condon to Roach, 9 November 1969.

144. Carl Sagan and Thornton Page, eds., *UFO's—A Scientific Debate* (Ithaca and London: Cornell University Press, 1972).

145. Andrew Jewett, *Science under Fire: Challenges to Scientific Authority in Modern America* (Cambridge and London: Harvard University Press, 2020); James Andrews, "Inculcating Materialist Minds: Scientific Propaganda and Anti-Religion in the USSR During the Cold War," in *Science, Religion, and Communism in Cold War Europe*, ed. Paul Betts and Stephen A. Smith (London: Palgrave Macmillan, 2016), 105–125.

146. UA, McDonald Papers, MS 412, Box 3, McDonald to Herbert Strentz, 11 August 1967.

147. UA, McDonald Papers, MS 412, Box 3, McDonald to Saunders, 27 November 1967.

148. APS, Condon Papers, Box O.6, Sagan to Condon, 29 September 1969.

149. Walter Sullivan, "Scientists Seek Air Force U.F.O. Data," *New York Times*, 28 December 1969: 18.

150. "James M'Donald A Cloud Physicist," *New York Times*, 16 June 1971: 48.

151. Ann Druffel, *Firestorm: Dr. James E. McDonald's Fight for UFO Science* (Columbus, NC: Wild Flower Press, 2003), 512–522.

152. Interview of Edward Condon by Charles Weiner on 1973 September 11, Niels Bohr Library & Archives, American Institute of Physics, College Park, MD USA, www.aip.org/history-programs/niels-bohr-library/oral-histories/4997-3.

153. APS, Menzel Papers, Box 7, Menzel to Paul E. McCarthy, 10 August 1972.

154. APS, Condon Papers, Box 9, Low to Condon, 16 October 1970.

CHAPTER 7

1. Arthur C. Clarke, "Whatever Happened to Flying Saucers?" *The Saturday Evening Post*, 1 June 1971: 10.

2. Charles H. Gibbs-Smith, "To Our Subscribers," *FSR* 18, no. 2 (1972): 2; "Achievement," *FSR* 17, no. 6 (1971): 1–2.

3. Editors, "Looking Back on the 60s, Forward to the 70s," *Merseyside UFO Bulletin* 2 (November–December 1969): n.p.

4. Walter Sullivan, "Despite Lack of Data from Pilots and Officials, Reports of UFO Sightings Are Many and Widespread," *The New York Times*, 21 October 1973: 65.

5. For local press coverage, see the UFO Research Committee's, *UFO Newsclipping Service* bulletin for 1973.

6. Jacques Vallee, "The UFO Wave of 1973: Some Early Statistics," *FSR* 19, no. 6 (1973): 15.

7. J. B. Delair, "Synopsis of the Great World-Wide UFO Wave of 1973," *The UFO Register* 5, Parts 1 and 2 (December 1974): 8–94.

8. J. Allen Hynek, *The UFO Experience: A Scientific Inquiry* (New York: Ballantine, 1972), 14.

9. David Webb, *1973—Year of the Humanoids*, 2nd ed. (Evanston, IL: Center for UFO Studies, 1976).

10. Charles Hickson and Calvin Parker, "Hickson, Parker: Robot Creatures Are Friendly," *Mississippi Press Daily*, 19 October 1973. In: *UFO Newsclipping Service Bulletin* 53/54 (September–October 1973).

11. Hickson later said he heard a voice in his head as the beings departed saying that they meant no harm and were peaceful.

12. Philip Mantle and Irena McCammon Scott, *Beyond Reasonable Doubt: The Pascagoula Alien Abduction* (Pontefract: Flying Disk Press, 2023), 9–25; O'Connell, *Close Encounters Man*, 275, 278–279.

13. Some of the more notable flaps and waves occurred in the United States (1947, 1952, 1957), France (1953), Latin America (1965, 1978), Canada (1989), and Belgium (winter 1989–1990). Vicente-Juan Ballester Olmos, "UFO Waves: An International Bibliography," 2015, self-published.

14. Martin S. Kottmeyer, "Did Life Magazine Help Spawn the 1952 UFO Wave?" *Magonia Supplement* 48 (21 October 2003): 1–3.

15. Interview with Paul Meehan, *TheoFantasique*, 19 May 2009, https://www.theo fantastique.com/2009/05/19/paul-meehan-saucer-movies-a-ufological-history-of-the-cinema/, accessed 11 July 2023; Paul Meehan, *Saucer Movies: A Ufological History of the Cinema* (Lanham, MD: Scarecrow, 1998).

16. This was the conclusion CUFOS came to at the time, according to a personal communication by Mark Rodeghier.

17. "Are UFO Sightings Linked to Sci-Fi Films?" *BBC Magazine*, 17 August 2009, http://news.bbc.co.uk/2/hi/uk_news/magazine/8205424.stm, accessed 1 July 2023.

18. Martin Kottmeyer, "UFO Flaps: An Analysis," http://tarnsitsandstations.blogs pot.com/2015/02/ufo-flaps-analysis-by-martin-kottmeyer.html, accessed 18 September 2021.

19. Andreas Killen, *1973 Nervous Breakdown: Watergate, Warhol, and the Birth of the Post-Sixties America* (New York: Bloomsbury, 2006), 261.

20. Moseley, *Shockingly Close*, 226.

21. Ibid., 232–233.

22. On these programs, see Swords, et al., *UFOs and Government*, 361–455.

23. Paolo Fiorino, "Italia 1971–1977: Verso un'ufologia 'ufficiale,'" *UFO: Rivista di informazione ufologica* 45 (December 2020): 25–39.

24. João Francisco Schramm, "A Força Aérea Brasileira e a investigação acerca de objetos aéreos não identificados (1969–1986): Segredos, tecnologias e guerras não convencionais" (MA thesis, University of Brasília, 2016).

25. Yu. V. Platov and B. A. Sokolov, "The Study of Unidentified Flying Objects in the Soviet Union," *Herald of the Russian Academy of Sciences* 70 (2000): 244–251.

26. Gildas Bourdais, "From GEPAN to SEPRA: Official UFO Studies in France," *IUR* (Winter 2000–2001): 10–13; David Rossoni, Eric Maillot, and Eric Déguillaume, "UFOs: An Assessment of Thirty Years of Official Studies in France," *Skeptical Inquirer* (January/February 2009): 47–51.

27. Claude Poher and Jacques Vallee, "Basic Patterns in UFO Observations," AAIA Paper 75-42, presented at the AIAA 13th Aerospace Sciences Meeting, Pasadena, CA, 20–22 January 1975.

28. In 2005 the department was renamed again, becoming the Groupe d'étude et d'informations sur les phénomènes aérospatiaux non identifies (Group for Study and Information on Unidentified Aerospace Phenomena) or GEIPAN. GEIPAN continues to operate today.

29. National Security Agency Declassified Documents, "French Government UFO Study," https://www.nsa.gov/Portals/70/documents/news-features/declassified-documents/ufo/french_gov_ufo_study.pdf, accessed 22 September 2021.

30. David Rossoni, Eric Maillot, Eric Déguillaume, *Les OVNI du CNES: 30 ans d'études officielles (1977–2007)* (Valbonne: Book-e-Book, 2007).

31. https://www.excite.co.jp/news/article/Tocana_201808_post_17875/, accessed 19 November 2021.

32. "GAP-Japan," *UFO Contactee* 1 (May 1985): 11–12.

33. "Editorial: Probing Beyond Frontiers Placed by Materialistic Science," *Kalpa-Nava* 10 (1986): 11.

34. AFU, run of *Malaysian UFO Bulletin*, 1980–1983.

35. AFU, Gordon Creighton Papers, Ahmad Jamaludin to Charles Bowen, 12 December 1980.

36. AFU, Gordon Creighton Papers, Ahmad Jamaludin, *A Summary of Unidentified Flying Objects and Related Events in Malaysia (1950–1980)*, self-published December 1981, 85.

37. Unless otherwise noted, details about developments in China are from Shi Bo, *Ufo-Begegnungen in China* (Berlin: Ullstein, 1997).

38. AFU, Gordon Creighton Papers, China/Paul Dong File, "Journal of UFO Research (JUR)," undated (ca. 1981).

39. Dong discussed his findings in "Extracts from Paul Dong's Fiedie Bai Wen Bai Da (Question and Answers on UFOs)," *FSR* 29, no. 6 (1984): 14–20. Quote is from p. 19.

40. Over the course of the late eighties and early nineties, more groups formed in both China and Taiwan. This included the China UFO Research Institute Network Centre, headquartered in Wuhan and the Taiwan UFO Science Association HQ in Taipei, chaired by Hoang-Yung Chiang, a PhD in biotechnology with a longstanding interest in ancient astronauts and "cosmic archaeology." AFU, Gordon Creighton Papers, Hoang-Yung Chiang (Chairman, Taiwan UFO Science Association) to Creighton, 3 December 1993.

41. John Rimmer, "ETH: A Look at the Alternatives," *Merseyside UFO Bulletin* 3 (January 1970), http://mufobmagazine.blogspot.com/2014/03/a-look-at-alternatives.html, accessed 29 November 2021.

42. Cabria, *Entre Ufólogos*, 75–136.

43. Kevin B. McCray, *Alien Thoughts: Voices of UFO Buffs of the 1960s and 1970s (and Beyond!)* (Mount Gilead: self-published, 2023), 31.

44. Personal communication, 30 November 2021.

45. Håkan Blomqvist, "Fifty Years in the UFO Movement," *Håkan Blomqvist's Blog*, 3 January 2020, https://ufoarchives.blogspot.com/2020/01/fifty-years-in-ufo-movement.html, accessed 3 December 2021.

46. Håkan Blomqvist, "The Founding of AFU," *Håkan Blomqvist's Blog*, 2 November 2019, https://ufoarchives.blogspot.com/2019/11/the-founding-of-afu.html, accessed 3 December 2021.

47. Information on the founding of CENAP comes from issues 33 and 34 of *CENAP-Report*, 1976.
48. *CENAP-Report* 1 (1976).
49. Charles H. Gibbs-Smith, "A Turning Point in UFO Investigation," *FSR* 18, no. 6 (1972): 6–8.
50. O'Connell, *Close Encounters Man*, 293–294.
51. See, for example, "From the Center for UFO Studies," *FSR* 21, no. 2 (1975): 32–34.
52. AFU, Luis Schönherr Collection, Presse Kommentare zum Thema UFOs; EKAHA-Randlochkarteien.
53. I. Grattan-Guinness, "Advice for Ufology," *FSR* 22, no. 4 (1976): 12–14. Quote from p. 14.
54. James Oberg, "The Failure of the 'Science' of Ufology," *New Scientist*, 11 October 1979, https://www.debunker.com/texts/ObergCuttySark.html, accessed 13 December 2021; Shirley McIver, "A Science of Ufology," *Magonia* (1984?), http://magoniamagazine.blogspot.com/2013/11/a-science-of-ufology-shirley-mciver-in_12.html#more, accessed 13 December 2021.
55. Gordon Creighton, "Interesting News from Russia," *FSR* 24, no. 1 (1979): 24–29; Nikita A. Schnee, "Ufology in the USSR," *FSR* 27, no. 1 (1981): 8–14; Gordon Creighton, "Dr. Felix Zigel and the Development of Ufology in Russia, Part 1" *FSR* 27, no. 3 (1981): 8–13, "Part 2," 27, no. 4 (1981): 13–19, "Part 3," 27, no. 4 (1981): 9–13; Jüri Lina, "UFO Study in the USSR," *FSR* 32, no. 4 (1987): 17–20.
56. "UFOIN," *FSR* 23, no. 2 (1977): 1–2; Jenny Randles, "The UFOIN Concept," *FSR* 25, no. 4 (1979): 28–29.
57. Shirley McIver, "UFO (Flying Saucer) Groups: A Look at British Membership," *Zetetic Scholar* 11–12 (1987): 39–60; Gregory L. Little, "Educational Level and Primary Beliefs About Unidentified Flying Objects Held by Recognized Ufologists," *Psychological Reports* 54 (1984): 907–910.
58. "International Congress in Turin: 1947–1987: Towards a Scientific Approach to the UFO Phenomenon," *Italian UFO Reporter* 6 (December 1987): 10–11. See also Gian Paolo Grassino and Edoardo Russo, "Italian UFO Research in the Eighties: A Review of Sightings, Activities, and Reflections," *Italian UFO Reporter* 11 (July 1989): 1–8.
59. Michael A. Persinger and Gyslaine F. Lafreniére, *Space-Time Transients and Unusual Events* (Chicago: Nelson-Hall, 1977); Michael A. Persinger, "Transient Geophysical Bases for Ostensible UFO-Related Phenomena and Associated Verbal Behavior?" *Perceptual and Motor Skills* 43 (1976): 215–221; "Geophysical Models for Parapsychological Experiences," *Psychoenergetic Systems* 1 (1975): 63–74.
60. John S. Derr, "Earthquake Lights: A Review of Observations and Present Theories," *Bulletin of the Seismological Society of America* 63 (1973): 2177–2187.
61. Michael A. Persinger, "What Factors Can Account for UFO Experiences?" *The Zetetic Scholar* 1 (1978): 92.
62. M. A. Persinger, "Neuropsychological Profiles of Adults Who Report 'Sudden Remembering' of Early Childhood Memories: Implications for Claims of Sex Abuse and Alien Visitation/Abduction Experiences," *Perceptual and Motor Skills* 75 (1992): 259–266; "Geophysical Variables and Behavior: LV. Predicting the Details of Visitor Experiences and the Personality of Experients: The Temporal Lobe Factor," *Perceptual and Motor Skills* 68 (1989): 55–65.

63. Claude Maugé, "Persinger's Tectonic Strain Theory: Strengths and Weaknesses," *Magonia* 24 (November 1986), http://magoniamagazine.blogspot.com/2013/11/persingers-tectonic-strain-theory.html#more, accessed 13 May 2022; Paul Devereux, "The Earth Lights Debate: For the Defence," *Magonia* 12 (1983), http://magoniamagazine.blogspot.com/2013/11/the-earth-lights-debate-for-defence.html, accessed 13 May 2022.

64. William Sims Bainbridge, "In Search of Delusion: Television Pseudocumentaries," *Skeptical Inquirer* 4 (1979): 33–39; L. Moddy Simms Jr., "We Came From Outer Space?" *Southern Quarterly* 16 (1977): 23–26.

65. Aldora Lee, "Public Attitudes Toward UFO Phenomena" in *Scientific Study of Unidentified Flying Objects*, 209–243.

66. Unless otherwise noted, all survey data comes from RR0, "Sondages d'opinions sur les ovnis," https://rr0.org/science/crypto/ufo/observation/Sondages.html#, accessed 16 December 2021.

67. Peter A. Sturrock, "Report on a Survey of the Membership of the American Astronomical Society Concerning the UFO Problem: Part 1," *Journal of Scientific Exploration* 8 (1994): 1–45; "UFO Reports from AIAA Members," *Astronautics and Aeronautics* 12 (1974): 60–64. The 1994 article is a reprint of the original article published in 1977. 36 percent of the AIAA questionnaires were returned, while 51.9 percent of those sent to AAS members were returned.

68. Phillis Fox, "Social and Cultural Factors Influencing Beliefs about UFOs" *UFO Phenomena and the Behavioral Scientist*, ed. Richard F. Haines (Metuchen, NJ and London: Scarecrow, 1979), 20–42; Lawrence W. Littig, "Affiliation Motivation and Belief in Extraterrestrial UFOs," *Journal of Social Psychology* 83 (1971): 307–308.

69. Cabria, *Entre Ufólogos*, 138–139.

70. Edoardo Russo, "What Do Italians Believe about UFOs? The CISU-Doxa Opinion Poll" *Italian UFO Reporter* 6 (December 1987): 1–3.

71. Donald I. Warren, "Status Inconsistency Theory and Flying Saucer Sightings," *Science* 170 (1970): 599–603. Quote is from p. 603.

72. Ron Westrum, "Witnesses of UFOs and Other Anomalies," in *UFO Phenomena and the Behavioral Scientist*, ed. Haines, 89–111.

73. Ron Westrum, "Social Intelligence about Anomalies: The Case of UFOs," *Social Studies of Science* 7 (1977): 271–302.

74. Michael Kelly Schutz, "Organizational Goals and Support-Seeking Behavior: A Comparative Study of Social Movement Organization in the UFO (Flying Saucer) Field" (PhD thesis, Northwestern University, 1973). Quote by Friedman is from pp. 225–226.

75. Shirley McIver, "The UFO Movement: A Sociological Study of Unidentified Flying Object Groups" (PhD thesis, University of York, 1984). Quote is from p. 215.

76. On Raël and the Raëlian movement, see Susan J. Palmer, *Aliens Adored: Raël's UFO Religion* (New Brunswick: Rutgers University Press, 2004). Thanks to Pierre Charles Dubreuil for his helpful input.

77. Benjamin E. Zeller, *Heaven's Gate: America's UFO Religion* (New York: New York University Press, 2014); Robert W. Balch, "Looking Behind the Scenes in a Religious Cult: Implications for the Study of Conversion," *Sociological Analysis* 41 (1980): 137–143; Robert W. Balch and David Taylor, "Seekers and Saucers: The Role of the Cultic Milieu in Joining a UFO Cult," *The American Behavioral Scientist* 20 (1977): 839–860.

78. Wendy Gale Robinson, "Heaven's Gate: The End," *Journal of Computer-Mediated Communication* 3 (December 1997), JCMC334, https://doi.org/10.1111/j.1083-6101.1997.tb00077.x.

79. Elizabeth Aileen Young, "The Use of the 'Brainwashing' Theory by the Anti-Cult Movement in the United States of America, pre-1996," *Zeitschrift für junge Religionswissenschaft* 7 (2012), https://sites.psu.edu/setisymposium2022/ ; Anson Shupe, David G. Bromley, and Susan E. Darnell, "The North American Anti-Cult Movement: Vicissitudes of Success and Failure," in *The Oxford Handbook of New Religious Movements*, ed. James R. Lewis (Oxford Handbooks Online, Oxford University Press, 2022); Massimo Introvigne, "Moral Panics and Anti-Cult Terrorism in Western Europe," *Terrorism and Political Violence* 12 (2000): 47–59.

80. Alexander C. T. Geppert, "The Post-Apollo Paradox: Envisioning Limits During the Planetized 1970s," in *Limiting Outer Space: Astroculture after Apollo*, ed. Alexander C. T. Geppert (London: Palgrave Macmillan, 2018), 3–26. Quote is from p. 6.

81. Marcello Truzzi, "The Occult Revival as Popular Culture: Some Random Observations on the Old and Nouveau Witch," *The Sociological Quarterly* 13 (Winter 1972): 16–36.

82. Roger Sandell, Peter Rogerson, and John Rimmer, "Ten Years On . . . The Editors Look Back on a Decade of Ufology," *MUFOB New Series* 10 (Spring 1978), http://mufobmagazine.blogspot.com/2014/03/10-years.html, accessed 22 May 2022.

83. Charles Bowen, "Thorny Topic: That 'Overlap'; Comment and Speculation," *Flying Saucer Review* 16 (1970): 23–24. Quote is from p. 24.

84. Jacques Vallee, *Passport to Magonia: From Folklore to Flying Saucers* (Chicago: H. Regnery, 1969). Quotes are from the 2nd edition published in 1993 by Contemporary Books, pp. 56–57.

85. Michel Monnerie, *Le naufrage des extra-terrestres* (Paris: Novelles éditions rationalists, 1979); *Et si les ovnis n'existaient pas?* (Paris: Les Humanoïdes associés, 1977).

86. Bertrand Meheust, *Soucoupes volantes et folklore* (Paris: Mercure de France, 1985); *Science-fiction et soucoupes volantes: une réalité mythico-physique* (Paris: Mercure de France, 1978).

87. For a good summary of the state of things in "the new ufology" by the mid-eighties, see Jacques Scornaux, "The Rising and the Limits of a Doubt," *Magonia* 15 (April 1984): 3–6.

88. *Magonia* 15 (April 1984).

89. Hilary Evans, *From Other Worlds: The Truth about Aliens, Abductions, UFOs, the Paranormal* (London: Carlton, 1988); *Gods, Spirits, Cosmic Guardians: A Comparative Study of the Encounter Experience* (Wellingborough: The Aquarian Press, 1987); *Visions, Apparitions, Alien Visitors* (London: Book Club Associates, 1984).

90. Edoardo Russo and Gian Paolo Grassino, "Towards a European Ufology: Where Is America Going To?" *Italian UFO Reporter* 8 (November 1988): 2–10.

91. AFU, Gordon Creighton Papers, Creighton to A. Pezarro, 7 September 1970.

92. AFU, Gordon Creighton Papers, Creighton to Jal N.D. Tata, 26 September 1983.

93. Eric Inglesby, *UFOs and the Christian* (New York: Regency, 1978); D. Scott Rogo, *The Haunted Universe: A Psychic Look at Miracles, UFOs, and Mysteries of Nature* (New York: New American Library, 1977).

94. Raymond W. Boeche, ed., *John Keel's Anomaly Newsletter, 1969–1976* (Lux et Veritas Books, undated); John A. Keel, "UFOs and Abominable Snowmen—What's Their Strange Connection?" *MALE* 19 (October 1969): 38–39, 74–76; "The Bedroom Invaders: Frightening New UFO-Pilot Mystery," *MALE* 19 (June 1969): 22–23, 94–96; "Strange Messages from Flying Saucers," *SAGA* 35 (January 1968): 22–25, 69–70, 72–73; "UFO 'Agents of Terror,'" *SAGA* 35 (October 1967): 29–31, 72–74, 76–79, 81. Quote is from "Bedroom Invaders," 95.

95. John A. Keel, *The Mothman Prophecies* (New York: Saturday Review Press, 1975).

96. John A. Keel, *Strange Creatures from Time and Space* (Greenwich: Fawcett, 1970).

97. David Clarke, "A New Demonology: John Keel and *The Mothman Prophecies*," in *Damned Facts: Fortean Essays on Religion, Folklore, and the Paranormal*, ed. Jack Hunter (Cyprus: Aporetic Press, 2016), 54–68.

98. John A. Keel, *Why UFOs: Operation Trojan Horse* (New York: Manor Books, 1970). Quotes from foreword and pp. 156 and 283.

99. John A. Keel, *Our Haunted Planet* (Greenwich: Fawcett, 1971).

100. John A. Keel, *The Eighth Tower* (New York: New American Library, 1971). Quotes are from the British version of the book entitled *The Cosmic Question* (London: Panther, 1978), 25–26, 133.

101. John A. Keel, "Aliens among Us," *UFO Report* 5 (November 1977): 28–29; "Mystery of the Alien Submarines," *SAGA* 47 (November 1973): 34–36, 92, 94.

102. Clarke, "A New Demonology."

103. O. I. Simpson, "Experimental UFO Hoaxing," *MUFOB New Series* 2 (March 1976): 3–6, 11–12.

104. Allen Greenfield, "Confessions of a Ufologist," *MUFOB New Series* 15 (Summer 1979), http://mufobmagazine.blogspot.com/2014/03/confessions.html, accessed 31 May 2022.

105. Donald H. Menzel and Ernest H. Taves, *The UFO Enigma* (Garden City, NY: Doubleday, 1977).

106. For the following history of CSICOP, see Kendrick Frazier, "History of CSICOP," in *The Encyclopedia of the Paranormal*, ed. Gordon Stein (Amherst, NY: Prometheus Books, 1996): 168–180, reprinted https://skepticalinquirer.org/history-of-csicop/, accessed 31 May 2022; Paul Kurtz, "CSCIOP at Twenty," *Skeptical Inquirer* (July/August 1996): 4–8; George P. Hansen, "CSICOP and the Skeptics: An Overview," *Journal of the American Society for Psychical Research* 86 (1992): 19–63.

107. Frazier, "History of CSICOP."

108. David J. Hess, *Science in the New Age: The Paranormal, Its Defenders and Debunkers, and American Culture* (Madison: University of Wisconsin, 1993).

109. APS, Philip J. Klass Papers (hereafter PJK), MS Coll 59, Ser. III-3, Sparks to Klass, 3 July 1973.

110. Library of Congress, Carl Sagan Papers, Box 29, Folder 4, Klass to Sagan, 1 December 1977.

111. APS, PJK, MS Coll 59, Ser. I-1, Klass to Girard, 29 March 1989.

112. APS, PJK, MS Coll 59, Ser. I-1, Cerny Correspondence, 1969.

113. APS, PJK, MS Coll 59, Ser. I-3, Klass to Van Dyke, 15 June 1976.

114. APS, PJK, MS Coll 59, Ser. I-2, Klass to Major, 1 April 1976.

115. APS, PJK, MS Coll 59, Ser. III-6, Klass to Lore, 11 June 1969.

116. APS, PJK, MS Coll 59, Ser. I-1, Klass to Bengtson, 20 December 1986.

117. Jenny Randles, "Not the ETH," *Magonia* 17 (October 1984): 3–7; *UFO Reality: A Critical Look at the Physical Evidence* (London: Robert Hale, 1983).

CHAPTER 8

1. On the the encounters between Moore, Bennewitz, Hansen, and Doty, see Curt Collins, "Cash-Landrum UFO Disinformation: Rick Doty & Bill Moore," *Blue Blurry Lines*, 22 June 2022, https://www.blueblurrylines.com/2022/06/cash-landrum-ufo-disinformation-rick.html, accessed 30 June 2022; Mark Pilkington, *Mirage Men: A Journey in Disinformation, Paranoia, and UFOs* (London: Constable & Robinson, 2010); Greg Bishop, *Project Beta: The Story of Paul Bennewitz, National Security, and the Creation of a Modern UFO Myth* (New York: Paraview Pocket Books, 2005).

2. Sources are not in complete agreement about when the two met, but this is the most widely accepted date.

3. Bishop, 266.

4. Ned Barnett, "Interview with John Lear—Part Two," *International UFO Library Magazine* 3, no. 4 (1995): 28–31, 67; John Lear, "The UFO Coverup," 25 August 1988 (first written 29 December 1987), http://www.sacred-texts.com/ufo/coverup.htm, accessed 21 March 2018.

5. John A. Keel, "UFO Kidnappers!" *SAGA* 33 (February 1967): 11–14, 50, 52–53, 56–60, 62. Quotes are from pp. 12, 16, and 62.

6. Húlvio Brant Aleixo, "Abduction at Bebedouro," *Flying Saucer Review* 19, no. 6 (1973): 6–14; "Bebedouro II: The Little Men Return for the Solder," *Flying Saucer Review* 21, nos. 3–4 (1975): 32–35; Walter Buhler, "Thoughts on the Bebedouro Case," *Flying Saucer Review* 21, nos. 3–4 (1975): 36–38.

7. Luis R. González, "Listado de casos de teleportación, levitación y similares en el siglo XX," *Cuadernos de Ufología* 30, no. 3a (2004): 159–188.

8. Walter Bühler, *40 Begegnungen mit Außerirdischen in Brasilien* (Wiesbaden: Ventla, 1975).

9. Alejandro Agostinelli, *Invasores: Historias reales de extraterrestres en la Argentina* (Buenos Aires: Editorial Sudamericana, 2009).

10. Roberto Enrique Banchs and Richard W. Heiden, "The Humanoids in Argentina," *The Journal of UFO Studies* 2 (1980): 58–71.

11. For a famous case from Italy, see Rino Di Stefano, *The Zanfretta Case: Chronicle of an Incredible True Story* (S.I.: Createspace Independent, 2014).

12. Bill Barry, "Kidnapped!"in *UFO Abductions: True Cases of Alien Kidnappings*, ed. D. Scott Rogo (New York: Signet, 1980), 28–43.

13. Coral and Jim Lorenzen, *Abducted! Confrontations with Beings from Outer Space* (Tucson: Berkley Medallion, 1977), 114–131.

14. D. Scott Rogo, "Introduction," in *UFO Abductions*, ed. Rogo, 3–4.

15. Details of the Patty Price case are from Lorenzen, *Abducted*, 9–24.

16. Ibid., 153.

17. "Tefatsupplevelserna sanna Hypno-analys har bekräftat," *Helsingborgs Dagblad*, 15 January 1959: 1–3. Also reported in Lorenzen, *Great Flying Saucer Hoax*, 57–58.

18. Details of Harder's biography are from https://senate.universityofcalifornia.edu/_files/inmemoriam/html/jamesharder.html and https://en-academic.com/dic.nsf/enwiki/2147981, accessed 14 July 2022.

19. Lecture "Do UFO Aliens Communicate with Humans?" UFO Symposium, Sand Diego, CA, 17 November 1979, https://archive.org/details/CEIVAnAudioHistoryOfAlienAbductionAndAnimalMutilation19571976Guide/53.mp3; Interview with the Intuition Network (undated), http://www.intuition.org/txt/harder.htm, accessed 14 July 2022.

20. University of Wyoming, American Heritage Center (hereafter UWAHC), R. Leo Sprinkle Papers, Box 23, Fol. 7, Harder memo, 23 September 1980.

21. Roger Luckhurst, *The Invention of Telepathy, 1870–1901* (New York: Oxford University Press, 2002); Alan Gauld, *A History of Hypnotism* (Cambridge: Cambridge University Press, 1992).

22. Daniel Pick, *Brainwashed: A New History of Thought Control* (London: Wellcome Collection, 2022); Charles S. Young, *Name, Rank, and Serial Number: Exploiting Korean War POWs at Home and Abroad* (New York: Oxford University Press, 2014); Susan L. Carruthers, *Cold War Captives: Imprisonment, Escape, and Brainwashing* (Berkeley: University of California Press, 2009). Quote is from Carruthers, p. 186.

23. UWAHC, Sprinkle Papers, Box 23, Fol. 7, "Hidden UFO Experiences" and the Pendulum Technique, July 1977.

24. R. Leo Sprinkle, *Soul Samples: Personal Explorations in Reincarnation and UFO Experiences* (Columbus, NC: Granite, 1999), 7–58.

25. UWAHC, Sprinkle Papers, Box 20, Fol. 9, Sprinkle to Max Edwards, 21 April 1970 and 8 June 1970.

26. UWAHC, Sprinkle Papers, Box 23, Fol. 12, Paola Harris Rome, Personal Experience Part #4, 18 December 1998.

27. R. Leo Sprinkle, "Hypnotic and Psychic Implications in the Investigation of UFO Reports," in *Encounters with UFO Occupants*, Coral and Jim Lorenzen (New York: Berkley Medallion, 1976), 256–338.

28. R. Leo Sprinkle, "Hypnotic Time Regression Procedures in the Investigation of UFO Experiences," in *Abducted!* Lorenzen, 191–222. Quote from p. 205.

29. David M. Jacobs, "A Brief History of Abduction Research," *Journal of Scientific Exploration* 23 (2009): 69–77.

30. UWAHC, Sprinkle Papers, Box 20, Edmonds to Sprinkle, 16 February 1986.

31. UWAHC, Sprinkle Papers, Box 20, Sprinkle to Dan and Aileen Edwards, 11 August 1981.

32. R. Leo Sprinkle, "Psychotherapeutic Services for Persons Who Claim UFO Experiences," *Psychotherapy in Private Practice* 6 (1988): 151–157.

33. Conversation with author, 12 and 26 January 2019.

34. Ann Druffel and D. Scott Rogo, *The Tujunga Canyon Contacts* (Englewood Cliffs, NJ: Prentice-Hall, 1980). On Druffel's background, see https://www.coasttocoastam.com/guest/druffel-ann-6218/; http://www.xzonedirectory.com/druffel.htm, accessed 16 July 2022.

35. Raymond E. Fowler, *The Andreasson Affair: The True Story of a Close Encounter of the Fourth Kind* (Pompton Plains: Career Press, 1979/ebook 2015). Quote is from p. 76.

36. Betty and her new partner would later undergo more sessions about new encounters starting in 1980.

37. Budd Hopkins, "Sane Citizen Sees UFO in New Jersey," *The Village Voice*, 1 March 1976: 12–13.

38. UWAHC, Sprinkle Papers, Box 23, Fol. 37, Notes Budd Hopkins, [February 1978].

39. Budd Hopkins, *Missing Time: A Documented Study of UFO Abductions* (New York: Richard Marek, 1981). Quotes are from pp. 24 and 87.

40. On the Copley Woods case according to Hopkins and material related to the book *Intruders*, see Jim Schnabel, *Dark White: Aliens, Abductions, and the UFO Obsession* (London: Penguin, 1994); Budd Hopkins, *Intruders: The Incredible Visitations at Copley Woods* (New York: Random House, 1987).

41. Hopkins, *Intruders*, 197, 202.

42. Debbie Jordan and Kathy Mitchell, *Abducted! The Story of the Intruders Continues* (New York: Carroll & Graf, 1994). Quote from Debbie Jordan-Kauble, "Open Letter to Anyone Who Will Listen," *Paratopia* 1 (2011): 32.

43. Patrick Huyghe, *Swamp Gas Times: My Two Decades on the UFO Beat* (New York: Paraview, 2001), 255.

44. David M. Jacobs, *The Threat* (New York: Simon & Schuster, 1998); Budd Hopkins, "What They're Doing to Us," *International UFO Reporter*, September/October 1987: 4–9.

45. Budd Hopkins, "Toward a 'Supportive Spirit,'" *UFO* 5 (1990), reprinted in *Missing Time: A Documented Study of UFO Abductions*, 50–53. Quote is from p. 51.

46. Budd Hopkins, *Witnessed: The True Story of the Brooklyn Bridge UFO Abductions* (New York: Pocket Books, 1996).

47. Carol Rainey, "The Priests of High Strangeness: Co-Creation of the 'Alien Abduction Phenomenon,'" *Paratopia* 1 (2011): 11–21. Quote is from p. 15.

48. For details, see https://emmawoodsbooks.com/david-m-jacobs/ and https://www.expandingfrontiersresearch.org/items-1/emma-woods-special-collection.

49. Unless otherwise noted, details about Laibow's involvement in alien abduction research is from Keith Basterfield, "Whatever Happened to Key Abduction Researcher Dr. Rima E. Laibow?" *Unidentified Aerial Phenomena: Scientific Research*, 2 January 2021, https://ufos-scientificresearch.blogspot.com/2021/01/whatever-happened-to-key-abduction.html, accessed 27 July 2022.

50. Rima E. Laibow, "Dual Victims: The Abused and the Abducted," *International UFO Reporter* 14 (May/June 1989): 4–9. Quote is from p. 9.

51. Huyghe, *Swamp Gas*, 151.

52. Budd Hopkins, "Some Thoughts on Psychiatrists and Investigators," *MUFON Journal* 263 (March 1990): 13–14.

53. Schnabel, *Dark White*, kindle edition, Loc: 3175–3317.

54. Laibow eventually pursued other interests, and in December 2021, a district court enjoined her from distributing the drug "nano silver" which she had claimed cured COVID-19 and the ebola virus. https://www.justice.gov/opa/pr/district-court-orders-new-jersey-defendants-stop-distributing-unapproved-nano-silver-products, accessed 28 July 2022.

55. Aphrodite Clamar, "Is it Time for Psychologists to Take UFOs Seriously?" *Psychotherapy in Private Practice* 6 (1988): 143–149.

56. Nathalie Zajde, "Die Schoah als Paradigma des psychischen Traumas," *Tel Aviver Jahrbuch für deutsche Geschichte* 39 (2011): 17–39; Ruth Leys, *Trauma: A Genealogy* (Chicago: University of Chicago Press, 2000).

57. José Brunner, *Die Politik des Traumas: Gewalterfahrungen und psychisches Leid in den USA, in Deutschland und im Israel/Palästina-Konflikt* (Berlin: Suhrkamp, 2014), 63–71.

58. Ann W. Burgess and Lynda L. Holstrom, "Rape Trauma Syndrome," *American Journal of Psychiatry* 131 (1974): 981–986.

59. American Psychiatric Association, "Post-Traumatic Stress Disorder," in *Diagnostic and Statistical Manual-III*, 3rd ed. (Washington, DC: APA, 1980).

60. Ron Westrum, "Post-Abduction Syndrome," *MUFON UFO Journal* 224 (December 1986): 5–6. Quote is from p. 6.

61. David M. Jacobs, *Secret Life: Firsthand Accounts of UFO Abductions* (New York: Simon and Schuster, 1992), Ch. 9, 57–59.

62. AFU, Cynthia Hind Papers, Case 1978, 18 October 1996.

63. Whitley Strieber, *Communion: A True Story* (New York: Beech Tree Books, 1987).

64. "Ted Seth Jacobs: An Interview with the Artist," *Beyond Communion*, 6 October 1999, http://www.beyondcommunion.com/communion/9910tsjacobs.html, accessed 30 July 2022.

65. UWAHC, Sprinkle Papers, Box 52, Series-II, Notes on telephone calls with Whitley Strieber, 29 April 1987 and 24 February 1988.

66. "Welcome to Our Newsletter," *The Communion Letter* 1 (Spring 1989): 1–2.

67. AFU, *The Communion Letter* enclosure, Spring 1991.

68. "Welcome," *Communion Letter*, 3.

69. Christopher D. Bader, "Supernatural Support Groups: Who Are the UFO Abductees and Ritual-Abuse Survivors?" *Journal for the Scientific Study of Religion* 42 (2003): 669–678. Bader studied the UFO Contact Center International based in Seattle, Washington.

70. Brenda Denzler, *The Lure of the Edge: Scientific Passions, Religious Beliefs, and the Pursuit of UFOs* (Berkeley: University of California Press, 2001), 165–166, 238.

71. Karla Turner, *Into the Fringe: A True Story of Alien Abduction* (New York: Berkley Books, 1992). Turner, a former college instructor, first considered her own abduction experiences after reading books by Strieber and Hopkins. From May 1988 to summer 1989, she and her family recalled encounters with aliens dating back to their childhoods. She later went on to profile eight women who had their own alien abduction experiences. Turner believed firmly that the alien visitors were dissembling, vicious, and even capable of murdering and eating their victims.

72. Roper Organization, *Unusual Personal Experiences: An Analysis of the Data from Three National Surveys* (Las Vegas: Bigelow Holding Corporation, 1992).

73. Lloyd Stires, "3.7 Million Americans Kidnapped by Aliens?" *Skeptical Inquirer* 17 (Winter 1993): 142–144; Philip J. Klass "Additional Comments about the 'Unusual Personal Experiences' Survey," 145–146.

74. Russo and Grassino, "Towards a European Ufology." In the 1990s, two periodicals were founded—Kevin McClure's *Abduction Watch*, launched in 1997 out of Leeds in the United Kingdom and the *European Journal of UFO and Abduction Studies*, launched in 1999. Both adopted a skeptical approach to the topic.

75. Paolo Fiorino, "Le Abduction in Italia," *UFO: Rivista di Informazione Ufologica* 3 (June 1988): 35–37.

76. T. E. Bullard, "A Comparative Study of Abduction Reports Update," in *Alien Discussions: Proceedings of the Abduction Study Conference*, ed. A. Pritchard, D. E. Pritchard, John E. Mack, P. Kasey, and C. Yapp (Cambridge, MA: North Cambridge Press, 1994), 45–48.

77. В.И. Голц, *Рукопись, Навлюдения ААЯ (НЛО) в СССР (Сборник Соовщений Н 13)* (Samizdat, Leningrad, 1984).

78. Antonio Ribera, "Do Abductees Fit into a Certain Pattern?" *Flying Saucer Review* 29 (1984): 20–22.

79. Erik Saethre, "Close Encounters: UFO Beliefs in a Remote Australian Aboriginal Community," *Journal of the Royal Anthropological Institute* 13 (2007): 901–915. Saethre argued that these beliefs represented a syncretic integration of traditional spiritual ideas and images from popular culture at the time (e.g., *X-Files*).

80. Johannes Fiebag, *Kontakt: UFO-Entführungen in Deutschland, Österreich, und der Schweiz* (Munich: Langen Müller, 1994).

81. Archives of the Impossible (AI), Rice University, John E. Mack Papers, Mack to Hopkins, 28 January 1990; notes of meeting with Sagan, 2 August 1990. Note: I examined Mack's papers before they were moved to Rice University, so my citations may differ from those now being used.

82. Bridget Brown, *They Know Us Better Than We Know Ourselves: The History and Politics of Alien Abduction* (New York: New York University Press, 2007).

83. Daniel Mavrakis and Jean-Pierre Bocquet, "Psychoses et objets volants non indentifiés," *Revue canadienne de psychiatrie* 29 (1983): 199–201.

84. Ralph Blumenthal, *The Believer: Alien Encounters, Hard Science, and the Passion of John Mack* (Albuquerque: High Road Books, 2021), 283.

85. Lucas Richert, *Break on Through: Radical Psychiatry and the American Counterculture* (Cambridge, MA: MIT Press, 2019).

86. Denise H. Lajoie and S.I. Shapiro, "Definitions of Transpersonal Psychology: The First Twenty-Five Years," *Journal of Transpersonal Psychology* 24 (1992): 79–98.

87. Mark B. Ryan, *A Different Dimension: Reflections on the History of Transpersonal Thought* (Washington, DC: Westphalia, 2013), 5.

88. AI, Mack Papers, Final Report of Ad Hoc Committee, 25 May 1995; Mack response to ad hoc committee's draft report, 4 January 1995.

89. AI, Mack Papers, Final Report of Ad Hoc Committee.

90. Niall Boyce, "The Art of Medicine: The Psychiatrist who Wanted to Believe," *Lancet* 380 (2012): 1140–1141.

91. Karin Austin, Talk at the Second Archives of the Impossible Symposium Conference, 12 May 2023.

92. AI, Mack Papers, Transcript of interview with CDB Bryan, 16 July 1992.

93. C. D. B. Bryan, *Close Encounters of the Fourth Kind: Alien Abduction, UFOs, and the Conference at M.I.T.* (New York: Knopf, 1995); Andrea Pritchard, David E. Pritchard, John E. Mack, Pam Kasey, Caludia Yapp, ed., *Alien Discussions: Proceedings of the Abduction Study Conference Held at MIT, Cambridge, MA* (Cambridge, MA: North Cambridge Press, 1994). For reviews of Bryan's books, see Mack Papers, folder "CDB Bryan bookreviews."

94. AI, Mack Papers, Abduction Conference MIT, Mack opening remarks, 13 June 1992.

95. AI, Mack Papers, Abduction Conference MIT, Hall to Hans-Adam Liechtenstein, 7 July 1992 and Hopkins to Mack, et al., 23 June 1992.

96. Personal communication from Will Bueche.

97. Michael Jonathan Grinfield, "Space Alien Abductions: A Test of Wills, of Credibility," *Psychiatric Times*, October 1993: 11–12. Quotations from p. 12.

98. AI, Mack Papers, Mack response to ad hoc committee's draft report, 4 January 1995.

99. AI, Mack Papers, Hopkins to Mack, 27 November 1993.

100. John E. Mack, *Abduction: Human Encounters with Aliens* (New York: Scribner's and Macmillan, 1994). Quotation is from p. 413.

101. James Willwerth, "The Man from Outer Space," *Time* 143 (25 April 1994): 74. The quote from Ofshe comes from this article as well.

102. AI, Mack Papers, Note on conversation with Donna Bassett at the CSICOP's Conference, June 1994; Mack to Knapp, 8 September 1994 (unsent).

103. Final Report of Ad Hoc Committee, 25 May 1995.

104. AI, Mack Papers, Harvard Medical School Press Release, 3 August 1995; Tosteson to Mack, 18 July 1995.

105. Frederick Crews, *The Memory Wars: Freud's Legacy in Dispute* (London: Granta, 1995).

106. Sarah A. Hughes, *American Tabloid Media and the Satanic Panic, 1970–2000* (Cham: Palgrave, 2021).

107. Elizabeth Loftus, *The Myth of Repressed Memory: False Memories and Allegations of Sexual Abuse* (New York: St. Martin's Press, 1994); Richard Ofshe and Ethan Watters, *Making Monsters: False Memories, Psychotherapy, and Sexual Hysteria* (New York: Charles Scribner's, 1994); Lawrence Wright, *Remembering Satan: A Tragic Case of Recovered Memory* (New York: Knopf, 1994).

108. On Satanic ritual abuse claims, see David Frankfurter, "The Satanic Ritual Abuse Panic as Religious-Studies Data," *Numen* 50 (2003): 108–117; J. S. La Fontaine, *Speak of the Devil: Tales of Satanic Abuse in Contemporary England* (Cambridge: Cambridge University Press, 1998), 99–107.

109. Nicholas P. Spanos, "Past-Life Identities, UFO Abductions, and Satanic Ritual Abuse: The Social Construction of Memories," *International Journal of Clinical and Experimental Hypnosis* 42 (1994): 433–446. He was not alone in this. See Ronald C. Johnson, "Parallels Between Recollections of Repressed Childhood Sex Abuse, Kidnappings by Space Aliens, and the Salem Witch Hunts," *Issues in Child Abuse Accusations* 6 (1994), http://www.ipt-forensics.com/journal/volume6/j6_1_ 4.htm, accessed 21 July 2014.

110. Nicholas P. Spanos, *Multiple Identities and False Memories: A Sociocognitive Perspective* (Washington, DC: American Psychological Association, 1996), 127. See also Nicholas P. Spanos, Patricia A. Cross, Kirby Dickson, and Susan C. DuBreil, "Close Encounters: An Examination of UFO Experiences," *Journal of Abnormal Psychology* 102 (1993): 624–632.

111. Steven E. Clark and Elizabeth F. Loftus, "The Psychological Pay Dirt of Space Alien Abduction Memories," *Contemporary Psychology* 40 (1995): 861–863. Quote is from p. 862.

112. Leonard S. Newman and Roy F. Baumeister, "Toward an Explanation of the UFO Abduction Phenomenon: Hypnotic Elaboration, Extraterrestrial Sadomasochism, and Spurious Memories," *Psychological Inquiry* 7 (1996): 99–126.

113. Caroline C. McLeod, Barbara Corbisier, and John E. Mack, "A More Parsimonious Explanation for UFO Abduction," *Psychological Inquiry* 7 (1996): 156–168.

114. Linda Billings, "John Mack and Abduction," *doctorlinda*, 2021, https://doctorli nda.wordpress.com/2021/08/25/how-the-media-covered-john-macks-abduct ion-research-part-1/, accessed 25 August 2021. See also her "Sex! Aliens! Harvard? Rhetorical Boundary-Work in the Media (A Case Study of Role of Journalists in the Social Construction of Scientific Authority)" (PhD diss., Indiana University, 2005).

115. Jack Brewer, *The Greys Have Been Framed* (North Charleston: CreateSpace Independent Publishing Platform, 2016); Robert Sheaffer, "Abductology Implodes," *Skeptical Inquirer* 35 (May/June 2011): 25–27; Joseph J. Stefula, Richard D. Butler, and George P. Hansen, "A Critique of Budd Hopkins' Case of the UFO Abduction of Linda Napolitano," unpublished paper, 1993.

116. David Halperin, "Jerome Clark's 'UFO Encyclopedia'—Thomas Bullard's 'Abduction Phenomenon,'" *David Halperin*, 15 November 2018, https://www. davidhalperin.net/jerome-clarks-ufo-encyclopedia-thomas-bullards-abduction-phenomenon/?fbclid=IwAR055iRoa_mAZOX3xTEroZrDBffaj_56Rxr0dP15syyW 60lENz3eMgWW_oQ, accessed 14 August 2022.

117. Guilio Perrotta, "Clinical Evidence in the Phenomenon of Alien Abduction," *Annals of Psychiatry and Treatment* 5 (2021): 107–115; Susan A. Clancy, *Abducted: How People Come to Believe They Were Kidnapped by Aliens* (Cambridge, MA: Harvard University Press, 2005); Richard J. McNally and Susan A. Clancy, "Sleep Paralysis, Sexual Abuse, and Space Alien Abduction," *Transcultural Psychiatry* 42 (2005): 113–122.

118. Katharine J. Holden and Christopher C. French, "Alien Abduction Experiences: Some Clues from Neuropsychology and Neuropsychiatry," *Cognitive Neuropsychiatry* 7 (2002): 163–178.

119. Richard C. McNally, "Explaining 'Memories' of Space Alien Abduction and Past Lives: An Experimental Psychopathology Approach," *Journal of Experimental Psychopathology* 3 (2012): 2–16. Quote is from p. 6

120. Lawrence Patihis, Lavina Y. Ho, Ian W. Tingen, Scott O. Lilienfeld, and Elizabeth F. Loftus, "Are the 'Memory Wars' Over? A Scientist-Practitioner Gap in Beliefs about Repressed Memory," *Psychological Science* 25 (2014): 519–530.

121. Tristan Sturm, "Hal Lindsey's Geopolitical Future: Towards a Cartographic Theory of Anticipatory Arrows," *Journal of Maps* 17 (2021): 39–45; Natasha Zaretsky, *Radiation Nation: Three Mile Island and the Political Transformation of the 1970s* (New York: Columbia University Press, 2018); Serhii Plokhy, *Chernobyl: The History of a Nuclear Catastrophe* (New York: Basic Books, 2018); Pramod K. Nayar, *Bhopal's Ecological Gothic: Disaster, Precarity, and the Biopolitical Uncanny* (Lanham, MD: Lexington, 2017); Adam Rome, *The Genius of Earth Day: How a 1970 Teach-In Unexpectedly Made the First Green Generation* (New York: Hill and Wang, 2013); Lawrence Badash, *A Nuclear Winter's Tale: Science and Politics in the 1980s* (Cambridge, MA: MIT Press, 2009).

122. Brendan I. Koerner, *The Skies Belong to Us: Love and Terror in the Golden Age of Hijacking* (New York: Crown, 2013); U.S. Department of Transportation, FAA, *Aircraft Hijackings and Other Criminal Acts Against Civil Aviation Statistical and Narrative Reports* (Washington, DC: FAA, 1986.

123. Jennifer Wallis, "Locating Sexual Abuse in the TV Movie, From Dangerous Dads to Day Care," in *Are You in the House Alone? A TV Movie Compendium, 1964–1999*, eBook ed., ed. Amanda Reyes (Manchester: Headpress, 2017), 75–83. Quote is from p. 75.

124. Paula S. Fass, *The End of American Childhood: A History of Parenting from Life on the Frontier to the Managed Child* (Princeton: Princeton University Press, 2016); Ian Hacking, "The Making and Molding of Child Abuse," *Critical Inquiry* 17 (1991): 253–288; C. Henry Kempe, Frederic N. Silverman, Brandt F. Steele, William Droegemueller, and Henry K. Silver, "The Battered-Child Syndrome," *Child Abuse & Neglect* 9 (1985): 143–154 (originally published in 1962, but republished several times in the eighties).

125. Paul M. Renfro, *Stranger Danger: Family Values, Childhood, and the American Carceral State* (New York: Oxford University Press, 2020); Ernest E. Allen, "Keeping Children Safe: Rhetoric and Reality," *Juvenile Justice* 5 (1998): 16–23; Paula S. Fass, *Kidnapped: Child Abduction in America* (New York: Oxford University Press, 1997).

126. Thomas E. Bullard, "UFO Abduction Reports: The Supernatural Kidnap Narratives Return in Technological Guise," *The Journal of American Folklore* 102 (1989): 147–170.

127. Brown, *They Know Us Better*, 73–74.

128. Daniel Pick, *Svengali's Web: The Alien Enchanter in Modern Culture* (London: Yale University Press, 2000).

CONCLUSION

1. Baasanjav Terbish, "Russian Cosmism: Alien Visitations and Cosmic Energies in Contemporary Russia," *Modern Asian Studies* 54 (2020): 759–794.

2. AFU, *Тоннел; Вестник; Неведомое; Аномалия; Аномалные явления; Дайжест нло и гуманоиды.*

3. Liu Zhen, "Is Anyone Out There?" *South China Morning Post*, 16 June 2018, http://www.scmp.com/news/china/society/article/2125466/anyone-out-there-days-when-ufo-fever-gripped-china, accessed 16 June 2018; "Das Ende des UFO-Booms," *DW.com*, 14 October 2005, http://www.dw.com/de/das-ende-des-ufo-booms/a-1739839, accessed 24 August 2022.

4. Angela Wang, "Americans Aren't Spotting as Many UFOs as They Used to, but That's Probably about to Change," *Insider*, 5 July 2019, https://www.insider.com/ufo-sightings-have-been-steadily-decreasing-2019-6, accessed 6 July 2019; Jennings Brown, "Our Skies are More Watched Than Ever, so Why Are Reported UFO Sightings on the Decline?" *Gizmodo*, 2 July 2018, https://gizmodo.com/our-skies-are-more-watched-than-ever-so-why-are-report-1827284430, accessed 24 September 2018; Philip Jaekl, "What Is Behind the Decline in UFO Sightings?" *The Guardian*, 21 September 2018, https://www.theguardian.com/world/2018/sep/21/what-is-behind-the-decline-in-ufo-sightings, accessed 24 September 2018; Linda Rodriguez McRobbie, "Why Alien Abductions Are Down Dramatically," *The Boston Globe*, 12 June 2016, https://www.bostonglobe.com/ideas/2016/06/11/why-alien-abductions-are-down-dramatically/qQ3zdBIc2tLAf3LVms8GLP/story.html, accessed 14 August 2017.

5. "FUFOR: Fund for UFO Research," *Anomaly Archives*, https://anomalyarchives.org/collections/file/fufor-fund-for-ufo-research/, accessed 24 August 2022; Håkan Blomqvist, "AFU in the 1990s," *Håkan Blomqvist's Blog*, 2 January 2018, https://ufoarchives.blogspot.com/2018/01/afu-in-1990s.html, accessed 4 January 2018; Announcement Disbanding COBEPS, *COBEPS*, http://www.cobeps.org/fr/inforespace.html, accessed 10 May 2014; Clarke and Roberts, *Flying Saucerers*, 31.

6. Announcement on https://bufora.org.uk/, accessed 10 June 2014; Nick Redfern, "Ufology: An Uncertain Future," *Mysterious Universe*, 17 January 2014, https://mysteriousuniverse.org/2014/01/ufology-an-uncertain-future/, accessed 24 August 2022; Edoardo Russo, "UFO Periodicals, a Possible Future," *Italian UFO Reporter* 4 (October 2009): 1; John Rimmer, "A Few Final Editorial Notes," *Magonia* 99 (April 2009): 2.

7. Jasper Copping, "UFOs Turn Out to be a Waste of Space," *Sunday Telegraph*, 4 November 2012: 5.

8. "James Carrion to Podcasters," *The UFO Trail*, 21 July 2014, http://ufotrail.blogspot.com/2014/07/james-carrion-to-podcasters-deception.html, accessed 14 December 2018; James Carrion, "Goodbye Ufology, Hello Truth," *The UFO Chronicles*, 6 April 2010, https://www.theufochronicles.com/2010/04/goodbye-ufology-hello-truth.html, accessed 9 June 2017.

9. Andrew Whalen, "What if Aliens Met Racists?" *Newsweek*, 29 April 2018, http://www.newsweek.com/ufo-sightings-mufon-2018-john-ventre-alien-extraterrestrial-905060, accessed 3 May 2018; Mike Damante, "MUFON Fails to Disavow Awful, Racist Comments from State Director," *Punk Rock and UFOs*, https://

www.punkrockandufos.com/blog/2017/5/29/mufon-fails-to-disavow-awful-rac
ist-comments-from-state-director, accessed 24 August 2022.

10. Terrence McCoy, "In US, Most UFO Documentation Is Classified. Not So in
Other Countries," *The Washington Post*, 6 September 2023, https://www.washing
tonpost.com/world/2023/09/06/ufo-brazil-documents-classified/, accessed 6
September 2023.

11. Vicente-Juan Ballester Olmos, "The Nature of UFO Evidence: Two Views" (2017),
Ballester Olmos, V.J. & Bullard, T.E. (2017), "The Nature of UFO Evidence: Two
Views, Pt. 1," https://www.academia.edu/33352049/THE_NATURE_OF_UFO_
EVIDENCE_TWO_VIEWS, accessed 9 June 2017.

12. Copping, "UFOs"; John Rimmer, "That's All, Folks . . ." *Magonia* 99 (2008),
http://magoniamagazine.blogspot.com/2014/02/thats-all-folks.html#more,
accessed 25 August 2022.

13. Personal communication; Michael Swords, "The Communications
Revolution: The End of Ufology and Anomalies Studies?" *The Big Study*, 23 March
2013, http://thebiggeststudy.blogspot.com/2013/03/the-communications-
revolution-end-of.html, accessed 25 August 2022; Ben McIntyre, "ETs Flown
Home—Chased Off by the Internet," *The Times*, 31 March 2006: 21.

14. Austin Weinstein and Pia Gadkari, "UFO Hunting in the Photoshop Age,"
Bloomberg, 18 September 2018, https://www.bloomberg.com/news/articles/
2018-09-18/ufo-hunting-in-the-photoshop-age, accessed 25 August 2022.

15. https://tothestars.media/pages/about, accessed 25 August 2022; Eghigian, "Year
of the UFOs."

16. Lukas K. Pokorny and Patricia Sophie Mayer, "'Like Armaggedon': Kōfuku no
Kagaku and the COVID-19 Pandemic," *Religions* 13 (2022): 480.

17. C. D. Bader, J. G. Melton, and J. O. Baker, *Survey of Attenders: International
UFO Congress Convention and Film Festival, 2010* (Association of Religion Data
Archives, 2021), DOI: 10.17605/OSF.IO/B3Z7V; Jeff Kripal, "Esalen and the
UFO," *Esalen*, 16 July 2021, https://www.esalen.org/post/early-esalen-ufos-and-
the-exploration-of-new-life, accessed 9 July 2023; Exploration David J. Halperin,
Intimate Alien: The Hidden Story of the UFO (Stanford: Stanford University Press,
2020); Andrew Marantz, "Silicon Valley's Crisis of Conscience," *The New Yorker*,
19 August 2019, https://www.newyorker.com/magazine/2019/08/26/silicon-
valleys-crisis-of-conscience, accessed 9 July 2023; D. W. Pasulka, *American
Cosmic: UFOs, Religion, Technology* (New York: Oxford University Press, 2019).
Nellie Bowles, "Where Silicon Valley Is Going to Get in Touch with Its Soul,"
New York Times, 4 December 2017, https://www.nytimes.com/2017/12/04/tec
hnology/silicon-valley-esalen-institute.html, accessed 10 July 2023.

18. NASA, Public Meeting on Unidentified Anomalous Phenomena, 31 May 2023,
https://www.youtube.com/watch?v=bQo08JRY0iM, accessed 10 July 2023;
Marissa E. Yingling, Charlton W. Yingling, and Bethany A. Bell, "Faculty
Perceptions of Unidentified Aerial Phenomena," *Humanities and Social Sciences
Communications* 10 (2023): https://doi.org/10.1057/s41599-023-01746-3; Tim
McMillan, "San Marino Could Become the U.N.'s New 'Geneva' for UFOs," *The
Debrief*, 17 September 2021, https://thedebrief.org/san-marino-could-become-
the-u-n-s-new-geneva-for-ufos/, accessed 10 July 2023.

19. In the interest of full disclosure, I serve on the advisory board of SUAPS.

20. Felix Richter, "I Want to Believe!" *Statista*, 14 February 2023, https://www.stati
sta.com/chart/29296/public-opinion-on-aliens-visiting-earth/, accessed 26
July 2023; Martijn Lampert, "Majority of Humanity Say We Are Not Alone in

the Universe" (Glocalities, 2017), https://glocalities.com/reports/majority-of-humanity-say-we-are-not-alone-in-the-universe, accessed 22 August 2023. Some of the points I make about COVID are raised by David Halperin, "Colares and Coronavirus—UFO Epidemic Revisited," *David Halperin Blog*, 28 August 2021, https://www.davidhalperin.net/colares-and-coronavirus-ufo-epidemic-revisited/, accessed 14 July 2023.

21. I am indebted to David Halperin for helping me express this point.

22. Matthew P. McAllister and Greg Eghigian, "Flying Saucers and UFOs in US Advertising During the Cold War, 1947–1989," *Advertising & Society Quarterly* 23 (2022); Niklas Alexander Döbler and Marius Raab, "Thinking ET: A Discussion of Exopsychology," *Acta Astronautica* 189 (2021): 699–711.

23. Simon Young, *The Boggart: Folklore, History, Place-Names, and Dialect* (Exeter: University of Exeter Press, 2022); Rebecca Charbonnaeu, "Imaginative Cosmos: The Impact of Colonial Heritage in Radio Astronomy and the Search for Extraterrestrial Intelligence," *American Indian Culture and Research Journal* 45 (2021): 71–94; Susan Claudia Lepselter, *The Resonance of Unseen Things: Poetics, Power, Captivity, and UFOs in the American Uncanny* (Ann Arbor: University of Michigan Press, 2016).

24. Jenny Andersson, *The Future of the World: Futurology, Futurists, and the Struggle for the Post-Cold War Imagination* (Oxford: Oxford University Press, 2018).

25. Diana Espírito Santo and Alejandra Vergara, "The Possible and the Impossible: Reflections on Evidence in Chilean Ufology," *Antípoda: Revista de Antropología y Arqueología* 41 (2020): 125–146.

BIBLIOGRAPHY

ARCHIVES
American Heritage Center
American Philosophical Society
Archives for the Unexplained
John E. Mack Papers
British National Archives, Kew
NICAP.Org
Niels Bohr Library & Archives, American Institute of Physics
Northern Ontario UFO Research and Study
Project 1947, Sign Historical Group
Project Blue Book Archive
Sign Oral History Project
University of Arizona, Special Collections
US National Archives, Library of Congress

UFO NEWSLETTERS, BULLETINS, AND MAGAZINES
Abduction Watch
Аномалные явления
Аномалия
APRO Bulletin
APRO Newsletter
Caudernos de Ufología
CENAP-Report
Civilian Saucer Investigation Quarterly Bulletin
Civilian Saucer Investigation Quarterly Review
The Communion Letter
Дайжест нло и гуманоиды
European Journal of UFO and Abduction Studies
Fantastic Universe
Flying Saucer Review (FSR)
International UFO Library Magazine
International UFO Reporter
Italian UFO Reporter
IUR
Journal of UFO History
Journal of UFO Research

Kalpa-Nava
Lumiéres dans lu Nuit
Magonia
Magonia Supplement
Malaysian UFO Bulletin
Merseyside UFO Bulletin
MUFOB New Series
MUFON (UFO) Journal
Наблюдения аая (НЛО) в СССР
Неведомое
Nexus
Official UFO
Ouranos
Paratopia
Perspectivas Ufológicas
Phénomènes Spatiaux
The Saucerian Review
Saucers
SBEDV Boletim
Spacelink
Skywatch: Quarterly of the International Sky Scouts (S.A.) Durban
Space Review
Тоннел
UFO
UFO: Rivista di informazione ufologica
UFO Contactee
The U.F.O. Investigator
UFO Newsclipping Service
The UFO Register
Вестник
Weltraumbote

PUBLISHED SOURCES

Adamski, George. *Flying Saucers Farewell*. London and New York: Abelard-Schuman, 1961.

Adamksi, George. *Inside the Space Ships*. New York: Abelard-Schuman, 1955.

Agostinelli, Alejandro. *Invasores: Historias reales de extraterrestres en la Argentina*. Buenos Aires: Editorial Sudamericana, 2009.

Agrest, Matest M. "On the Development of the Idea of Paleocontacts in the USSR at the Beginning of the 1960s." *RIAP Bulletin* 8 (2002): 4–8.

Allen, Ernest E. "Keeping Children Safe: Rhetoric and Reality." *Juvenile Justice* 5 (1998): 16–23.

Andersson, Jenny. *The Future of the World: Futurology, Futurists, and the Struggle for the Post-Cold War Imagination*. Oxford: Oxford University Press, 2018.

Andrews, James. "Inculcating Materialist Minds: Scientific Propaganda and Anti-Religion in the USSR During the Cold War." In *Science, Religion, and Communism in Cold War Europe*, edited by Paul Betts and Stephen A. Smith, 105–125. London: Palgrave Macmillan, 2016.

Angelucci, Orfeo. *The Secret of the Saucers*. Stevens Point, WI: Amherst, 1955.

Arnold, Kenneth, and Ray Palmer. *The Coming of the Saucers: A Documentary Report on Sky Objects That Have Mystified the World*. Boise: Ray Palmer, 1952.

Aubeck, Chris. *Alien Artifacts, Vol. 1: From Antiquity to 1880*. Monee: Aubeck, 2022.

Badash, Lawrence. *A Nuclear Winter's Tale: Science and Politics in the 1980s*. Cambridge, MA: MIT Press, 2009.

Bader, Christopher D. "Supernatural Support Groups: Who Are the UFO Abductees and Ritual-Abuse Survivors?" *Journal for the Scientific Study of Religion* 42 (2003): 669–678.

Bader, Christopher D., J. G. Melton, and J. O. Baker. *Survey of Attenders: International UFO Congress Convention and Film Festival, 2010*. Association of Religion Data Archives, 2021, DOI: 10.17605/OSF.IO/B3Z7V.

Bainbridge, William Sims. "In Search of Delusion: Television Pseudocumentaries." *Skeptical Inquirer* 4 (1979): 33–39.

Balch, Robert W. "Looking Behind the Scenes in a Religious Cult: Implications for the Study of Conversion." *Sociological Analysis* 41 (1980): 137–143.

Balch, Robert W., and David Taylor. "Seekers and Saucers: The Role of the Cultic Milieu in Joining a UFO Cult." *The American Behavioral Scientist* 20 (1977): 839–860.

Banchs, Roberto. *Guía biográfica de la ufología Argentina*. Buenos Aires: Cefai Ediciones, 2000.

Barker, Gray. *They Knew Too Much about Flying Saucers*. New York: University Books, 1956.

Barry, Bill. "Kidnapped!" In *UFO Abductions: True Cases of Alien Kidnappings*, edited by D. Scott Rogo, 28–43. New York: Signet, 1980.

Bartholomew, Robert E., and George S. Howard. *UFOs and Alien Contact: Two Centuries of Mystery*. Amherst, NY: Prometheus, 1998.

Bender, Albert K. *Flying Saucers and the Three Men*. Clarksburg, WV: Saucerian Books, 1962.

Bennett, Colin. *Flying Saucers Over the White House: The Inside Story of Captain Edward J. Ruppelt and His Official U.S. Airforce Investigation of UFOs*. New York: Cosimo, 2010.

Bethurum, Truman. *Aboard a Flying Saucer: A True Story of Personal Experience*. Los Angeles: DeVors, 1954.

Bevir, Mark. "The West Turns Eastward: Madame Blavatsky and the Transformation of the Occult Tradition." *Journal of the American Academy of Religion* 62 (1994): 747–767.

Billings, Linda. "Sex! Aliens! Harvard? Rhetorical Boundary-Work in the Media (A Case Study of Role of Journalists in the Social Construction of Scientific Authority)." PhD diss., Indiana University, 2005.

Bishop, Greg. *Project Beta: The Story of Paul Bennewitz, National Security, and the Creation of a Modern UFO Myth*. New York: Paraview Pocket Books, 2005.

Bloecher, Ted. *Report on the UFO Wave of 1947*. Self-published: 1967, reproduced by Jean Waskiewicz and Francis Ridge, 2005.

Blumenthal, Ralph. *The Believer: Alien Encounters, Hard Science, and the Passion of John Mack*. Albuquerque: High Road Books, 2021.

Bo, Shi. *Ufo-Begegnungen in China*. Berlin: Ullstein, 1997.

Boffey, Philip M. "UFO Project: Trouble on the Ground." *Science* 161 (26 July 1968): 339–342.

Boyce, Niall. "The Art of Medicine: The Psychiatrist who Wanted to Believe." *Lancet* 380 (2012): 1140–1141.

Brown, Bridget. *They Know Us Better Than We Know Ourselves: The History and Politics of Alien Abduction*. New York: New York University Press, 2007.

Bourdais, Gildas. "From GEPAN to SEPRA: Official UFO Studies in France." *IUR* (Winter 2000–2001): 10–13.

Bowman, Matthew. *Interrupted Journeys: The Abduction of Betty and Barney Hill and the Fragmentation of America*. New Haven: Yale University Press, 2023.

Bravo, Eduardo. *Ummo: Los increíble es la verdad*. Sineu, Islas Baleares: Autsaider Cómics, 2019.

Brewer, Jack. *The Greys Have Been Framed*. North Charleston: CreateSpace Independent Publishing Platform, 2016.

Brooke, John L. *The Refiner's Fire: The Making of Mormon Cosmology, 1644–1844*. Cambridge: Cambridge University Press, 1994.

Brown, Timothy Scott. *Sixties Europe*. Cambridge: Cambridge University Press, 2020.

Brunner, José. *Die Politik des Traumas: Gewalterfahrungen und psychisches Leid in den USA, in Deutschland und im Israel/Palästina-Konflikt*. Berlin: Suhrkamp, 2014.

Bryan, C. D. B. *Close Encounters of the Fourth Kind: Alien Abduction, UFOs, and the Conference at M.I.T.* New York: Knopf, 1995.

Bühler, Walter K. *40 Begegnungen mit Außerdischen in Brasilien*. Wiesbaden: Ventla, 1975.

Bullard, Thomas E. *The Myth and Mystery of UFOs*. Lawrence: University Press of Kansas, 2010.

Bullard, Thomas E. "UFO Abduction Reports: The Supernatural Kidnap Narratives Return in Technological Guise." *The Journal of American Folklore* 102 (1989): 147–170.

Burgess, Ann W., and Lynda L. Holstrom. "Rape Trauma Syndrome." *American Journal of Psychiatry* 131 (1974): 981–986.

Burström, Mats Anders Gustafsson, and Håkan Karlsson. "The Air Torpedo of Bäckebo: Local Incident and World History." *Current Swedish Archaeology* 14 (2006): 7–24.

Cahn, J.P. "Flying Saucer Swindlers." *True*, August 1956: 36–37, 69–72.

Cahn, J.P. "The Flying Saucers and the Mysterious Little Men." *True*, September 1952, https://www.saturdaynightuforia.com/html/articles/articlehtml/anatomyofahoax-part11.html.

Campany, Robert Ford. *A Garden of Marvels: Tales of Wonder from Early Medieval China*. Honolulu: University of Hawaii Press, 2015.

Campbell, Bruce F. *Ancient Wisdom Revived: A History of the Theosophical Movement*. Berkeley: University of California Press, 1980.

Campbell, W. Joseph. *Getting It Wrong: Ten of the Greatest Misreported Stories in American Journalism*. Berkeley: University of California Press, 2010.

Campobasso, Craig. *The Extraterrestrial Species Almanac: The Ultimate Guide to Greys, Reptilians, Hybrids, and Nordics*. Newburyport, MA: MUFON, 2021.

Cantril, Hadley. *The Invasion from Mars: A Study in the Psychology of Panic*. New Brunswick and London: Transaction, 2005.

Canuti, Thibaut. *Histoire de l'ufologie française: 1 Le temps des soucoupistes*. Agniéres: Temps resent, 2011.

Canuti, Thibaut. *Histoire de l'ufologie française: 2 Le temps des officiels*. Agniéres: JMG éditions, 2019.

Carruthers, Susan L. *Cold War Captives: Imprisonment, Escape, and Brainwashing*. Berkeley: University of California Press, 2009.

Certeau, Florence Raulin. "Fraction of Civilizations That Develop a Technology That Releases Detectable Signs of Their Existence into Space, fc, pre-1961." In *The Drake Equation: Estimating the Prevalence of Extraterrestrial Life Through the Ages*, edited by Douglas A. Vakoch and Matthew F. Dowd, 219–220. Cambridge: Cambridge University Press, 2015.

Charbonnaeu, Rebecca. "Imaginative Cosmos: The Impact of Colonial Heritage in Radio Astronomy and the Search for Extraterrestrial Intelligence." *American Indian Culture and Research Journal* 45 (2021): 71–94.

Charbonneau, Rebecca. *Mixed Signals: Cold War Communication with Extraterrestrial Intelligence*. New York: Polity Press, 2024.

Ciardi, Marco. *Il mistero degli antichi astronauti*. Rome: Carocci, 2017.

Clamar, Aphrodite. "Is it Time for Psychologists to Take UFOs Seriously?" *Psychotherapy in Private Practice* 6 (1988): 143–149.

Clancy, Susan A. *Abducted: How People Come to Believe They Were Kidnapped by Aliens*. Cambridge, MA: Harvard University Press, 2005.

Clark, Jerome. *Hidden Realms, Lost Civilizations, and Beings from other Worlds*. Canton, MI: Visible Ink Press, 2010.

Clark, Jerome, ed. *The UFO Encyclopedia*, 3rd ed., vols. 1–2. Detroit: Omnigraphics, Inc., 2018.

Clark, Steven E., and Elizabeth F. Loftus. "The Psychological Pay Dirt of Space Alien Abduction Memories." *Contemporary Psychology* 40 (1995): 861–863.

Clark, Stuart. *Thinking with Demons: The Idea of Witchcraft in Early Modern Europe*. Oxford: Oxford University Press, 1999.

Clarke, Arthur C. "Review of Desmond Leslie and George Adamski, *Flying Saucers Have Landed*." *Journal of the British Interplanetary Society* 13 (1954): 119–122.

Clarke, Arthur C. "Whatever Happened to Flying Saucers?" *The Saturday Evening Post*, 1 June 1971: 10.

Clarke, David. *The National Archives Research Guide (UFOs)*. Sheffield: Sheffield Hallam University Research Archive, 2008.

Clarke, David. "A New Demonology: John Keel and *The Mothman Prophecies*." In *Damned Facts: Fortean Essays on Religion, Folklore, and the Paranormal*, edited by Jack Hunter, 54–68. Cyprus: Aporetic Press, 2016.

Clarke, David, and Andy Roberts. *Flying Saucerers: A Social History of UFOlogy*. Loughborough: Alternative Albion, 2007.

Cocconi, Giuseppe, and Philip Morrison. "Searching for Interstellar Communications." *Nature* 184 (1959): 844–846.

Colavito, Jason. *The Cult of Alien Gods: H.P. Lovecraft and Extraterrestrial Pop Culture*. Amherst, NY: Prometheus Books, 2005.

Condon, Edward U. *Final Report of the Scientific Study of Unidentified Flying Objects*. New York: Bantam Books, 1969.

Condon, E. U. "UFO Trouble in *Science*." *Science* 161 (30 August 1968): 844.

Condon, E. U. "UFO's I Have Loved and Lost." *Proceedings of the American Philosophical Society* 113 (December 1969): 425–427.

Cooke, Michelle. "Little People and Leprechauns: Creatures of Cultural Folklore." *Journal of Chickasaw History and Culture* 15 (2013): 21–33.

Craig, Roy. *UFOs: An Insider's View of the Official Question for Evidence*. Denton: University of North Texas Press, 1995.

Crews, Frederick. *The Memory Wars: Freud's Legacy in Dispute*. London: Granta, 1995.

Crouch, Tom D. "Dream of Aerial Navigation." In *Astride Two Worlds: Technology and the American Civil War*, edited by Barton C. Hacker, 205–244. Washington, DC: Smithsonian Institution Scholarly Press, 2016.

Crowe, Michael J. *The Extraterrestrial Life Debate, 1750–1900: The Idea of a Plurality of Worlds from Kant to Lowell.* Cambridge: Cambridge University Press, 1986.

Dänekin, Erich von. *Chariots of the Gods? Unsolved Mysteries of the Past.* New York: G. P. Putnam's Sons, 1970.

Daley, Jason. "The Screenwriting Mystic Who Wanted to be the American Führer." *Smithsonian Magazine*, 3 October 2018, https://www.smithsonianmag.com/history/meet-screenwriting-mystic-who-wanted-be-american-fuhrer-180970449/.

Darrach, H. B., Jr., and Robert Ginna. "Have We Visitors from Space?" *Life*, 7 April 1952: 80–96.

Daston, Lorraine, and Katharine Park. *Wonders and the Order of Nature, 1150–1750.* New York: Zone, 1988.

Davies, Owen. *The Haunted: A Social History of Ghosts.* Basingstoke: Palgrave Macmillan, 2007.

Davies, R. E. G. *Airlines of the United States since 1914.* Washington, DC: Smithsonian Institution Press, 1998.

Davis, Isabel, and Ted Bloecher. *Close Encounter at Kelly and Others of 1955.* Evanston, IL: Center for UFO Studies, 1978.

Déguillaume, Eric. "UFOs: An Assessment of Thirty Years of Official Studies in France." *Skeptical Inquirer* (January/February 2009): 47–51.

Denzler, Brenda. *The Lure of the Edge: Scientific Passions, Religious Beliefs, and the Pursuit of UFOs.* Berkeley: University of California Press, 2001.

Derr, John S. "Earthquake Lights: A Review of Observations and Present Theories." *Bulletin of the Seismological Society of America* 63 (1973): 2177–2187.

Di Stefano, Rino. *The Zanfretta Case: Chronicle of an Incredible True Story.* S.I.: Createspace Independent, 2014.

Dick, Steven J. "The Drake Equation in Context." In *The Drake Equation: Estimating the Prevalence of Extraterrestrial Life through the Ages*, edited by Douglas A. Vakoch and Matthew F. Dowd, 1–20. Cambridge: Cambridge University Press, 2015.

Dick, Steven J. *Life on Other Worlds: The 20th-Century Extraterrestrial Life Debate.* Cambridge and New York: Cambridge University Press, 1998.

Dick, Steven J. *Plurality of Worlds: The Origins of the Extraterrestrial Life Debate from Democritus to Kant.* Cambridge: Cambridge University Press, 1982.

Döbler, Niklas Alexander, and Marius Raab. "Thinking ET: A Discussion of Exopsychology." *Acta Astronautica* 189 (2021): 699–711.

Dorsch, Kate. "Reliable Witnesses, Crackpot Science: UFO Investigations in Cold War America, 1947–1977." PhD diss., University of Pennsylvania, 2019.

Druffel, Ann. *Firestorm: Dr. James E. McDonald's Fight for UFO Science.* Columbus, NC: Wild Flower Press, 2003.

Druffel, Ann, and D. Scott Rogo. *The Tujunga Canyon Contacts.* Englewood Cliffs, NJ: Prentice-Hall, 1980.

Drury, Nevill. *The New Age: The History of a Movement.* New York: Thames & Hudson, 2004.

Dunphy, Seamus. "UFO Fever in America's Historical Newspapers: The Mysterious Airships of 1896–1897." *The Readex Blog*, http://www.readex.com/blog/ufo-fever-america's-historical-newspapers-mysterious-airships-1896-97.

Durant, Frederick C. *Report of Meetings of Scientific Advisory Panel on Unidentified Flying Objects Convened by Office of Scientific Intelligence, CIA: 14–18 January*

1953. Washington, DC: Central Intelligence Agency, OSI Operations Staff Washington, 1953.

Eby, Cecil D. *The Road to Armageddon: The Martial Spirit in English Popular Literature, 1870–1914.* Durham, NC: Duke University Press, 1987.

Edwards, Kathryn A. "The History of Ghosts in Early Modern Europe: Recent Research and Future Trajectories." *History Compass* 10 (2012): 353–366.

Eghigian, Greg. "The Year of the UFOs." *Smithsonian Air & Space Magazine,* February 2020, https://www.airspacemag.com/space/year-ufos-180973965/.

Evans, Hilary. *From Other Worlds: The Truth about Aliens, Abductions, UFOs, the Paranormal.* London: Carlton, 1988.

Evans, Hilary. *Gods, Spirits, Cosmic Guardians: A Comparative Study of the Encounter Experience.* Wellingborough: The Aquarian Press, 1987.

Evans, Hilary. *Visions, Apparitions, Alien Visitors.* London: Book Club Associates, 1984.

Esquerre, Arnaud. *Théorie des événements extraterrestres: Essai sur le récit fantastique.* Paris: Librairie Arthème Fayard, 2016.

Faria, J. Escobar. *Discos voadores: Contatos com sêres de outros planêtas.* São Paulo: Melhoramentos, 1959.

Fass, Paula S. *The End of American Childhood: A History of Parenting from Life on the Frontier to the Managed Child.* Princeton: Princeton University Press, 2016.

Fass, Paula S. *Kidnapped: Child Abduction in America.* New York: Oxford University Press, 1997.

Fernandez, Gilles. "The Coming of the (Term) 'Flying Saucers.'" *Sceptiques vs. les Soucoupes Volantes,* 15 March 2017, http://skepticversustheflyingsaucers.blogs pot.com/2017/03/the-coming-of-flying-saucers-term.html.

Festinger, Leon, Henry W. Riecken, and Stanley Schachter. *When Prophecy Fails.* Minneapolis: University of Minnesota Press, 1956.

Fiebag, Johannes. *Kontakt: UFO-Entführungen in Deutschland, Österreich, und der Schweiz.* Munich: Langen Müller, 1994.

Finley, Stephen C. *In and Out of This World: Material and Extraterrestrial Bodies in the Nation of Islam.* Durham, NC: Duke University Press, 2022.

"First Soviet-American Conference on Communication with Extraterrestrial Intelligence (CETI)." *Icarus* 16 (1972): 412–414.

Flournoy, Theodore. *From India to the Planet Mars: A Case of Multiple Personality with Imaginary Languages.* Princeton: Princeton University Press, 2015.

Fort, Charles. *The Book of the Damned.* New York: Tarcher/Penguin, 2016.

Fowler, Raymond E. *The Andreasson Affair: The True Story of a Close Encounter of the Fourth Kind.* Pompton Plains: Career Press, 1979/ebook 2015.

Fox, Phillis. "Social and Cultural Factors Influencing Beliefs About UFOs." In *UFO Phenomena and the Behavioral Scientist,* Metuchen: Scarecrow, 1979, edited by Richard Haines, 20–42.

Frazier, Kendrick. "History of CSICOP." In *The Encyclopedia of the Paranormal,* edited by Gordon Stein, 168–180. Amherst: Prometheus Books, 1996.

Frankfurter, David. "The Satanic Ritual Abuse Panic as Religious-Studies Data." *Numen* 50 (2003): 108–117.

Friedman, Stanton T. *Top Secret/Majic: Operation Majestic-12 and the United States Government's UFO Cover-Up.* Cambridge, MA: Da Capo, 1996.

Fry, Daniel W. *Alan's Message: To Men of Earth.* Los Angeles: New Age, 1954.

Fry, Daniel W. *The White Sands Incident.* Los Angeles: New Age, 1954.

Fuller, John G. "Flying Saucer Fiasco." *Look,* 14 May 1968. https://www.project1947.com/shg/articles/fiasco.html.

Fuller, John G. *The Interrupted Journey: Two Lost Hours "Aboard a Flying Saucer."* New York: The Daily Press, 1966.

García, Ignacio Cabria. *Entre ufólogos, creyentes y contactados: Una historia social de los OVNIs en España.* Santander: Cuadernos de Ufología, 1993.

Gardner, Martin. *Fads and Fallacies in the Name of Science.* New York: Dover, 1957.

Garthoff, Raymond L. "Foreign Intelligence and the Historiography of the Cold War." *Journal of Cold War Studies* 6 (2004): 21–56.

Gauld, Alan. *A History of Hypnotism.* Cambridge and New York: Cambridge University Press, 1992.

Geppert, Alexander C. T. "The Post-Apollo Paradox: Envisioning Limits During the Planetized 1970s." In *Limiting Outer Space: Astroculture after Apollo*, ed. Alexander C. T. Geppert, 3–26. London: Palgrave Macmillan, 2018.

Gerovitch, Slava. *Soviet Space Mythologies: Public Images, Private Memories, and the Making of a Cultural Identity.* Pittsburgh: University Pittsburgh Press, 2015.

Gibbons, Gavin. *They Rode Space Ships.* London: Neville Spearman, 1957.

Ginna, Robert E., Jr. "Saucer Reactions." *Life,* 9 June 1952: 20–26.

Gollin, Alfred M. "England is No Longer an Island: The Phantom Airship Scare of 1909." *Albion* 13 (1981): 43–57.

Golowin, Sergius. *Götter der Atom-Zeit: Moderne Sagenbildung um Raumschiffe und Sternenmenschen.* Bern: A. Francke, 1967.

Голц, В.И. *Рукописъ, Навлюдения ААЯ (НЛО) в СССР (Сборник Соовщений Н 13).* Leningrad: Samizdat, 1984.

Golubev, A.V. "НЛО над планетарием: эпистемологическая пропаганда и альтернативные формы знаний о космосе в СССР в 1940–1960-е годы;" *История* 54 (2021): 5–16.

Goodrick-Clarke, Nicholas. *Black Sun: Aryan Cults, Esoteric Nazism, and the Politics of Identity.* New York: New York University Press, 2002.

Gordon, Richard. "*Superstitio,* Superstition, and Religious Repression in the Late Roman Republic and Principate (100 BCE–300 CE)." *Past and Present* 199 (2008): 72–94.

Grinfield, Michael Jonathan. "Space Alien Abductions: A Test of Wills, of Credibility." *Psychiatric Times* (October 1993): 11–12.

Gross, Loren. *UFO's: A History 1952—August.* Fremont: Loren Gross, 1986.

Gulyas, Aaron John. *Extraterrestrials and the American Zeitgeist.* Jefferson, NC: McFarland & Co., 2013.

Haas, Angela. "Miracles on Trial: Wonders and Their Witnesses in Eighteenth-Century France." *Proceedings of the Western Society for French History* 38 (2010): 111–128.

Hacking, Ian. "The Making and Molding of Child Abuse." *Critical Inquiry* 17 (1991): 253–288.

Hague, Angela. "Before Abduction: The Contactee Narrative of the 1950s." *The Journal of Popular Culture* 44 (2011): 439–454.

Haines, Richard F., ed. *UFO Phenomena and the Behavioral Scientist.* Metuchen: Scarecrow, 1979.

Hallet, Marc. *A Critical Appraisal of George Adamski: The Man Who Spoke to the Space Brothers.* Self-published, 2016.

Halperin, David. "Frank R. Paul—'The Man Who Created Flying Saucers.'" 17 May 2019. https://www.davidhalperin.net/frank-r-paul-the-man-who-created-flying-saucers/.

Halperin, David. *Intimate Alien: The Hidden Story of the UFO*. Stanford, CA: Stanford University Press, 2020.

Hanegraaff, Wouter J. *New Age Religion and Western Culture: Esotericism in the Mirror of Secular Thought*. Leiden: Brill, 1996.

Hansen, George P. "CSICOP and the Skeptics: An Overview." *Journal of the American Society for Psychical Research* 86 (1992): 19–63.

Hayes, Matthew. *Search for the Unknown: Canada's UFO Files and the Rise of Conspiracy Theory*. Montreal: McGill-Queen's University Press, 2022.

Heard, Gerald. *The Riddle of the Flying Saucers: Is Another World Watching?* London: Carrol & Nicholson, 1950.

Henry, Victor. *La Langage Martien*. Paris: J. Maisonneuve, 1901.

Hess, David J. *Science in the New Age: The Paranormal, Its Defenders and Debunkers, and American Culture*. Madison: University of Wisconsin Press, 1993.

Heuyer, Georges. "Note sur les psychoses collectives." *Bulletin de l'Académie Nationale de Médecine* 138 (1954): 487–490.

Hippler, Thomas. *Governing From the Skies*. London: Verso, 2017.

Holden, Katharine J., and Christopher C. French. "Alien Abduction Experiences: Some Clues from Neuropsychology and Neuropsychiatry." *Cognitive Neuropsychiatry* 7 (2002): 163–178.

Holland, Steve, and Roger Perry. *The Men Behind the Flying Saucer Review*. Middleton, DE: Bear Alley Books, 2017.

Holman, Brett. "The Air Panic of 1935: British Press Opinion between Disarmament and Rearmament." *Journal of Contemporary History* 46 (2011): 288–307.

Homan, Brett. "Constructing the Enemy Within: Rumours of Secret Gun Platforms and Zeppelin Bases in Britain, August–October 1914." *British Journal for Military History* 3 (2017): 22–42.

Hopkins, Budd. *Intruders: The Incredible Visitations at Copley Woods*. New York: Random House, 1987.

Hopkins, Budd. *Missing Time: A Documented Study of UFO Abductions*. New York: Richard Marek, 1981.

Hopkins, Budd. "Sane Citizen Sees UFO in New Jersey." *The Village Voice*, 1 March 1976: 12–13.

Hopkins, Budd. *Witnessed: The True Story of the Brooklyn Bridge UFO Abductions*. New York: Pocket Books, 1996.

Horsfall, Sara. "The Experience of Marian Apparitions and the Mary Cult." *The Social Science Journal* 37 (2000): 375–384.

Howard, Dana. *Diane: She Came from Venus*. London: Regency, 1955.

Howard, Dana. *My Flight to Venus*. San Gabriel: Willing, 1954.

Howard, Dana. *Over the Threshold*. Los Angeles: Llewellyn, 1957.

Hughes, Sarah A. *American Tabloid Media and the Satanic Panic, 1970–2000*. Cham: Palgrave, 2021.

Hutchison, Phillip J., and Herbert J. Strentz. "Journalism Versus the Flying Saucers: Assessing the First Generation of UFO Reportage, 1947–1967." *American Journalism* 36 (2019): 150–170.

Huyghe, Patrick. *Swamp Gas Times: My Two Decades on the UFO Beat*. New York: Paraview, 2001.

Hynek, J. Allen. J. "The Condon Report and UFOs." *Bulletin of the Atomic Scientists* 25 (April 1969): 39–42.

Hynek, J. Allen. *The UFO Experience: A Scientific Inquiry*. New York: Ballantine, 1972.

Hynek, J. Allen. "UFOs Merit Scientific Study." *Science* 21 (1966): 329.

Inglesby, Eric. *UFOs and the Christian*. New York: Regency, 1978.

Introvigne, Massimo. "Moral Panics and Anti-Cult Terrorism in Western Europe." *Terrorism and Political Violence* 12 (2000): 47–59.

Iwasaka, Michiko, and Barre Toelken. *Ghosts and the Japanese: Cultural Experience in Japanese Death Legends*. Logan: Utah State University, 1994.

Jacobs, David M. "A Brief History of Abduction Research." *Journal of Scientific Exploration* 23 (2009): 69–77.

Jacobs, David M. *Secret Life: Firsthand Accounts of UFO Abductions*. New York: Simon and Schuster, 1992.

Jacobs, David M. *The UFO Controversy in America*. Bloomington: Indiana University Press, 1975.

Jacobs, David M., ed. *UFOs and Abductions: Challenging the Borders of Knowledge*. Lawrence: University Press of Kansas, 2000.

Jankovic, Vladimir. *Reading the Skies: A Cultural History of English Weather, 1650–1820*. Chicago: University of Chicago Press, 2000.

Jewett, Andrew. *Science Under Fire: Challenges to Scientific Authority in Modern America*. Cambridge: Harvard University Press, 2020.

John, Richard R. *Network Nation: Inventing American Telecommunications*. Cambridge, MA: Belknap Press, 2010.

Johnson, Ronald C. "Parallels Between Recollections of Repressed Childhood Sex Abuse, Kidnappings by Space Aliens, and the Salem Witch Hunts." *Issues in Child Abuse Accusations* 6 (1994): 41–47.

Johnston, Sarah Iles. *Restless Dead: Encounters Between the Living and the Dead in Ancient Greece*. Berkeley: University of California Press, 1999.

Jordan, Debbie, and Kathy Mitchell. *Abducted! The Story of the Intruders Continues*. New York: Carroll & Graf, 1994.

Jung, C. G. *Ein moderner Mythus: Von Dingen, die am Himmel gesehen werden*. Zürich: Rascher-Verlag, 1958. [Translated as *Flying Saucers: A Modern Myth of Things Seen in the Skies*. New York: MJF Books, 1978.]

Kaiser, David, and W. Patrick McCray. "Introduction." In *Groovy Science: Knowledge, Innovation, and American Counterculture*, edited by David Kaiser and W. Patrcik McCray. Chicago: University of Chicago Press, 2016, 1–10.

Keel, John A. "Aliens Among Us." *UFO Report* 5 (November 1977): 28–29.

Keel, John A. "The Bedroom Invaders: Frightening New UFO-Pilot Mystery." *MALE* 19 (June 1969): 22–23, 94–96.

Keel, John A. *The Eighth Tower*. New York: New American Library, 1971.

Keel, John A. "The Man Who Invented Flying Saucers." 1983. http://greyfalcon.us/The%20Man%20Who%20Invented%20Flying%20Saucers.htm.

Keel, John A. *The Mothman Prophecies*. New York: Saturday Review Press, 1975.

Keel, John A. "Mystery of the Alien Submarines." *SAGA* 47 (November 1973): 34–36, 92, 94.

Keel, John A. *Our Haunted Planet*. Greenwich, CT: Fawcett, 1971.

Keel, John A. *Strange Creatures from Time and Space*. Greenwich: Fawcett, 1970.

Keel, John A. "Strange Messages from Flying Saucers." *SAGA* 35 (January 1968): 22–25, 69–70, 72–73.

Keel, John A. "UFO 'Agents of Terror.'" *SAGA* 35 (October 1967): 29–31, 72–74, 76–79, 81.

Keel, John A. "UFO Kidnappers!" *SAGA* 33 (February 1967): 11–14, 50, 52–53, 56–60, 62.

Keel, John A. "UFOs and Abominable Snowmen—What's Their Strange Connection?" *MALE* 19 (October 1969): 38–39, 74–76.

Keel, John A. *Why UFOs: Operation Trojan Horse*. New York: Manor Books, 1970.

Kellermann, Kenneth I., Ellen N. Bouton, Sierra S. Brandt. *Open Skies: Historical & Cultural Astronomy*. Cham: Springer, 2020.

Kempe, C. Henry, Frederic N. Silverman, Brandt F. Steele, William Droegemueller, and Henry K. Silver. "The Battered-Child Syndrome." *Child Abuse & Neglect* 9 (1985): 143–154.

Keyhoe, Donald. *The Flying Saucers Are Real*. New York: Fawcett, 1950.

Killen, Andreas. *1973 Nervous Breakdown: Watergate, Warhol, and the Birth of the Post-Sixties America*. New York: Bloomsbury, 2006.

King, George. *You are Responsible!* London: Aetherius, 1961.

Klarer, Elizabeth. *Beyond the Light Barrier*. Aylesbury: Howard Timmins, 1980.

Koerner, Brendan I. *The Skies Belong to Us: Love and Terror in the Golden Age of Hijacking*. New York: Crown, 2013.

Komons, Nick A. *Bonfires to Beacons: Federal Civil Aviation Policy under the Air Commerce Act, 1926–1938*. Washington, DC: U.S. Department of Transportation, 1978.

Kottmeyer, Martin S. "Did Life Magazine Help Spawn the 1952 UFO Wave?" *Magonia Supplement* 48m (21 October 2003): 1–3.

Kraspedon, Dino. *My Contact with Flying Saucers*. London: Neville Spearman, 1959.

Kripal, Jeffrey. *Authors of the Impossible: The Paranormal and the Sacred*. Chicago: University of Chicago Press, 2010.

Kripal, Jeffrey. "Esalen and the UFO." *Esalen*, 16 July 2021, https://www.esalen.org/post/early-esalen-ufos-and-the-exploration-of-new-life, accessed 9 July 2023.

Kurihara, Ken. *Celestial Wonders in Reformation Germany*. London: Pickering & Chatto, 2014.

Kurlander, Eric. *Hitler's Monsters: A Supernatural History of the Third Reich*. New Haven: Yale University Press, 2018.

Kurtz, Paul. "CSCIOP at Twenty." *Skeptical Inquirer*, July/August 1996: 4–8.

La Fontaine, J. S. *Speak of the Devil: Tales of Satanic Abuse in Contemporary England*. Cambridge: Cambridge University Press, 1998.

Lajoie, Denise H. and S. I. Shapiro. "Definitions of Transpersonal Psychology: The First Twenty-Five Years." *Journal of Transpersonal Psychology* 24 (1992): 79–98.

Lamont, Peter. *Extraordinary Beliefs: A Historical Approach to a Psychological Problem*. Cambridge: Cambridge University Press, 2013.

Lamont-Brown, Raymond. *Phantoms, Legends, Customs, and Superstitions of the Sea*. Glasgow: Brown, Son & Ferguson, 1989.

Lee, Gloria. *The Changing Conditions of Your World by J.W. of Jupiter Instrumented by Gloria Lee*. Palos Verdes Estates: Cosmon, 1962.

Lee, Gloria. *Why We are Here by J.W. A Being from Jupiter Through the Instrumentation of Gloria Lee*. Los Angeles: DeVross & Co., 1959.

Lepselter, Susan Claudia. *The Resonance of Unseen Things: Poetics, Power, Captivity, and UFOs in the American Uncanny*. Ann Arbor: University of Michigan Press, 2016.

Leslie, Desmond, and George Adamski. *Flying Saucers Have Landed*. London: Panther, 1957.

Levy, David H. *The Man Who Sold the Milky Way: A Biography of Bart Bok*. Tucson: University of Arizona Press, 1993.

Lewis, James R., ed. *The Gods Have Landed: New Religions from Other Worlds*. Albany: State University of New York Press, 1995.

Leys, Ruth. *Trauma: A Genealogy*. Chicago: University of Chicago Press, 2000.

Lindell, Jeffrey A. "The Real Foo Fighters: A Historical and Physiological Perspective on a World War II Aviation Mystery." *Skeptic Magazine* 17 (2012): 38–43.

Littig, Lawrence W. "Affiliation Motivation and Belief in Extraterrestrial UFOs." *Journal of Social Psychology* 83 (1971): 307–308.

Little, Gregory L. "Educational Level and Primary Beliefs About Unidentified Flying Objects Held by Recognized Ufologists." *Psychological Reports* 54 (1984): 907–910.

Loftus, Elizabeth. *The Myth of Repressed Memory: False Memories and Allegations of Sexual Abuse*. New York: St. Martin's Press, 1994.

Lorenzen, Coral E. *The Great Flying Saucer Hoax: The UFO Facts and Their Interpretation*. New York: William-Frederick Press, 1962.

Lorenzen, Coral E., and Jim Lorenzen. *Abducted! Confrontations with Beings from Outer Space*. Tucson: Berkley Medallion, 1977.

Luckhurst, Roger. *The Invention of Telepathy, 1870–1901*. New York: Oxford University Press, 2002.

Machado, Severino. *Los platillos volantes ante la razón y la ciencia*. Madrid: Machado, 1955.

Mack, John E. *Abduction: Human Encounters with Aliens*. Scribner's and Macmillan, 1994.

Mack, John E. *Passport to the Cosmos: Human Transformation and Alien Encounters*. New York: Crown, 1999.

Mantle, Philip, and Irena McCammon Scott. *Beyond Reasonable Doubt: The Pascagoula Alien Abduction*. Pontefract: Flying Disk Press, 2023.

Martin, Dan. *The Watcher: Seven Hours Aboard a Space Ship*. Clarksburg: Saucerian Publications, 1969.

Marwick, Arthur. *The Sixties*. London: Bloomsbury Reader, 1998.

Mavrakis, Daniel, and Jean-Pierre Bocquet. "Psychoses et objets volants non indentifiés." *Revue canadienne de psychiatrie* 29 (1983): 199–201.

McAllister, Matthew P., and Greg Eghigian. "Flying Saucers and UFOs in US Advertising During the Cold War, 1947–1989." *Advertising & Society Quarterly* 23 (2022): https://doi.org/10.1353/asr.2022.0028.

McCray, Kevin B. *Alien Thoughts: Voices of UFO Buffs of the 1960s and 1970s (and Beyond!)*. Mount Gilead: Self-published, 2023.

McCurdy, Howard E. *Space and the American Imagination*. Baltimore: Johns Hopkins University Press, 2011.

McLeod, Caroline C., Barbara Corbisier, and John E. Mack. "A More Parsimonious Explanation for UFO Abduction." *Psychological Inquiry* 7 (1996): 156–168.

McIver, Shirley. "UFO (Flying Saucer) Groups: A Look at British Membership." *Zetetic Scholar* 11–12 (1987): 39–60.

McIver, Shirley. "The UFO Movement: A Sociological Study of Unidentified Flying Object Groups." PhD thesis, University of York, 1984.

Mclagan, R.C. "Ghost Lights of the West Highlands." *Folklore* 8 (1897): 203–256.

McNally, Richard C. "Explaining 'Memories' of Space Alien Abduction and Past Lives: An Experimental Psychopathology Approach." *Journal of Experimental Psychopathology* 3 (2012): 2–16.

McNally, Richard C., and Susan A. Clancy. "Sleep Paralysis, Sexual Abuse, and Space Alien Abduction." *Transcultural Psychiatry* 42 (2005): 113–122.

Meehan, Paul. *Saucer Movies: A Ufological History of the Cinema*. Lanham: Scarecrow, 1998.

Meerloo, Joost A. M. "Le syndrome des soucoupes volantes." *Médecine et Hygiène* 794 (September 1967): 992–996.

Meheust, Bertrand. *Soucoupes volantes et folklore.* Paris: Mercure de France, 1985.

Meheust, Bertrand. *Science-fiction et soucoupes volantes: une réalité mythico-physique.* Paris: Mercure de France, 1978.

Melton, J. Gordon. "A History of the New Age Movement." In *Not Necessarily the New Age: Critical Essays,* edited by Robert Basil, 35–53. Buffalo: Prometheus Books, 1988.

Menger, Howard. *From Outer Space to You.* Clarksburg: Saucerian Books, 1959.

Menzel, Donald H. *Flying Saucers.* Cambridge: Harvard University Press, 1953.

Menzel, Donald H. "The Truth About Flying Saucers." *Look* 16 (17 June 1952): 35–39. www.project1947.com/fig/look61752.htm.

Menzel, Donald H., and Ernest H. Taves. *The UFO Enigma.* Garden City, NY: Doubleday, 1977.

Menzel, Donald H., and Lyle G. Boyd. *The World of Flying Saucers: A Scientific Examination of a Major Myth of the Space Age.* Garden City, NY: Doubleday, 1963.

Meurger, Michel. "Zur Diskussion des Begriffs 'modern legend' am Beispiel der 'Airships' von 1896–97." *Fabula* 26 (1985): 254–273.

Michel, Aimé. *Flying Saucers and the Straight-Line Mystery.* New York: Criterion, 1958.

Michael, Aimé. "Les tribulations d'un chercheur parallèle." *Planète* 20 (January–February 1965): 31–39.

Michel, Aimé. *The Truth about Flying Saucers.* New York: Pyramid, 1956.

Miller, James. "Seeing the Future of Civilization in the Skies of Quarouble: UFO Encounters and the Problem of Empire in Postwar France." In *Imagining Outer Space: European Astroculture in the Twentieth Century,* edited by Alexander C. T. Geppert, 245–264. Basingstoke: Palgrave, 2012.

Mitchell, Helen, and Betty Mitchell. *We Met the Space People.* Clarksburg: Saucerian Books, 1967.

Monnerie, Michel. *Le naufrage des extra-terrestres.* Paris: Novelles éditions rationalists, 1979.

Monnerie, Michel. *Et si les ovnis n'existaient pas?* Paris: Les Humanoïdes associés, 1977.

Moseley, James W., and Karl T. Pflock. *Shockingly Close to the Truth: Confessions of a Grave-Robbing Ufologist.* Amherst, NY: Prometheus, 2002.

Moskowitz, Sam. "The Origins of Science Fiction Fandom: A Reconstruction." In *Science Fiction Fandom,* edited by Joe Sanders, 17–36. Westport, CT: Greenwood, 1994.

Muhammad, Elijah. *Message to the Blackman in America.* Phoenix: Secretarius MEMPS, 1965, 1973.

Muhammad, Elijah. *The Mother Plane.* Phoenix: Secretarius MEMPS, 1992.

Muhammad, Elijah. *The True History of Master Fard Muhammad.* Phoenix: Secretarius MEMPS, 1996.

Nadis, Fred. *The Man from Mars: Ray Palmer's Amazing Pulp Journey.* New York: Penguin, 2013.

Nall, Joshua. "Constructing Canals on Mars: Event Astronomy and the Transmission of International Telegraphic News." *Isis* 108 (2017): 280–306.

National Academy of Sciences. *Review of the University of Colorado Report on Unidentified Flying Objects.* National Academy of Sciences, 1969.

Nayar, Pramod K. *Bhopal's Ecological Gothic: Disaster, Precarity, and the Biopolitical Uncanny.* Lanham, MD: Lexington, 2017.

Nelson, Buck. *My Trip to Mars, the Moon, and Venus*. West Plains: Quill, 1956.

Nerone, John. *The Media and Public Life: A History*. Cambridge and Malden: Polity, 2015.

Neufeld Michael J. *The Rocket and the Reich: Peenemünde and the Coming of the Ballistic Missile Era*. New York: Free Press, 1995.

Newman, Bernard. *The Flying Saucer*. New York: Macmillan, 1950.

Newman, Leonard S., and Roy F. Baumeister. "Toward an Explanation of the UFO Abduction Phenomenon: Hypnotic Elaboration, Extraterrestrial Sadomasochism, and Spurious Memories." *Psychological Inquiry* 7 (1996): 99–126.

North, John. *The Norton History of Astronomy and Cosmology*. New York: W. W. Norton, 1995.

Oberg, James. "The Failure of the 'Science' of Ufology." *New Scientist*, 11 October 1979, https://www.debunker.com/texts/ObergCuttySark.html.

O'Connell, Mark. *The Close Encounters Man: How One Man Made the World Believe in UFOs*. New York: Dey St., 2017.

Ofshe, Richard, and Ethan Watters. *Making Monsters: False Memories, Psychotherapy, and Sexual Hysteria*. New York: Charles Scribner's, 1994.

Palmer, Susan J. *Aliens Adored: Raël's UFO Religion*. New Brunswick: Rutgers University Press, 2004.

Pasulka, D.W. *American Cosmic: UFOs, Religion, Technology*. New York: Oxford University Press, 2019.

Patihis, Lawrence, Lavina Y. Ho, Ian W. Tingen, Scott O. Lilienfeld, and Elizabeth F. Loftus. "Are the 'Memory Wars' Over? A Scientist-Practitioner Gap in Beliefs about Repressed Memory." *Psychological Science* 25 (2014): 519–530.

Pauwels, Louis, and Jacques Bergier. *The Morning of the Magicians*. Rochester, VT: Destiny, 2009.

Penny, Alan John. "The SETI Episode in the 1967 Discovery of Pulsars." *European Physical Journal H* 38 (2013): 535–547.

Perrotta, Guilio. "Clinical Evidence in the Phenomenon of Alien Abduction." *Annals of Psychiatry and Treatment* 5 (2021): 107–115.

Persinger, Michael A. "Geophysical Models for Parapsychological Experiences." *Psychoenergetic Systems* 1 (1975): 63–74.

Persinger, Michael A. "Geophysical Variables and Behavior: LV. Predicting the Details of Visitor Experiences and the Personality of Experients: The Temporal Lobe Factor." *Perceptual and Motor Skills* 68 (1989): 55–65.

Persinger, Michael A. "Neuropsychological Profiles of Adults Who Report 'Sudden Remembering' of Early Childhood Memories: Implications for Claims of Sex Abuse and Alien Visitation/Abduction Experiences." *Perceptual and Motor Skills* 75 (1992): 259–266.

Persinger, Michael A. "Transient Geophysical Bases for Ostensible UFO-Related Phenomena and Associated Verbal Behavior?" *Perceptual and Motor Skills* 43 (1976): 215–221.

Persinger, Michael A. "What Factors Can Account for UFO Experiences?" *The Zetetic Scholar* 1 (1978): 92.

Persinger, Michael A., and Gyslaine F. Lafreniére. *Space-Time Transients and Unusual Events*. Chicago: Nelson-Hall, 1977.

Petersen Michael B. *Missiles for the Fatherland: Peenemünde, National Socialism, and the V-2 Missile*. New York: Cambridge University Press, 2009.

Pick, Daniel. *Brainwashed: A New History of Thought Control*. London: Wellcome Collection, 2022.

Pick, Daniel. *Svengali's Web: The Alien Enchanter in Modern Culture*. London: Yale University Press, 2000.

Pilkington, Mark. *Mirage Men: A Journey in Disinformation, Paranoia, and UFOs*. London: Constable & Robinson, 2010.

Platov, Yu. V., and B. A. Sokolov. "The Study of Unidentified Flying Objects in the Soviet Union." *Herald of the Russian Academy of Sciences* 70 (2000): 244–251.

Plokhy, Serhii. *Chernobyl: The History of a Nuclear Catastrophe*. New York: Basic Books, 2018.

Pokorny, Lukas K., and Patricia Sophie Mayer. "'Like Armaggedon': Kōfuku no Kagaku and the COVID-19 Pandemic." *Religions* 13 (2022): 480.

Pooley, Jefferson, and Michael J. Socolow. "War of the Words: *The Invasion from Mars* and its Legacy for Mass Communication Scholarship." In *War of the Worlds to Social Media: Mediated Communication in Times of Crisis*, edited by Joy Elizabeth Hayes, Kathleen Battles, and Wendy Hilton-Morrow, 35–56. New York: Peter Lang, 2013.

Popp, Richard K. "Information, Industrialization, and the Business of Press Clippings, 1880–1925." *The Journal of American History* 101 (2014): 427–453.

Posard, Marek N., Ashley Gromis, and Mary Lee. *Not the X-Files: Mapping Public Reports of Unidentified Aerial Phenomena Across America*. Santa Monica: RAND Corporation, 2023.

Pritchard, A., D. E. Pritchard, John E. Mack, P. Kasey, and C. Yapp, eds. *Alien Discussions: Proceedings of the Abduction Study Conference*. Cambridge: North Cambridge Press, 1994.

Rainey, Carol. "The Priests of High Strangeness: Co-Creation of the 'Alien Abduction Phenomenon.'" *Paratopia* 1 (2011): 11–21.

Randles, Jenny. *UFO Reality: A Critical Look at the Physical Evidence*. London: Robert Hale, 1983.

Reeve, Bryant, and Helen Reeve. *Flying Saucer Pilgrimage*. Amherst, WI: Amherst Press, 1957.

Renard, Jean-Bruno. "La sacralization de la science." In *Nouvelles idoles, nouveaux cultes: Dérives de la sacralité*, edited by Claude Rivière and Albert Piette, 82–98. Paris: L'Hartmann, 1990.

Renfro, Paul M. *Stranger Danger: Family Values, Childhood, and the American Carceral State*. New York: Oxford University Press, 2020.

Ribera, Antonio. *Objetos desconocidos en el cielo*. Barcelona: Argos, 1961.

Richert, Lucas. *Break on Through: Radical Psychiatry and the American Counterculture*. Cambridge: MIT Press, 2019.

Rieger, Bernhard. "'Modern Wonders': Technological Innovation and Public Ambivalence in Britain and Germany, 1890s to 1933." *History Workshop Journal* 55 (2003): 153–176.

Roberts, Peder. "The White (Supremacist) Continent: Antarctica and Fantasies of Nazi Survival." In *Antarctica and the Humanities*, edited by Peder Roberts et al., 105–124. London: Palgrave, 2016.

Robinson, Wendy Gale. "Heaven's Gate: The End." *Journal of Computer-Mediated Communication* 3 (December 1997), JCMC334, https://doi.org/10.1111/j.1083-6101.1997.tb00077.x.

Rogo, D. Scott. *The Haunted Universe: A Psychic Look at Miracles, UFOs, and Mysteries of Nature*. New York: New American Library, 1977.

Rome, Adam. *The Genius of Earth Day: How a 1970 Teach-In Unexpectedly Made the First Green Generation*. New York: Hill and Wang, 2013.

Roper Organization. *Unusual Personal Experiences: An Analysis of the Data from Three National Surveys*. Las Vegas: Bigelow Holding Corporation, 1992.

Rossoni, David, Eric Maillot, Eric Déguillaume. *Les OVNI du CNES: 30 ans d'études officielles (1977–2007)*. Valbonne: Book-e-Book, 2007.

Roth, Christopher F. "Ufology as Anthropology: Race, Extraterrestrials, and the Occult." In *E.T. Culture: Anthropology in Outerspaces*, edited by Debbora Battaglia, 38–93. Durham, NC: Duke University Press, 2005.

Rulier, François. "Les juristes à la rencontre d'une vie intelligente extra-terrestre: composition d'une astroculture disciplinaire dans les années 1950 et 1960." *Sociétés & Représentations* 57 (2024): in press.

Ruppelt, Edward J. *The Report on Unidentified Flying Objects*. Garden City, NY: Doubleday, 1956.

Ryan, Mark B. *A Different Dimension: Reflections on the History of Transpersonal Thought*. Washington, DC: Westphalia, 2013.

Saethre, Erik. "Close Encounters: UFO Beliefs in a Remote Australian Aboriginal Community." *Journal of the Royal Anthropological Institute* 13 (2007): 901–915.

Sagan, Carl, and Thornton Page, eds. *UFO's—A Scientific Debate*. Ithaca: Cornell University Press, 1972.

Saler, Benson, Charles A. Ziegler, and Charles B. Moore. *UFO Crash at Roswell: The Genesis of a Modern Myth*. Washington, DC: Smithsonian Institution Press, 1997.

Sanarov, Valerii I. "On the Nature and Origin of Flying Saucers and Little Green Men." *Current Anthropology* 22 (1981): 163–167.

Santo, Diana Espírito, and Alejandra Vergara. "The Possible and the Impossible: Reflections on Evidence in Chilean Ufology." *Antípoda: Revista de Antropología y Arqueología* 41 (2020): 125–146.

Santos, Rodolpho Gauthier Cardoso dos. *A Invenção dos discos voadores: Guerra Fria, imprensa ciêcia no Brasil (1947–1958)*. São Paulo: Alameda, 2017.

Saunders, David R., and R. Roger Harkins. *UFOs? Yes! Where the Condon Committee Went Wrong*. New York: Signet, 1968.

Schatzman, Évry. "Les soucoupes volantes." *La Penseé* 36 (1951): 87–90.

Schatzman, Évry. "Les soucoupes volantes, vertes, possibilities, illusions." *Science et Vie* 403 (1951): 216–220.

Schatzman, Évry. "Une mystification: Les soucoupes volantes." *L'Education nationale* 7 (26 April 1951): 10.

Schechner, Sarah J. "Comets and Meteors." In *The Oxford Guide to the History of Physics and Astronomy*, edited by John L. Heilbron, 65–66. Oxford: Oxford University Press, 2005.

Schechner Genuth, Sarah. *Comets, Popular Culture, and the Birth of Modern Cosmology*. Princeton: Princeton University Press, 1997.

Schivelbusch, Wolfgang. *The Railway Journey: The Industrialization of Time and Space in the 19th Century*. Berkeley: University of California Press, 2014.

Schmidt, Reinhold O. *The Kearney Incident and to the Arctic Circle in a Spacecraft*. Hollywood: Reinhold O. Schmidt, 1959.

Schmitt, Jean-Claude. *Ghosts in the Middle Ages: The Living and the Dead in Medieval Society*. Chicago: University of Chicago Press, 1998.

Schnabel, Jim. *Dark White: Aliens, Abductions, and the UFO Obsession*. London: Penguin, 1994.

Schöpfer, Siegfried. *Fliegende Untertassen—Ja oder Nein?* Lüneburg: Carola Von Reeken, 1980 (original 1955).

Schorsch, Christof. *Die New-Age-Bewegung: Utopie und Mythos der neuen Zeit.* Gütersloh: Gütersloher Verlag Haus Mohn, 1988.

Schramm, João Francisco. "A Força Aérea Brasileira e a investigação acerca de objetos aéreos não identificados (1969–1986): Segredos, tecnologias e guerras não convencionais." MA thesis, University of Brasília, 2016.

Schutz, Michael Kelly. "Organizational Goals and Support-Seeking Behavior: A Comparative Study of Social Movement Organization in the UFO (Flying Saucer) Field." PhD thesis, Northwestern University, 1973.

Scully, Frank. *Behind the Flying Saucers.* New York: Henry Hold & Co., 1950.

Scully, Frank. "Scully's Scrapbook." *Variety,* 12 October 1949: 61 and 23 November 1949: 24.

Shalett, Sidney. "What You Can Believe about Flying Saucers." *Saturday Evening Post,* 30 April 1949: 20–21, 136–139 and (7 May 1949): 36, 184–186.

Sharples, John. "Sky and Stardust: The Flying Saucer in American Popular Culture, 1947–1957." *Cultural and Social History* 12 (2016): 81–98.

Sheaffer, Robert. "Abductology Implodes." *Skeptical Inquirer* 35 (May/June 2011): 25–27.

Sheaffer, Robert. "The Trent Photos—'Best' of All Time—Finally Busted?" *Skeptical Inquirer* 39 (2015), https://skepticalinquirer.org/2015/01/the-trent-ufo-photosbest-of-all-timefinally-busted/

Shklovskii, I. S., and Carl Sagan. *Intelligent Life in the Universe.* San Francisco: Holden-Day, 1966.

Shough, Martin. "Return of the Flying Saucers: A Fresh Look at the Sighting that Started it All." *Darklore* 5 (2017): 69–99.

Shupe, Anson, David G. Bromley, and Susan E. Darnell, "The North American Anti-Cult Movement: Vicissitudes of Success and Failure." In *The Oxford Handbook of New Religious Movements,* edited by James R. Lewis. Oxford Handbooks Online, Oxford University Press, 2022.

Sievers, Edgar. *Flying Saucer über Südafrika: Zur Frage der Besuche aus dem Weltenraum.* Pretoria: Sagittarius, 1955.

Silberstein-Loeb Jonathan. *The International Distribution of News: The Associated Press, Press Association, and Reuters, 1848–1947.* New York: Cambridge University Press, 2014.

Simms, L. Moddy, Jr. "We Came from Outer Space?" *Southern Quarterly* 16 (1977): 23–26.

Simpson, Christopher. *Science of Coercion: Communication Research and Psychological Warfare 1945–1960.* New York: Oxford University Press, 1994.

Smith, Ernie. "The Long, Strange History of People Filing Flying Saucer Patents." *Atlas Obscura,* 27 October 2017, https://www.atlasobscura.com/articles/flying-saucer-patents-alexander-weygers.

Spanos, Nicholas P. *Multiple Identities and False Memories: A Sociocognitive Perspective.* Washington, DC: American Psychological Association, 1996.

Spanos, Nicholas P. "Past-Life Identities, UFO Abductions, and Satanic Ritual Abuse: The Social Construction of Memories." *International Journal of Clinical and Experimental Hypnosis* 42 (1994): 433–446.

Spanos, Nicholas P., Patricia A. Cross, Kirby Dickson, and Susan C. DuBreil. "Close Encounters: An Examination of UFO Experiences." *Journal of Abnormal Psychology* 102 (1993): 624–632.

Sprinkle, R. Leo. "Hypnotic and Psychic Implications in the Investigation of UFO Reports." In *Encounters with UFO Occupants*, edited by Coral Lorenzen and Jim Lorenzen, 256–338. New York: Berkley Medallion, 1976.

Sprinkle, R. Leo. "Hypnotic Time Regression Procedures in the Investigation of UFO Experiences." In *Abducted!* Coral E. and Jim Lorenzen, 1977, 191–222.

Sprinkle, R. Leo. "Psychotherapeutic Services for Persons Who Claim UFO Experiences." *Psychotherapy in Private Practice* 6 (1988): 151–157.

Sprinkle, R. Leo. *Soul Samples: Personal Explorations in Reincarnation and UFO Experiences*. Columbus, NC: Granite, 1999.

Stires, Lloyd. "3.7 Million Americans Kidnapped by Aliens?" *Skeptical Inquirer* 17 (Winter 1993): 142–144.

Stilo, Giuseppe. *Un cielo ross scuro. 1947–1949: l'arrivo dei dischi volanti sull'Italia e sul mundo*. Turin: Edizioni UPIAR, 2017.

Stoczkowski, Wiktor. *Des hommes, des dieux et des extraterrestres: Ethnologie d'une croyance modern*. Paris: Flammarion, 1999.

Story, Ronald. *The Space-Gods Revealed: A Close Look at the Theories of Erich von Däniken*. New York: Harper & Row, 1976.

Story, Ronald, ed. *The Encyclopedia of UFOs*. Garden City, NY: Doubleday & Co., 1980.

Stothers, Richard. "Unidentified Flying Objects in Classical Antiquity." *The Classical Journal* 103 (2007): 79–92.

Strentz, Herbert Joseph. "A Survey of Press Coverage of Unidentified Flying Objects, 1947–1966." PhD diss., Northwestern University, 1970.

Strieber, Whitley. *Communion: A True Story*. New York: Beech Tree Books, 1987.

Stringfield, Leonard H. *Inside Saucer Post . . . 3–0 Blue*. Cincinnati: CRIFO, 1957.

Sturm, Tristan. "Hal Lindesy's Geopolitical Future: Towards a Cartographic Theory of Anticipatory Arrows." *Journal of Maps* 17 (2021): 39–45.

Sturrock, Peter A. "Report on a Survey of the Membership of the American Astronomical Society Concerning the UFO Problem: Part 1." *Journal of Scientific Exploration* 8 (1994): 1–45.

Sturrock, Peter A. "UFO Reports from AIAA Members." *Astronautics and Aeronautics* 12 (1974): 60–64.

Sullivan, Walter. *We Are Not Alone: The Search for Intelligent Life on Other Worlds*. New York: McGraw-Hill, 1964.

Sullivan III, Woodruff T. *Cosmic Noise: A History of Early Radio Astronomy*. New York: Cambridge University Press, 2009.

Sullivan III, Woodruff T. "The History of Radio Telescopes, 1945–1990." *Experimental Astronomy* 25 (2009): 107–124.

Swords, Michael D. "Project Sign and the Estimate of the Situation." *Journal of UFO Studies* 7 (2000): 27–64.

Swords, Michael, Vicente-Juan Ballester Olmos, Bill Chalker, Barry Greenwood, Richard Thieme, Jan Aldrich, and Steve Purcell. *UFOs and Government: A Historical Inquiry*. San Antonio: Anomalist Books, 2012.

Syon, Guillaume de. *Zeppelin! Germany and the Airship, 1900–1939*. Baltimore: Johns Hopkins University Press, 2002.

Szwed, John F. *Space Is the Place: The Lives and Times of Sun Ra*. New York: Pantheon, 1997.

Taylor, James. "Written in the Skies: Advertising, Technology, and Modernity in Britain since 1885." *Journal of British Studies* 55 (2016): 750–780.

Terbish, Baasanjav. "Russian Cosmism: Alien Visitations and Cosmic Energies in Contemporary Russia." *Modern Asian Studies* 54 (2020): 759–794.

Tessicini, Dario, and Patrick J. Boner, ed., *Celestial Novelties on the Eve of the Scientific Revolution, 1540–1630*. Florence: Leo S. Olschki, 2013.

Thiering, Barry, and Edgar W. Castle. *Some Trust in Chariots: Sixteen Views on Erich von Däniken's Chariots of the Gods?* Folkstone: Bailey Brothers & Swinfen, 1973.

Toronto, Richard. *War Over Lemuria: Richard Shaver, Ray Palmer, and the Strangest Chapter of 1940s Science Fiction*. Jefferson, NC: McFarland, 2013.

Truzzi, Marcello. "The Occult Revival as Popular Culture: Some Random Observations on the Old and Nouveau Witch." *The Sociological Quarterly* 13 (Winter 1972): 16–36.

Turner, Karla. *Into the Fringe: A True Story of Alien Abduction*. New York: Berkley Books, 1992.

United States. *Symposium on Unidentified Flying Objects. U.S. House of Representatives, Committee on Science and Astronautics, 29 July 1968*. Washington, DC: U.S. Government Printing Office, 1968.

United States Department of Transportation, FAA. *Aircraft Hijackings and Other Criminal Acts Against Civil Aviation Statistical and Narrative Reports*. Washington, DC: FAA, 1986.

Vallee, Jacques. *Forbidden Science: Journals 1957–1969*. Berkeley: North Atlantic Books, 1992.

Vallee, Jacques. *The Invisible College: What a Group of Scientists has Discovered About UFO Influence on the Human Race*. San Antonio: Anomalist, 1975.

Vallee, Jacques. *Passport to Magonia: From Folklore to Flying Saucers*. Chicago: H. Regnery, 1969.

Vallee, Jacques. "The Pattern Behind the UFO Landings." *Flying Saucer Review, Special Issue: The Humanoids* 1 (October-November 1966): 8–27.

Vallee, Jacques, and Chris Aubeck. *Wonders in the Sky: Unexplained Aerial Objects from Antiquity to Modern Times and Their Impact on Human Culture, History, and Beliefs*. New York: Jeremy P. Tarcher/Penguin, 2009.

Van Duzer, Chet. *Sea Monsters on Medieval and Renaissance Maps*. London: British Library, 2013.

Van Tassel, George W. *I Rode a Flying Saucer: The Mystery of Flying Saucers Revealed*. Los Angeles: New Age, 1952.

Verga, Maurizio. "Making the Saucers Popular: Cartoons and Comics in the 1947 Press." *Cielo Insolito* 3 (2017): 9–27.

Verga, Maurizio. *Flying Saucers in the Sky: When UFOs Came from Mars*. Self-published: Maurizio Verga, 2022.

Versluis, Arthur. *American Gurus: From American Transcendentalism to New Religion*. New York: Oxford University Press, 2014.

Wallis, Jennifer. "Locating Sexual Abuse in the TV Movie, From Dangerous Dads to Day Care." In *Are You in the House Alone? A TV Movie Compendium, 1964–1999*, edited by Amanda Reyes. Ebook edition, Manchester: Headpress, 2017.

Walsham, Alexandra. "Sermons in the Sky: Apparitions in Early Modern Europe." *History Today* 51 (April 2001): 56–63.

Wang, Jessica. "Science, Security, and the Cold War: The Case of E.U. Condon." *Isis* 83 (1992): 238–269.

Wang, Jessica. "Scientists and the Problem of the Public in Cold War America, 1945–1960." *Osiris* 17 (2002): 323–347.

Warren, Donald I. "Status Inconsistency Theory and Flying Saucer Sightings." *Science* 170 (1970): 599–603.

Watson, Nigel, ed. *The Scareship Mystery: A Survey of Worldwide Phantom Airship Scares (1909–1918)*. Northamptonshire: Domra, 2000.

Watson, Nigel. *UFOs of the First World War: Phantom Airships, Balloons, Aircrafts, and Other Mysterious Aerial Phenomena*. Gloucestershire: The History Press, 2014.

Webb, David. *1973—Year of the Humanoids*. 2nd ed. Evanston, IL: Center for UFO Studies, 1976.

Webb, Walter N. "Occupant Encounter in New Hampshire." *APRO Bulletin* 22 (January–February 1974): 5–7.

Westrum, Ron. "Social Intelligence about Anomalies: The Case of UFOs." *Social Studies of Science* 7 (1977): 271–302.

Westrum, Ron. "Witnesses of UFOs and Other Anomalies." In *UFO Phenomena and the Behavioral Scientist*, edited by Richard F. Haines. Metuchen: Scarecrow, 1979, 89–111.

"What Were the Flying Saucers? Eyewitnesses Believe They Saw Secret Aircraft." *Popular Science* 159 (August 1951): 74–75, 228.

White, John Peter. *The Past Is Human*. Sydney: Angus & Robertson, 1974.

Wiechmann, Gerhard. *Von der deutschen Flugscheibe zum Nazi-UFO: Metamorphosen eines medialen Phantoms 1950–2020*. Paderborn: Brill/Schöningh, 2022.

Williamson, George Hunt, and John O. McCoy. *UFOs Confidential! The Meaning Behind the Most Closely Guarded Secret of All Time*. Corpus Christi: Essene, 1958.

Winter, Alison. "The Rise and Fall of Forensic Hypnosis." *Studies in History and Philosophy of Biological and Biomedical Sciences* 44 (2013): 26–35.

Wiroth, Manuel. *Ovnis sur la France: histoire et étude du phénomène des années 1940 à nos jours*. Agnières: Éditions Le temps présent, 2017.

Wohl, Robert. *A Passion for Wings: Aviation and the Western Imagination, 1908–1918*. New Haven, CT: Yale University Press, 1994.

Wohl, Robert. *The Spectacle of Flight: Aviation and the Western Imagination, 1920–1950*. New Haven, CT: Yale University Press, 2005.

Wojcik, Daniel. "Spirits, Apparitions, and Traditions of Supernatural Photography." *Visual Resources* 25 (2009): 109–136.

Wright, Lawrence. *Remembering Satan: A Tragic Case of Recovered Memory*. New York: Knopf, 1994.

Yingling, Marissa E., Charlton W. Yingling, and Bethany A. Bell. "Faculty Perceptions of Unidentified Aerial Phenomena." *Humanities and Social Sciences Communications* 10 (2023): 246, https://doi.org/10.1057/s41599-023-01746-3.

Young, Charles S. *Name, Rank, and Serial Number: Exploiting Korean War POWs at Home and Abroad*. New York: Oxford University Press, 2014.

Young, Elizabeth Aileen. "The Use of the 'Brainwashing' Theory by the Anti-Cult Movement in the United States of America, pre-1996." *Zeitschrift für junge Religionswissenschaft* 7 (2012): https://sites.psu.edu/setisymposium2022/,

Young, Simon. *The Boggart: Folklore, History, Place-Names, and Dialect*. Exeter: University of Exeter Press, 2022.

Zajde, Nathalie. "Die Schoah als Paradigma des psychischen Traumas." *Tel Aviver Jahrbuch für deutsche Geschichte* 39 (2011): 17–39.

Zaretsky, Natasha. *Radiation Nation: Three Mile Island and the Political Transformation of the 1970s*. New York: Columbia University Press, 2018.

Zeller, Benjamin E. *Heaven's Gate: America's UFO Religion*. New York: New York University Press, 2014.

Ziegler, Charles A. "UFOs and the US Intelligence Community." *Intelligence and National Security* 14 (1999): 1–25.

Zuñiga, Diego. *Los Ovnis: La prensa escrita en la difusión de creencias populares. Memoria para optar al título de periodista*. Santiago: Universidad de Chile, 2003.

INDEX

For the benefit of digital users, indexed terms that span two pages (e.g., 52–53) may, on occasion, appear on only one of those pages.

Note: Figures are indicated by an italic *f* following the page number.

Ouranos, 108
Oz factor, 257–58
Ozma, Project, 186

Page, Thornton, 72, 189–90, 211–12
paleovisitology, 176–81, 248–49
Palmer, Ray, 52–56
parapsychology, 247, 252, 257–58, 276, 304
Parker, Calvin. *See* Pascagoula encounter
Pascagoula encounter, 220–21
Pereira, Jader, 149–50
Persinger, Michael, 238–39
photographs, 67–68
Pilkington, Mark, 262
Poher, Claude, 191–92, 226–27
Powers, William, 190
Price, Patty, 270–72
Program for Extraordinary Experiences Research (PEER), 297, 302
psychiatry, 164, 165–68, 182, 240, 273–74, 280, 284, 288, 303. *See also* Mack, John; trauma
psychology, 272, 281–82, 284, 285–86, 293, 294–95, 301–2, 303
psychopathology. *See* psychiatry
psychosocial hypothesis, 184, 248–50
psychotherapy, 276–77, 282–85, 293–94, 299
public opinion, 50, 68, 107–8, 111, 239–42
pulp fiction. *See* science fiction

Quintanilla, Hector, 191

race, 119, 122, 124, 125, 127–28, 139–40, 144, 146, 147, 149–50, 162–63, 167, 180, 254–55, 264, 310–11, 315, 316–17
racism. *See* race
radio astronomy, 185–86
Raël, 244–45, 246–47
Ragaz, J. Heinrich, 104–5
Rainey, Carol, 283–84
Randi, James, 253–54
Randle, Kevin, 270
Randles, Jenny, 238, 257, 291
Reeve, Bryant and Helen, 117, 118*f*, 120–21, 124, 128–29, 130, 132, 134–35
Rehn, Gösta, 100–1, 159–61

religion, 105–6, 117, 136, 153–55, 180, 181, 182–84, 185, 241, 242–47, 278
Relman, Arnold, 300
Ribera, Antonio, 104, 174, 292–93
Rimmer, John, 217–18, 230–31, 310
Robertson Panel, 72–74
robot, 156, 220–21, 265*f*
Rockefeller, Laurance, 297
Rodeghier, Mark, 250
Rogerson, Peter, 162
Rogo, Scott, 268, 278
Roper poll, 292
Roswell, 19, 84–85, 259, 261
Ruppelt, Edward, 50, 58
Russia, 309–10. *See also* USSR
Russo, Edoardo, 94, 250

Sagan, Carl, 136, 186, 192, 211–12, 214, 255, 293, 302
Salisbury, Frank, 101–2, 267*f*
Sanders, Jacqueline, 152
Satanic ritual abuse, 300–1
Saturn, 122, 138
Saunders, David, 196, 198, 204, 205–6, 209, 237
Scarnaux, Jacques, 249
Schatzman, Évry, 93
Schiaparelli, Giovanni, 42
Schmidt, Reinhold, 136
Schönherr, Luis, 237
Schutz, Michael Kelly, 242–43
science, 211–12, 235–42, 243–44, 296, 297, 313–14
science fiction, 42–43, 52–54, 59, 177, 243–44
Scully, Frank, 62–65, 92–93
Search for Extraterrestrial Civilizations. *See* SETI
secularization, 27–28
Sesma, Fernando, 137–38
SETI, 185–89
Shalett, Sidney, 56–57, 60
Shaver mystery, 52
Shklovskii, Iosef, 187
Sievers, Edgar, 140–41
SIGN, Project, 57–59
Silence Group, 122, 128
Silva, Antônio da, 264
Simon, Benjamin, 166–68, 167*f*
SIOANI, 225

Villas Boas, Antônio, 157–62
Vorilhon, Claude. *See* Raël
V-rocket, 15–16

Walter, Werner, 234–35
Walton, Travis, 266–67
War of the Worlds broadcast, 44–45,
    48, 62, 76
Warren, Donald, 241–42
Washington, DC, flap of 1952, 69–71
wave of 1973, 218–21
waves, theories of, 221–23
Webb, David, 220
Webb, Walter, 4–7, 164
Well, H.G., 36, 44
Welles, Orson, 44–45

Weltraumbote, 104–5
Westrum, Ron, 242, 287, 292
Williamson, George Hunt, 126–28
wonders, 24–31
Woods, Emma, 284
World War II, 22, 51, 57–58, 86, 183,
    285–86. *See also* foo fighters,
    V-rocket

X-Files, 64–65, 262

Zamora, Lonnie, 147–49
Zeppelin, Ferdinand von.
    See dirigible
Zigel, Felix, 237–38
Zimbabwe, 287–88